An

Unforgettable Woman

The Life and Times of Rosa Newmarch

Rose Newmarch c.1916

An Unforgettable* Woman

The Life and Times of Rosa Newmarch

A portrayal, based on Rosa's unpublished autobiography and
her daughter Elsie's unpublished account of the life of Rosa,
together with their letters and additional research by the author

*Sibelius described Rosa Newmarch to Harriet Cohen
as '*une femme inoubliable*'

Lewis Stevens

Matador
5 Weir Road
Kibworth Beauchamp
Leicester LE8 0LQ, UK
Tel: (+44) 116 279 2299
Fax: (+44) 116 279 2277
Email: books@troubador.co.uk
Web: www.troubador.co.uk/matador

ISBN 978 1848766 709

British Library Cataloguing in Publication Data.
A catalogue record for this book is available from the British Library.

Typeset in 11pt Garamond by Troubador Publishing Ltd, Leicester, UK

Matador is an imprint of Troubador Publishing Ltd

Printed and bound in the UK by TJ International, Padstow, Cornwall

For Renée

CONTENTS

LIST OF ILLUSTRATIONS

"Little minds soon come to terms with themselves and the world, and then fossilise; but others flourish, and are always alive and in motion[...] It is persistent, uninterrupted activity that constitutes the superior mind."

Schopenhauer

This quotation is set at the beginning of Rosa Newmarch's biography of Henry Wood; it applies equally to Rosa herself.

PREFACE

Rosa Newmarch was an extraordinary woman. Nowadays she is best known as the programme writer for the Promenade Concerts from 1908 to 1918, and in collaboration with Eric Blom until 1927, when the BBC took over the Proms. But equally important was that she was instrumental in bringing to the concert going public, music by many Russian composers and also Czech composers, particularly Janáček. In fact, Janáček's music was hardly known in Britain until Rosa Newmarch organised his visit to Britain in 1926. Although she hoped to see his operas performed in Britain during her lifetime, that was not to be. The first performance of one of his operas in Britain was not until 1952. Since that time, Janáček's operas have become some of the most popular in this country. Rosa Newmarch was also a great friend of Sibelius and had the insight to realise that he would become one of the greatest composers of the first half of the twentieth century. She helped organise all five of his visits to England.

At a time when middle class Victorian families brought up their daughters to sing, play the piano and embroider, she became very much a woman in a man's world. Apart from two years at art college, she had no formal higher education but was brought up in a family very well connected with the world of the arts and literature. She visited Russia several times between 1897 and 1915, often travelling alone or with a friend, and then after the Russian Revolution doing the same in Czechoslovakia until 1937. Rosa Newmarch was brought up bilingual, and by 1911 she had mastered so many languages that she became a member of the Polyglot Club. She was also one of the first six members of the School of Russian Studies at the University of Liverpool. From the time she was about twenty until her death at the age of eighty-two she was a prolific author, publishing twenty-three books and numerous articles. She put her linguistic skills to good use translating into English from French, German, Russian and Czech. Rosa had a very wide circle of acquaintances and friends in the musical world, including Balakirev, Cui, Rimsky-

Korsakov, Sibelius, Greig, Elgar, Bantock, Busoni, Lamond, Shaliapin, and Sir Henry Wood. She had boundless energy, the ability to take control of difficult situations and was a great initiator or facilitator. Her interests and writings were not confined to music but extended into art and poetry. She published two books of her own poems and wrote another on Russian poetry.

In 1934, when she was seventy-six, she decided, albeit reluctantly, to write her autobiography, commenting: 'I do not presume to suggest that the captious, critical atmosphere which surrounded my youth has robbed the world of anything valuable, but I know that it is responsible for the inferiority complex which has hitherto restrained me from writing anything about myself. I have always secretly despised autobiography as the consolation of those who begin to realize that it is likely to be the only kind of record they will ever get! Why, then, have I rashly changed my reasoned conviction that it is, on the whole, more honourable to pass out "unhonour'd and unsung" than to sound one's own "last post", lustily blowing one's trumpet to the end? I do not know. One thing is definitely borne in upon me: at my age I cannot afford to dally with this autobiographical brain-wave. It is part of the tide that must be utilized now or never...'

The somewhat apologetic tone of this quote is not unlike the way many writers begin to justify their autobiography. The novelist Daphne du Maurier condemned all examples of this literary form as self-indulgent. George Orwell thought an autobiography could only be trusted 'when it reveals something disgraceful' saying 'A man who gives a good account of himself is probably lying.' At the time when Rosa began her autobiography she was also writing two other books: *The Music of Czechoslovakia* and *Jean Sibelius: A Short Story of a Long Friendship*. Both were completed and published in 1942 and 1939 respectively, whereas the autobiography was incomplete at the time of her death. By the mid-1930s, Rosa's health was declining and she must have lacked some of the stamina of her former years. Perhaps her apparent reluctance to write an autobiography meant that she accorded it a lower priority than the other works.

Some years after her death, her daughter Elsie, who lived with her and had been her close companion on many of her trips abroad, and who also acted as her secretary and helper, completed the account of Rosa's life, but after several attempts, she failed to get it published. Whilst their combined work covers most of Rosa's professional life, it only touches briefly on her personal life, which led one publisher to comment: 'It is that the portrait of your mother never quite comes to life. Remarkable and vital woman that she was, she remains within these pages but a shade of her true self. [...] the essential spark is missing.'

Rosa Newmarch wrote many accounts of the lives of other musicians including the first biography of Henry Wood in 1904; in it she refers to Wood's admiration for John Ruskin. Ruskin said of his own autobiography, *Praeterita*, 'It is – as you say – the "natural" me, only carefully peeled.' The Woods and the Newmarches became great family friends. Henry Wood wrote his autobiography, *My Life in Music*, about the same time as Rosa was writing hers. It is even possible they may have conferred. Reading Rosa Newmarch's autobiography, one is left wondering whether its "peelings" might bring out the "essential sparks".

AUTHOR'S CONTRIBUTION

Since the 1960s, Rosa's typescript, with Elsie's revision, has been filed away in a case along with many of her papers. Many authors have continued to refer to Rosa's writings and it was through a happenstance that I became aware of her writings. Before writing a short article for the newsletter of The Dvořák Society for Czech and Slovak Music on Rosa Newmarch, I contacted her sole surviving granddaughter, Renée Bodimeade, to see if she had more information about her grandmother. When I visited her, she revealed a 'treasure chest' with not only the autobiography but also many letters and artefacts, all of which she made readily available to me. With the passage of time, I feel that Rosa's life and writings have, if anything, become more fascinating and it is possible to see her contribution to the music scene in a more historical perspective. A book by Philip Bullock has been published entitled *Rosa Newmarch and Russian Music in Late Nineteenth and Early Twentieth-Century Music (2009),* a new edition of her poetry, *Horae Amoris: The Collected Poems of Rosa Newmarch* edited by John Holmes and Natasha Distiller, was published in 2010 and a further book on letters between Newmarch and Sibelius by Philip Bullock is in preparation. All three are indications of an increased interest in Rosa Newmarch.

My account of Rosa Newmarch's life is based on her unpublished autobiography, which concludes shortly after 1900, her daughter Elsie's account of the later parts of her professional life (1900 to 1940), many of Rosa's letters, her granddaughter Renée's recollections, and further research on my part.

Lewis Stevens
Sheriffmuir
Dunblane

NOTES ON THE TEXT

(i)   Transliteration. The transliteration of Russian from Cyrillic which has been used is the system adopted by the *New Grove Dictionary of Music and Musicians* except when quoting from articles or letters, where the authors' spellings have been retained.

(ii) Quotations. Many instances in this account include long quotations, particularly of letters and from unpublished material primarily by Rosa and Elsie Newmarch. In order to readily identify these, they are indented and use a different font.

(iii) Biographical Notes. An asterisk is used in the text against the names of individuals who are included in the Biographical Notes on pages 315–323.

ACKNOWLEDGEMENTS

First of all, I am very grateful to Rosa Newmarch's granddaughter Mrs Renée Bodimeade for encouraging me to work on Rosa's biography and also for making available to me so much material relating to Rosa Newmarch in her possession. This included Rosa's unpublished incomplete autobiography, her daughter Elsie Newmarch's biography, a large number of Rosa's and Elsie's letters, and many photographs, portraits and illustrations in her possession. During the two years in which I was working on the biography, I visited Mrs Bodimeade in her home on a number of occasions, and we were able to discuss Rosa's interesting life. Although only twelve when Rosa died, she did have some vivid recollections from her childhood, and she also recalled the recollections of her mother, Mrs Gwendoline Newmarch, dating back to when Rosa's husband, Henry Charles Newmarch, was alive. Each time I visited her, she managed to find some new artefact of Rosa's including her silver cigarette case in which Rosa kept her black Russian cigarettes.

I am also very grateful to my friend Peter Stott, who carefully read the whole manuscript and made many helpful suggestions and detailed comments. Dr Philip Bullock and the Reverend Jim Benson also read the whole manuscript and made many useful suggestions and Peter Taylor advised on technical aspects of the illustrations. My sister, Jo Barsoux, translated a difficult handwritten letter from Jean Lahor.

For chapters 24 and 25, on *Meeting Janáček* and *Janáček's Visit to England*, in addition to Elsie Newmarch's unpublished account, I have also drawn on Zdenka Fischmann's *Janáček-Newmarch Correspondence* (Rockville, Maryland: Kabel Publishers, 1986) and on John Tyrrell's book *Janáček, Years of a Life, Volume 2 (1914-1928)* (London: Faber and Faber, 2007).

Finally, I am indebted to my wife, Dr Evelyn Stevens, for listening patiently to the story as it unfolded and for many suggestions. By the time she met Mrs Renée Bodimeade when she visited us in May 2010, she was sufficiently familiar with Rosa's life to discuss it with Renée as though she knew the family.

The photographs and illustrations are from the following sources: Nos. 5-9, 12-14, 17-19, 21, 23-26, 28, 29, 31, 32, 37-47, from Mrs Bodimeade's collection; 1, 3, 20, 22, 33-35, the author's; 2, from a portrait by Samuel Laurence, c.1840; 4, from a portrait by Condé published in the *European Magazine*, December 1792; 10, *Views of Leamington* (Rock & Co., London, 1860); 11, Martin Billing, Son and Co. Livery St,

Birmingham, 1832; 15 and 16, *A History and Description of the Parish or Whitnash*, by J. Young, 1865; 27, *Russian Memories* by Olga Novikoff, 1917; 30, from a portrait by Fred Yates, 1904; 36, Cornish Brothers, 37 New St. Birmingham, 1900; the Frontispiece, Claude Harris, 122 Regent St London, 1916.

CHAPTER 1: FOREBEARS AND RELATIVES

Rosa Jeaffreson was born on 18 December 1857, the youngest child in a well-educated upper-middle-class Victorian family with eight children; four brothers followed by four sisters. She was seven years younger than her nearest sibling, her eldest was eighteen years older. Her father, Samuel John Jeaffreson (1814-1870), was a Cambridge-educated physician, and her mother, Sophie née Kenney (1814-1872), was the daughter of the English dramatist James Kenney (1780-1849). (See Jeaffreson Family Tree.)

The Jeaffresons were a well-established family that can be traced back to Norman times. The original Norman name is believed to have been Fitz-Geoffrey and there is evidence it was changed to Jeaffreson at that time in the 'Provisions of Oxford' (1258). Since the time of Henry VIII, the Jeaffreson families were country gentry, squires and parsons living for the most part in the eastern counties. Younger sons went into the army, the church or, more frequently, the medical profession. One of the more adventurous Jeaffresons was John Jeaffreson of Pettistree (b.1590), who, with his friend Thomas Warner, made a joint expedition to the West Indies and founded a colony there in 1623-4. He was subsequently appointed Lieutenant of the island of St Kitts, where he acquired a large estate and became a wealthy man. With advancing prosperity, he also acquired St Andrew's House, Holborn and considerable property in the eastern counties, including Dullington House in Cambridge and Rowshall in Clopton, Suffolk. He christened his only son Christopher, after the island on which the boy was to inherit his father's estate, thus introducing the name Christopher, which has persisted in every generation of the family since 1650.

In Victorian times, the strong family tradition of scholarship, the ministry and medical practice continued. Samuel's father, the Rev. Christopher William (1770-1846), friend of Samuel Wesley, was a Cambridge-educated classical scholar who became Rector of Tunstall and Iken, Suffolk and later chaplain to the Marquis of Hertford. Another relative, John Cordy Jeaffreson (b. 1831 Framlingham, Suffolk), graduated from Oxford in 1852 and published numerous novels and also the book *The Real Lord Byron*. Rosa's brother, William Julius, studied at Uppingham School and Lincoln College Oxford and eventually became Master of Radley College. Her great uncle, John Jeaffreson, was a surgeon in Islington. Her father's cousin, Henry Jeaffreson, practiced at St Bartholomew's Hospital, and his brother William was an oculist. Rosa's brothers James Russell and Christopher Samuel both became medically qualified, the latter specialising in eye diseases at Newcastle Infirmary. Rosa's son became a general practitioner. In her autobiography, Rosa counted fifteen medical men in four generations of her father's family.

1. Jeaffreson Family Tree

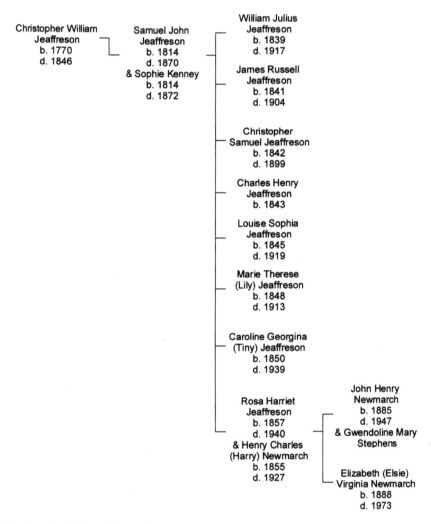

Distinguished though her father's side of the family was, Rosa always found it more exciting to learn about her mother's forebears. Rosa's mother, Sophie, was the daughter of the dramatist James Kenney (1780 -1849) and his French wife, Louisa

Mercier. Tracing the family tree on Sophie's mother's side is all the more complex because Louisa married twice, and for her first husband, Thomas Holcroft, it was his third marriage. All three families, the Kenneys, the Merciers and the Holcrofts, included literary figures well known in their day. Rosa's interest was also heightened by the fact that the families were respectively of Irish, French and English descent. Although Rosa was only a relation by marriage to the Holcrofts, her mother Sophie had one Holcroft half-brother and two Holcroft half-sisters. The ties with the Holcrofts were sufficiently strong that one of Rosa's elder sisters, Marie Therese (Lily), referred to herself as Lily Holcroft Jeaffreson. The three families will be described in turn and the complex relationships are set out in the Mercier Family Tree.

2. James Kenney (1780-1849)

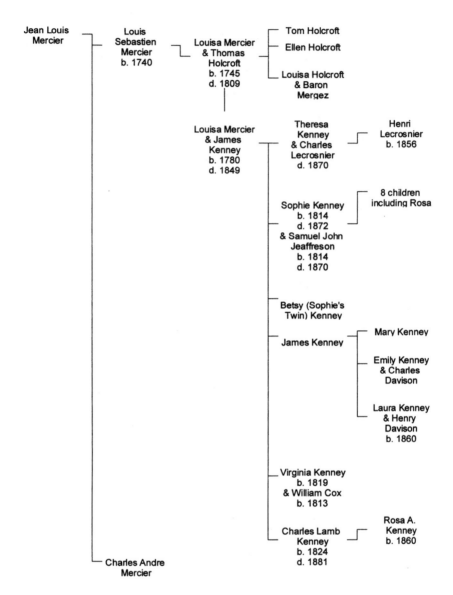

3. Mercier Family Tree

James Kenney, Rosa's maternal grandfather, wrote over forty dramas and light operas, which were in vogue between 1803 and 1845. He was born in Ireland, son of a manager and part-proprietor of Boodles, a well known sporting club, which was one of a number of gaming houses that opened in London in the eighteenth century and which, many years later, became gentlemen's clubs. The club was established in 1762 and called Boodles after the name of its headwaiter. When the Kenney family arrived in England around 1800, James's father took it over, and under his management, some of the most influential English establishment figures of the day retired behind the club's portals to indulge in gaming, drinking and other pursuits. Early members included Beau Brummell, friend of the Prince Regent and leader of fashion, the politician Charles James Fox; the philosopher David Hume; the economist Adam Smith; and the historian Edward Gibbon. More recently, members have included the actor David Niven; Ian Fleming, the creator of James Bond, who is said to have based his fictional club 'Blades' on Boodles; and John Profumo, the disgraced former politician and charity worker. Sir Winston Churchill was elected an honorary member.

James's father intended his son's career to be in banking, but James's leaning was towards the theatre. After his early successes as a playwright (*Raising the Wind*, his first two-act farce was staged when he was only twenty-three). James became one of the most prolific and popular playwrights of the early nineteenth century, producing over forty dramas and operas and numerous songs and poems. One of his plays, *The Pledge*, or *Castilian Honour*, had a command performance before the young Queen Victoria.

Among James Kenney's friends were the essayist Charles Lamb (1775-1834), the poet and art collector Samuel Rogers (1763-1855), and the writer and dramatist Thomas Holcroft (1745-1809). Charles Lamb wrote the epilogue to Kenney's play *Debtor and Creditor*. The circumstances leading to James's marriage are quite involved.

Thomas Holcroft
from a portrait by Condé
published in the European Magazine, December 1792

4. Thomas Holcroft (1745-1809)

In 1783, Thomas Holcroft wrote a column on the theatre for the *English Review* and subsequently went to Paris a number of times in search of new plays and books worth translating. During these trips, he wrote several articles for the *Morning Herald* and established close friendships with French writers, including Louis-Sébastien Mercier. Holcroft had first married in 1765, but his wife died soon afterwards, and he remarried. His second wife bore him three children, William, Sophy and Fanny (1780-1844), but she died shortly after the third child was born. With the onset of the French Revolution, according to Rosa's account, 'probably about 1789 – Sébastien Mercier sent his daughter Louisa to England under the care of his friend and widower, Tom Holcroft, who proposed to her and offered her the shelter and the safety of his home.' Thomas, then forty-five, married Louisa, probably in her late teens. Rosa adds, 'I cannot find any published confirmation of this story, but, if it is true, gratitude may have played a leading part in the affair. Louisa Mercier, who had been brought up in a literary circle, might have seen her future husband, Thomas Holcroft, the author of *The Road to Ruin* in a favourable light.' Thomas Holcroft's memoirs state, '3rd March 1799, Informed Col. Barry of the business of to-morrow; viz. my marriage with Louisa, and received his hearty congratulations.'[1]

5. Louisa Mercier (Rosa's grandmother)

In June 1799, Holcroft left for Hamburg, where he stayed for over a year, and then went on to Paris, returning to England in 1802[2]. He wrote his memoirs up to his fiftieth year in three volumes and these were edited and supplemented after his death in 1809 by the essayist William Hazlitt (1778-1830). Louisa is favourably mentioned in them[3]:

> Before Mr Holcroft left England he married Louisa, the daughter of his friend Mercier. Of his marriage with this lady, it is needless to say any more at present than that Mr Holcroft found all that happiness in it which he had promised himself

from the union with a young, sensible, accomplished and affectionate wife.

Louisa bore him three children, Tom, Ellen and Louisa, and supported him throughout their ten years of marriage and final illness, as the account[4] shows:

> If any thing could exceed the patient courage with which he passed through this trying scene, it was the affectionate, unwearied assiduity with which Mrs Holcroft attended him night and day, through the whole. For the last six weeks she scarcely once quitted his bedside for a quarter of an hour together. The task was one, to which duty and affection were alone equal. In any other circumstances, her strength would have failed under such exertions: but Mr Holcroft was not satisfied unless she was with him, and that consideration prevailed over every other.

He died aged sixty-three on 23 March 1809. Louisa, now well into her thirties, married James Kenney. There were six children by her second marriage: Theresa, the twins, Sophie and Betsy, James, Virginia and Charles, making a total of nine children altogether. Although Louisa first married an Englishman and then an Irishman, she was very conscious of her French heritage. The family lived in England most of the time, but they spent periods in France, and when Louisa was giving birth, she preferred to be in France for her confinement. The awareness of French heritage was very evident in subsequent generations: Rosa and her mother were both bilingual.

6. Louis-Sébastien Mercier

One of Rosa's maternal great-grandfathers was Louis-Sébastien Mercier (1740-1814). He was born of humble origin. His father, Jean-Louis Mercier, was an artisan, who polished swords and metal weaponry. Louis-Sébastien and his brother Charles-André lost their mother as young children and their father married again. It was said within the family that they were of noble lineage, having descended from the Duc de Vendôme and Gabrielle d'Estrée, though it is difficult to find evidence to substantiate this. Henri IV (b.1553, d. 1610), King of France (1589-1610), fathered four children by his mistress Gabrielle D'Estree (1571-1599). The conjecture is that Louis-Sébastien Mercier may be an indirect descendent of their son César, Duc de Vendôme (1594-1665). According to Rosa's account, 'By patronage in high places Sébastien's grandfather was established in the Palais-Royal as a sword-maker and privileged to call himself *l'armurier du roi*. There were many "spurious" offspring in the vast royal retinue.'

Although Jean-Louis Mercier had modest means, his son Louis-Sébastien was given a good education and embarked on a literary career, writing over 60 dramas. A number of his books have been re-issued, an indication that they are still read today. Also he merits an entry in *Le petit Larousse* as '*litterateur francais, auteur d'un très curieux Tableau de Paris*'. *Le Tableau de Paris* (1781-1788) was first published in two volumes by the Société Typographique de Neufchâtel in June 1781 in Switzerland. These Swiss publishers accepted for publication works which under French censorship would not have been permitted: books calculated to annoy the King, to question God, or merely to give the facts of history in a manner more entertaining and possibly more truthful than the official version. The book met with immediate success although until 1783 it was sold only surreptitiously by hawkers, after which it was freely available for public sale. In 1933 a selection from the *Tableau* was translated into English by Helen Simpson and published; this was reissued in paperback in 1999[5].

In politics Mercier was a moderate, and as a member of the Convention he voted against the death penalty for Louis XVI. During the Reign of Terror he was imprisoned, but was released after the fall of Robespierre. He had little time for philosophy or science, believing that modern science had not made any real advances; he even maintained that the earth was a circular flat plain around which revolved the sun. To quote Helen Simpson, 'he blasphemed against the three demigods of philosophy, Newton, Locke and Descartes.' After the Revolution he came to England frequently. On his death in 1814, he left an incomplete and unpublished book entitled *Parallel between Paris and London*. He is commemorated in a street named after him, Rue Sébastien Mercier in the 15th arrondissement of Paris.

James Kenney, Rosa's maternal grandfather, wrote a large number of plays, and occasionally some were very successful stage works. By his writing he managed to make a living and bring up a large family. For a time the Kenneys lived in France, partly perhaps for economy's sake. Their eldest daughter, Theresa, was middle-aged when she married Charles Lecrosnier, and they lived in a villa outside Paris. Both had a talent for painting, but according to Rosa, whereas Theresa's watercolour copies of masterpieces in the Paris galleries may have brought her a modest remuneration, Charles's landscape sketches, hastily thrown on canvas, led nowhere. They had a son, Henri, late in life, a similar age to Rosa, whom she describes as handsome but lamentably spoilt.

7. Charles Lecrosnier

Rosa's mother, Sophie, had a twin sister, Betsy, but little is known about her. Rosa's uncle James is also only given a passing mention in Rosa's autobiography. He died young and financially impoverished. There is no mention of his wife although he had three daughters: Mary, Emily and Laura. After James's death, Mary and Emily went to live with James's half-sister Louisa and her husband, Baron Mergez, and Laura went to stay with Theresa and her husband in Paris. According to Rosa, both Mary and Emily were unusually talented girls. Mary was a talented pianist, and had she a more suitable temperament and stronger physique, she might have become a professional pianist. She was for many years the organist at St Matthias, West Brompton. Emily married Charles Davison, son of J. W. Davison* and Laura married his brother Henry. Henry and Laura had three sons and two daughters. Virginia, married comparatively late to a widower art dealer William Cox and lived in London, who clearly had an important influence on Rosa's musical development in her early years.

In 1824, when Charles, their youngest child, was born, Rosa's grandparents were living in Bellevue near Paris. The writers Charles and Mary Lamb came to stay with them and the former stood godfather to the newborn baby, named Charles Lamb Kenney. Charles had a variety of occupations, including assistant foreign editor on *The Times,* secretary to Sir Joseph Paxton (1803-1865) and later private secretary to Ferdinand de Lesseps (1805-1904) before returning to journalism as dramatic critic on *The Standard.* He also wrote librettos for a number of light operas. He died in 1881 and is buried in Brompton Cemetery.

Besides Sophie's brothers and sisters, there was a half-brother, Tom, and two half-sisters, Ellen and Louisa, from Rosa's grandmother Louise's first marriage to Thomas Holcroft. Of these, Rosa describes her aunt Louisa Holcroft, who married Baron Mergez, as follows:

> Baroness Mergez as I recollect her was a tall dignified white-haired lady, extremely deportment-conscious, whose expression, usually stern, could on rare occasions relax into a most kindly and tender smile. She was a strange mixture of ungrudging liberality in big things and almost peasant-like parsimony in matters of everyday life. I think before her marriage when the family lived at home with her mother and stepfather [James Kenney] she kept the family of excitable half-brothers and sisters in order. Her husband, the Baron, was a choleric, weather-beaten cavalry officer of the old school.

8. Baron Mergez

Their house in Touraine, Le Petit Plessis, was a ramshackle chateau, towering and be-pinnacled, which would have cost thousands to restore. The land was valuable and rich in vineyards and orchards. From time to time my mother went on a visit to her half-sister and took one of us with her. The Merges had only one child, a delicate boy who died in his teens, and this absence of an heir, combined with a lack of capital, probably accounted for what in our youth we regarded as Aunt Louisa's parsimony.

The Mergez, who were as generous as they were close-fisted, had adopted Mary and Emily, the two elder daughters of my uncle James who had died comparatively young and who, after the Kenney fashion left very little behind [...] She [Emily] was the jolliest of companions in whom all the hectic Kenney dash and vivacity of her generation seemed to have concentrated itself. Her greatest passion was for horses.

The preponderance of English physicians and scholars among Rosa's father's relatives contrasts with the literary and artistic relatives of French and Irish descent on her mother's side. How her parents met and how their differing backgrounds influenced Rosa's upbringing is described in the next chapter.

Notes

1. William Hazlitt, *The Life of Thomas Holcroft* (London: Constable, 1925), vol. 2, p.248.

2. Ibid. 292.

3. Ibid. 117.

4. Ibid. 309.

5. Helen Simpson, *The Waiting City: Paris 1782-88*, an abridgement of Louis-Sébastien Mercier's *Le Tableau de Paris* (London: Harrap, 1933).

CHAPTER 2: EARLY YEARS

In Rosa's autobiography, she explains how her parents met and then her recollections of her childhood. Shortly after her father had obtained his medical degree, he accompanied the family of the Chandos Leigh (1791-1850), First Baron of Stoneleigh Abbey, Warwickshire, as travelling physician on a 'grand tour'. Her mother was also a member of a retinue without which the aristocracy seldom ventured abroad in those days, as Rosa describes:

> She [Sophie] must have been ridiculously young – not more than eighteen – to take upon herself the responsibilities of a governess, but my grandfather, James Kenney, although he wrote one or two successful works for the theatre, seems to have always been a poor man, and I remember my mother telling me how she and her sisters resolved to get work as early in life as possible in order to relieve the situation at home. [It would seem likely that she was more than eighteen. Rosa's parents were both born in the same year, and by then her father was medically qualified.] She may well have owed her post partly to her personal charm, but probably also to the fact that she was already an excellent linguist and likely to be useful on that account. There was also in the Leigh [party] following another young governess, a Miss Urquhart, and a youthful Cambridge graduate, just in orders, the Rev. James Young, who went as travelling chaplain to the Leighs. It is not surprising that by the end of the tour these four young people had paired off: Dr Jeaffreson became engaged to Miss Sophie Kenney and the Rev. James Young to Miss Urquhart. I mention this, because later on, the Youngs and the Jeaffresons, after years of friendship, became still more closely linked by ties of intermarriage. [In 1874, the daughter of Rev. James Young, Edith Mary Young married the Rev. Herbert Herman Jeaffreson, the nephew of Samuel Jeaffreson.]
>
> Very shortly after the return to England my father started as a consultant in London. Eventually he should have made a most successful career. He had a perfect 'bedside manner' polished and sincerely sympathetic; he was imposing looking, over six feet high, and always dressed in the dignified frockcoat and pepper-and-salt trousers in which physicians of those days felt it incumbent upon them to appear at any hour of the day or night. Moreover he kept to the low waistcoat and frilled

shirt, immaculately gauffered, almost a survival from the eighteenth century. He was probably the last man to carry a snuff-box. Apart from external attractions his medical attainments were much above the average, and he was highly reputed for his almost unerring powers of diagnosis. But the practice came slowly, and the family quickly in those early years of married life. It is improbable that he had any capital with which to play a waiting game. He decided, too soon many of his friends thought, to move from Half-Moon St. [off Piccadilly, London], to Leamington Spa, where living was cheaper and the facilities for education of his children excellent. My mother assuredly regretted leaving London and a large circle of interesting friends for any 'Little Peddlington', no matter how bright, healthy and socially comme il faut it might prove. She must however have been consoled by the fact that the many invalids who frequented our Warwickshire Spa soon found out that a physician of the first rank had come among them. My father became quickly prosperous and even affluent for those times in which the country consultant's fee rarely exceeded the modest guinea [£1.05]. Here, in Leamington, I was born in 1857, the youngest child of a family of eight.

9. Samuel Jeaffreson, Rosa's father (1814-1870)

In the west end of London, Samuel Jeaffreson appears to have been less fortunate in attracting a large clientele to his practice than his cousin Henry Jefferson working on the east side of London at St Bartholomew's Hospital, who developed a larger consultancy practice than many of his professional contemporaries. The probable date of the family's move from Half-Moon St, London to 29 Landsdowne Place, Leamington was between the births of Louisa in 1845 and that of Lily in 1848, since only the youngest three daughters were christened at All Saints Church, Leamington: Marie Therese (Lily) on 15 December 1848, Caroline Georgina (Tiny) on 7 April 1851, and Rosa Harriet on 8 February 1858. .

10. All Saints Church , Leamington, c 1860

Most of the houses in Landsdowne Place (now the north end of The Parade) were built in the 1830s. George Morley, describing them in 1887, wrote: 'The houses had balconies to them, as indeed they have at the present time, and were well suited for the abodes of the wealthy families who took up their residences in Leamington. The demand for these edifices being great, the whole block … was completed and the two hotels – viz., Clarendon Hotel at the north, and the Landsdowne Hotel at the south made a befitting finish to this row of mansions.'[1]

Dr Samuel Jeaffreson had his surgery at the house, but he also became honorary physician to the Warneford Hospital soon after his arrival in Leamington. At the Warneford, he had a large and successful consultancy practice and became one of the earliest and best known of the Leamington physicians and a well known public figure in the town, not only as a physician. He was one of two medical practitioners who actively campaigned for the implementation of the Public Libraries Act in Leamington. In 1850, the Public Libraries Act became law after much opposition from Conservatives who objected to rates levied on the middle classes being used to finance libraries for the poor. The borough councils had to obtain the consent of two thirds of the local ratepayers who voted in a referendum, and if approved, a rate of no more than a halfpenny in the pound could be levied. In practice it meant that it was difficult to set up a good public library without additional support.

In 1865, he became President of the British Medical Association on the occasion of its visit to Leamington. In November 1866, he resigned his consultancy at the Warneford Hospital and was succeeded in the post by his eldest son, Dr. James Russell Jeaffreson.

From a photo by Martin Billing, Son & Co.]   *[Livery Street, Birmingham.*

THE WARNEFORD HOSPITAL, ESTABLISHED 1832.

11. The Warneford Hospital, Leamington, established 1832

Rosa was seven years younger than her nearest sister and, as she explains, 'Having been born belated it was natural that my mother felt reluctant to open a nursery and school-room expressly for me'. It appears that her older siblings received the early stages of their education in the schoolroom at home. Rosa's education seems to have been less regular in the early stages. Although both schoolroom and nursery had been closed, a nurse and governess were nevertheless employed. Ann Letts, who was from Northampton and thirty-seven when Rosa was born, served the family for many years as family nurse. After Samuel and Sophie died, she would continue to serve the family as housekeeper. Rosa described her as follows: 'a wonderful virtue of loyalty seems to have been inherent in her family, for she had two sisters who lived for half a century in the service of families in our neighbourhood, and who like her, died at their post. She was particularly devoted to me and to my sister nearest to me in age.'

12. Ann Letts, the family's devoted housekeeper

Being so much younger than the rest of the family, Rosa often played alone but, as she described, her mother ensured that life was never dull: 'Her lively wit, compounded of French and Irish elements, her quick temper, her warm affections, and her perspicuous and unsparing criticism of her own, and other people's children, kept us wide awake. [...] No mother could have been more anxious that her children should be beautiful, clever and good –I believe I have put her desires in the right order.'

She was encouraged to read from an early age, and her mother, who regarded herself more French than English, spoke French to her from as early as she could remember. There was always a governess in the house, generally a middle-aged German lady, as Rosa's mother was keen they should be more than bilingual. Rosa found these governesses somewhat intimidating and described them as 'exemplary monuments of *Wohlanständigkeit* (decorum)'. At one stage, when her eldest sister had gone to Russia and her other sisters were studying in Paris, she felt particularly lonely. Partly for this reason, and partly because her mother did not want her to pick up the local accent, a prim, genteel middle-aged spinster from Nottinghamshire was employed as governess to teach her the rudiments of the English language. Her stay, however, was short-lived. Rosa's father was a busy man and had to drive to neighbouring counties for consultations and as a result was often away from home for several days together. When he did get home at a reasonable hour, he would enjoy a chat with Rosa. On one occasion, he asked Rosa what she had learned from the nursery governess. Rosa recited a poem and a riddle:

The spotted 'orse is put away,
The 'oop, the top, the kite, the ball,
This is the Lord's most 'oly day,
On which we never hought to play.

Although not showing displeasure at the time, her father was concerned that she would completely lose control of her aspirates. Shortly after this incident, the governess left, and for a time her education was of her own making.

13. Rosa as a child

Rosa enjoyed reading and there was a wide range of books at her disposal in the house: French and English classics, fiction, sporting books collected by sporting brothers, philosophical and controversial theology, and, in her father's consulting room, medical treatises. An author she singled out was George Sand*, having read many of her novels by the age of eleven.

When her father was out for many hours at a time and there was a roaring fire in the consulting room, she found that the 'stodgy looking books were full of human interest and astonishing revelations.' This led to aspirations to become a doctor, but these were extinguished by a letter from her eldest brother with the 'usual arguments of the day' against a woman becoming a doctor. A chance incident also led to the closing of her father's bookshelf to juvenile research. As Rosa described: 'At lunch the conversation turned upon an old friend of my parents who was suffering from a slow and tragic mental deterioration. Eager to show that I could contribute something to the subject I chipped in with: "I suppose it is a case of the slow atrophy of the grey matter, erroneously spoken of as 'a softening of the brain', etc." My father's eyebrows shot up in puzzled surprise. "My dear child, don't chatter about things you don't understand." "But I do understand, Papa, I've read about it in 'Solly on the Brain.' " [*The Human Brain, its Configuration, Structure, Development and Physiology; Illustrated by Reference to the Nervous System in the Lower Order of Animals.* Samuel Solly, 1836]

14 Louisa Sophia Jeaffreson, Rosa's eldest sister

There is little indication of any formal school education in Rosa's autobiography other than that she attended a boarding school and left at the age of seventeen. She became interested in music from an early age and as a small child lying in bed recalled catching fragments of music emanating from the drawing room. Even then, she felt she had a clear feeling for style and knew when the performers passed from Bach to Mozart or from Chopin to Schumann. She seems to have had piano lessons but little formal musical education. However, there was always music-making in the house. Her eldest sister, Louisa, was an excellent pianist who studied under Theodor Kullak (1818-1882) in Berlin, and another sister, Lily, studied singing with Romain Bussine (1830-1899) in Paris and then entered the Royal Academy of Music in London.

Besides the music at home, the family often visited her mother's sister, Virginia. Late in life, Virginia married William Cox, a picture dealer who owned a gallery at 53-4 Pall Mall, opposite Malborough House, and also 'a charming old fashioned villa enclosed with a high-walled garden at Oak Villa, Old Brompton Rd, and later a house in Wimpole Street.' It was when visiting her aunt's house that she listened to, and learned more about, music. Virginia was a fine amateur pianist who had studied in Paris under Chopin's pupil Adolph Gutman (1819-1882). She had more of the Irish humour and happy repartee than any other member of the Kenney family of her generation. On a deeper level, Virginia expressed herself in music. Rosa remembers as a six-year old child waking in the night and secretly creeping down the stairs to hear her playing. Initially to her it was just music, but later she came to distinguish style and later still she could put names to the pieces. She felt she had a good musical ear, although in the family she was not considered to have special musical aptitude, and this gave her a deeply concealed inferiority complex concerning music.

Through her aunt Virginia, Rosa often heard about some of the Westmorland Quaker families that Virginia had come to know during her time as a governess. On occasions when these families were in London, they would visit Aunt Virginia. Amongst them was Mr William Henry Wakefield, brother of Mrs Cropper (née Fanny Alison Wakefield). On one occasion when Mr Wakefield visited Aunt Virginia, Rosa remembered how they discussed Mr Wakefield's daughter Mary's singing voice and the difficulties of limiting her activities to non-professional engagements. Mary Wakefield was a very promising singer, but this was considered an unsuitable profession, particularly for a Quaker family. The discussion made a big impression on Rosa, only a girl at the time, because her elder sister Lily was contemplating a singing career at the time. On another occasion, about 1877, Aunt Virginia organised a party at her house in Mary's honour, with a view to her being heard by James Davison (1813-1885)*, a music critic and friend of Virginia. It was the first time Rosa met Mary Wakefield, and the latter's singing made a big impression. They were not to meet again for over twenty years, by which time Mary was running the Westmorland Music Festival.

Many members of the musical and theatrical profession visited her aunt at Oak Villa, and she gleaned much from their overheard discussions and conversations. The regular visitors included the music critics James Davison* (1813-1885) and Henry Chorley* (1808-1872), the journalist Horace Mayhew (1816-1877) and the actors – the rising stars – Henry Irving* (1838-1905) and Henry James Montague (the stage name of Henry James Mann, 1844-1878). Also visiting were Colonel H L Bateman (1812-1875), who ran the Lyceum Theatre from 1871, and his daughters, Kate, Isabelle and Virginia, all fine actresses.

About this time, James Davison[2] would have been in his late fifties; he was music critic of *The Times* from 1846-1878 and editor of *Musical World* from 1843-*c.*1880. Henry Chorley[3] was editor of the *Athenaeum.* Both were writers on music with strong and often idiosyncratic views, and Rosa was later to make that her career as a writer on music. They may have been influential at this formative stage of her development.

On one occasion, Rosa explains how the talk at the dinner centred on the ambitions of these two promising actors. 'Irving looked ripe for tragedy, but it was the fascinating, self-assured Montague who was to make contact with it all too soon, dying at the early age of 34. Both men were anxious for my mother to see them in their respective roles and promised tickets for their performances. Montague was playing *The Liar* as far as I can remember, and Irving in *Petruchio*, with Ellen Terry at the Queen's Theatre. When he [Irving] said goodnight to me, he added in his hollow voice: "Bring the child to the theatre too." My mother and my aunt began to explain that I was far too young for such late hours, etc. "But she'll enjoy it," said Irving, as though it was the only thing that mattered. So the child went.' Subsequently, when the family returned to live in London after her father's death, Rosa rarely missed seeing Irving in his most popular parts: Charles I, Richelieu, and Hamlet.

From Rosa's account of actors' and music critics' visits to her aunt's house, it seems that she listened attentively to the conversations and took in much of what was discussed: 'The elderly and erudite writers gathered at table in my aunt's house might have been amused had they known what was going on in the head of the small Tater-like child drinking in their wisdom with some of the enjoyment with which they imbibed their wine […]'

At home in Leamington, acting was one of the great delights of Rosa's childhood, and one her mother greatly encouraged in the family. There was a good supply of props and a wardrobe adequate for many roles, from Hamlet to Sam Weller, Cinderella and Joan of Arc. Although the children were not encouraged to expect an audience; it was largely done for the family's amusement. However, on occasions they had the added encouragement from the playwright and producer Eliza Keating, a friend of the family. She lived in Birmingham where she did a good deal of work in the Birmingham Theatre, arranging and dramatising stories for the stage. Her published dramatisations show that she had a particular flare in working with children: *Cinderella* (1860), *Charade Plays for the Parlour* (1865), *Beauty and the Beast* (1864) and *Home Plays: Drama for Boys: a series of comedies comprising male characters only* (1862).

Other visits Rosa particularly remembered from her childhood were to the Rev. James Young and family. Her parents had kept up the friendship ever since both couples had accompanied Baron Leigh on 'the grand tour'. From 1846, Rev. James Young became the Rector at Whitnash near Leamington, a short walk from the Jeaffreson's, where he ran a small preparatory school with a dozen or so pupils.

15. Reverend James Young

The school enjoyed a reputation for enlightened educational practice well above the average rectory school at that time[4]. For example, emphasis was placed on the value of natural history, with excursions into the countryside to collect flowers, butterflies and birds' eggs in moderation. There was a private printing press on which boys practised typesetting, and in winter they attended dancing classes in Leamington. Each Christmas, the boys recited to their parents in Latin, Greek, French, German and English, and for the years 1851-1870, the *Recitations* were printed, with the help of a local printer. The Jeaffresons often visited them and participated in their various dramatic activities. In the winter of 1868, when Rosa was just eleven, the Youngs put on an ambitious, well-rehearsed performance of Schiller's *The Lay of the Bell*. Friends of the Youngs down from Oxford played some of the major parts. The women singers included Rosa's sister Lily, who had a light soprano voice, and her cousin Emily Kenney, who later married James Davison's son. Rosa took the part of a peasant girl. The performance was directed by John Stainer (1840-1901), who at this time was Professor of Music at Oxford University, and who later became well known as a composer and the organist at St Paul's Cathedral. The performance was such a success that it had to be repeated for several nights, and hence brought in a considerable sum for the church restoration fund.

16. Whitnash School

Thus by the time Rosa was twelve, she had read widely, acted, listened to music made in the home, had become a theatre goer, and had met important figures in the arts of the day.

In the spring of 1868, her father's health was causing her mother anxiety. His illness was later that year diagnosed as diabetes with complications. In the days before the discovery of insulin, diabetes was practically regarded as hopeless. So by the summer of 1868, Rosa's father was advised to take a longer holiday than usual. By now, her elder brother James was a qualified doctor and able to look after the practice while his father was away.

His holiday involved going abroad for about a month as travelling physician to Anthony Ashley Cooper*, who by then had inherited the title of Seventh Earl of Shaftesbury. Rosa's father described the tour in letters he sent to Rosa's eldest sister,

Louise, who was in Odessa at the time. The trip involved taking the boat to Calais, travelling on to Brussels and Cologne, then by train via Frankfurt-am-Main and a further twelve miles to Homburg. Thus rested from heavy work, her father returned in better health and took up practice again with the assistance of Rosa's brother, who had now settled in Leamington. Her father was now on a prescribed diet, presumably one low in carbohydrate. Rosa comments: 'To be a diabetic was to be condemned to perish of slow starvation. But at this time he was still far from the rapid wasting, the lethargy, and attacks of coma which occur in the later stages of the complaint.'

Rosa's father had seldom spent a holiday with the family, but in the autumn of 1868, he joined them for a second period of rest and change of scene on the south coast of England. But by the autumn of 1869, his condition had worsened; he was suffering from dyspnoea (difficulty in breathing) and showed signs of weakening circulation. Sir Thomas Watson*, a distinguished consultant, examined him. He diagnosed dilatation of the aorta and ordered him to winter abroad, which Rosa described:

[My Father] together with my mother and my third sister started for Cannes. My eldest sister was winding up her time in Eastern Europe with a yachting trip in the Black Sea, and who had just become engaged to a navel man, was to join them in the South of France. I was left at home with my second sister and the old nurse. Then about Christmas time something happened which caused me to suddenly feel grown up: my mother sent for me. I was to go to Cannes at once, either in the care of Nurse [Ann Letts] – or she in mine. I was barely twelve and naturally felt elated at the prospect of the journey before I had time to realise its significance. But before we had reached Cannes I had the prevision that the object of our journey was not gay. I remember I kept it to myself and asked no questions, but inwardly I surmised that we had been sent for because my father wanted to see me again, and my mother needed Nurse in the hour of trial before her. We stayed a few days at a hotel in Paris near my aunt Theresa's flat in the Rue Montaigne, where Theresa was nursing her husband in the last weeks of his life. It was the first time I had come in contact with mortal illness, and the closely overhanging shadow of death; and although my uncle welcomed me with a sweet smile – he was a gentle, melancholy soul – five minutes was obviously as much as he could bear of my presence, and I crept, mouse-like, out of the sick-room feeling that of the quality known as 'animal spirits'.

One small incident of the visit lodged in my memory. My aunt was sending me out to do an errand for her, and as I stood at the door of her flat receiving her final instructions, a remarkable looking man, bearded, and muffled in a merino scarf, came down the public staircase. He saluted us, made some enquiry about the invalid, and passed on. "That was Leon Gambetta*", said my Aunt as soon as he was out of hearing, "Deputy for Paris. He lives upstairs." This was in the last days of 1869; ten years later he was President of the Republic.

Rosa and Ann Letts travelled on to Cannes to where her father was staying, and Rosa's account continues:

My joy in the lovely scenery of the Mediterranean, in the rich variety of colours which steeped the sky and mountain and sea – such contrast to the red clay and lush, monotonous greens of our Warwickshire meadows – was dimmed from the first by the recognition that my forebodings as to my father's state were true. Nobody told me in words that we should go home without him, but I realised it. I knew nothing about invalids then, but have learned much since, and I think he was one of the most patient and unobtrusive of sick men. He was still able to get up and be settled for some hours a day in an arm-chair by a window which looked out on the sparkling seas, dancing their polychrome ballet on a perpetual flickering of turquoise ultramarine, or beryl and topaz, shot with glittering sparks from sunrise to sunset. All was planned to give him cheerfulness and distraction, but how wearisome it could be to a man weary and weak from malnutrition and perfectly aware of the adverse course of his own symptoms! This I discovered one day when I was sitting alone with him. I, too, tried like everybody else to cheer him with praises of the luminous blue sky and the lovely amethystine outlines of the Esterelles mountains. "Yes, my child," he said, "It is very beautiful, but it tires me out. I long for the grey sky and a wet Warwickshire lane". A moment later he added: " Don't tell them I said so."

I did not live my whole life at Cannes in the atmosphere of the sick room. I was too young to take a very responsible share in the nursing and was often sent out with kind friends for long excursions. How thankful I was to be a bi-lingual child! I could be friends with the Belgians who lived in the flat overhead and had two delightful young folk – a pretty girl nearly seventeen, and a fine boy of fifteen who looked well on horseback and was good at all manly sports. I could talk to the boatman, the bathing men, the cabman and even our old cook-char, who was forty and looked eighty, and spoke nothing but patois. But by far the most interesting and adventurous of my companions during my three or four month visit were the daughters of an English doctor who resided there all year round, the youngest of whom was about my own age. She was a good looking, absolutely fearless type of

English girl and we took long rambles together, up into the lovely, juniper scented hills above the town where we often sat and chatted with the gangs of workmen imported from Grisons to make a new railway line. They talked only Romanche [dialect spoken in the Grisons, Switzerland and adjacent parts of Italy], and were said to be an 'exceedingly dangerous bunch'. Or we wandered seawards and gazed across the intervening miles of blue, satin-smooth waters that divided us from the Iles des Lerins, sometimes coaxing one of the boatmen to take us for a short sea-trip. The chief boatman at Cannes at that time was a certain Rombaldi, a picturesque mariner, reputed to be the cousin of Giuseppe Garibaldi, and certainly very like the pictures of him. [...]

Their father's devotion to mine during the last weeks of his life was wonderful. My mother would have been completely exhausted but for the help of this kind friend, always at hand by day and night, when he would make up an impromptu bed on the drawing room floor. The end came on.

My uncle Charles Lecrosnier died a few weeks earlier in Paris. My aunt was overwhelmed with sorrow.

Rosa and her mother and sister left Cannes shortly after her father died on 2 April 1870. They stayed in Paris with the recently bereaved Aunt Theresa until late August. By that time, Rosa had witnessed not only family loss and mourning, but also the outbreak of the Franco-Prussian war (1870-71). Rosa's account continues:

Aunt Theresa had a villa outside Paris. From the highest terrace of its sloping garden there was a fine view over the Park of St Cloud with Mount Valerien in the background. Here she suggested that my mother should come for a long visit on her way home from Cannes. It was natural that the two recently widowed sisters should wish to console each other, but I am not sure that it was a success. My mother was already seriously affected, her sorrow profound, but comparatively resigned. My aunt's grief was frenetic, and to us young folk, incomprehensible and unreasonable. Life at the villa was often stormy and difficult, but it was certainly interesting. I am sure that my sister and I mourned our father in our quiet inexpressive way, and that [cousin] Henri mourned his; but the human heart between ages of twelve and twenty naturally craves as much sunlight as shadow. We could not help enjoying our long walks in the surrounding parks, our steamboat trips on the Seine, the racket of the fair at Meudon and occasional days among the shops and galleries of Paris.

My cousin had a tutor several mornings a week. He was a highly intellectual gentle, fair-haired type of Frenchman, and the first specimen of a rampant communist I had ever come across. I sometimes shared the lessons and picked up something of French literature and a little Latin. I am afraid we used to pick on the tutor to talk politics, and then he would cast horrible pictures upon the screen of the immediate future; pictures of Paris in flames, of gutters running with blood, of the return of the Carmagnole. [La Carmagnole refers to a triumphantly sarcastic song about the fates of the Queen of France, Marie Antoinette and those who supported the French monarchy.] On the other hand it was difficult to foresee what part he intended himself to play in the coming revolution, for he was dead against taking the life of anything, even the most persistent and irrepressible wasp was immune in his presence. Discussion ran high until our pet green parrot, at liberty on her perch, would start screaming like a fury of the Halles, and flying in a bee-line would alight on one of our heads, generally the tutor's. She was called Mrs Gill, after the heroine of a song then much in vogue which ran:

Mrs Gill is very ill
And nothing will improve her
Unless she sees the Tuileries
And toddles through the Louvre.

Alas! Poor Mrs Gill, our tiny beloved bantam cock, and our solid pair of Barbary ducks, who fancied themselves no heavier than humming birds and looked surprised and aggrieved when they fluttered onto twigs of standard roses which promptly let them down – all fell victims to the Prussian invaders before many months had passed over our heads [...]

In France during the summer of 1870 shadows of tragic events were growing daily more imminent. On either side of my aunt's house we had interesting neighbours. On the one hand the widow of the painter Flandrin [Jean-Hippolyte (1809 –64) who won the Prix de Rome for his painting in 1832. He is best known for his monumental decorative paintings often in churches, but he also painted a large number of portraits] and her family; on the other the popular novelist Jules Sandeau (1811-1883), librarian at Saint-Cloud, who in earlier years had collaborated with George Sand in a novel Rose et Blanche, and from whom after their liaison had come to an abrupt end, she stole half his name as well as most of his heart. Sandeau was at that time about sixty and far from a hero of romance; homely rather inclined to a middle-aged spread, he had always a genial smile of greeting for us young folk, though we may have been sometimes rather noisy neighbours for a literary man. No biographical dictionary contains, I think, any reference to Sandeau's marriage. He was long in recovering from the blow of George Sand's defection, but in 1870 there was no trace about him of the broken-hearted and deserted lover.

Moreover there was certainly a lady, spoken of as his wife, who seemed completely at home as mistress of the villa. The summer of 1870 was hot, and this lady, stout and dark, and once undoubtedly comely, slouched about most of the day in a *peignoir* [dressing gown] and might easily be taken for a respectable though somewhat dishevelled *femme de ménage.* [...]

My mother and aunt frequently went next door in the evening and sat over a cup of coffee or a sirop[fruit juice] in the garden. They enjoyed talking to the novelist whose conversation had much of the charm of his literary style: a tendency to extreme sensibility, almost sentimentality, tempered by an ironic vein and a subdued gaiety. Long years had passed since his first successes, but his novels (*La Roche aux Mouettes*) kept their freshness and his plays (*Mademoiselle de la Seglière* and *Gendre de Monsieur Poirier*) were not forgotten by the Paris public. It was said that his books appealed greatly to the Empress Eugenie. But in July 1870, our elders next door were more preoccupied with politics than literature. Much was taking place at Saint-Cloud of which Sandeau — though not a politician — must have knowledge. Over the hedge of laurels and deflowered lilacs which divided the two gardens we caught echoes of anxious and impassioned discussions, on those warm evenings [...]

The actual 'eve of war' was July 18th. That evening my mother called over the hedge from Jules Sandeau's garden that we might come in to hear some news: history in the making. There were one or two friends there, including a staff officer whose name I never heard. Gravely, but with suppressed exultation, this gentleman told us that at 10 pm on the 14th a council had been called at Saint-Cloud, and that the pendulum had swung wholly to the side of the war party. Furthermore he told us that the Emporer would not make a public departure for the front in spite of the enthusiam which the news of the declaration of war against Prussia was certain to evoke. The actual declaration took place on 19th July. And on the 28th, advised by Sandeau and his friends, we saw him leave Saint-Cloud with the Prince Imperial a sick and unhappy man, with no escort of the Cent-Gardes, glorious in blue and silver, but hidden in a corner of a closed carriage; his features drawn by physical pain and mental anguish, his complexion sallow with ill-health, his whole attitude bespeaking dejection and foreboding. Did he realise that Niel's report made to him two years earlier — that fifteen days would amply suffice for the assemblage of all the army reserves was untrustworthy? That the mysterious new weapon — the *mitrailleuse* — about which the soldiers were whispering such hopeful prognostications would be misapplied during the first actions of the war. That 450,000 Germans were ready at the end of a fortnight to face not much more than half that number of French troops on the Rhine-Moselle frontier?

The days that immediately followed the declaration of war were full of hectic excitement for us young people, who shared with the majority of the French nation an almost vainglorious faith in the brief campaign and splendid victory. The blast of the bugles and the roll and tuck of the drums resounded all day long through the streets and leafy avenues of Sèvres, Meudon and Saint-Cloud; the long-forbidden, spirited, Marseillaise became once more the favourite song of the populace and the military, and soon almost silenced the time and amateurish marching song, *Partant pour la Syrie*, which had been the vogue under the second Empire, probably more because it owed its authority to Queen Hortense, mother of Napoleon III, than on account of its literary or musical merit. Soldiers were bivouaced (*sic*) under the trees and squares and avenues, and on every available yard of green sward around us. The uniforms of the French army were picturesque in those days and were made familiar to all children by those coloured broad sheets bought for a few coppers in kiosks and newspaper shops. Near to us were drafts of *voltigeurs* [light infantry soldiers] and *zouaves* [also infantry soldiers]. We used to give them cigarettes and chocolates just as over forty years later we delighted to treat our own Tommies under similar circumstances. I remember that I was specially signalled out for good natured chaff. A few days before war broke out, romping about in the garden with my cousin Henri, he accidentally caught me in the eye with a stick. For nearly a week I was bandaged, and the soldiers used to salute me with :*"en viola une qui a déja vu la guerre."* [Here is a girl who's already seen the war.] Nothing lacking in audacity, I laughed back : *"Si, l'on m'a donné un billet d'aller et retour pour Berlin; et me voici de retour, légèrement blesée!"* [Yes, I was given a return ticket to Berlin, and here I am, back again, slightly injured.]

But our youthful confidence was not altogether shared by my mother who had lived too long in England to have kept an entirely one-sided view. Staunch as she was to France she was not a whole-hearted believer in the regime of the second Empire. After the battle of August 6th, when the Crown Prince of Prussia inflicted a severe blow on MacMahon's troops, she began to feel uneasy, and by the 17th or 18th of the month, after Napoleon III had arrived at Chalons, and was discussing with Trochu and MacMahon the next move to be taken against the ever-swelling hosts of Germany, and the almost equally threatening aspect of political affairs in Paris, she decided that the sooner she set our faces homewards the better. Whatever we younger ones felt then about turning our backs on France in the hour of her adversity, we afterwards recognised the wisdom of this determination. Two of her daughters were with her in France, and two were in England; my eldest brother who had not seen my mother since our father's death two months previously, was anxiously awaiting her return in order to wind up the family affairs; my second brother was still provisionally nursing the family practice in Leamington; my third brother – also a medical man – had already volunteered for the Red Cross service in France. All three had married and she had not seen her first grandchild. It was natural that my mother should feel an urge to return and knit up the family again in so far as was possible. I do not remember the exact date on which we crossed the Channel, but I think it was almost immediately after the Emperor had appointed General Trochu Governer of Paris – about August 17th, 1870.

17. Rosa's Mother, Sophie née Kenney (1814-1872)

Notes

1. George Morley, *History of Royal Leamington,* written for the *Leamington Spa Courier* (Leamington: 1887-9).

2. Charles Reid, *The Music Monster: A Biography of James William Davison, Music Critic of the Times of London, 1846-78* (London: Quartet Books, 1984).

3. Robert Bledsoe, *Henry Fothergill Chorley: Victorian Journalist* (Aldershot: Ashgate Publishing Ltd, 1998).

4. Donald Leinster-Mackay, D.P. *The Rise of the English Prep School* (London: Falmer Press, 1984) p.80.

CHAPTER 3: LEAVING HOME

The period from 1870 when Rosa, her sister Caroline Georgina (Tiny) and her mother returned from France after her father's death, to the time of her marriage to Henry (Harry) Charles Newmarch in 1883 is only very sketchily described in Rosa's autobiography. The events leading up to her father's death are fully described, but Rosa's mother's death is hardly mentioned. Sophie Jeaffreson died just under two years after her husband on 28th February 1872 at the age of fifty-eight. She died at the family home in Landsdowne Place, and the cause of death is recorded as *morbis cordis*, the term then used to describe heart disease but also as the 'catch-all' phrase for death by natural causes when the exact cause was not evident. The informant was the family servant Anne Letts. Thus Rosa was orphaned at the age of fourteen, but she hardly touches upon what it was like to be an orphan or how she was educated.

18. Rosa Newmarch in her late teens

Rosa and her mother lived in London after their return from France, as she described:

> After my father's death, my mother had no immediate wish to return to Leamington. Also her generous and hospitable nature suffered a shock for she felt more than she need have done the change in her pecuniary situation. For the moment she took a small and dismal furnished house in the Fulham district where we were dumped with our accumulated luggage [though later returning to the family home in Leamington].

Although Rosa's brother James maintained the practice at Landsdowne Place, Leamington for a short time before moving the short distance to Clarendon Square, it was effectively its end as a family home.

The nature or place of Rosa's schooling at this stage is not clear. At one point in her autobiography she wrote that she left school at about the age of nineteen, and in another that she left school in 1874 when she would have been seventeen. She referred to being at boarding school. It seems most probable that London was her home for the rest of her teenage years. In Victorian middle and upper class families, the norm for girls was to have private tuition from a governess, and then at the stage when boys might go off to public schools, to remain at home to be educated mainly in fashionable 'accomplishments' such as French, drawing, painting, singing, dancing, and the piano. For boys, but not girls, there was the further prospect of Oxbridge. However, in the later part of the century, girls' education was taken more seriously and schools such as Cheltenham Ladies' College (founded 1854) and Roedean (founded 1885) offered girls an education broadly the same as for boys of the same class, with an emphasis on academic subjects and outdoor games. The Girls' Day School Trust was formed in 1872 to provide affordable day school (non-boarding) education for girls. Oxford and Cambridge began taking women students in the 1870s after the founding of the first women's colleges. However, although they were able to attend lectures and take examinations, women were not able to become full members of the university, and therefore graduate, until 1920 at Oxford and 1946 at Cambridge. Queens College, London opened in 1848 and admitted women. The first medical school in the United Kingdom to train women, the London School of Medicine for Women, was established in 1874. Rosa did think about becoming a doctor, as mentioned in Chapter 2, but her brother advised her that it was not a suitable career for a woman.

After leaving school, probably between 1876-8, Rosa entered Heatherley's School of Art in Newman Street, off Oxford Street, and studied there for about two years. During her time at Heatherley's, she also spent time in Paris. This is evident from a letter from her nephew Henry Davison (son of James) written to Rosa's daughter Elsie, after Rosa's death. He refers to seeing Rosa in Chur, Switzerland with her sister and also staying in Paris at her Aunt Theresa's in June 1877. In her autobiography, Rosa says little about any interest in art, although her descriptions of the countryside in France suggest she was a keen observer. The illustrations on envelopes that she drew and sent to her future in-laws between 1875 and 1878, and the sketch entitled *Un Pieux Mesange,* show her ability to sketch and her sense of humour.

19. Rosa's illustration on an envelope posted to her future sisters-in-law, in February 1876

She says little about her interest in art but much about her interest in music, so it is not clear how she came to choose art rather than music for further study. It is possible that her schooling, which she does not describe, may have been an influencing factor. Apart from schooling, it is clear that she was surrounded by relatives and acquaintences who were deeply interested in the visual arts, music and literature. Heatherley's Art School was founded in 1845, the oldest independent art school in London and is among the few art colleges in Britain that even today focus purely on portraiture, figurative painting and sculpture. It was the first school to admit women on equal terms with men, and this may have been a factor in her choice. Among Heatherley's former students were Burne Jones, Rossetti, Millais, Lord Leighton, Russell Flint, Michael Ayrton and Sickert. The conductor Henry Wood, who later became Rosa's close friend, also studied at Heatherley's, attending evening classes. In his autobiography, he does not give the dates, but it can be deduced that it must have been around the early 1890s, i.e. much later than when Rosa attended. Of her time at Heatherley's, Rosa reflected:

> This experience, however, forced me to conclude that painting was not my natural vocation. No doubt the time spent over study was formative, and helped me to acquire broad comparative views which guided me in critical work in later years. My real leanings were to a literary life, a desire which had been fostered in early years by my mother, who unfortunately died in 1871 [28 February 1972 according the death certificate]. I later took every opportunity to acquire some practical knowledge of journalism, and wrote several articles for provincial newspapers.

Thus some time around 1880 Rosa returned to Leamington to live with her sisters Marie Therese (Lily) and Georgina Caroline (Tiny) at 60 South Parade (later renamed Clarendon Avenue), just round the corner from Landsdowne Place, together with her mother's old housekeeper, Ann Letts, and a servant, Ellen King. By this time, her eldest sister, Louise, was married. Lily studied singing at the Royal Academy of Music; she had a charming but light soprano voice. When she returned to Leamington, she taught singing and became well known as a teacher of singing in the Midlands and had many promising and successful artists among her pupils. In the 1881 census, Lily's occupation is given as 'Artist Professor of Singing' and Rosa's as 'Artist Painter'; Tiny is without occupation. Lily continued living there as a singing/music teacher after Rosa had moved back to London.

When Rosa returned to Leamington, she taught painting and drawing and in her spare time took up stained-glass work and painting on china, accomplishing some work for Mortlock, a firm founded in 1746 with a pottery gallery in Oxford St from 1796 to 1933. Not primarily a manufacturer of china, they employed independent decorators to paint the intricate designs on their china. They have been described as the most important china retailer in London in the early nineteenth century. Also during this period, she began to implement her 'leanings to a literary life', writing several articles for provincial newspapers.

20. Clarendon Avenue (formerly South Parade) –Rosa's home in the early 1880s

Rosa now began to develop her early interest in music. She had many opportunities to hear music both in the home and at concerts. She enjoyed her Aunt Virginia's playing and would also join in with the music making of her elder sisters. In her teens, when she was living in London, she became a regular concert-goer. She was a frequent occupant of the one-shilling seats (5p in decimal coinage but equivalent to about £3 in 2011) at the Popular Concerts at St James's Hall, Regent Street. The St James's Hall opened in 1858 and held regular Pops Concerts organised by the Philharmonic Society on Monday and Saturday nights for forty seasons. (The Philharmonic Society was founded by a group of professional musicians in 1813 at a time when there were no professional orchestras in London. Initially it met in Hanover Square, but from 1869 concerts were held in St James's Hall.) They were a source of musical enjoyment for those who could not afford the ticket prices on other days. When the Queen's Hall opened towards the end of the 1890s, it attracted audiences away from the St James's Hall, which closed about 1900 and was demolished in 1905. Rosa reminisced about her early concert days in the 1870s:

> As I began my career as a concert-goer before I was in my teens, I can look back a long way on my own and other people's enthusiasms. My impression is that apart from operatic furore, the raptures of the seventies and eighties were very decorous and self controlled as compared with what was soon to follow. Music at the time –good music – was the privilege of a small and superior minority. Take the habitual frequenters of the 'Pops', St James's Hall housed the entire batch of us and, we believed that the elite of us –the esoteric core – perched on the backless benches of the orchestra or stifled under the balcony in the comfortless space allotted to the one shilling ticket holders. We came perforce early –and what a coming that was, dear children of the present generation. Forty minutes ride from Bayswater in a nice draughtless horse-drawn bus, with a door that was kept jealously closed by a genial and witty cockney conductor, and a litter of noisome but comfortable straw underfoot. No harassed and irritable autocrat in uniform shouting his orders from the step to the public inside and outside his little kingdom on wheels; no row of straphangers jazzing on your feet; no unseemly demands for "fares please"; no obligation to be perpetually passing coppers and all too-nimble 'threepennies' to and fro as in a weary game of hunt-the-thimble. With our miniature scores under our arms – no self-respecting amateur went to a concert without a miniature score – we met our fellow enthusiasts and went on our way to St James's Hall
>
> From the orchestra or top gallery we watched the privileged stall-holders slowly and solemnly taking their accustomed seats – I had almost written pews. Browning, genial and always a refreshing sight to me, as he watched and wondered if it was at the 'pops' that he learnt 'sliding in semi-tones', till he 'sink to the minor' and how to 'blunt it into a ninth', and so come to his resting place in C major, and other fearsome bits of musical erudition far above my comprehension in those far off days. I Leighton, beautiful to look upon, an aesthetic asset to any concert room. His sister Mrs Matthews, a genuine music-lover, whose outlook was wide enough and sympathies broad enough to carry her on into a new musical dispensation, for she became a regular attendant at the concerts of the Queen's Hall Orchestra as long as failing health permitted[2].

She attended recitals given by Anton Rubinstein, Hans von Bulow, Eugène d'Albert and Busoni. She also recalled the first performances of *Lohengrin* at Covent Garden in 1875, with Christine Nilsson (1843-1921) as Elsa, and *Aida* in June 1876 with

Adeline Patti (1843-1919), and concert performances of Wagner given at the Royal Albert Hall in 1877.

By today's standards of education, where academic achievements great or small are characterised by exams and qualifications subject to audit and the award of certificates, Rosa's education appears very unstructured. By the time she left Heatherley's School of Art, she probably had few, if any, formal qualifications. Yet she had gained cultural experiences surpassed by very few of her contemporaries or university students today. She had read widely, had met many important literary figures and artists, and gained practical experience in journalism. But perhaps most importantly, she had gained the confidence to educate herself further, the drive to get things done, and to rise to a challenge.

Notes

1. Refers to the poet, Robert Browning and his poem *Abt Vogler*, the last verse of which is:

    Well, it is earth with me; silence resumes her reign:
    I will be patient and proud, and soberly acquiesce.
    Give me the keys. I feel for the common chord again,
    Sliding by semitones till I sink to the minor,—yes,
    And I blunt it into a ninth, and I stand on alien ground,
    Surveying awhile the heights I rolled from into the deep;
    Which, hark, I have dared and done, for my resting-place is found,
    The C Major of this life: so, now I will try to sleep.

2. Lord Frederic Leighton (1830-1896) was a very successful Victorian artist and sculptor and a close friend of Robert and Elizabeth Barrett Browning. Leighton's sister Augusta Winnburg Leighton married Arthur Matthews in 1859.

CHAPTER 4: HENRY CHARLES NEWMARCH

Rosa began her autobiography in 1934, when she was in her mid-seventies. Realising that at that age she might need to press on with it, she began with a quotation by Armado from Shakespeare's *Love's Labour's Lost* 'Devise wit, write pen: for I am for whole volumes in folio.'

There is little doubt from Rosa's writing that she does not lack inspiration. She recalls many events and anecdotes from the past with great eloquence, but when it comes to events relating to her husband Henry (Harry) Charles Newmarch, her accounts are terse and sometimes inconsistent. Also, her eloquence appears to desert her. There is scarcely anything about Harry's personality or the nature of their relationship either in Rosa's autobiography or the biography that her daughter, Elsie, continued. It seems most unlikely that over the forty-four years of their marriage Harry ever went to concerts or exhibitions with Rosa. Nor did he accompany her on any of her trips abroad. Her letters to Harry written on these trips are generally business-like in tone and never inquire after his welfare. Their first meeting place, and the subsequent marriage, appears to have resulted from a friendship between their parents. In Rosa's autobiography and the biography that Elsie continued, Harry is mentioned only on four occasions. The first referred to their marriage:

> In 1884 [the actual date was 19 June 1883] I married Henry Charles Newmarch, second son of Rev. Charles Newmarch, rector of Leverton, Lincolnshire. The two families had known each other for many years, as my father-in-law had been guardian to a young and delicate boy who came to live with us in the care of my father, and later with my brother who took over the practice in Leamington. Life in the country rectory with eight daughters and two sons to educate offered little opportunity for travel or the study of the arts. But both my husband and I enjoyed the interests and pleasures of country life – fishing, walking, riding and driving. However, though his work as a surveyor and estate agent took him often to the country we decided to make our home in London, and I was once able to enjoy the musical life of the city.

Their marriage took place at the Parish Church of Leamington Priors after their family friend James Reynolds Young, Rector of Whitnash, had announced the banns. At the time, Rosa was living in Leamington and Henry's residence is given as St Giles in the Field, Bloomsbury. Among the witnesses were Rosa's brother James Russell Jeaffreson and Henry's sister Emily. Rosa was friendly with Henry's sisters for sometime before her marriage and they were exchanging Christmas cards by 1875 or earlier. The 1881 census entry shows that Henry was living in London before they were married, at 95 Finborough Rd, Kensington, with his brother Francis and sisters Emily, Lucy and Isabella. Thus Rosa and Henry had both lived in London at some point before 1883, when they decided to make their married home in London.

21. Henry Charles Newmarch and his son John

The second mention of her husband in Rosa's autobiography is nearly twenty years later, when she was in discussion with Henry Wood about introducing performances of Russian music in England. As a 'coda' to Wood's letter to Rosa, he adds: 'I do hope it will be fine on Sunday for I am looking forward to a "ride" with your husband.' This was at a time when the family were all bicycle-minded; Henry Newmarch and his son John would go cycling with Henry Wood in Richmond Park.

The third reference is at a time when Rosa was completing her book *Poetry and Progress in Russia* in 1907. After working on it, she felt she needed a break and went with her friend Bella Simpson first to Paris and then on to Italy. It was decided to let their house in Campden Hill temporarily, as by that time their son John, a medical student, was studying in the hospital, their daughter, Elsie, had left school and was about to study in the Sorbonne and 'her husband had agreed to make his home with his sisters during our absence.' It rather sounds as though Rosa made the arrangements and Henry was obliged to comply.

The final reference to her husband is written by Elsie: 'When in 1928, after the death of her husband, Rosa Newmarch and I decided to move to a flat it was with great regret that Bella Simpson, who had lived with us and been her constant companion for nearly forty years, left us to join her widowed sister.'

There is little in either Rosa's autobiography, or Elsie's account, from which one might draw clues about Henry's personality.

Henry Newmarch was brought up in a rectory as a member of a large family with eight sisters and one brother. He trained as a surveyor estate agent. The latter term is probably used of someone who managed estates, rather than the present day usage for someone acting as an agent for buying and selling houses. When he lived in Kensington with his older brother and three sisters, and before his marriage, his occupation in the 1881 census is given as land agent and surveyor. His brother was a civil servant and junior clerk at the India Office, and the three sisters living at the same address all gained their income from stocks.

It appears that Henry was more than an ordinary land agent; one reference is to work he carried out in 1887 in Knightbridge, as the architect for Albert Gate Court, a fairly standard example of the mansion flat genre built in red brick with stone dressings and an iron balcony. The report[2] of this development indicates that Henry Charles Newmarch FSI of Lincoln's Inn Fields designed these residences, which were subsequently built by James Baker of Cadogen Terrace.

About twenty years later, in 1917, there is a reference to Henry in a quite different context as a second lieutenant, 3/6th Battalion of the County of London Volunteer Regiment in the First World War, by which time he would have been in his early sixties. Rosa refers to this in one of her letters quoted in Chapter 19.

Henry died in 1927, before Rosa's youngest granddaughter, Renée Bodimeade (née Newmarch), was born. Although Renée did not know Henry, her mother Gwendoline Mary Newmarch (née Stephens), Rosa's daughter-in-law, knew him from the time of her marriage in 1920 until Henry's death. She described him to Renée as a kindly man who may have had difficulty in coping with a dominating and forthright wife such as Rosa. She related how each year the Newmarch family used to leave London for an annual holiday on the south coast. One year, the family were just ready to depart on such a holiday when Henry rather sheepishly told Rosa that they could not go because they had no money as it had all been lost. It is only possible now to surmise how it was lost, but probably as a result of bad investments. Rosa's response was that from then on she would control the finances, and it gave her the pretext for which she was looking to earn money in her own right. This account seems very plausible in the light of information in the 1881 census that all three of Henry's sisters were supported by income from stocks, and it seems probable that some of Henry's income was also from stocks.

Mismanagement of financial affairs accords with Erik Tawaststjerna's accounts of Rosa Newmarch in his biography of Sibelius[3]. In the course of his description of a train journey made by Sibelius, Granville Bantock and Rosa Newmarch, he states: 'Mrs Newmarch herself was nothing if not decisive: after her husband had mismanaged their financial affairs, she took them into her own hands'

It seems likely that Henry did not share Rosa's great love for music. He was undoubtedly interested in country sports. When Sibelius came to visit the Newmarch family, Rosa states: 'Sometimes he [Sibelius] would come to our house, where – though he and my husband had no language in common – each discovered in the other the true sportsman.'[4] Henry was evidently a keen fisherman.

When in 1926 Rosa organised Janáček's visit to England, she wrote encouraging him to bring his wife, Zdenka, on the visit, but Janáček declined. It is perhaps ironic that Rosa should encourage Janáček to bring his wife, with whom his relationship had been, for most of their married life, very cool, when Rosa herself never had her husband accompany her to any of the functions held during Janáček's visit to London. However, by 1926 there may well have been health reasons for Henry not to be present at these functions.

It seems likely that soon after Rosa's and Henry's marriage in 1883, they began to live what might be described as 'parallel lives'. Rosa pursued her interests in music, the arts and writing, while Henry's interests outside his work lay in outdoor pursuits, but both lived in the same house and shared their children's upbringing. Music came to dominate Rosa's life, particularly as she developed her career as a music writer. In 1885, their son, John, was born and was followed in 1888 by their daughter, Elsie. In between their births, Rosa met Bella Simpson, who did share her passion for music and became her companion on her travels and at musical events for at least twenty years. She lived with the family until Henry's death in 1928.

Notes

1. *Love's Labour's Lost* Act 1, Scene 2, Lines 178-9.

2. John Greenacombe (Ed), *Survey of London : Knightsbridge* (Athlone: Continuum International Publishing Group, 2000) vol. 45, pp.53-63.

3. Erik Tawaststjerna, *Sibelius 1904-1914* (London: Faber and Faber, 1986) vol.2, pp.42-3.

4. Rosa Newmarch, *Jean Sibelius: A Short Story of a Long Friendship* (London: Goodwin and Tabb, 1944) p.15.

CHAPTER 5: LIFE IN LONDON 1883-1897

After Rosa and Henry were first married, they lived at 24 Leamington Road Villas, Westbourne Park. In September 1885, their first child, John Henry, was born. Rosa continued to be a regular attender at the Royal Philharmonic Concerts given in the old St James's Hall and it was when travelling to and from these concerts that she made the acquaintance of a near neighbour and enthusiastic music lover like herself. Miss Bella Simpson lived two doors away at 20 Leamington Road Villas with her older sister, Frances, and her widowed mother Mary, together with an Irish servant and also, according to the 1881 census, a five-year-old grandchild. The child was born in India but it is not clear who his parents were. The family's income appears to have been entirely from annuities, as no one was in employment. Bella, twelve years older than Rosa, was brought up in Birmingham where her father became a theatre manager. However, at the time of Bella's birth, he is described as a comedian. Bella had been a regular Philharmonic Society concert-goer from the time she first attended with her mother in 1871, but even before that, when they lived in Birmingham, she had been to many of the Birmingham Musical Festival concerts. She was present at Thalberg's last recital in Birmingham on 10 December 1863. At some point Bella and Rosa discovered they had a mutual friend in the playwright Eliza Keating. Eliza had been an intimate friend of the Simpson family when they lived in Birmingham and Bella Simpson's father was a theatre manager. Eliza encouraged the Jeaffreson children in play-acting when they lived in Leamington (referred to in Chapter 2).

Rosa and Bella developed a friendship almost immediately. Writing to Bella about a week after their first meeting, Rosa begins: 'Dear Miss Simpson, At this rate the first volume of our correspondence will soon be completed' and continues, 'in sweet music is such art, that it either cements a friendship very quickly and firmly, or – and the reverse side is not so pretty but as true – makes people deadly enemies in a few hours! I am looking forward very much to seeing you on Monday [...] always yours truly Rosa Newmarch.' In her autobiography she wrote:

22. The Newmarch's first home at Leamington Road Villas.

In this case it established a long and lasting friendship with Bella Simpson – nay more than a friendship, for she became one of the family and lived with us for over forty years. [...] The programme of the concert [10 March 1887] at which we sealed our friendship was typical of many we enjoyed together; I see that it contained a slip quoting a letter from Sir Arthur Sullivan, from Monte Carlo, which reads: "with very great regret I am compelled to ask the forbearance of the Directors to excuse me from conducting the first, and perhaps the second, Philharmonic Society's Concerts this season. I am quite ill with nervousness; I think the late earthquake is the cause [the earthquake struck on 22 February 1887 and was felt from Leghorn to Paris] with all its attendant terrors, and the suspense we were in." Mr George Mount took his place, and the soloist was Madame Clara Schumann in her husband Robert's Piano Concerto in A minor, and the programme included a Brahms symphony.

The programme for that concert was inscribed by Bella and Rosa years later: 'Fifty years close friendship began. Bella Simpson & Rosa Newmarch. Concert where I met Rosa.'

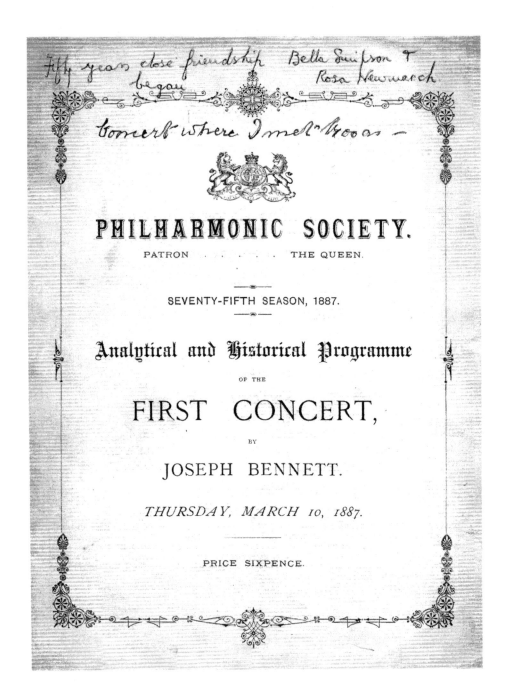

Fifty years close friendship begun Bella Simpson & Rosa Newmarch.

Concert where I met Rosa —

PHILHARMONIC SOCIETY.

PATRON . . . . . . THE QUEEN.

SEVENTY-FIFTH SEASON, 1887.

Analytical and Historical Programme

OF THE

FIRST CONCERT,

BY

JOSEPH BENNETT.

THURSDAY, MARCH 10, 1887.

PRICE SIXPENCE.

23. The Concert at which Rosa and Bella first met

Other performers that Rosa particularly remembered were the pianist Vladimir de Pachmann* and the composer Edvard Grieg and his wife. Rosa often met Pachmann and was in raptures on hearing him perform, as can be discerned from her letter to Bella on 3 June 1887. Now addressing her as 'My dearest Bella', she wrote, after visiting Pachmann:

> I never criticise Pachmann – I can't – and therein lies perhaps the great charm of his playing to me. For once in a way listening to music ceases to be in any way an intellectual exercise; my feelings get the better of my judgement. I forgot that there is a piano, a programme, a concert room; I forgot the medium of sound; technical perfections or imperfections are nothing to me; I don't hear them; only I am conscious of giving myself up to the *music*, the soul of the music utterly and completely. It penetrates me, touches me profoundly and renews my enthusiasm, without which, as George Sand says, one can accomplish nothing. I know at that moment the power that music has in my life. I should be a little ashamed of what might be taken for gush if I did not feel that you know.

In the letter she also referred to herself and Bella learning the Brahms piano duets to play together. Later in 1887, an exchange of letters between Rosa and Bella shows how the friendship has deepened. From 52 Clarendon Avenue Leamington, where she was presumably staying with her sisters, Rosa wrote:

> My dearest Bella
>
> Thank you for both your letters –so like yourself that it seemed almost as though you were saying rather than writing all the sweet things to me. I am so sorry about poor little Johnkin; but have told them not to give him any more beef-tea. Dear your letters touch me and make me feel rather remorseful. I am not worthy indeed of such a warm and true affection; but I am too weak to refuse it; only I hope I shall not disappoint you later on. You have more faith in me than I have in myself. I am afraid I cannot say I am coming home on Saturday. I think I am *more likely* to stay till next week; but not far into it. I am glad you enjoyed the flowers. If you only knew how much pleasure it gives me to bring more interest and happiness into your life. I do not think any trouble – that I may legitimately take – too much, if it gives you any pleasure dear Bella. Only we must be careful that we do not absorb each other to the exclusion of other duties. There can come no real happiness out of a friendship that is founded on anything approaching to selfishness. I don't want to appropriate you; to influence you too much, or have the monopoly of your affection and interests.

You have given me more – so much more – than I ever could have hoped or expected. It was lovely in the fields yesterday. As far as sport went we did not do great things, but the delight, to me of sitting in the meadows and first drinking in all the sights and sounds I had not seen or heard for so long! I wish you could be here. I will try to gather you some forget-me-nots tomorrow, but I fear they are getting over.

I should certainly ask you to do anything dear, if I was in want of anything. Thank you so much too, for going to see dear John. [Her son, aged two.] I expect his father would be very glad to have the same attention paid to him! Perhaps you may see him on Sunday. After all there is some doubt of our going to Seascale.

Dear me: how late it is getting I must go out at once.

With much love and a kiss (the sands of the sea are terribly diminished!)

Ever my dearest, Yours Rosa'

And on 31 December 1887, Bella wrote from 20 Leamington Road Villas:

Dearest Rosa

I must send you a line however stupid – so that my wishes for a happy New Year may meet you first thing to-morrow. Darling I do so hope that it may be a happy and prosperous year for you and yours and that it may bring you ever increasingly all the happiness you need – that we two may continue true and fast friends throughout and for many more to come is my one and heartfelt wish – I couldn't bear not just to see you to-night for I had so hoped to spend the evening with you, the last one of a year you have made so happy and eventful for me. I am glad I came in for you made me feel it was just what I wanted, just to see you and kiss you once more – God bless you darling now and ever. Yrs Bella.'

In 1888, Rosa was expecting her second child. Elizabeth Virginia (Elsie) was born in September 1888. It was also in 1888 that Rosa first met Grieg. She went to Grieg's first public performance in England at St James's Hall on 3 May 1888, by which time she must have been five months pregnant. She described her impressions:

I first met Grieg and his wife about this time, and retain a vivid picture of them at a recital in 1888. Never out of Noah's Ark could one behold two such lovable, but quaint, strange beings as the Griegs. When they sat at the piano to play duets together this was the impression they gave me; of course they were not likenesses, only impressions made out of the same piece of material – though what the nature of it was one could not say. He always played in a dress suit at an afternoon concert, possibly fashioned during their leisure hours among the Norwegian mountains, and she appeared to have borrowed his clothes for the occasion! But how came such breezy, robust, open-air sort of music to be the production of anything so strange and weird? As a musical afternoon it was delightful, more like spending a day at home with them than being at a concert. 'Chopin of the North' indeed, as critics of the day dubbed him. For myself I could never see much to compare between them. Grieg's music, in spite of a certain national tendency to melancholy is healthy above all things, vigorous and clear, the direct outcome of a sane mind influenced by nature pure and simple. One might as well compare a bunch of mountain-ash berries to a spray of stephanotis as draw comparisons between Grieg and Chopin.

The concert on 3 May was entirely devoted to works by Grieg and included his piano and violin sonatas in F major and in C minor, a number of piano solos played by his wife Nina, and a number of his songs. Rosa had loved Grieg's music since her schooldays and liked to play his piano music. Many years later in 1906 she edited a biography of Grieg entitled *Grieg and His Music* by Theophilus Finck. By that time she had become editor of a series of monographs, *Living Masters of Music*, published by John Lane.

Besides time spent at concerts, Rosa also managed to become acquainted with important literary figures living in London. From her childhood days she had been encouraged to write by her mother, whose early death deprived Rosa of a literary *confidante*. On returning to London after her marriage, she was once again in the midst of many literary friends in much the same way as she had been during her earlier years at her Aunt Virginia's. She renewed her acquaintance with the two daughters of the architect G. T. Robinson* and became a frequent visitor to their house in Gower Street. She had known the Robinson family from her childhood when the Robinson's also lived in Leamington.

The Robinson's house in Gower Street was a gathering place for a number of well-known literary figures: Walter Pater (1839-1894), English essayist and art and literary critic; J A Symonds (1840-1893), English poet and literary critic; Robert Browning (1812-1889), English poet and playwright; Arthur Strong (1863-1904), librarian and Arabic scholar; Arthur O'Shaughnessy (1844-1881), poet born in London of Irish parents; and Justin McCarthy (1830-1912), an Irish nationalist, historian, novelist and MP. McCarthy, as a politician, was a Liberal Home Ruler, but his bent was really as a writer. His early works were novels, but his most important writing was *History of Our Times* (vols i-iv 1879-80 and vol. v 1897). Although Rosa includes O'Shaughnessy as one of those who gathered at the Robinson's in Gower

Street, she would not have encountered him there after her marriage in 1883 since he had died in 1881. There were also gatherings of friends at her home in Leamington Road Villas, who included the Robinsons, Arthur Strong, Franklin Clive (a bass singer in the Doyle Carte Opera Company), Vernon Lea*, Esther Wood and many others[1].

These meetings gave Rosa the encouragement and opportunity to formulate ideas and seek a means of expression in verse, in critical essays, or in some form of creative work. At this time, she made regular trips to the British Museum for research and study, until she joined the London Library (founded 1841), which enabled her to take out books *ad lib* for work at home.

Her first book to be published was an English translation from German of Hermann Deiters's biographical sketch of Johannes Brahms. Music, in many ways, was her first love and she was particularly fond of Brahms's music, which she mentions in a number of her letters to Bella Simpson. In 1880, Deiters's short book had been published in Germany, the first biography of Brahms. Deiters had previously revised a biography of Mozart and translated the biography of Beethoven by Alexander Thayer (1817-1897), before deciding to write a biographical sketch of Brahms. He wrote to Brahms in 1880 asking specific points and received an unhelpful reply: 'I really know absolutely no dates or years concerning myself: but here, naturally, I also cannot try to look up old letters, etc. Having said that, I need hardly add that I dislike talking about myself, or dislike reading anything that concerns me personally [...] I cannot answer your specific questions. Except: J.B., born 1834 in Altona on the 7 March (not, as often stated, on the 7 May in Hamburg).'[2]

It is perhaps not surprising, in view of Brahms's lack of help that, according to Styra Avins 'most of the facts of Brahms's life [in Deiters book] were incorrect.[2]' So perhaps in retrospect this was not the best start to Rosa's publishing career. Brahms lived until 1897, and in the period between 1880 and 1887, when Rosa's translation was completed, Brahms was still very much an active composer. To cater for this, Rosa added a chapter of descriptive notes of some twenty additional works (30 pages in a book totalling 160 pages). Rosa sent the last pages of her manuscript to the publishers, T. Fisher Unwin, in March 1887 and the book was published in 1888, shortly after her daughter Elsie was born.

In 1891, the Newmarch family had moved house from Leamington Road Villas to 52 Campden Hill Square. The addition of a second child to the family, and also accommodating Bella Simpson, may have necessitated a move to a larger house.

Since childhood, Rosa had a latent interest in the people and culture of Russia. She found 'Boris Godounov' and 'Ivan the Terrible' her substitutes for characters more popular with her contemporaries, such as 'Bluebeard' and the princesses in the 'Arabian Nights'. She attributes this interest to a little book published by the Society for the Promotion of Christian Knowledge on Russia and the Russian People that she stumbled on in the family library in their house in Leamington. As she says: 'It was full of thrilling horrors about Ivan the Terrible, who wanted to marry Queen Elizabeth, and I doubt if it promoted any Christian knowledge, but it served to acquaint a girl of nine with the names of Ivan and Boris Godounov, the great Patriarch Nicon, and other personalities and events which were not commonly known in school rooms of that period.' When they moved to London, it was one of the treasures that disappeared, which she greatly regretted. Although her sister visited southern Russia, staying in Odessa, she learnt little of the life of the people and nothing of the language, and so had little influence on Rosa's urge to find out more about Russia.

By 1894, Rosa was dimly aware of a new and vigorous movement going on in the Russian musical world. Whilst spending an Easter holiday in Belgium, she came across a copy of *Alexandre Borodine* written in French by an enthusiastic amateur, Alfred Habets, who was a successful mining engineer by profession working in Liège. The book, really not more than a pamphlet, opened a new world to Rosa. At the time, she knew something of Glinka, Tchaikovsky and Rubinstein, the last both as pianist and composer, but of Borodin, Cui, Balakirev, Rimsky-Korsakov and Musorgsky she was hardly aware. At the time in Russian musical circles, there was a fierce debate about the dominance of 'foreign' music over Russian music. Much of the music performed in the theatres and concert halls was Italian, German or French; music composed by Russians was performed at inferior venues with inferior orchestras. The New Russian School of Music was formed in the 1850s and advocated the importance of national music. Its proponents included the 'Mighty Five' or *kuchka*, mentioned above.

Habets had taken as a basis of his essay a biographical notice that Vladimir Stasov dedicated to the memory of his friend Borodin immediately after his premature death in 1887. To this he had added a collection of Borodin's letters, six to Madame Borodin and one to César Cui. They were written when he went to Germany in 1877 to visit Liszt in Weimar. They describe their conversations and Liszt's opinion of the new Russian school of music. Habets translated the biography and letters from Russian into French with the aid of two Russian students in Liège, one of whom was a pupil of Borodin, probably at the Academy of Medicine at St Petersburg. Rosa decided that this biography of a composer, though little known in England, was of sufficient interest to musicians there to warrant its translation. However, she felt the need to set the biography in the context of the developments in Russian music at that time, and so she decided to contact the author of the primary source, Vladimir Stasov, then the director of Fine Arts at the Imperial Library in St Petersburg. She corresponded with him, and with the information he provided she was able to write a Translator's Preface, which is a good resumé of the developments of Russian music from the eighteenth century. She did not undertake any detailed criticism of the music since at the time she knew it only through the medium of piano arrangements, and much of it had not been performed in concerts in England.

She began by describing how Habets visited Saint Isaac's Cathedral in St Petersburg and was profoundly impressed with the touching and characteristic music of the Greek ritual and the *à capella* singing of the famous choir. He also found the folk music captivating. Surely, Habets thought, people who can produce this music must have composers capable of moulding its wealth of national melody into some permanent and beautiful art forms. However, when he visited a Russian family to discuss music, to his dismay he was told that Tchaikovsky and Rubinstein alone represented modern music in Russia; composers of the New School met with little success. In the course of the preface, Rosa was able to summarise the opposing forces at play in Russian music. She probably communicated with Stasov in French at this stage. He had travelled widely in Europe, including a stay in London, and, like all educated Russians at that time, probably spoke well-nigh perfect French and probably one or two more European languages.

Having completed the manuscript, Rosa tried a number of publishers who all rejected it. She felt so strongly about the importance of the New Russian School of Music, with whose music she felt the world should become acquainted, and she had expended so much time and effort compiling the preface that she decided the only course was to spend a little money and go in for what nowadays might be called 'vanity publishing'. The book was published by Digby, Long and Co, London in 1895 and lavishly distributed to the press. Although reviews were not numerous, they were on the whole favourable. *The Times*[3] review stated that it had been well translated by Mrs Newmarch; it then went on to describe the book as follows: 'It consists of two sections, the first a very interesting and sympathetic memoir of the exceedingly original Russian genius whose music is almost completely unknown in England, and the second a vivid sketch of Liszt as he appeared to Borodin.' Unfortunately the book did not sell well, and within a short time the publisher indicated they were going to remainder it. Rosa had been comforted when the musical press began to quote from it and she could not bear to see her hard work lost, so she went to the publisher, took all their stock and managed to sell it to another firm. Whether or not its sales then improved is not clear, but the book was reprinted in paperback in 2005 by AMC Press, Boston, USA.

Rosa continued to correspond with Stasov, and he sent her articles of his own and of other Russian writers. At her request that the articles should be in French or German, his reply was forthright: her attitude to Russian art was amateurish and indolent, and the only way to master the subject seriously was to learn Russian. Rosa was never the person to shy away from a challenge, and by this time she was passionate about Russian culture. However, she did at first try to find an easy way out. She visited John Theophilus Naaké, the keeper of Russian books and manuscripts at the British Museum and author of *Slavonic Fairy Tales Collected and Translated from Russian, Polish, Serbian and Bohemian*, (1874), to ask him to recommend someone who might translate an article she had received from Stasov. He recommended a Madame N. (so-called in Rosa's autobiography), adding that she was an extremely poor but well-educated Russian and Rosa must to be sure to pay promptly the fee she asked.

It is not clear why Rosa refers to her as Madame N. She came out of Russia in 1881 possibly for political reasons. Russia, in the early and mid-nineteenth century, was a place of increasing tension and dramatic political, economic, and social changes. Industrialisation created big wealth disparities and entirely new classes of people as the old aristocratic power system transformed into a plutocratic one. Russian monarchs realised that serfdom and the social structure was not sustainable and would end in a bloody rebellion. The problem was to implement reforms that were both effective and politically realistic. In the 1860s, a movement known as the Nihilist Movement developed in Russia. The term nihilist was originally coined by Ivan Turgenev in his 1862 novel *Fathers and Sons*. Nihilists favoured the destruction of human institutions and laws, based on the idea these were artificial and corrupt and needed to be wiped out in order to start anew. It culminated in the assassination of Csar Alexander II in 1881.

Madame N. sometimes appeared careworn, but was at times vivacious. She spoke and wrote English fluently. What pleased Rosa most, both then and later on, was her evident enjoyment in any job she undertook. The arrangement seemed promising until Rosa opened the packet containing her first translation and found that 'Not one single word was it possible to decipher of Madame N.'s cryptic and impenetrable handwriting. It took me days to unravel and transliterate the manuscript into clear readable English.' Rosa then decided she might just as well learn Russian. This decision came at about the time when she developed heart trouble. The doctors' diagnoses varied between angina pectoris and 'functional derangements due to indigestion'. The recommended remedy was rest and dosing with digitalis. When the attacks came, they often lasted hours but sometimes days. Rosa used this to escape 'futile social engagements' and begin the study of Russian.

Learning Russian at the end of the nineteenth century was not straightforward. There were few English people studying the language and those who were came into one of two categories: military officers who were working for the government grant which allowed them a year's residence in Russia and young men seeking employment in the oil, wood or mining industries in Russia. In both cases they were generally interested solely in becoming sufficiently fluent in Russian to get by. The teaching of Russian at King's College London began in 1889 with the appointment of Nicolas Orloff. The inclusion of Russian teaching was based on the belief prevailing at the time that Russia's expansionist policy posed a serious threat to British interests in India and so Russian language should be treated as a subject for future members of the Indian Army and Civil Service[4]. Those like Rosa, purely interested in the literature and art of the country, were few. About this time, she made the acquaintance of the Slavonic scholar William Richard Morfill (1834-1909). He had travelled much in Slavonic countries and, in 1889, was appointed university reader in Russian at Oxford. He wrote a number of grammars of Slavonic languages and books on Slavonic literature. In the years to come, he became one of her literary *confidantes*. Both he and Mme N. told her that to find someone enthusiastic about Russian language and literature was a truly stimulating experience. Such grammar books as were available at the time all had some shortcomings or were not suited to Rosa's needs. Mme N. was aware of the books currently available but felt it better to develop the necessary grammar herself as the lessons progressed.

Mme. N. came to the Newmarchs' house at Campden Hill Square twice a week for several months and although she was by nature reserved, during that period a genuine friendship developed between her and Rosa, who not only learned the language but also much about the culture. She mastered the Cyrillic alphabet quite quickly, being fascinated by calligraphy and obviously enjoyed writing in the new script. A major hurdle, she recalls, was getting to grips with the Russian verb, its tenses, aspects, moods and inflections, all of which Mme N. felt had to be taken in one sitting. Rosa became quite attached to her, as her sensitive account shows, and later when Mme N. left the country Rosa could not replace her.

As we proceeded I learnt many things from Mme. N. besides the rudiments of Russian grammar. She talked to me a great deal about her country, its customs, its literature and art (I think she was not specially interested in music, but her husband had been a painter of some distinction), and when I confided to her my intention of visiting it before the year was out, she gave me some very useful and, as I afterwards found, reliable and just information. She took off the keen edge of its unfamiliarity so that I lost no time in feeling at home there. She had been in England some years before I knew her, having come, as I think, for political reasons in the troubled year of 1881; but I never asked her any indiscreet questions. Her quiet voice, restrained manner and veiled expression, all gave the impression that she would not harm a fly; only now and then I caught a flash of northern fire in her usually mild blue eyes which made me suspect she might be an extinct volcano, almost –but not quite – incombustible. Her youth must have coincided with the most active Nihilist period [...] There were moments when she talked with the awful sincerity and point-blank frankness of Russians about the lowest depths of human souls [...]

She was a true Slav in her unconsciousness of time and would come pounding up Campden Hill Square, arriving too breathless to gasp out her apologies. I suspected that she had often walked from Bloomsbury to Notting Hill on nothing but a cup of tea to save the bus fare [...] She was proud, but when she knew me better she would condescend to stay and share my lunch [...] I grew to respect her, and was sincerely grieved, not to say remorseful, when I heard of her departure, I hope, to a happier world. It happened that I was a long time abroad and had not heard of her failure to find sufficient work, which probably meant that she often went short of warmth and food [...] I tried in vain to find her equal as a teacher.

In the autumn of 1896 and the following spring, Rosa made the acquaintance of a number of Russians visiting England for the first time. It seems that her book *Borodin and Liszt* had made more impression in Russia than in England and she had become recognised as a Russophile; this was in part due to Vladimir Stasov and his intellectual circle. The Newmarchs' house became something of a meeting place for Russian intelligentsia, who probably felt more at ease there than they would have in their own country. Among those whom she mentions were Anofriev, a journalist; Andrei Krasinsky, a medical man; Vladimir Strakhov, a promising young occulist; Tarassov, a professor who wrote about Russian art and Pavel Nikolayevich Milyukov, a politician and the founder, leader, and most prominent member of the Constitutional Democratic party, known as the Kadets. Milyukov was a great lover of music and in those days not so deeply preoccupied with politics so they used to go to some of the best London concerts.

These friends practically planned Rosa's first visit to Russia. During the summer of 1897, there was an International Congress of Medicine to be held in Moscow, and as a number of the participants would be from England, it was considered an opportune time to make a tour. Rosa was being urged to go with a friend or at least fellow countrymen with whom she could travel; the hospitality and entertainment laid on for the Congress would be extended to her even though she would not be a participant. Should she fall ill or have any further heart problems, she would not be isolated and could be assured of medical help close at hand. As she remarks: 'It sounded a most promising proposition, but its fulfilment, although delightful in almost every particular, was entirely different to what they kindly planned.' Friends and relatives thought it insane for a woman prone to heart attacks to embark on such an enterprise, some suggesting that she would return home via Siberia if at all. If there were any specific concerns expressed by her husband about leaving him and two children aged nine and twelve for such a trip lasting about three months then they are not disclosed in her autobiography. Bella Simpson, with her love of music, would make the ideal travelling companion. She would have liked a few more months with Mme. N. to give her Russian that extra polish, but otherwise why put off realising her ardent wish to see Russia?

24. John and Elsie Newmarch

Notes

1. Letter to Rosa dated 2 February 1934 from Mrs Esther Wood, author of *Dante Rossetti and the PreRaphaelite Movement* (London: Sampson Low Marston & Co. 1894).

2.   Styra Avins, *Johannes Brahms: Life and Letters* (Oxford: OUP, 1997), pp.560-2.

3.   *The Times*, 17 May 1895.

4.   I. W. Roberts, *History of the School of Slavonic and East European Studies 1915-1990* (London: School of Slavonic and East European Studies, 1991), p.3.

CHAPTER 6: THE FIRST JOURNEY TO RUSSIA, 1897

The Twelfth International Congress of Medicine was held in Moscow from 19 to 26 August 1897. Unlike international scientific congresses nowadays, where delegates are jetted in for a few days for a plethora of presentations, followed perhaps by a post-conference tour before returning home, in the late nineteenth century the pace was somewhat slower. An American doctor, Victor Clarence Vaughan, gave a fascinating account of his experience as a delegate at this Moscow conference[1]. He and his family landed in Antwerp in early June with their bicycles and made their way leisurely through Europe by train, sightseeing en route, arriving in Moscow in August in time for the congress and returning home in September. A number of excursions were arranged in connection with the Congress, such as a trip to the Caucasus lasting up to 30 days and costing seven and a half guineas, not including the cost of steamers on the Black Sea nor of stagecoaches on the Georgian Road[2]. So when Rosa, accompanied by Bella Simspon, set off several days before the start of the conference, making their way across Europe with a number of stops en route, they were travelling in much the same way as many of the delegates.

The first leg of their journey was to Liège, where Rosa made her personal acquaintance with Alfred Habets, whose book, *Borodin and Liszt*, she had translated. At the time, Habets was not in the best of health, having experienced a severe shock which had brought on a slight stroke. Recently he and his wife had been driving in the environs of Liège in an open Victoria when the horse had taken fright, throwing Mme Habets violently from the carriage and killing her instantly. He was a man of great charm and both he and his wife were devoted to music; he was president of the musical committee of the Société d'Emulation of Liège. He had been in daily contact with both Borodin and César Cui when they visited Belgium and had become particularly fond of Borodin as a person, and of his music. However, he modestly explained that although he had written a book on Borodin, it was through the patronage of Comptesse Mercy-Argenteau (see Marie-Clotilde-Elizabeth Louise de Riquet*) that the New Russian School became known in Belgium.

Rosa told Habets that she and Bella were on their way to Russia. He congratulated them and somewhat envied them, having been to Russia twelve years earlier, but he knew that his health was now such that he would not be able to travel there again.

After spending a pleasant two days with Habets, they began the second stage of their journey.

Rosa had already told Stasov that she intended to pay him a visit at the Imperial Public Library in St Petersburg, and he replied cordially, indicating he would do all he could to help her with her studies. However, in mid-August he would be away on holiday and he suggested they visited Moscow first and then continued to St Petersburg in September. That suited their plans, as they wanted to see their Russian friends who would be in Moscow during August for the Medical Congress. They still had a little time before then so they decided to stop in Berlin and Warsaw on the way.

In Berlin, Rosa found the heat intolerable and felt quite ill during the first night there. Bella began to feel anxious lest Rosa's heart, which had behaved well so far, should become irregular. She asked the porter to phone a doctor, which he reluctantly did. 'It is as I thought,' he said, 'he is just sitting down to his *Mittagessen*, and will not be coming until four o'clock.' So for four hours Rosa sustained herself with digitalis, weak tea and cognac. As she said: 'It was evidently the treatment needed, for towards five o'clock I was sitting up and, although Coué[3] was as yet unknown, I was asseverating cheerfully and repeating a formula of my own: I am much better – I shall sleep –I shall leave Berlin tomorrow.' When the porter knocked at about 7pm to say the doctor would come immediately, she sent a polite message to say that the patient had made a miraculous recovery after a course of auto-suggestion lasting seven hours.

The next day, they set out for Warsaw. Rosa was always thankful to find herself in a Latin or Slavonic country; she had no particular liking for Germany. This feeling would later become even stronger after the First World War and became very evident when she met Sibelius a decade later and was reluctant to communicate in German, although she was quite familiar with the language.

On arrival in Warsaw, Rosa stated: 'I made an act of thanksgiving for finding myself at last in a Slavonic country!' She did not say whether this involved prostrating herself on Polish soil. Her first experiences of Warsaw were off-putting – with initial difficulties at the hotel, which her Russian friends had recommended, and struggling with language. Things soon improved however, as is evident from her account.

Its [the hotel's] entrance was picturesque and intriguing, but it filled me with distrust. [...] An unusually vain-glorious concierge directed us to one of the little houses and opened the door of what was evidently the room reserved for us. We were followed by a most villianous-looking man, swivel-eyed and badly marked with smallpox. The room was small, with two dingy beds in it and approached by a tiny, dark, whiffy hall in which I presently discovered another bed – an unspeakable couch. The window which gave on to the busy courtyard was so low down that any passerby could have stepped over the sill into our room. I shook my head and emphatically said: "*Nie hochu*" (I don't want it), *Ich will es nicht, Pas tout du monde*, etc. The hotel proprietor appeared on the scene. He commanded some ten words of French: the head porter in the disguise of a high military official aired six words of German; the villainous person was voluble in Polish. Among many charms of the room pointed out to me was the fact that he, the villainous one, would sleep in the little cubby-hole at my door and be always at my beck and call. Now I am not one of those travellers who go about in the expectation of being robbed and murdered, and I had already heard from my sister and Mme. N. about *Koridorny* or corridor men, who in the less fashionable hotels often entirely replaced the west-european chamber maid, sleeping on a mat or a bench outside one's door ready to serve one night or day. But the prospect of that white-faced deeply pitted squinting unfriendly person, with his unclean looking whiskers, as a servant, clinched the matter. I exchanged a glance with Bella Simpson and we firmly grasped our travelling bags and prepared to depart. I could quite understand that in this exclusively Polish inn they did not care to struggle with my halting, and perhaps not too intelligible, Russian [...] However our firm gesture of departure brought about a change of heart in our host. He took us away from that part of the building with its little rooms, which may well have been the cells of an old monastry, along a gloomy passage and up endless stairs (there was no lift) to a more modern part of the hotel. Here we were ushered into a fine large room looking out on to a wide thoroughfare. Our particular corridor man proved to be a small, sturdy, cheerful fellow who talked Russian willingly and fluently. He afterwards told me that he had been a batman to an officer in the Russian army. In no time our luggage followed us, was unstrapped and opened, our dusty travelling coats taken away and brought back clean, while Russian tea with lemon and *sukhary* (rusks) appeared on the table. We had indeed hit on a handy man and one of the most attractive ladies' maids I ever came across. By some miraculous intuition he seemed to understand my feeble Russian; took charge of our passports, posted my letters faithfully, and made the sun to shine upon us once again.

Warsaw took me altogether by surprise. I had looked for tragedy, dull resignation, injured pride, smouldering resentment –perhaps apathy; I found the stage set for a harlequinade; a city peopled by a vivacious, bustling, mobile population. I think that Poland under the old regime was not always well served by her exiles, at least those I had chanced to meet in Paris and other European centres. They were not by any means all political martyrs, but they hugged a grievance very close and talked of the sorrows of Poland more perhaps than dignity demanded[4]. In my youth it was very much the fashion to espouse the Polish cause on sentimental rather than historic grounds. In every school a copy of Miss Jane Porter's *Thaddeus of Warsaw* was to be found. It was generally the most be-thumbed and tattered of the few works of fiction permitted in young ladies' seminaries [...] It coloured my views of East-European history for many years to come [...] Jane Porter wrote this in 1831, but so greatly did she impress the sensibility of a schoolgirl of fourteen that when I first saw Warsaw in 1897, I half expected to meet gaunt forms in 'threadbare uniform coats'; to contemplate 'a variety of wretched yet noble-looking visages' and to find at every street corner the prototype of her hero 'with melancholy and bravery stamped on his emaciated features' and although his hat was rusty and 'his hands without gloves' his aspect always that of a perfect gentleman and his step that of a military man. So long can the glamour of a sentimental historical novel blind us to changes of time! I met none of these seedy and oppressed ghosts of the past in the *stare miasto* [old town] or in the beautiful Saxon gardens. I saw instead an extremely well-dressed population, moving as briskly as high-stepping horses, with a similar suggestion of swagger, and an irresistable energy in their looks and actions which betokened the purposeful, intelligent race which they have proved to be. The Poles at home were far more impressive, even in 1897, than in the lachrimose frequenters of foreign cities. One feared for the stability of Poland immediately after her independence. One need fear no more . Her steady resuscitation, without sensationalism, one of the post-war miracles[5].

As to the city itself, the Vistula is its life-giving artery. On the dazzling day I first saw it, like a flowing mass of light it cut its pathway through the capital – the heart of Poland –past the Old City and the New, where the buildings come down to the edge of the water on its left bank, and on its right skirting the green Alexander Park. The river is spanned by five arches of the Alexander Bridge, a beautiful example of a modern bridge (1865), its lattice ironwork giving it an unaccustomed grace. Apart from the hostile political feeling which was not visible on the surface, Warsaw as the meeting place of two civilisations the Latin and the Byzantine has a unique charm.

Whilst Rosa found Warsaw interesting, she had not a single acquaintance there, which is perhaps surprising given the huge number of people she knew, and she was keen to move on to Russia, the promised goal of her pilgrimage, where she had many friends and much she hoped to achieve.

Rosa and Bella took the train from Warsaw to Moscow. Her description of the journey is in fascinating contrast with travel today. Her Baedeker travel guide suggested the journey from Warsaw to Moscow offered little of interest for the traveller. This was not the case for Rosa; the scenery and the whole experience she found exciting.

The alternations of forests of dark delphinium-blue firs, their edges gallooned by silver birch, extensive swamps, and districts rich in waving cornfields offered such exquisite contrasts of colour that I never once felt its monotony. The old towns through which we passed –Minsk, Kasnoie, Smolensk – scenes of fierce battles between the Russians, the Poles and Lithuanians, often showed interesting architectural features – examples of the timber period in Russian architecture. The sluggish waters of the Berezina recalled to mind Napoleon's disastrous campaign in 1812 and the terrible crossing of the river near Studianka[6]. We stopped at Smolensk, where the French emperor paused for three or four days making a final effort to reorganise the remnants of his vast invading host. Smolensk had known various sharp vicissitudes: as 'key of the gate of Russia' the town had been tossed to and fro between Russia and Poland like a shuttlecock; Boris Godounov had rebuilt its ancient walls at the end of the 16th century; Potemkin, the favourite of Catherine the Great was born there. It was by no means a dull itinerary.

In those days it was customary to stop at some of the bigger stations long enough to get out of the train and eat a meal in comfort while at a standstill. One entered a large hall and experienced some surprise at the preparations as for a mayoral banquet; *zakouska* [starters] of every description, dried eels, caviar, the delicious smoked *Syg*[7]; soups steaming hot in tureens –fish soup, and *stschi, bortch* eaten cold with sour cream; *pirozhki*, small pies or croquettes, filled with egg, fish, or cabbage and mince, which go with the soup course; many unfamiliar fish, hot and cold – sturgeon, starlet, fish pies very superior to our *réchauffée* of boiled cod smothered in mashed potatoes and pasty white sauce; varieties of meat, roast or boiled; poultry and game, including ptarmigan and the tasty hazel hen from the forests. The choice is bewildering, and though the time allowed was liberal enough to satisfy most appetites, and three bells at least were rung before the train departed, the vacillating glutton can be left behind [...] Of course I am writing of the past; the spreads may now be curtailed.

For economy's sake we travelled in an ordinary Russian sleeping car with four berths. At night my friend and I occupied the lower ones and over my head was a lady who built herself in with bags and cases. She appeared a quiet and rather shabby little person when I saw her climb into her berth. Almost immediately after we had dimmed our lights, we became aware of sounds as of mice or rats scampering over paper. It continued for several hours. Every moment I fancied that some of them might drop from above and canter like Queen Mab's team of 'atomies' across my nose, and although I am not frightened of the 'inferior rodent' the strain of expectancy grew unbearable.

When we arrived at the *douane* I gasped at the spectacle of the dowdy little body who had gone to bed moth-eaten and rusty as an autumn blackbird and now stepped out of the train in fashionable silks and laces, carrying all her suit cases containing her former shabby envelope, like a butterfly unwilling to part with its chrysalis. It seemed a transparent kind of trick, but her face when she came back to her berth expressed triumph. She spent the rest of the night carefully folding, while we passed the remaining hours of darkness in calling down maledictions on her vanity. She must have been buying a whole trousseau in Berlin.

My first experiences at a Russian custom house were more ludicrous than painful. The French speaking officials alluded to by my Baedeker, must have all been on holiday, but I consoled myself by thinking how good it was to struggle in Russian with the fierce-looking, bearded man who signed to me to open one of my bags. I was confessionally minded, but it is not easy to confess accurately and fluently in a strange language. I had been told that all kind of imported wines and spirits were very expensive in Russia, and the wines of the Crimea and Caucasus unpalatable to Westerners, so I took a couple of bottles of whisky to last me during my visit. These I produced at once, to the evident amusement of the customs official, who pushed them back into my arms. I made out the remarks which accompanied his gesture to be: "You require these for the journey –English wine?" "Scotch" I replied "Good (*Kharasho*)! Take them." Not until I was back in the train did I realise that two bottles of "Particular Old Scotch" was rather an ample allowance for the time remaining before my arrival in Moscow. The rest of my luggage appeared to contain no contraband. But wait! What is this? I had a folding travelling bath with me and a piece of mackintosh to spread on the floor under it. What could this be? "This is dress material?" "Certainly not!" "What do you use it for then?" "To put under a bath", I replied, but I made a howler in using the word *vanya*, a public bath-house instead of *vanna*, a hip-bath, which might have meant something to an official. "Impossible"! *Nievozmozhno* !" In a tinkling two or three *douaniers* were on he spot. My piece of mackintosh was undergoing a kind of third degree examination; folded and refolded, sniffed – being brand new it smelt horribly – laid on the dirty floor of the custom house, discussed from every point of view, and just as I was thinking I should have to find my bath and demonstrate its uses to puzzled officials, they gave up in despair and pushed it back into my holdall.

Strange that at the very confines of the promised land we should be laughing over such absurd incidents as these and forgetful of the thrilling issues close at hand.

We arrived at the terminus of Smolensk[8] and were met by one of our friends, Vladimir Petrovich Strakhov, junior house surgeon at the Ophthalmic Hospital. With him was a striking looking man, dark and dignified, a typical Ukrainian, the senior house surgeon, and a third older man, the chief consultant and medical director of the same establishment. He had come out of courtesy to help two complete strangers, and outside the station his *équipage* was waiting to take us to our hotel. I could never get quite used to this high-sounding name, which in reality applied to any kind of two-horsed carriage without a license plate and with a liveried coachman. One almost expects outriders and a military escort to accompany an equipage. The Professor's roomy landau with its pair of elderly stallions and astounding and almost globular coachman, brought us at last to the steps of the Hotel Continental, with so much shouting and whip-cracking that I felt immensely important. I might have been the advance guard of the British Medical Association itself.

Notes

1. Victor C. Vaughan, *A Doctor's Memories* (Indianapolis: The Bobbs-Merrill Co., 1926), pp.153-5.

2. The International Congress in Moscow [From our special correspondent in St Petersburg], *British Medical Journal* (14 August 1911), 410-411.

3. The Coué method, introduced by the psychotherapist, Émile Coué (1857-1926) is a method of psychotherapy and self-improvement based on auto-suggestion. It centres on a routine repetition of a particular expression according to a specified ritual, in a given physical state and in the absence of any sort of allied mental imagery, at the beginning and at the end of each day.

4. From 1795 until 1918, Poland was partitioned between Russia, Austria and Prussia and did not exist as a country, only as a nation.

5. This account was written about 1935 before the German army overan Poland in World War II.

6. After the retreat from Moscow in 1812, Napoleon's engineers managed to construct

two makeshift bridges at Studianka, and on 26 November the bulk of his army began to cross the river. On 29 November, the Russians pressed from the east, and the French were forced to burn the bridges, leaving some 10,000 stragglers on the other side.

7. *Syg* [сиг] = whitefish.

8. *Belorussky vokzal,* the station in Moscow where trains from Smolensk arrive.

CHAPTER 7: MOSCOW 1897

Although Rosa's prime reason for going to Russia was to meet Stasov and work in the St Petersburg Library, she never regretted first visiting Moscow, and she felt that Moscow was the core of Russian life. But there had been much cruelty enacted in the past; when she walked home to her rooms in the evenings through Red Square and down the silent business streets of the *Kitai Gorod*, she may have shuddered to remember the very earth must be saturated with the blood of those sacrificed to Ivan the Terrible's barbarity. Still, Moscow remained for her a hospitable city. As she put it:

> My affection for the old capital was love at first sight. On the other hand, although in course of time I gave to St Petersburg respect and friendship, I was always subject there to moods of uneasiness, which crept over me like chilly, miasmic, moral mists. The orientalism of Moscow put its spell on me; whereas Peter's window turned to the west had its blinds too often pulled down to be cheerful. [...] Why should I have felt the sense of well-being in Moscow, with its tradition of violence, cruelty and bloodshed is difficult to say. Maurice Baring in his *Mainsprings of Russia* has penetrated far into this unaccountable problem of 'the fascination of Russia' despite of, or perhaps because of, all her weaknesses, defects and asperities. The spell is there not to be analysed, never to be annulled; 'once you have felt you will never be free of it. The aching melancholy song which Gogol says wanders from sea to sea throughout the length and breadth of the land, will forever echo in your heart and haunt the recesses of your memory.'

Already in 1897 Rosa sensed a feeling of unrest and that changes must occur in the governance of the country. This was seventy-two years after the failed Decembrist uprising and eight years before the 1905 revolution, which has been regarded as the dress rehearsal for the 1917 revolution. On meeting Vladimir Stasov, he would talk about the 'general holocaust to come'. He spoke prophetically of what must inevitably be the end of the existing regime, reminding her eloquently by quoting Ezekiel: 'behold a whirlwind came out of the north, a great cloud, and a fire infolding itself [...] Remove the diadem and take off the crown [...] I will overturn it'(Ezekiel, I, iv; XXI, xxvi, xxvii). Like all liberals in Russia, he ardently wished that freedom would come to his people, but he had misgivings as to how and when it would come. He used to say that he feared the *otsebyatinnost* (Отсебятиност) – the beside-itselfness of the Russians. Rosa, as an outsider, hoped it would come through reformation rather than revolution and found it hard to believe when the inevitable change came some years later with such violence.

During her first days in Moscow, she was not dwelling on such gloomy thoughts; the August sun shone all day on the peerless white walls, on gilded cupolas, spires and towers, on the gleaming tiles, green and red, on architectural forms unfamiliar to western Europeans. The summer heat had driven most of the inhabitants to their dachas, although Moscow did not look deserted on the eve of a fête – the reception of the Twelfth World Medical Congress. At night the public gardens, Alexandrovsky and Sokolniky Parks were beautifully illuminated, their finely grown specimen fir trees exhaling a cool and bracing fragrance. Every day friends came to take them out and they never felt themselves a tax upon them because their hospitality was all spontaneously given. Rosa was surprised to find that most men of the professional classes spoke only Russian, though some had a small French or German vocabulary, so it was gratifying for her to find how well her Russian carried her.

Initially they stayed at the Hotel Continental, chosen from a list sent to Rosa before she left England. News soon spread among the hotel staff that 'the English visitor' was interested in Tchaikovsky, who had died four years earlier, and was even writing articles about him. By now Tchaikovsky was a household name in Moscow, and no sooner did Rosa and Bella appear in the dining room than the powerful mechanical organ was switched on. At the time this was very up-to-date technology, being second only to the one in the Hermitage Restaurant. So their meals were eaten to the accompaniment of Tchaikovsky's *Sérénade Mélancolique,* the *Pathétique Symphony,* or the *1812 Overture.* After they had been in the hotel a couple of days, the manager told them that their rooms were required the following day as they had been booked for the organising committee of the Medical Congress. This took them rather by surprise; they presumed they could have the rooms for an indeterminate period. With nearly 8000 medical guests in town, it might have been difficult to find new accommodation, but with advice from their friends, they moved to a hotel in the old town (*Kitai Gorod*). These friends were worried about them moving to a small commercial hotel frequented only by Russian merchants and thus unaccustomed to foreign visitors. However, the proprietor of the hotel had been a patient of Dr Nicolai Pravasoud, one of their medical friends and he phoned the proprietor who assured him that the ladies could have a fine large room. Although there were disadvantages, especially as none of the hotel staff spoke a language other than Russian, the hotel had no restaurant, and they would have to order food to be brought into their room, nevertheless it had the advantage that Rosa would have to speak Russian. They found the staff very helpful so long as they could make themselves understood.

From their room, high up in the hotel, they had a wide view across the narrow street. Opposite stood a church with walls decorated with bright coloured frescos representing scenes from the life of Christ and five onion-shaped cupolas in deep royal blue, each surmounted with a gilt Byzantine cross. Stretching further towards the low lying hills and beyond a long range of buildings in palest salmon crowned by a roof of blue-green, was an endless vista of cupolas, their golden crosses flashing and shimmering through the haze of the still, burning August noon.

Rosa had not come to Moscow with any expectation of hearing serious music at that season of the year, nor had she brought any introductions to members of the music profession, most of whom she expected would be away for their summer holidays. However, quite unexpectedly, she made some interesting contacts. Before leaving England she had completed a series of articles on Tchaikovsky, based on Nikolai Dmitrievich Kashkin's pamphlet *Reminiscences of P.I. Tchaikovsky* (published 1896). These appeared in a new musical weekly, *The Musician*, on 14 and 21 July, and on 4 and 11 August 1897. Nicolai Dmitriyevich Kashkin (1839-1920) was music critic of the *Moskovsky Viedomostny* from 1886-1897, and at one time both he and Tchaikovsky were professors at the Moscow Conservatoire. Rosa had previously corresponded with him to seek his permission to use his *Reminiscences* as the basis for her articles on Tchaikovsky. She was therefore very surprised when there was a loud knock on her door at 7.30am and an elderly man in a loose alpaca coat with wild eyes and unkempt hair appeared. Kashkin entered, oblivious that it was not the calling hour, wanting to tell her about Peter Ilich Tchaikovsky. Walking round and round the table he poured forth a stream of lively reminiscences. Kashkin, she realised, was not a great music critic – he was too enthusiastic about his friend, Tchaikovsky to assess his music critically – but he had a gift of word painting and a quick memory. She found his talk wonderfully inspired and inspiring. Much of what he told her she was later able to incorporate into Part 1 of her first book on Tchaikovsky[1].

At her suggestion that he could write a wonderful biography of his friend, a great portrait in words, a pendant to Kouznietsov's painting, Kashkin became excited, thinking it a good idea, but in a few moments he sprang up and left as hastily as he arrived. As Kashkin left, he snatched up a small manuscript from the table, which Rosa had been anxious to show him during a pause in his oration – a pause that never occurred. As he was leaving, he asked the rhetorical question 'Your writing? It shall be published next week.' It was not clear to Rosa whether he meant the suggested Tchaikovsky's biography or Rosa's article that he had snatched up entitled *The Appreciation of Russian Music in England*. Neither was actually published. Some days later, she heard that he had been wandering day and night in the woods around Moscow, probably seeking inspiration for the suggested biography. She recalled Kashkin's anecdotes of sylvan excursions with Nikolay Rubinstein and Tchaikovsky, but she was devastated when she learnt that her article had been lost on one of these excursions, for it had been written in Russian with much labour and some help from Mme. N. It had taken a full three weeks to complete, and when it was finished she did not have time to make a copy, and now it was lost forever – her first article written in the Russian language.

As to the second possibility of Kashkin writing a biography of Tchaikovsky, it seems most likely that the idea rapidly evaporated with the announcement that Tchaikovsky's younger brother Modest (1850-1916) was writing *Zhizn Piorta Ilicha Tchaikovskavo (Life of Tchaikovsky)*, published in three volumes between 1900 and 1902. Rosa was to translate an abridged version of this into English a few years later[2].

Another useful contact Rosa made whilst in Moscow was with Peter Ivanovich Jurgenson*, the head of the publishing firm *Muzikal'naya Torgovlya P Yurgensona*. Peter Jurgenson proved to be a useful friend, and it was through him that Rosa made contact with Modest Tchaikovsky, which led to her translating his biography of the composer. In 1897, Peter Ivanovich Jurgenson was still head of the firm, but it was with his son Boris, who, with his brother Gregory, took over the management of the business, that Rosa became most friendly and with whom she had subsequent dealings.

Rosa and Bella were able to take advantage of social events put on for the delegates of the Medical Congress, and their friends also took them sightseeing. The worries her friends at home had about her health and whether the enterprise would prove too much for her were so far unfounded. They attended a church festival and an open-air concert.

On 15th August, the Feast of the Assumption of the Blessed Virgin, the Mass was celebrated by the Metropolitan of Moscow. The Grand Duke Sergius and his wife Princess Ella attended the service. A cordon of soldiers kept a clear space in front of the ikonostasis[3]. Our friends who took us made some explanation to the officer in charge who allowed us to slip under the rope and stand between the guards. It was not altogether a comfortable position for the crowd pushed to and fro, and I felt sorry for the soldier beside me, a short sturdy lad of Finnish type, who had his work cut out to hold back the restless multitude immediately behind us. The Grand Duke Sergius was not popular. He was however a fine figure of a man, and in his showy uniform stood with a certain stolid, sulky dignity near to his wife Princess Ella, sister of the Tsaritsa. This Princess, both then and later, was well beloved of the Russian people. The Grand Duke Sergius was assassinated in Moscow in 1905, after which his widow became a lay sister in a convent. The Metropolitan, though old and fragile was an imposing personality, his beard and long hair reaching to his shoulders, were silvery white; it seemed to cost him great effort to prostrate himself and to rise from his knees even with the assistance of two priests. After the service the Metropolitan stood up on the Ambo[4] or semi-circular platform that juts out from the Royal gates to the Nave. A small proportion of the congregation then filed before the Metropolitan who held out his hand in order that they might individually kiss his ring, containing a relic, and receive his blessing. We were among the few admitted to the privilege.

Rosa wrote a detailed letter to her sister-in-law Emily describing not only the visit to the cathedral, but also a visit to the Kremlin and some reflections on her Russian friends.

Moscow

August 15th/27th

My dear Emily,

I am going to reserve my account of our church dissipations for *you*, if you will kindly send my letter on to Harry when you have done with it. Today, being the festival of the Assumption, was a very great day in the Uspensky Sabor or Cathedral of the Assumption, the chapel in the Kremlin where the Tsars are crowned and married. But last night the Eve of the Festival was very interesting in its way. Our two doctor friends, Nikolaï Gregorievich, and Vladimir Petrovich took us to the final meeting of the Congress in the Great Theatre. We heard Lombroso, Virchow*, Leyden and various other medical celebrities; then they rushed back to their hospitals to make an afternoon round of their wards and came back to our rooms where we had the Samovar boiling and regaled them with tumblers of tea and real English biscuits. After that we went off, two and two, in droshkys to Xram Christa Spasitelia, or "Temple of the Saviour" which is the modern church of Moscow, built in commemoration of 1812. It is a large building, in white stone with five golden cupolas, and is most effective in the distance; and inside it is gorgeously decorated and the pictures are not Byzantine, but by modern artists. But it has not the interest artistic or historical of the Kremlin churches[5]. The music, however, is very good. The services are extremely difficult for an outsider to follow. Nobody has a book, and the congregation stands for 3 or 4 hours, except when some of the very devout *really* prostrate themselves. The poor people and the women are the most devout, and though one has a certain admiration for it (and it is certainly the chief distraction and interest in their rather hard lives) it strikes one at times as rather overdone. Many of the educated men are not very orthodox, I think, and do not go much to church, but there *are* an immense number of men of all classes in the churches. I think, for instance, our kind friend Nikolaï Gregorievich is what one would call 'a good churchman' but quite simple and unostentatious about it. However, I must be descriptive. In this large church there are places where it is possible to have a chair if they know you are a foreigner, as they understand that we are not accustomed to stand for such hours. After the service we saw that the bell-tower "Ivan Veliki" was illuminated, and part of the Kremlin near the Cathedral of the Assumption, so we all went up into the Kremlin, but could not get into the Cathedral; people were standing in crowds at the doors. I never saw anything so beautiful. It was a perfect night — like a *southern* night, the coloured lights on the bell-tower were just enough to light up the gold and silver and blue and green cupolas of the different churches, and from the Terrace we looked over Moscow, lit up with thousands of lights, and saw them reflected in the river below us. It is like a dream, or a wonderful Eastern story. We could hardly tear ourselves away from the Kremlin. But at last we felt we *must* go home and to bed as Nikolaï Gregorievich said he should call for us at 9 this morning for the great service in the Cathedral of the Assumption. By the time we had finished our breakfast — we made our own — he had come and we hurried off as fast as the heat would allow, but when we got to the Kremlin already the people were assembled in rows to see the arrival of the Metropolitan of Moscow who was to officiate. The Cathedral was full apparently, and a line of policemen kept guard lest the people should break through, because not only the Metropolitan but Grand Duke Serge and Grand Duchess Elizabeth were expected.

However the good doctor spoke to one of the various swell officers with a dozen crosses on, and the chief officer immediately placed us in front of the police and as the service proceeded he took us up towards the Ikonstasis until we were afterwards in the place (2). I show you on my little plan.

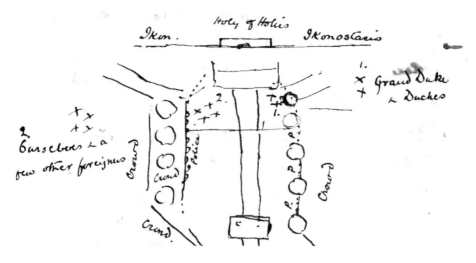

25. Rosa's Plan of the Cathedral of the Assumption, Moscow

The Metropolitan, is a very old, but intellectual and benign looking man. Two Archbishops accompanied him, and a host of deacons with voices nearly as deep as the bell of Ivan Veliki itself. The dresses and vestments I ought to say – of all the officiating clergy were pale blue and gold brocade. The metropolitan was invested with a white silk cassock, and over that pale blue satin garments embroidered with gold and crimson flowers. He combed out his white hair and beard with a large tortoiseshell comb before wearing his mitre which was apparently of gold filigree work, inlaid with sacred pictures and jewels. But they all wear the Russian top-boots underneath which strikes one as very peculiar. The service lasted till after 12 o'clock, and there was no hope of sitting down [...] [a page is missing here]

We shall feel quite low spirited when we leave for Petersburg. Russian men are very nice. They accept women as intellectual equals, and are very proud of what their women-kind are doing in the intellectual way. They will discuss all kinds of things without reserve and at the same time they are <u>truly</u> polite. Less bowing and scraping than in France and Germany, but they never think of letting you do a thing for yourself that they can do for you. They all appear to me in the light of charming, ideal younger brothers. We have four really intimate friends [...] Of ladies I have not seen so much except at functions. They appear very cordial and nice. One lady I wanted to know is still in the country. One of the older doctors wives is an invalid, one away for a time, the other men are bachelors. It is bedtime now. Much love to all the sisters –

Yours affect RN.

After leaving the cathedral, the temperature outside was 90° F and Rosa thought she had succumbed to sunstroke. By the time they were back at the hotel, Rosa's temperature was 100°F, she had a bad headache and she was hoping she did not become delirious and have to leave Bella trying to communicate by sign language. They told the landlord to phone one of their medical friends. Very soon, two surgeons were at her side and they pronounced it *grippe* (Russian flu). The treatment – bed, big doses of quinine in capsules, lemon tea with a little cognac. The surgeons, not realising Rosa understood the language, made some disparaging remarks in Russian: 'You must write her a prescription. In England there is always a prescription. She will think we are doing nothing for her.' To which the reply came in Russian: 'There will be no prescription', and the corridor man was promptly sent to the chemists for quinine. Rosa was in bed for three days with the doctors visiting her two to three times a day and Bella nursing her. Fortunately Bella did not succumb to flu; this she attributed to the fact that whereas Rosa kissed the Metropolitan's ring, Bella only bowed over his hand.

Once Rosa had recovered, Nikolai Pravasoud, one of the surgeons, announced that he would come to fetch her for an outdoor concert at the Rond de Sokolniky given in honour of the Medical Congress. She gave an account of this in her 'Letter, from Moscow' dated 23 August and published in *The Musician* (1 September 1897), from which this is an extract:

On Saturday evening a concert of Russian music was organised in the beautiful surroundings of the Sokolniky Park. From five o'clock in the evening all tramcars, which run between Moscow and this suburban park, were exclusively reserved for members and guests of the Congress. Consequently, when we arrived a few minutes before the beginning of the concert at 8 p.m., the large pavilion, erected last year at the time of the Coronation, was crowded with an expectant audience, neither sitting nor standing room being available. The pavilion, as I said, was quite full, but directly the Russians saw that we were strangers, they insisted on giving up their seats to us and pushing us to the front that we might have a good view of the performers. The orchestra was excellent, consisting almost entirely of members of the Opera band under the conductorship of M. Litvinov, a musician well known in Moscow. The programme, which consisted of three sections, with intervals of 20 minutes, included works by Glinka, Rubinstein, Borodin, Dargomijsky, Tchaikovsky, Weniawsky, Rimsky-Korsakov, Glazunov, and Moussorgsky. The programme was not, however given in its entirety.

The programme was interrupted by the excitement of the arrival of Professor

Virchow, a famous German pathologist, who was given a royal ovation, after which it proved difficult to resume the concert. Rosa's account continued:

It was midnight before everything had been played and sung, and everything available eaten and drunk. An amiable doctor insisted on driving us home in his light carriage, behind a pair of big, fast-trotting chestnuts. In a few minutes we had left the illuminated gardens and dark pinewoods of the Sokolniky behind us. The babel of half-a-dozen different languages was lost in the rattle of the cobbled-paved streets of Moscow; and as conversation was impossible I sat and gazed in admiration at the astounding circumference of the fashionable Muscovite coachman who sat in front of us, clothed in a black cloth cassock and a biretta, with an Oriental embroidered girdle round his portly figure.

Rosa was keen not only to experience the sites that visitors are usually taken to, but also to see what life was like for typical, not-so-well-off Russians. One of their friends, a young schoolmaster and democrat called Anofriev, was anxious to show them how working people lived and took them to some curious places, as Rosa described:

The one I liked best was not frequented by the poorest of the poor, but by the artisan class and some of the lesser *bourgeoisie*: people who had a little but not very much money in their pockets. We used to get a slab of cold fish with horseradish sauce – not the elegant creamy preparation that accompanies the Sunday sirloin at home, but the root roughly scraped and covered with malt vinegar, a hunk of black bread and *kvas* [fermented mildly alcoholic beverage made from black or rye bread] for very few kopeks, the equivalent of six or sevenpence in England [2½ to 3p]. Those who happened to be well off at the moment could add a slice of ham. The proprietor took me into the kitchen to inspect the huge fish which were always fresh and well boiled. There were two or three varieties of what he described as *osseotr* or *bieluga* (kinds of sturgeon), the latter very large with flesh as white and firm as veal. The company at this unpretentious and moderately clean eating-house appeared thoroughly respectable. They stared a little at our west European clothes, but they were never impertinent or resentful. As I watched them eat their cheap and sufficient meal, laughing and discussing their own topics, some reading the papers to those who could not read, I thought of the exaggerated notions we had in England as to the lives of the miserable half-starved down-trodden lower classes in Russia under the rule of the Tsars. Poverty, degradation, unhealthiness there certainly was, and a vast amount of drunkenness: but there was, too, plenty of cheerfulness.

My friends sometimes scolded me for walking home after dark, but I never felt the least nervousness in the streets of Moscow. If people got drunk it seemed to be the fuddled kind of drunkenness which drove them to take refuge in the gutter, or on doorsteps, in order to sleep it off. Off course if intoxication took the form of maudlin, religious sentiment it was more dangerous to its victims for they would often stand in perilous places to look up at an ikon and cross themselves. On the whole one felt just as safe on foot as being driven by a very stupid *izvostchik* (cabman). For honesty, the Russian cabmen compared favourably with Londoners of Victorian days. One bargained with them before getting into one of their queer little four-wheeled vehicles, and at least on one occasion an *izvostchik* offered to give me back half the stipulated fare because the house I directed him to go to proved to be in the next street. There were nearly as many cabs as pigeons in the streets of Moscow and by daylight there was no difficulty in selecting a fairly good horse and comparatively clean cab. At night it was a matter of luck [...]

Living in the modest commercial hotel, their money went twice as far as it would have done had they stayed at the Continental or Slaviansky Bazaar, so Rosa and Bella prolonged their stay from week to week and grew more disinclined to leave Moscow. However, the day came when an urgent summons arrived from Vladimir Stasov, now back in St Petersburg after his summer holiday: 'I am back in the Imperial Library. There is plenty of work waiting to be done. Come.' So remembering the real object of their journey, knowing that in Russia the summer is short and wanting to return home before the winter set in, they reluctantly made preparations for their journey north.

All their kind friends were on the platform to take leave of them and the compartment seemed full of parting gifts. At the last moment, Nikolaï Grigorevich Pravasoud, a kind doctor who had looked after her during her bout of *grippe*, thrust into her arms a huge parcel containing a gleaming tea urn, a samovar, just like the one of his that she had admired. 'May you use it for many years!' he said to her. 'But not if you drink tea without sugar; cure yourself of this dreadful habit, Madame Roz, and live to be an old woman.'

Rosa had made real friends in Moscow, but sadly never met any of them again, as she reflected in her autobiography.

Very often I wake in the night full of self-reproach and wonder as to the destinies of that little group of people who made life in Moscow such a happy experience.

What has befallen them in these topsy-turvy years? When I returned to the old city in 1910 and 1915 I tried each time to trace some of my old friends, but their footsteps had utterly vanished in a way which I think would be impossible in a less illimitable country than Russia; for my visits occurred before the revolution. I have met a good many Russian acquaintances in strange places, fulfilling strange occupations, but not one of the original Muscovite group. One feels happier about those whom one knows for certain died before the worst of the ordeal; who did not survive to see their ideal hopes thwarted and the work of years reduced to futility. I am far from refusing to believe that there may be ameliorations and, in certain directions, even progress under the present regime; but I am sure that none of the progressives I knew at the beginning of the century ever foresaw the turns and twists which the path of freedom was going to take when revolution –their idea of revolution – had been accomplished. For bloodshed and a brief terrible reign of revenge and wanton destruction they may have been prepared; but when the storm was over they believed the sun of freedom would shine upon a regenerated and ennobled Russia. That may yet come; but the pioneers of fifty or even thirty years ago never foresaw the intervening years; could never have imagined a drab, mechanised, unsoaring Russia. Most of the realists I knew in the 'nineties' were, in their hearts dreamers.

Notes

1. Rosa Newmarch, *Peter Ilich Tchaikovsky, His Life and works with extracts from his writings, and the diary of his tour abroad in 1888* (London: Grant Richards, 1900).

2. Rosa Newmarch, *The Life and Letters of Peter Ilich Tchaikovsky* (London: John Lane, 1906). This has been reprinted a number of times up to the present day.

3. A wall of ikons and religious paintings separating the nave from the sanctuary.

4. An elevated platform or pulpit in early Christian churches from which part of the service was chanted.

5. The order to build the cathedral was signed by Tsar Alexander I in 1812, but it was not completed until much later, being consecrated 1883 at the crowning of Tsar Alexander III. In 1931, it was dynamited on Stalin's orders. With the fall of Communism it was rebuilt, starting in 1992 and completed in 2000.

CHAPTER 8: THE IMPERIAL PUBLIC LIBRARY, ST PETERSBURG

A day before travelling north to St Petersburg, Rosa received a note from Stasov:

Honoured Madam

Home from the country this morning (for two and a half days) I found your letter awaiting me, and write to say that I shall expect you at the Library on Monday next, August 25th, or if necessary the 26th. But it would be best if you came to us at I o'clock. Looking forward to making your acquaintance,

Vladimir Stasov[1].

The Imperial Public Library was established in 1795 by Catherine the Great. From 1932-1992, the library was renamed the State Public Library, and from 1992, the National Library of Russia. Vladimir Vassilievich Stasov (1824-1906) was employed by the library from 1856, and from 1872 until his death was Head of the Department of Fine Arts, preferring to remain in that post rather than accept the post of Director of the Library, with the restrictions to his freedom it would inevitably bring. Prior to 1856, he was in the civil service before being appointed secretary to Prince A.N. Demidov, an undemanding post that between 1851 and 1854 allowed him to spend thirty months abroad. In 1854, he began working in the Imperial Library under the new director, Baron Korff, and shortly after, the Head of the Department of Art, V.I. Soboldhchikov, suggested he should compile a systematic catalogue of the art and Rossica collections. The Rossica collection was a large collection of foreign books touching on Russia. This not only gave him the chance to catalogue the collection, but also to immerse himself in reading much of it.

The library provided an ideal environment for Stasov's own research. He is often thought of as a music critic, but his interests were much wider. When the first collected edition of his writings, *Sobranie sochinenii,* was published in 1894 in three volumes, two of the volumes were devoted to art history, criticism and biographical studies of architects, painters and sculptors, while less than half a volume was devoted to 'Music and the Theatre'. He was best known for his championship of Russian artists and particularly the New Russian School of Music, although he had a wide knowledge of the arts of other nations. In 1856, Stasov made the acquaintance of Balakirev and soon began to play an inspirational rôle in Russian music, and in Russian art generally. The painter and sculptor Ilya Repin (1844-1930) and the sculptor Mark Antokolsky (1843-1902) regarded him as their teacher, and he was closely associated with Kramskoy's Free Artists' Co-operative of 1863. In 1874, Stasov, together with the president of the Architects' Society, was responsible for the memorial exhibition in St Petersburg for the painter Victor Alexandrovich Hartmann (1834-1873). The exhibition became famous with Musorgsky's composition *Pictures at an Exhibition*. According to Valkenier, Stasov saw himself 'as the driver of a *troika* that would bring Russian culture to the world stage. Repin, Musorgsky and Antokolsky were its horses[2].'

Rosa started to communicate with Stasov in 1896 and for the following decade until his death they remained in close touch and became great friends. He was very much her mentor in her understanding of Russian arts and music and there were numerous exchanges of letters. After his death, consideration was given to his biography, and, with that in mind, Stasov's last surviving brother, Dmitri, a well known St Petersburg barrister, begged Rosa for the loan of the letters. Stasov left a vast number of papers and to complete a full biography would be a large undertaking. Instead, a plan evolved as an interim measure, to bring out a volume of short appreciations by a chosen group of friends, of whom Rosa was one. Rosa left the letters with Dmitri Stasov until such time as they were needed, and he left them safely deposited in the Imperial Public Library, but their whereabouts now are not known, nor has any comprehensive biography of Stasov ever been produced. So, when writing her autobiography in the 1930s, Rosa recalled her visit to St Petersburg in 1897 without the aid of the letters[3].

After her arrival in St Petersburg, Stasov phoned Rosa at the Hotel d'Angleterre, where she and Bella were staying, suggesting that they met in the Imperial Library rather than at his home, as the Stasov family were still away in their country house at Pargolova about twenty miles from the Finnish border on the road to Viborg. Her first sight of Stasov was when he came out of his private study and walked down the corridor to meet her. She described him as an impressive kingly-looking man of gigantic stature with a long white flowing beard, who received her with grudging condescension. He explained that he was always busy and rarely showed visitors around the library. Once in his study, she found scattered on the floor on either side of his writing chair several sheets of manuscript, obviously an article for some review. He gestured to an attendent to pick up the papers and put them in order. She felt that perhaps his ungracious reception was because his work had been interupted at a critical moment, for it was the only time when she saw him behave like a *chinovnik* or bureaucrat; he particularly disliked the 'jack-in-office' type of government official. He was an imposing figure, and Madame N. had told her that Stasov had several nicknames among the intelligentsia and students who frequented the library; some referred to him as 'the Bogatr' or hero – the type of doughty knight so magnificently portrayed by ViktorVasnetsov (1848-1926) in his famous picture *The Three Heoes of Old*.

26.Vladimir Stasov, 1873

When Stasov asked what kind of study she meant to pursue at the library, Rosa explained that she was somewhat of a beginner and wanted a preliminary list of books from which she might 'snatch out their vitals' as rapidly as possible as she could only stay for a limited period of time. He seemed obviously disappointed that she was only a beginner in the subject of Russian art. He was occasionally frank to the point of rudeness. *"Quelle ignorance, Madame,"* he exclaimed one day when they were talking about the gradual defection of the National School of Music from the leadership of Balakirev (1837-1910) to the paramount influence of Mitrofan Belyayev (1836-1904), who was at that time barely a name to her. She was particularly ashamed of being ignorant of the polemics of the moment, but they ended by laughing at his indignation and her stolidity. Years later, he hinted at his first impression of her, believing then that she was merely an amiable woman who had come to Russia out of superficial curiosity and doubting the seriousness of her purpose. In time he drastically revised this view on seeing that she was both serious and determined; they were to become unshakeable friends.

On arriving at the library on her second day, Rosa expected to receive a ticket for the public reading room and to be handed over to some minor official who understood French or German. She was astonished when an attendent led her upstairs and along the same corridor as on the previous day. On that floor there was a series of rooms opening out of each other and terminating in Stasov's private study. In the room next to his own, Stasov was waiting for her. The big writing table was already piled with books. 'Here are a few useful things to begin with,' he said, 'you can spend the morning looking through them and as we are next door neighbours, if you want any special information you can come and ask me.' The bear of yesterday was the prince charming of today.

Her primary aim was to find out all she could about Russian music and composers, particularly from the time of Glinka onwards. She found that there were practically no complete biographies of the precursors of the modern Russian school of music: Glinka and Dargomyzhsky. She was surprised as their operas were in the regular repertory of the opera houses of Moscow and St Petersburg, and Glinka had died in 1857 and Dargomyzhsky in 1869. The former left a diary which was completed by his sister and published with the addition of some letters in 1887. His sister's reminiscences formed a personal memoir of the founder of the Russian national opera, but there was no attempt at a critical study of his work. M.F. Findeisen, the editor of the *Russian Musical Gazette*, had published the first section of his ambitious biography of Glinka in 1896, but it only covered the early years of the musician's life. Stasov's exhaustive articles on Glinka in the third volume of his *Collected Works*, was still the most authoritative and finished account of his life and work. Much the same state of things existed as regards

Dargomyzhsky, whose interesting autobiography, a clear revelation of his independent and progressive outlook on music, Stasov had brought out as early as 1875 in *Russkaya Starina* (The Russian Past, also printed in Vol. III of the *Collected Works*).

There was no comprehensive account of Balakirev's circle or 'the Mighty Handful' or *kuchka*, but Stasov knew exactly where to lay hands on all the authoratative articles on contemporary Russian music and he ensured that Rosa was always well supplied with current literature periodicals. He was anxious that she should not limit her studies too strictly to music, but pursue them concurrently with other subjects. For example, he showed her two editions of Musorgsky's *Boris Godunov* together with Pushkin's poems, pointing out from where the libretto was taken, and several reproductions of pictures relating to the subject with notes on costumes and decorations of the period. This enabled her to relate the music to literature and pictorial art without spending much time searching for cross references. Reflecting some forty years later, she realised that what she most valued during the first period of study in Russian was the unique chance of a leisurely perusal of scores to which she could not get access elsewhere. Besides Glinka's *A Life for a Tsar* and his then almost unknown *Ruslan and Lyudmila,* she came across for the first time his very touching and dramatic incidental music to Nestor Koukolnik's tragedy *Prince Kholmsky,* which contains two beautiful songs sung by the Jewish heroine, Rachel.

She copied and translated these Russian songs and was later able to use them to illustrate lectures that she started to give in 1900. It was an essay by César Cui, entitled *Russky Romancy* (Russian Songs), that she discovered in the library that gave her the idea for her lectures. She felt Cui was a penetrating but not always just music critic. He undervalued Musorgsky and Tchaikovsky, who were at the opposite poles as song writers, finding the former unrefined in his direct nationalism, while Tchaikovsky seemed to him a colourless cosmopolitan. Cui himself was usually at his best when treating a French text.

A book to which she often referred was Stasov's *Russkia Narodnie Ornament* (Russian National Design and Ornament), published in 1872 with the help of a generous patroness of the fine arts, the Grand Duchess Helena Pavlovna. It is a useful account of design for all the various Russian schools: Kiev, Novgorod, Moscow, etc. Stasov had worked to preserve the old traditions in the peasant arts and took immense trouble to supply the rural and provincial schools of needlework with authentic Russian patterns.

With her desk outside Stasov's, she was aware of the many comings and goings of visitors. On occasions she would see him shutting the door on sniffling females, but more often she would be aware of well known musicians, painters and literary men knocking on his door. When showing the latter out, he would bring them to her table and introduce them. Among those whom she met in this way were the painter Ilya Repin (1844-1930), the publisher and patron of music Mitrofan Petrovich Belyayev (1836-1904), the composer Alexander Glazunov (1865-1936), the singer Fyodor Shaliapin (1873-1938) and Stasov's colleague in the library, Professor Liberio Sacchetti (1852-1916). She described an encounter with Belyayev in detail:

Mitrofan Petrovich Belyayev was a wealthy timber merchant and patron of music. In 1885 he had founded a publishing firm which bears his name, and the Russian Symphony Concerts, devoted entirely to national music. He was a frequent visitor to Stasov. I was aware of his hurried, but rather pompous passage through the room I worked in, and the sound of his somewhat self-important voice, long before I came into personal touch with him, which was not I believe until 1900. At our one and only interview I burnt my boats! It came about in this way. Among the songs I took home to England after my first visit to Russia was Rimsky-Kosakov's delicate little lyric *Ty I Vy*; the poem turning on the subtle meaning of the pronouns 'thou and you' though translatable into French, it was extremely difficult to render in English, the affectionate and familiar use of the second person singular having completely fallen out of custom. The song had immense success when first sung at my lectures by Mrs Olga Wood (née Ouroussova) , Sir Henry Wood's first wife. I received a great number of inquiries as to where the song could be bought and whether an English text existed. One day the spirit moved me to make a passably singable translation for my programmes. It was actually a paraphrase rather than a translation of the original poem. On my next visit to Russia I took the song back with me, and told Rimsky-Korsakov that I had laid irreverent hands on the words, but that the success of the 'romance' had gone far to justify my action. We also discussed with Stasov the possibility of getting half-a-dozen modern Russian songs translated and republished with English text by some reputable British publisher. The question of copyright between the two countries was then the most difficult to disentangle. Some of the older songs – like *The Red Sarafan* – had already appeared in more than one English version; but only those interested in contemporary Russian music in the early years of the twentieth century know how difficult it was even to order works from Russia and be sure of getting the right ones. So many of the titles were not yet translated, and no publisher thought of filling a window with Russian music as was frequently done ten years later. Rimsky-Korsakov seemed pleased at the idea of one or two of his songs being made easily accessible to the English public, and I was anxious to grately him. But he shook his head over *Ty i Vy*, reminding Stasov that it was published by Belyayev who guarded his copyrights jealously. He was, in fact, one of the two or three leading publishers who had established a branch business in Germany so that they could make sure that their rights of publication were respected. We finally decided that perhaps an exception could be made for this charming lyrical bagatelle if I spoke to Belyayev and 'asked prettily' for his permission to have it brought out in an English edition. But the interview was a failure. Belyayev seemed in no mood even to discuss the question; he brusquely refused to consider any aspect of it which involved the appearance of the song in an English edition. If, he argued, 'Rimsky' liked the words I would mention the price for them then he would buy them, and perhaps if it ever came to reprinting the song they might appear under the Russian and German texts. Equally I felt they might remain in a pigeon-hole in Belyayev's Leipzig publishing house for the rest of my life and Rimsky-Korsakov's. I replied that my text was not for sale; I was out for propaganda, not for commerce. I suppose Belyayev and I had what Stasov would have called the 'camel temperament' . The capitalist jumped up, flushed with anger, and without the least gesture of salutation strutted hastily out of the room, flung himself into his open Victoria waiting outside and went whirling down the *Nesvsky Prospect* in a cloud of dust like a disgruntled chieftain escaping in his chariot. I only mention the absurd incident over bars of music as demonstrating some of the difficulties of the well-intentioned enthusiast at the beginning of his or her career. In later years I might have seen Belyayev's point of view in a different light, but he died in 1904 before we had a chance to meet again.

At the time she met Glazunov, at the age of thirty-six, he was the youngster of the New Russian School of Music. She felt that his impassive dignified serenity meant that he rarely quarreled with Stasov, always leaving best of friends. Stasov also appreciated Glazunov's service in revising and completing many works of Borodin after the latter's death.

In time she was to become a great friend of Shaliapin and she described her first encounter with him at the library:

One morning a striking figure walked into the room where I was busy: a tall, magnificently built young man, typically north Russian, with oat-coloured hair and well-opened deep blue eyes, strolled leisurely past me to Stasov's door, pausing to glance at some books displayed in a glass case under the window. He knocked and walked into the inner room with the assurance of a visitor certain of his welcome. When he came out, ten minutes later, Stasov came with him and, passing my table, stopped to introduce him: 'Mmne. Rosa Newmarch – Feodor Ivanovich Shaliapin'.

At the time the great singer was still at the beginning of his career. In 1894 he sang –as far as I know –for the first time in St Petersburg at the summer Theatre in the Aquarium, and the following year he appeared at the Maryinsky Theatre, but hardly with the success that his superb voice and powers of dramatic expression already merited. It was only the year before I first met him, in 1897, that a wealthy patron of Russian opera, Mamantov, by paying a large indemnity for his services, succeeded in transferring Shaliapin from the Imperial Opera House at St Petersburg to his private Opera Company in Moscow, where he lept into fame in his first season [...] Of course on the occasion of our first meeting my name meant nothing to Shaliapin. His broad face and expansive brow, which he can stamp at will with the images of Ivan Sousanin, from *A Life for the Tsar*, of the demented Boris, of Ivan the Terrible and Dosithei from *Khovanchina*, – reflecting the whole gamut of conflicting emotions, from nobility of purpose, to distraught remorse, from insane cruelty to religious fanaticism – seemed at the moment almost a *tabula rasa*, inexpressive as a moon; an empty stage awaiting some swift, unpredictable change of scene. Nor could I then foresee a time when we would really be friends; when I should be a guest in his house and respond to his half-teasing, half-caressing, and wholly unconventional nickname – *Baboushka* (Grannie dear).

Among the officials at the library, the one Rosa came to know best was Liberio Sacchetti. He was of Italian descent and the son of a music teacher in Keuzar, Tambov. In 1866, he studied at the St Petersburg Conservatoire, where he first joined the violincello class under the direction of Karl Davidov (1838-1889). He remained at the Conservatoire, and later in 1886 he was appointed to the newly founded chair of Musical History and Aesthetics. Rosa described his role at the library:

Two years before my visit to Russia, Professor Sacchetti had been called to the Imperial Public Library as assistant librarian to Stasov. It would be difficult to imagine two temperaments less suited to run together in double harness. Sacchetti had a reverence for classicism in his blood, and although the section of his Universal History of Music entitled *The Music of the Slavonic Races* is a most useful, reliable and comprehensive piece of work, it is void of any special enthusiasm for the subject. His nationalism was luke warm and he was careful to avoid any sparks from Stasov's fiery enthusiasm which might inflame it. He was an admirable and balanced writer and teacher, but useless as a propagandist [...] Mme. Sacchetti on the contrary held her own very well as a practical aid to Vladimir Vassilich; she smiled her way through his electrical storms, and assured in speech and movement; moreover she had a splendid memory and could lay her hands on any book in the Library at a moment's notice.

Personally the time I spent with the Sacchettis in their own home was very helpful to me. It was good to escape occasionally from the atmosphere of impassioned nationalism which pervaded the Stasov household, and to discuss music in general. Not that the interests of Sacchetti were exclusively musical. A good many literary men used to drop in during the evening; among them V.D. Spassovich whose *Literary Sketches and Portraits* were being much read at the time. His conversation and literary style were expressive and clear, so that in spite of one's own imperfect knowledge of Russian it was a pleasure to have speech with him and read his essays especially those which concerned Byron's influence upon Poushkin and Lermontov. I cannot remember that he spoke English very well, but he must have had a good knowledge of our language, judging from his familiarity with our literature. Picking up a volume of works after many years reminded me that I disagreed with him for taking too seriously my cousin John Cordy Jeaffreson's smug piece of bookmaking, *The Real Lord Byron*, which had appeared in 1882.

Besides spending much time in the Imperial Public Library, Rosa was able to find time to go to the opera and report on the musical scene in St Petersburg in two *Letters from St Peterburg*, which were published in England in the new weekly magazine, *The Musician*[4,5]. In these she reported seeing Glinka's *A Life for the Tsar* and Tchaikovsky's operas *The Oprichnik* and *Eugene Onegin*. Rimsky-Korsakov had just finished his opera *Sadko* and although there was not a performance whilst she was still in St Petersburg, she was able to obtain an early copy of the score and from it gave a detailed decription of the opera for readers in England. She also wrote about Russian church music.

Notes

1. Rosa Newmarch's unpublished autobiography.
2. Elizabeth Valkenier, (1990) *Ilya Repin and the World of Russian Art (Studies of the Harriman Institute)* (New York: Columbia University Press, 1990), p.32.

3. A number of letters between Rosa Newmarch and the Stasovs were sold at Southeby's in May 2003 for £900. These comprise five letters from Vladimir Stasov written between August 1897 and March 1900, twe;ve signed by Stasov's brother Dmitri between 1907 and 1913, one by Pauline Stasov dated 1910, and one by Stasov's daughter. The letters from Vladimir Stasov thank her for sending a copy of her book on Borodin and Liszt and express delight that Sir Henry Wood is making Russian composers better known in England. One invited her to the Imperial Library at St Petersburg and arranged to meet her in London in 1900, and another informed her that he had asked Likhatschoff to send her a copy of his book on Russian women, in which she would find some interesting biographical information. However, these are undoutedly only a small fraction of the correspondence between the two.

4. Rosa Newmarch, Letter from St. Petersburg, *The Musician*, 1/20 (22 September, 1897), 373.

5. Rosa Newmarch, Letter from St. Petersburg, *The Musician*, 1/21 (29 September, 1897), 387-8.

CHAPTER 9: THE STASOV FAMILY

As soon as the Stasov family returned to St Petersburg, Rosa was invited to spend the evening with them. It was her first introduction to family life in Russia, for all her friends in Moscow happened to be bachelors. It was a chance for her to see a Russian family as she had read about in Russian novels and biography. The Stasovs were a quintessential family of the Russian intelligentsia. Stasov's father, Vassily Petrovich Stasov (1769-1848), was a well known architect responsible for many important buildings and monuments in St Petersburg, including the New Hermitage erected in 1839-52, the Barracks of the Pavlovski Regiment, the Narva Triumphal Gate, the Moscow Triumphal Gate, and the statues of Mikhail Kutuzov and Mikhail Barklai de Tolli, both sculpted by Boris Orlovsky. Vassily Petrovich used to live half the year in St. Petersburg and during the summer months at Tsarsky Selo, where he was occupied with the restoration of the Imperial Palace and also with the building of a cathedral.

The family consisted of five brothers and two sisters. At an early age they were all taught foreign languages, drawing and music. From 1830, they received piano lessons from Anton Gerke, regarded as the best piano teacher in St Petersburg, who ten years later taught Musorgsky.

After the death of Vassily Petrovich in 1848, his children took a flat in St Petersburg and lived there for several years. By the time Rosa first visited them, the household was seven in number. The flat itself had been exchanged for a smaller one. Nicholas, the eldest brother, died in 1879 and Nadejda in 1895. Dmitri (1828-1918), the youngest, had married and left home. He was a lawyer and held progressive political views and later defended several revolutionaries in court. He also took part in the founding of the Russian Musical Society. His daughter, Elena Stasova (1873-1966), taught at a workers' evening school in St Petersburg and joined the Communist Movement in 1898. By 1912 she was one of the leaders of the Bolsheviks in Petrograd (as it was then named) and became personal secretary to Lenin. She was exiled to Siberia from 1913-1916. After the Russian Revolution in 1917, she was made responsible for Soviet relations with other Communist parties of the world.

The household in 1897, when Rosa visited them, consisted of Alexander, the eldest of the family, Margaret Stasov (née Clark) widow of Nicholas, and her daughter, Marie, also Miss Clark, Margaret's sister. There was also Natalia Pivovarova, the godchild of Stasov's sister Nadejda, who had adopted and educated her, and Mlle. Ernestine, whose surname Rosa never knew and who lived with the family for years, first as a governess and later as special companion to Marie, who was not quite sound mentally.

Marie was a particular favourite of Stasov. Impatient, irate and truculent as he often was, he would instantly break off an argument, or aesthetic altercation, and control himself at the first indication that it was distressing to Marie. Her puckered brow and wistful lost look would bring him at once to her side when, with infinite patience, he would try to make her understand what it was all about, that nobody was really angry and it was only her 'noisy bear of an uncle who made all the row'. She was exceedingly sensitive to music, and among the pianists who loved to play for her pleasure, Balakirev, the elusive mystic, was her devoted servant in this respect. Probably he shared the popular belief that God was on the side of the mentally afflicted.

These seven people were permanent inhabitants of the flat, but from time to time Rosa was introduced to an adopted nephew or niece who lived there temporarily and pursued studies at university or high schools, because, as Vladimir Vassilievich would explain, their parents 'were living away',[6] a term that she came to understand as implying exile. Most of the family had occupations and worked hard and those who were unable to earn were cared for by the rest. The accommodation of so many people under one roof was a source of curiosity for Rosa until she realised that the divan bed, common in England, solved this problem for the Stasovs as for most Russian families. There appeared to be only one proper sitting room, a fine big drawing room with lofty windows, in one corner of which was a full concert grand. In many other rooms, a comfortable divan, discreetly draped and heaped with cushions, showed that the rooms could be used as a bedsit. As to Vladimir Vassilievich, his room was also the library. As virtually the head of the family, though not the eldest, he boasted that he kept up the old tradition of Russian hospitality to strangers: food and shelter for the unexpected guest and no questions asked. Mme. N. had already told Rosa in London the tale of a man knocking at Stasov's door late in the night following the assassination of Alexander II, claiming sanctuary, being let in according to custom, supping, sharing the library and leaving in the early hours of the morning unquestioned. She also added that when the police paid a domiciliary visit, shortly afterwards they were reprimanded for their pains by 'a high personage' who said they should have known that the 'Stasovs' loyalty was beyond all doubt.' Although she could not verify this story, she could well imagine the old man justifying his time-honoured custom and refusing to be interrogated.

When Rosa and Bella Simpson were first invited there, the only additional visitors were the youngest of the Stasov brothers, Dmitri, and his intelligent, warm-hearted and charming wife. Dmitri was a prosperous and highly regarded barrister. They lived in a flat of their own in Fontanka. One other unforgettable personality whose presence pervaded all the hospitable gatherings with a dominating influence was Stasov's late sister, Nadejda. Thanks to Repin's living portrait of her, Nadejda, still seemed to share all the joys and sorrows of the family life, although she had passed away just two years before Rosa's visit. The portrait now hangs in the Russian Museum, St Petersburg. Rosa described the painting and Nadejda's work on women's emancipation:

Nadejda had suffered much physically and emotionally in her long life, dedicated to the service of others, for she had been an untiring pioneer in the feminine cause in Russia. Fatigue and disillusionment had dimmed the fire and light in her steady, faithful eyes and she was not a beautiful woman but her mouth was firm and sweet, and her high forehead framed between two smooth braids of dark hair gave her an almost Quakerish look. Repin painted her with her arms crossed and her fine long-fingered hands showing white upon her black dress.

Nadejda worked tirelessly for women's emancipation in Russia. She was selfless, courageous and a gentle person. Doubtless she was of the past, but she firmly believed in the future of Russian womanhood, although her programme for the freedom of her sex did not include the practice of abortion nor the denial of a living God. She played an important part in the progressive movement of the sixties, when, after the accession of Alexander II, Russia witnessed a blossoming of generous and humane impulses, liberalisation, and improved conditions for peasants, including, in 1861, the emancipation of the serfs.

She and other women had been working individually on behalf of their sex, but now decided to form a common fund and work in unison. They started unpretentiously with a modest capital of £50, and in the course of a few years they inaugurated such invaluable institutions as the Society for Providing Cheap Dwellings for Working Women, the Kalinkinsky Hospital, the Magdalene House, and the Sunday Schools, they finally attained the apex of their ambitions with the establishment of the Higher Educational Classes for Women. They met with many rebuffs, and saw the peremptory extinction of more than one of their organisations. The Minister of Education, Count Tolstoy, was a hardened reactionary and a master of the art of diplomatic procrastination, and although the women had many of the university professors on their side, nothing would be done without his authority. He scoffed at the idea of founding a Women's University, and made it clear that the women might not hope for the assignment of any locality in which to open their projected Higher Educational Classes, nor obtain financial support from the government. Once or twice when their scheme seemed to be progressing, the machinations of the extreme Nihilist party once again put back the hand of the clock. The 'advanced' faction opened a series of lectures at their own risk, known as the 'Alarchinsky Classes', while the moderates inaugurated a course in the Vladimirsky district. There was less rivalry than might have been expected between the two classes, and some of the pupils attended them both.

In January 1870, the Vladimirsky classes were opened thanks to the generosity of the various professors who offered to lecture gratuitously. Count Tolstoy himself attended the opening ceremony and was particularly gracious to Nadejda Stasov. "Your heart may well rejoice" he remarked to her "your perseverance has triumphed". With characteristic modesty and quick wit she answered *sotto voce:"Ce que femme veut Dieu le veut"* No doubt the change in the attitude of the minister and the government was due to anxiety over the increasing emigration of Russian women to foreign universities. A special commission inquiring into this question two years later admitted, while deploring, this exodus of educated women students and recommended that as the Vladimirsky classes were hardly sufficient to meet the needs of the country, Higher Classes for Women should be founded in the capitals and provincial university towns of Russia.

In 1878, largely thanks to the intervention of the liberal and enlightened Prince of Oldenburg, Alexander II assented to a new educational scheme, although he still refused his consent to the creation of a University for Women. The Women's Higher Classes were based upon a surer footing than the Vladimirsky lectures. But Count Tolstoy gave only half-hearted approval to the project and managed to delay his formal sanction of the plan for eleven years. It was not until 1889 that these Higher Classes acquired a proper legal status. Count Delianov, who had succeeded Count Tolstoy as Minister of Education, closed the existing Higher Classes before carrying out the new plan, pending a long inquiry into the general question of women's education. When, finally, the classes were reopened their entire constitution was changed. Purged of all it owed to individual initiative it became a government machine. The old committee that played the leading part in the foundation of the Vladimirsky courses and the earlier activities of the Higher Classes for Women, of which Nadejda was a prominent member, saw their labours ended.

She died of a stroke in her 74th year. It seems she was the first woman to receive a public funeral in Russia. A concourse of women followed the procession and bore her coffin from the church to her grave in the Alexander Nevsky cemetery. Her death left a sense of irremediable loss in Vladimir Stasov's life. One of his most interesting books is the volume he dedicated to her memory in 1899; it is not only a biography of his sister, but a history of the women's movement in Russia from 1860-1895.

Stasov's widowed sister-in-law, Margaret Stasov, and her sister Miss Clark intrigued Rosa. They were descendants of British settlers and neither they nor their parents had been to England, yet they both spoke perfect English. They were full of curiosity about England, still imagining social life there to be as it was in the eighteenth century. These untravelled Russians fell easy victims to malicious propaganda. They were particularly shocked about what they heard about poor Tommy Atkins [Tommy Atkins was a term for a common soldier in the British Army that was already well established in the nineteenth century, but is particularly associated with World War I]. 'Is it true,' they asked Rosa in a horrified whisper, 'that ladies never walk alone in England because of your soldiers?' When Rosa laughed aloud, they looked confused, but followed on, incredulous of Rosa's vindications of the British Army, 'But they were terribly brutal; we hear they toss up the Boer babies and catch them on their bayonets?' Rosa reminded them that that was an old indictment of Cossack customs that had evidently come home to roost in a new form. Tracing these slanders to their origin, Rosa found it came from a German colleague of a friend who had been in England for three years.

CHAPTER 10: MEETING STASOV'S FRIENDS

Had Rosa Newmarch visited Russia a few years earlier, she would have met at the Stasov home the novelist and playwright Ivan Turgenev (1818-1883) and the composers Borodin (1833-1887), Musorgsky (1839-1881), and Anton Rubinstein (1829-1894). She had, of course, heard Anton Rubinstein perform earlier in London. She was, however, fortunate enough to meet a number of those eminent in the field of music and art, including many composers of the New Russian School of Music (César Cui, Balakirev, Rimsky-Korsakov, and Glazunov), the painter Ilya Repin, then President of the Academy of Arts, and Ilya Ginsburg (1859-1939), the foremost pupil of the sculptor Antokolsky.

Among Ginsburg's works were busts of Tolstoy, Anton Rubinstein, Repin, Stasov and the Russian chemist, Dmitri Mendeleyev (Rosa described Ginsburg's work in detail in her book *The Russian Arts*[1]). Stasov was a great admirer of Antokolsky, regarded as one of the most original sculptors of his generation. Rosa does not appear to have met Antokolsky, who died in Homburg in June 1902. After his death, Rosa received a tribute to Antokolsky from Stasov. Following excuses for being in arrears with his correspondence and explaining that Antokolsky was a great and revered friend of his for over thirty years, and a great artist who inaugurated a new era in Russian national art, he wrote:

I had the consolation of arranging his obsequies, and making them as impressive and triumphal as possible. As you know the Jews in Russia are on a totally different footing to that which they enjoy in other European countries. Nevertheless I was able to obtain permission to organise this funeral ceremony on a scale unheard of in Russia. My dear friend died in Homburg, and on the arrival of his body in Petersburg it was received with honours far exceeding anything that had been paid to it in Vilna, Kovno or other towns through which it had passed, where the population is chiefly Israelite. Here, the coffin was met at the station and, accompanied by thousands of people, was borne to the great Synagogue, preceded by the choir of the Synagogue singing their chants and litanies in the public streets. With great pomp the body was carried through the Nevsky Prospekt itself, and afterwards taken by special train to the Hebrew cemetery outside the town. (Can you imagine anything so unheard of as this public funeral for a Jew?) Many excellent and touching orations were spoken at the grave; I among those who spoke though I have neither the habit nor the aptitude for oratory.

Since July, I have been working without break on the preparation of a book, which will contain extracts from his autobiography, and reproductions of all his works in phototype. This is the labour with which I have been occupied unceasingly for the past five months.

Later Rosa described, in her autobiography, her first meeting with Balakirev:

It was at a gathering at the Stasov home, that Milly Balakirev (1837-1910) emerged from his voluntary seclusion, and, forgetting all his mystical preoccupations showed himself once more the inspired pianist, the fiery persuasive Balakirev of twenty years earlier. It was then listening to his playing that I realised the power and fascination of the man to whom Glinka had pointed as the successor of his work.

On what appears to be the same occasion, Taruskin[2], quoting Rosa[3], describes the situation slightly differently:

When Milly Balakirev, the one Russian composer who might fit anyone's narrowest definition of a 'nationalist' was introduced to Rosa Newmarch in 1901, he sat down at the piano to play her a kind of *profession de foi* in tones: Beethoven's *Appassionata*, Chopin's B minor sonata, and Schumann's G major sonata. Not a Russian note in the lot and yet it characterises Balakirev and his old "kuchka" far better than their usual chauvinist label.

From this second quotation it appears that Rosa did not meet Balakirev until her second visit to St Petersburg in 1901. Earlier in the 1870s, Balakirev had gone through a personal crisis of self-doubt and in 1871 fell under the influence of a soothsayer who turned him from a free-thinker into a fanatically superstitious Christian[4]. He withdrew from his friends and musical activity and took a job on the Russian railways. Four years later, he gradually returned to his musical activities but remained somewhat a recluse.

Of the younger musicians in Russia at this time, Modest Musorgsky was the one for whom Stasov had the greatest admiration. But for the ill fate which kept the young officer so long from his true vocation, and the physical sufferings which led him to drink himself into an early grave, Stasov maintained that Musorgsky should have made one of the greatest reputations of his day, because he had the true vein of innovating genius that distinguished him from composers better equipped than himself as regards technique. Certainly the ultimate success of his songs and music dramas in his own and other countries justified Stasov's high hopes for his future fame. It was during this visit to Russia that Stasov made his prophecy to me, then a half-hearted believer in Musorgsky's genius. Stasov would not introduce me to the operas until he thought me ripe for the honour. Then he would go through the early edition of *Boris Godounov* and *Khovanstchina*, already issued with Rimsky-Korsakov's revisions. 'Love them or hate them' Stasov would say, seeing my doubtful enthusiasm; 'but you will find more vitality in Musorgsky than any of our contemporary composers. These operas will go further afield than the rest, and you will see their day when I shall no longer be here to follow them to Germany and France, and perhaps England.' Speaking of *Boris Godounov*, he would declare that 'within this work burns too keen a flame of life to be extinguished by neglect. Musorgsky, I assure you, experienced and visualised each scene as he wrote it. Shakespeare and Pushkin created in the same way, and believe me, *Boris Godounov* will never drop into oblivion[5].'

Rosa did not see a performance of *Boris Godunov* until 1908 in Paris, when, in the face of many difficulties and some opposition, Diaghilev and his assistant Michael Calvocoressi produced it at the Grand Opera and were greatly rewarded for their enterprise. By then she was ready to appreciate the opera and felt that, with the highly trained chorus from the Imperial Opera of Moscow, with a conductor so completely in sympathy with the music as Felix Blumenfeld, with soloists such as Madame Ermolanke in the part of Marina, M. Smirnov as the False Dimetrius, M. Altchevsky as Prince Shouisky and Shaliapin in the title role, the performance came as near perfection as human talent could bring it. Such an enthralling performance gave her an urge to see the same offered to the London public.

She first became aware of Rimsky-Korsakov's name from Stasov's *Life and Letters of Borodin*, which she had translated, and she was so charmed by the glimpses revealed of the determined and high-spirited sailor-musician that she wrote to him asking for information about his largely unknown works. The biographical sketch of the composer, in Russian, that Stasov had sent her was another incentive to learn the language. She wrote her first article on Rimsky-Korsakov for *The Musical Standard*[6], which appeared to arouse more interest in Russia than in England.

Later, in 1897, she made the acquaintance of the composer at the house of his sister-in-law, Mme. Molas. Mme. Molas was a gifted singer and her sister Mme. Rimsky-Korsakov a talented pianist. Long before works by Cui, Musorgsky, Borodin and Rimsky-Korsakov were heard at the Imperial Opera, Mme. Molas was performing their works at those intimate drawing room gatherings often held at the Stasov house.

Rosa's first sight of 'Rimsky', as all his friends called him, was somewhat of a surprise; his long white beard, his spectacles, and the natural gravity of his demeanour gave him a slightly severe and pedagogic air. She wondered where he kept hidden away the exquisite fancy and dainty humour that brightened every page of *The Snow Maiden* and the *Christmas Eve Revels*. Outwardly he had the semblance of a serene and passionless philosopher; inwardly his mind was full of fantastic folklore of Russia and the East. His natural reserve, and the fact that he spoke no language fluently but his own, made him rather inaccessible, but she managed to arrive at an interchange of thoughts. Like many of his compatriots he had a great admiration for British constitutional government and individual liberty of thought. He would have liked to have visited England and always took a great interest in the career of the conductor, Henry J. Wood, of whose ability he had heard much from Russian visitors to London. Long and varied experience had made Rimsky-Korsakov a skilled conductor and Rosa often regretted that London audiences had not had the opportunity to hear any of his works conducted by himself, although Henry Wood was already introducing them to English audiences.

One memorable evening spent at the Stasov's house at Pargolova, within a short journey of St Petersburg on the borders of Finland, lingered clearly in Rosa's memory.

Here on one sunny evening in June a party was organised in my honour. It was a real Russian country house, built of wood, with a broad veranda, a porch decorated with rough carvings of horses' heads leading to the front door. This opened directly into a spacious sitting room simply furnished with a couch and plain wooden chairs. In the middle stood a full-sized grand piano which had been hauled up from St Petersburg by road a few days before. The garden boasted few flowers, but was chiefly spring turf and fir and larch trees. Here we sat an hour or two in that pleasant outdoor intimacy which draws people so speedily together. Indeed a memorable gathering: Stasov in national dress which like Tolstoy, he loved to wear in the country, a red cotton blouse embroidered in quaint designs, and loose breeches tucked into high boots below the knee. Glazounov, large and imperturbable occupying the largest of the garden chairs, Cui in immaculate summer attire, making smart and interesting comments in perfect French, Sigismund Blumenfeld looking like a typical Polish noble, Repin bronzed and picturesque, a true Cossack type with eyes both keen and mystical, and Rimsky-Korsakov quiet and self-effacing, a listener rather than a talker on these occasions, exchanging now and then a warm, affectionate word with our host. A very gay party sat down to do justice to lavish Russian hospitality in a large dining room simply appointed as a convent rectory. After dinner came music. Cui and his pretty daughter played and sang through his latest work, a setting of Pushkin's unfinished tragedy *A feast in the Year of the Plague*. Glazounov played his latest pianoforte sonata; Sigismund Blumenfeld sang some of Musorgsky's satirical songs in which he makes fun of the musical tastes and music critics of his day, with less expenditure of means but with quite as much malice as Richard Strauss in *Ein Heldenleben*. Rimsky-Korsakov himself took no part in the music, but we heard an arrangement for four hands of a Suite from his opera *Tsar Saltan*.

A train of small Finnish carts, with their muscular cat-like ponies, had scrambled up from the village to take the guests to the station. One of these ponies was reported by the servants to be unbroken and skittish. One after another the guests departed, carefully choosing the most sober ponies and drivers. The Rimsky-Korsakovs and my friend and I lingered on after the others had gone, and we left the house together. There were still two carts and two ponies waiting; which was the more dangerous? Rimsky made a rush for the first, helped his wife into the primitive, springless vehicle and drove off in the perfect light and sapphire-blue night. 'I hope you have chosen the right horse', he called back merrily as they disappeared over the brow of the steep hill. My friend and I followed with Hobson's Choice. All went well until we reached the steepest part of the descent, then crack! A vision of pony's heels in unpleasant proximity! We had a kicker, and no doubt about it! The laconic Finn descended from his seat on the shafts, a few fresh knots were tied in the broken rope-harness, and on we went again. At the station we found Rimsky-Korsakov still waiting for the train, and we travelled to Petersburg together. It was past midnight, but the midnight of a northern June; fantastic, exciting though the light of day haunted the night and kept it wide-eyed and sleepless. Mutual farewells were said, and plans discussed, including Rimsky-Korsakov's visit to England, but alas this was not accomplished.

It is uncertain whether Rosa saw Rimsky-Korsakov again, but she wrote the biographical entry for him for the second edition of *Grove's Dictionary of Music and Musicians*. She had many letters from him concerning his work as Professor of Composition and Instrumentation at the St Petersburg Conservatoire and details of his later compositions.

Sergius Lyapunov (1859-1924) was yet one more member of the circle who foregathered at Stasov's house. He was undoubtedly attracted to the National School led by Balakirev, with whom he formed a close friendship until the latter's death in 1910. During the long period of Balakirev's almost complete withdrawal from social life, Lyapunov and Dmitri Stasov, Vladimir's brother, were closer to him than any other friends. It was through Lyapunov that colleagues kept in touch with Balakirev during his last days.

In his compositions, Lyapunov made very effective use of folk elements and of his *Solemn Overture*, which was performed by Henry Wood at a Promenade Concert in 1901 Rosa Newmarch retained a lasting impression of a work; fresh and original in melodic inspiration.

Glazunov was perhaps the one of the circle Rosa Newmarch came to know best in England. On his first visit to England in 1897, he conducted the Royal Philharmonic Orchestra in a performance of his Fourth Symphony[7]. He became a frequent visitor to England, especially as a conductor. In an article, Rosa recalled a small luncheon party which she gave for Glazunov on one of his early visits, when Henry Wood and his wife, Olga, a compatriot of the composer, Dr Charles Maclean and Mrs Hertz (probably the wife of the conductor, Alfred Hertz) were guests.

He was a delightful companion, modest, simple and quite imperturbable. He was anxious to visit Oxford, so a few days later they journeyed there, together with Mengelberg, conductor of the Amsterdam [Concertgebow] Orchestra. I had arranged for Professor Morfill to meet us and show our Russian friend round some of the colleges. At Magdalen we met the then President, Dr Warren, a charming man who took them all over the college himself; but his French, like Professor Morfill's Russian, was quite unintelligible; though I am sure their academic knowledge of the languages may have been quite extensive! [Professor Morfill was an expert and had written grammars on Slavonic languages and was very interested in the structure of languages, but it seems likely that his experience of the spoken languages was limited.] I came away feeling that because Glazunov and I had talked Russian together, he thought I must be Madame Glazunov, and he promised to call on us when visiting St. Petersburg![5]

Notes

1. Rosa Newmarch, *The Russian Arts* (London: Herbert Jenkins, 1916), pp.252-4.
2. Richard Taruskin, (1997) *Defining Russia Musically* (Princeton: Princeton University Press, 1997) p.xv.

3. Rosa Newmarch (1914) *The Russian Opera* (London: Herbert Jenkins, 1914), pp. 199-200.

4. David Brown, D. (2006) *Tchaikovsky: The Man and His Music* (London: Faber and Faber, 2006), p.289.

5. Rosa Newmarch, unpublished autobiography.

6. Rosa Newmarch, 'Rimsky-Korsakov: A Biographical Sketch,' *The Musical Standard* (6 March 1897), pp.152-3.

7. Robert Elkin, *Royal Philharmonic* (London: Rider and Co.,1946), p.93.

CHAPTER 11: SPREADING THE WORD

Rosa Newmarch was enthusiastic about Russian music before she visited Russia, and by the time she returned to London in the autumn of 1897, she was even more fired up and keen to do all she could for its promotion. She encouraged the performance of Russian music, gave a series of lectures on the subject, and continued writing articles in music journals on Russian composers.

At the time, the twenty-eight-year-old conductor Henry Wood, then very much a rising star, had been conducting the Promenade Concerts for three seasons. He had already included in these concerts some performances of Russian music by Arensky, Borodin, Cui, Dargomyzhsky, Glazunov, Rimsky-Korsakov, Serov, and Tchaikovsky. The first time a work by Musorgsky was given at a symphony concert in the Britain was in February 1898[1]. Wood had also given the first British performance of Tchaikovsky's opera *Eugene Onegin* in 1892. Clearly he was someone Rosa must get to know. Before visiting Russia, she had taken the step of writing to Henry Wood, complimenting him on his performances of Russian music at the Queen's Hall, and had received an appreciative reply[2]. He thanked her and said that he thought Russian music very original and splendidly scored, but he did not want to do too much yet as it took time for audiences to become sufficiently appreciative of it, but in due course he would do so.

The first meeting between Rosa and Henry Wood took place in the autumn of 1897. This important event was to lead to a life long friendship. Their recollections are described in their autobiographies, written some time later, so it is interesting to compare them[3,4]. Rosa's description follows:

Of course I can remember 'little Henry J. Wood' pulling himself – not I think entirely unaided – on to his organ stool at the Fisheries Exhibition in 1883; but our real friendship began on a late autumn morning in 1897, when I had returned from my first musical tour in Russia. I had brought back with me a few scores by Glinka, Moussorgsky and Rimsky-Korsakov – then very much unknown to the general public in England. I wanted the 'Prom' audience to enjoy what I had been enjoying myself in Moscow and Petersburg. On the doorstep of his flat in Langham Place I collided with a vivacious, tremendously energetic young man – the conductor himself. Heaven knows how long we discussed music on the pavement! Well, I took those precious scores to Henry Wood not because I was particularly infatuated with his conducting, or because I had any axe to grind myself – it was many years before I had any official connection with Queen's Hall – but because I already knew that he had the spirit of real propaganda; he already thought for the future.

In Henry Wood's *My Life in Music*[4], he recollected meeting her on the steps of Queen's Hall in 1908, where she made herself known to him as he was about to enter the concert hall. 'You will not know me, Mr Wood,' she said by way of introduction. 'My name is Rosa Newmarch; I am deeply interested in what you are doing for Russian music. I have been living in Russia.' 'Then you must meet my wife,' he replied. 'She is Russian by birth.' He explained that they became lifelong friends.

Memories can be notoriously fallible. In this case, Henry Wood's dating of the meeting is eleven years late, he was not married to a Russian wife until the year after the meeting he described, and whether the location was the steps of Wood's flat or Queen's Hall is uncertain, although both were situated in Langham Place. Arthur Jacobs discusses the discrepancies in Wood's autobiography and possible reasons for it in an entertaining forward to his biography[5].

At the time, the names of Russian composers such as Musorgsky, Balakirev, Rimsky-Korsakov, Glazunov, and Dargomyzhsky were not familiar to the average concert-going audience, unlike Russian writing, where Tolstoy, Chekhov, Gogol, Dostoyevsky, and Turgenev were more generally known. These authors were known through Constance Garnett's translations. Garnett (1861-1946) was a near contemporary of Rosa Newmarch and in a way promoted Russian literature by her translations, as did Rosa for Russian music. Garnett visited Russia in 1893, meeting Tolstoy, and subsequently translated works by Tolstoy, Gogol, Dostoyevsky, Pushkin, Chekhov, Turgenev, and Ostrovsky.

Henry Wood gave singing lessons, and on 10 July 1898, he married his Russian-born pupil Olga Meikoff. He referred to her as Princess Olga Ouroussoff. According to Arthur Jacobs, she was most probably the illegitimate daughter of Princess Sofiya Ouroussoff[6]. After they were married, they inaugurated a series of recitals billed as 'Mr and Mrs Henry J. Wood's Vocal Recitals' in which Olga sang and Henry accompanied on the piano. Developing the educational potential of this, Rosa began giving a series of illustrated lectures on Russian composers. At these lectures the illustrations would be of Olga's singing in Russian and occasionally in French with Henry accompanying at the piano, at times assisted by the singer H. Lane Wilson. The first of these lectures, entitled *The Art Songs of Russia,* was given on 26 April 1900 at the Steinway Hall, Wigmore Street. The Steinway Hall opened in 1875 and after 1925 became known as the Grotrius Hall. The programme included songs by Glinka, Dargomyzhsky, Rubinstein, Balakirev, Borodin, Cui, Musorgsky, and Tchaikovsky. Most of the translations in the programme notes were by Rosa Newmarch. The lecture was repeated a year later on Monday 18 March at Leighton House, Kensington and also in the South Place Institute, Finsbury. Olga was full of admiration for Rosa's interest and enthusiasm for Russia and its music and had already read her book, *Borodin and Liszt*.

Although the audiences were initially small, the music critics of the day were complimentary as reported in *The Times, The Sunday Times, The Star* and *The Atheneum*. To quote one: 'Lectures are frequently the means of producing an amount of pain and weariness not compensated for by the amount of instruction they convey, but Mrs Newmarch has an entirely admirable sense of fitness of things in lectures, and as she knows her subject thoroughly, she mingles biography and criticism in exactly the right proportions and never loses the attention of her listeners for a moment.' Not only was there favourable comment on Rosa's lecturing, but also on Olga's singing. To quote another critic: 'There is unusual elegance in the vocal method, there is "temperament" enough and to spare, but perhaps the chief attraction lies in the delicate and unerring power of suggestion which is Mrs Wood's very enviable gift. She uses no coarse or even strong colouring, yet her refinement lacks no vital element of strength. The quality of her art is brought into vivid relief when one compares her interpretation of such as Tchaikovsky's *Ballroom Meeting* with that of more than one famous dramatic singer.' Rosa, Olga, and Henry worked well as a team. Rosa also translated a number of the songs into English so that they might more readily be sung by English singers. Of the three venues at which the first series of lectures were given, Rosa liked Leighton House least, not liking its décor, whereas the South Place Institute was the venue with the most enthusiastic music public. As the lectures became more popular, new venues in the provinces were included and the support team enlarged to include the singers Miss Granger Kerr and Louis Arena, a Russian tenor. Since Henry Wood had so many other commitments, Richard Epstein also acted as piano accompanist.

Not only did Rosa increase the number of venues, but she also increased the scope of the lectures. With the formation of the Anglo-Russian Literary Society, she added further lectures entitled *The Popular Poets of Russia* and *Life and Legend in Russian Art* that were given at the Imperial Institute. The former included the poets Koltsov, Nakressov, and Nikitin, and for the latter the Russian art ranged from the introduction of iconography by Greek monks at the close of the tenth century to the realistic national school. For these she gradually acquired a fine collection of slides, many of them coloured, of representative pictures from the principal galleries in Moscow and Petersburg. This must have been quite a feat at the time because the process for producing photographic coloured lanternslides was invented in Germany by Agfa only in 1916.

From January 1900 until April 1905, Rosa gave a series of five papers to meetings of the Musical Association (now the Royal Musical Association). The meetings were held at the Royal College of Organists, Bloomsbury, chaired by Sir Hubert Parry or Dr Charles Maclean. The first sets out the overall development of Russian opera and then dealt with the period from earliest times up to the operas of Glinka. The second considered operas of Dargomyzhsky, Musorgsky, and Serov; the third with Borodin, the fourth with Tchaikovsky, and the fifth with Rimsky-Korsakov. These lectures were also given with musical illustrations for which the singers were again Mrs Henry Wood and Miss Grainger Kerr and the piano accompanist was Richard Epstein. All five papers were published by the Musical Association[7].

In addition to lecturing, Rosa Newmarch wrote prolifically. During this period, she spent much time writing and researching Tchaikovsky and his music. Before she went to Russia, she had been in contact with Nikolai Kashkin and met him in Moscow. He had agreed that she could use his *Reminiscences of P.I. Tchaikovsky* and she wrote a series of articles that were published in *The Musician* in 1897[8]. Hermann Laroch* (1845-1904), a Russian music and literary critic, edited and published *Collective Writings of Tchaikovsky* in 1898. Laroch had been a lifelong friend of Tchaikovsky's; they had been music students together and Tchaikovsky had dedicated three pieces to him. Rosa made extracts from these collective writings which showed Tchaikovsky's musical tastes and sympathies. Later, at the suggestion of her friend, the music critic C. A. Barry (1830-1915), she made a translation of the diary of Tchaikovsky's tour abroad in 1888. She had also heard that the authorised *Life and Letters of Tchaikovsky* being compiled by his brother Modest was likely to be long delayed, and so she contacted the publisher, P. Jurgenson, whom she met whilst in Moscow, to seek permission to reprint the diary in book form suitable for the English public. She was then able to compile the information from these three different sources in her book *Tchaikovsky: His Life and Works*, published by Grant Richards in 1900[9]. Although forgotten today, between 1900 and 1935 the firm of Grant Richards was a very innovative publisher. Good at fostering hidden talent they published works by Shaw, Joyce, and A.E. Housman. Rosa was aware of the book's shortcomings at the time, writing in the preface: 'No one can be more conscious than myself of the patchy nature of its construction.' Nevertheless, it was the first book on Tchaikovsky in English and was favourably reviewed in the *New York Times* on 1 December 1900. The book's dedication was 'To Henry J.

Wood who has helped to realise so many of Tchaikovsky's masterpieces, and to his wife.' Wood responded in a letter saying that he was delighted with the book but felt that he had not done enough to deserve her warm words[10]. This book has now been superseded by more recent biographies. In 1908, it was republished, edited and expanded to 418 pages, including a section on 'The relation of Tchaikovsky to art-questions of the day' and an analysis of selected works by Edwin Evans. This was apparently without Rosa's involvement[11]. There was sufficient interest for the book to be reissued up to 1969 and it is still being reprinted today. However, it was not to be the final word on Tchaikovsky from Rosa Newmarch as a much larger book was to be published six years later.

At the time Rosa was writing there was far less information about Tchaikovsky's life than at present; there have been a number of recent biographies of Tchaikovsky[12-14]. Although his brother Modest published over 5000 of Tchaikovsky's letters in three volumes between 1900 to 1902, he set himself as the curator of Tchaikovsky's legacy and suppressed or destroyed documentary evidence of Tchaikovsky's homosexuality. He carefully excluded anything that pointed too markedly to his brother's sexuality and perhaps by association his own. According to Brown, the word 'homosexual' only found its way into English medical, social, and legal parlance in the late 1890s. He goes on to suggest that Rosa was probably aware of his 'heterodox erotic inclinations during her sojourns in Russia'. And this is discreetly alluded to in her writings, describing him as a 'gentle and sensitive artist, possessed with an almost feminine craving for approval and encouragement[15]'. And later, at the time of his marriage, Rosa wrote: 'Even his most intimate friends had very little clue to the mysterious catastrophe which seemed to have broken up his life. M. Kashkin, who knew his tender-heartedness and the almost feminine sensibility of his nature, was filled with the gravest apprehensions, which, as it afterwards proved were not without foundation[16].'

Stasov visited London in 1900 and met Rosa regularly during his stay. On one occasion they met at the Newmarchs' house, where Rosa entertained him together with Henry and Olga Wood, Norman and Adine O' Neill, and Professor Morfill. Rosa also made a return visit to Russia in 1901, although she does not mention this in her autobiography[17]. During the period between her return from Russia and 1905, she also managed to write a number of articles on music in Russia. The subjects included Liszt[18], Berlioz[19], and Schumann[20] in Russia, Musorgsky[21], Serov[22], two further articles of Tchaikovsky[23-24], and articles on Turgenev[25] and Russian poets[26].

By 1903, Rosa was becoming more widely known as a writer, and about this time came to know the publisher John Lane (1854-1925). He was the co-founder of The Bodley Head publishers with offices in London and New York; his nephew Allen Lane later founded Penguin Books. John Lane was a man of many artistic interests and was keen to publish books on music that would meet the demand of the growing concert-going public as well as musicians. He invited Rosa to become the editor of a series of monographs he was planning entitled *Living Masters of Music*, which she accepted. In the preliminary announcement it was stated that 'the distinguishing feature of the books will be that touch of intimacy which gives contemporary biography its greatest value and vitality. As far as possible, each volume will be confided to a writer who is actually acquainted with the personality and the work of the musician he is invited to depict.' So, who better to start the series than the editor herself with a book on her great friend Henry Wood. Against the argument that Henry Wood might be considered rather young to feature in this series, her view was 'If he has attained greatness in his own line at thirty five, why wait until he is an octogenarian before having the courage to say so.'

The series included twelve volumes in all, as follows:

Volume	Subject	Author	Publication Date	Reprinting
I	Henry Wood	Rosa Newmarch	1904	
II	Edward Elgar	R.J. Buckley	1905	2001
III	Richard Strauss	Ernest Newman, with a personal note by Alfred Kalisch	1908	1921,1969, 2001
IV	Paderewski	Edward A Baughan	1908	2008
V	Alfred Bruneau	Arthur Hervey	1907	
VI	Joseph Joachim	J.A. Fuller Maitland	1905	2008
VII	Edvard Grieg	H. T. Finck	1908	1922,1929, 2007
VIII	Theodore Leschetizsky	Annette Hullah	1906	1923
IX	Giacomo Puccini	Wakeling Dry	1906	2008
X	Claude Debussy	Mrs Franz Liebich	1908	1925, 2001
XI	Granville Bantock	H.C. Anderton	1915	
XII	Edward MacDowell	Lawrence Gilman	1906	2007

Many are still referred to today, and as can be seen, most have been reprinted. The most recent printings are generally 'print on demand'. Each was about 20,000 words, with appropriate illustrations, and as they were published at the then popular price of 2/6 (12½p, equivalent to about £7 today based on the Retail Price Index), the fee paid to the author of each volume could of necessity only be small, even for those days, and not likely to attract writers as a remunerative proposition. John Lane felt the series was 'destined to be a great factor in modern musical life'. For the editor, it was no easy task to select and then persuade writers of a high standard to undertake these volumes. At the time, the demand for music books amongst the general public was small, and John Lane was certainly enterprising. Such a series was something of an innovation, but he hoped to meet the requirements of an ever-growing number of music enthusiasts who were filling the Queen's Hall, the Albert Hall and other concert halls in the provinces.

Though things generally went smoothly, there were a few hiccups, as her daughter Elsie Newmarch described[27]:

> Though John Lane undoubtedly had every confidence in his editor's judgement, one small contretemps seems to have occurred. He was anxious, probably with the American market in mind, to include the then popular conductor and composer, Sousa, in the series. I remember that the proposal caused Rosa Newmarch some trepidation and concern, for though she realised that such a book might well be acceptable and saleable in America, to include it in the series might raise protests here, which could be bad for the rest of the volumes. 'Our terms are not high', she writes in a letter to John Lane, 'and the prestige of the series has so far been its chief recommendation to writers of any standing. We must not jeopardise its reputation for the sake of one volume'. Already she had not been very happy about the authorship of the Elgar monograph, feeling that this outstanding British composer should have been written about by a writer of wide experience. 'I am not small in my views', she continues, 'or afraid of expressing my opinion as I hope you realise; but I am of the opinion that it was an error of judgement on our part to introduce a second-rate writer in the series, it would be still worse to follow it up by a distinctly second-rate –though immensely popular musician.'

Sousa was not included in *Living Masters of Music*. The 'second-rate writer' was the Birmingham journalist R. J. Buckley, who interviewed Elgar in September 1903. According to Percy Young, the monograph on Elgar, published in 1904, was authoritative to that date, the proofs having been read by Elgar himself, so perhaps

Rosa's fears on this issue were unfounded, or based on prejudice[28].

Ernest Newman was a writer who at first felt it difficult in the midst of other more remunerative work to take on a volume and give the research, time and expense involved for such a small fee. But when the music critic Alfred Kalisch, well known for his dilatory ways where work was concerned, failed month after month to produce his manuscript, Newman agreed to complete the volume on Richard Strauss. Grieg was invited to write about Tchaikovsky, but he declined, saying he was too occupied at the time[29].

Rosa Newmarch's *Henry Wood* was the first to appear in print. The reviews were enthusiastic, as the following selection shows: The *Morning Post*, 'Apart from its biographical interest, the volume is remarkable on account of the author's knowledge and critical acumen, as well as the excellence of its literary style'; *Musical News*, 'Perfect tact and an excellent temper [...] a practical and brilliant writer [...] The most important and successful of all her prose writings'; *Pall Mall Gazette*, 'Mrs Newmarch's writing has a very readable quality.'

It would be difficult to quarrel with the readability of the book, but it is adulatory in tone rather than critical. Rosa Newmarch undoubtedly had a flair for writing, and she must have been able to compose quickly in order to produce the large number of articles and books published in such a short space of time. There are, however, occasional signs that she was not always thorough with her research. Arthur Jacobs, the most recent biographer of Henry Wood, makes the positive comments that her personal description of Wood is vivid and paints a picture of mental and physical vigour[30]. Also she refers to Olga correctly[31] as the daughter of Princess Sofie Ouroussov, though not herself as a princess. On the negative side, Wood deceived her over particulars of his birth, an excusable mistake on her part. Less excusable, however, is her statement: 'In all, Mr Wood has conducted forty six operas, grand and comic, and it is no exaggeration to say that the whole *repertoire* of the lyric stage is at his finger-ends[32].' 'Forty six' is a case of 'over egging'; it is an overestimate.

Besides all her writing and lecturing, Rosa Newmarch found time to sponsor a piano trio from Moscow. The Moscow Trio, David Schor (piano), David Krein (violin), and Rudolph Erlich (cello), arrived in London in 1903 after a successful tour of Paris. They came without an agent, simply writing to Rosa and a few friends. After hearing them play, Rosa felt sure that if she could get the right people to come to their concert, their eventual success could be as great as when Joachim performed at the 'Pops' concerts. With great enthusiasm and energy, she wrote to the music critics in the press, and with the help of her friend the singer Miss Grainger Kerr, she sent out dozens of tickets. Although few sold for their first concert, it was sufficient for the word to get around, and they were in immediate demand to give further concerts.

None of the trio spoke English and two of them spoke only Russian and did not want to sign any contracts without Rosa being present to interpret for them. So, initially she effectively became their agent. However, she felt should could not continue as an impresario in addition to all her other commitments, and she was able to place them with the agent Mrs Ethyl Robinson. The Trio came the following year and repeated their successes in both London and Manchester. Rosa singled out their performance of Tchaikovsky's elegiac *Trio in A minor* as outstanding.

Besides all the activities mentioned in this chapter, Rosa was embarking on what was to become her largest and most successful work of translation, that of Tchaikovsky's letters.

Notes

1. Rosa Newmarch, 'Modeste Moussorgsky', *The Musical Standard* (19 Feb, 1898), p.118.

2. Reginald Pound, *Sir Henry Wood* (London: Cassell, 1969), pp.62-3.

3. From a speech Rosa Newmarch gave at a dinner given by Sir Henry Wood on 26 September 1937 at the Langham Hall to members of his orchestra.

4. Henry Wood, *My Life in Music* (London: Gollancz, 1938), p.231.

5. Arthur Jacobs, *Henry Wood: Maker of the Proms* (London: Methuen, 1994), pp.xxi-xxiii.

6. Ibid. pp.58-9.

7. Rosa Newmarch, 'The Development of National Opera in Russia', *Musical Association* 1900-1905, pts 1-5.

8. Rosa Newmarch, Peter Ilich Tchaikovsky, *The Musician*, 1/10 (14 July 1897): 192-4, 1/11 (21 July 1897): 212-3, 1/12 (28 July 1897): 231-3, 1/13 (4 August 1897): 251-3, 1/14 (11 August 1897): 272-3, and 1/15 (18 August 1897): 291-3.

9. Rosa Newmarch, *Tchaikovsky: His Life and Works, with Extracts from his Writings, and the Diary of his Tour abroad in 1888* (London: Grant Richards, 1900) pp.249.

10. Pound, *Wood*, p.78.

11. Philip Ross Bullock, *Rosa Newmarch and Russian Music in the Late Nineteenth and Early Twentieth-Century England* (Farnham, Surrey: Ashgate, 2009), p. 108.

12. Roland Wiley, *Tchaikovsky* (Oxford: OUP, 2009).

13. David Brown, *Tchaikovsky: The Man and His Music* (London: Faber and Faber, 2007).

14. Anthony Holden, *Tchaikovsky* (London: Bantam Press, 1995).

15. Malcolm Brown, 'Tchaikovsky and His Music in Anglo-American Criticism, 1890s-1950s', in Sophie Fuller and Lloyd Whitesell (eds), *Queer Episodes in Music and Modern Identity* (Urbana: University of Illinois Press, 2002), pp.138-9.

16. Rosa Newmarch, *Tchaikovsky: His Life and Works* (London: Reeves, 1908), p.69.

17. Bullock, *Newmarch*, p.10.

18. Rosa Newmarch, 'Liszt in Russia', *The Musical Monthly Record*, 1 Apr. 1902, pp.64-5.

19. Rosa Newmarch, 'Berlioz in Russia', *The Musical Monthly Record*, 1 Jul. 1903, pp.122-3.

20. Rosa Newmarch, 'Schumann in Russia', *The Musical Monthly Record*, 1 Oct. 1902, pp.185-6.

21. Rosa Newmarch, 'Modeste Moussorgsky', *The Musical Standard*, 19 Feb. 1898, pp118-9.

22. Rosa Newmarch, 'Serov' *Zeitschrift der Internationalen Musicgesellschaft*, Jan, 1903, pp.177-180.

23. Rosa Newmarch, ' Tchaikovsky and Tolstoy', *Contemporary Review*, Jan. 1903, pp.112-8.

24 Rosa Newmarch, 'Tchaikovsky's Last Visit to England', *Musical Times*, 1 Feb. 1904, pp.95-7.

25. Rosa Newmarch,' Some New Letters of Tourgeniev, *Altantic Monthly*. Nov. 1899, pp.691-705.

26. Rosa Newmarch, 'The Popular Poets of Russia', *Proc. Anglo-Russian Lierary Soc.* 5 Mar. 1901, pp.19-48.

27. Biography of Rosa Newmarch, Elsie Newmarch's unpublished version.

28. Percy Young, *Elgar O. M* .(London: Collins, 1955), p.116.

29. Letter from Grieg to Rosa Newmarch, dated 25 Oct. 1905, Kristiana, *Sotheby's Music Catalogue* 22 May 2003, p.51.

30. Jacobs, *Wood*, p. 93.

31. Rosa Newmarch, *Henry J. Wood* (London: John Lane, 1904), p.9.

32. Ibid. p.8.

CHAPTER 12: TCHAIKOVSKY'S LIFE AND LETTERS: THE TOUR DE FORCE

After Tchaikovsky's death in 1893, his brother Modest (1850-1916) began working on *The Life and Letters of Peter Ilich Tchaikovsky* [Жизнь Петра Ильича Чайковского]. This was an enormous task because there were some 6000 letters from over 800 people to Tchaikovsky, while his own letters addressed to various people, together with extracts from his diary, accounted for another 4000 documents, in addition to many other annotated manuscripts. The completed work was published by P. Jurgenson, Moscow, in three volumes in 1900. This was followed very shortly by a German translation by Paul Juon, *Das Leben Peter Iljitsch Tschaikowsky*.

Rosa Newmarch's book, *Tchaikovsky, his Life and Works with Extracts from his Writings, and the Diary of his Tour Abroad in 1888*, published in 1900 was the most comprehensive on Tchaikovsky published in English at the time, and within two years it had sold out. Interest in Tchaikovsky's music both in England and America was clearly increasing, judging by the requests for Rosa's book. A year later, Jurgenson approached her on the subject of a translation of Modest Tchaikovsky's *The Life and Letters of Peter Ilich Tchaikovsky*, but negotiations with an American publishing firm eventually fell through[1]. At the time Rosa saw two alternative courses of action: either to revise her book using the new information from Modest's book, or to make a complete translation of it, the former being the easier task. However, there was no doubt in Rosa's mind that the latter would be of greater value in the long run. She corresponded with Modest Tchaikovsky concerning the possibility of bringing out an abridged English edition of his *The Life and Letters of Peter Ilich Tchaikovsky*. Judging by Modest's reply, he was willing and grateful that the work should be abridged, and happy that the task of translating it into English and revising it should be in her capable hands. This must have seemed to her a huge undertaking, especially as she had other writing and lecturing commitments at the time.

Rosa asked the publisher John Lane whether he would consider an English translation of Modest's *Tchaikovsky*. On 28 March 1904, John Lane wrote to her concerning the Tchaikovsky memoirs and letters indicating that he would be pleased to pay her thirty-five guineas on publication, *i.e.* for translating, arranging and editing these letters selected from the new *Life*, which had just appeared in Russia in two volumes. This was by no means a very remunerative proposition, but the demand was not likely to be very high and thus not a rewarding one for the publisher. [On the basis of the Retail Price Index, thirty-five guineas in 1903 is equivalent to approximately £2800 in 2011].

Before embarking on the translation there was a practical issue to consider. The 3000 letters amounted to nearly 2000 pages, which, while valuable to the specialist, was far too much for the more general reader. The German edition, already published, had been abridged by about one third of its original length. A significant proportion of the letters were to people quite unknown to the British and American public, and many concerned local issues. Rosa comments: 'While admiring the patient and pious industry which has raised so colossal a monument to Tchaikovsky's memory, I cannot but feel that it would be unreasonable to expect of any nation but its own a hero-worship so devout that it could assimilate a *Tchaikovskiad* of such prodigious dimensions'[2]. Rosa's abridged translation, published in 1906, ran to 782 pages. Her selection was judged favourably by the *New York Times* reviewer Richard Aldrich[3]: 'Mrs Newmarch has retained quite enough to give a complete view of Tschaikovsky's life and activities, even his intimate relations.' Rosa Newmarch carefully selected the material, trying as far as possible to maintain the autobiographical character of the book, wherever feasible letting Tchaikovsky himself tell the story of his life.

On 24 November 1905, John Lane wrote to her enclosing a cheque for thirty-seven guineas, thirty-five for the Tchaikovsky book and two guineas for the editorial fee for a book on MacDowell[4]. At this early stage, few copies had sold, but with advertising he hoped for more sales. He also complimented her on the editorial work which had been very helpful.

Whilst the initial response was slow, by the end of November 1905, John Lane was able to report favourable reviews in the *Westminster Gazette* and the *Birmingham Post* and a 'brilliant notice of Mr Grave's.' Charles L Graves (1856-1944) was the music critic for the *Spectator*, later its assistant editor, and he wrote a biography of Sir George Groves (editor of *Groves Musical Dictionary*). He wrote to Rosa Newmarch: 'The book is enormously interesting. It was impossible to do justice to it in a single article, so that I was obliged to concentrate attention on one aspect of it […] I can only repeat what I have already said, that musicians and music-lovers owe you a deep debt of gratitude for your labours. I am rejoiced to think that I have in a small way helped to dispel the misgivings that you may have entertained as to the result and value. My only regret is that the size and price of the book must necessarily limit its circulation and place it out of the reach of many of the intelligent middle-class people who are the backbone of the musical world here and elsewhere.'

The composer and conductor, Granville Bantock wrote:

First let me congratulate you on your monumental achievement. Your Tchaikovsky book is a fine contribution to the literature of music, and leads me to marvel at the perseverance and energy with which you have tackled such a formidable task. I am reserving an hour a day for reading the book, for I feel justified in allowing myself the selfish pleasure as a reward for hours of diplomatic strategy among the musical mammons of Birmingham [...] Your book, to change the metaphor, will be to me an oasis in the desert! Tchaikovsky was to me a real musical soul, and many profitable lessons are to be gathered from his life and works. I am grateful to you for this opportunity of becoming better acquainted with his individuality.

The book was generally welcomed as a fascinating self-revelation of a great artist. There was praise for its musical interest, for the translations, and for the skill in literary craftsmanship that served the editor well in the delicate task of abridgement. The book has undoubtedly stood the test of time; it was reissued in hardback in 1924, 1970, and 2001, and in paperback in 1973 and 2004, and remains valuable today. In 1995, Boynton Stevenson argued that her translation was made on the basis of the previous German version and contained a number of errors and miscomprehensions[5]. Conversely, G.S. Smith praised the translations she made in the book *Poetry and Progress in Russia* published only one year later[5].

On the other hand, Vladimir Stasov, who viewed Tchaikovsky as composing more in the European tradition, was less complimentary. A shade of reserve marked his attitude towards Tchaikovsky. In the early days of the composer's career, when he was still much attracted towards the national opera and the modern forms of symphonic music, their intercourse had been friendly, as can be gathered from the musician's letters to Stasov published in *The Life and Letters*. However, by 1883, in an essay entitled *Our music in the last 25 years,* Stasov complimented Tchaikovsky on certain aspects of his music but condemned others. He described Tchaikovsky as an extremely gifted musician, although influenced by his conservatory training as a disciple of Anton Rubinstein. [Stasov had little sympathy for Rubinstein as a composer though he recognised him as an outstanding pianist.] He was at his best as an orchestral composer, good with instrumental music, not always successful in handling folk material and least gifted at vocal composition. He was critical of his operas. Summing up Tchaikovsky's total output, he wrote, 'A few works are first-rate and highly original; the remainder are mediocre and weak.'[6]

As time went on and Tchaikovsky stood more and more aloof from the national school, of which Stasov was the literary champion, it was inevitable that the differences of opinion between them should become accentuated. In 1900, Stasov wrote to Rosa, looking forward to her forthcoming book but expressing the view that notwithstanding all Tchaikovsky's faults and all his breadth, he was a composer of considerable merit and talent although rarely original. By the spring of 1906, when she had sent him a copy of her English edition, Stasov clearly still had great reservations about Tchaikovsky but was pleased to see that they were both in agreement about the more essential issues. Nevertheless, she felt sure that in his heart of hearts he would rather she had bestowed the time and immense labour in other directions. He wrote:

> I have read all you have ever written about Tchaikovsky; you are afraid that we shall not agree as to his talents and musical physiognomy generally; but I have observed with great satisfaction that this is not the case, and that in the more essential matters you and I think almost exactly alike. But I cannot sympathise with all Tchaikovsky's ideas, not with his evaluations of other musicians, be they Russian or foreigners. He prefers Mozart to Beethoven, which to me is impossibility, although I have great admiration for parts of the Requiem and Don Juan. What shocks me in Tchaikovsky is his utter inability to understand what is really great in Glinka and the new Russian School; the latter he did not understand in the least. He thought Balakirev, Moussorgsky, Borodin and Rimsky-Korsakov were men of talent, but only amateurs *au fond*.

Rosa was also complimented by Madame Olga Novikoff*, who paid tribute to the great services she had rendered to the artistic world by publication of her two volumes on Tchaikovsky and her later works *The Russian Opera* and *The Russian Arts*: 'We Russians must always think of Mrs Rosa Newmarch's efforts to bring about an artistic entente between Russia and England'[7].

27. Olga Novikoff in 1876

About 1906, an effort was made to form a Russian society to promote a better understanding between the two countries. By this time, Rosa was more widely known as an authority on Russian arts, especially after the publication of *The Life and Letters of Peter Ilich Tchaikovsky,* and she chaired the inaugural meeting held at the Hotel Russell. In a letter to her sister, she spoke of it as 'very stormy, for a few people came with the intention of trying to be disagreeable. I managed, however, to get all the resolutions carried by the meeting; one notice in the *Daily Mail* headed "A Firm Lady Chairman" would amuse you! But I have had such nice letters since from both Russian and English friends; one from Princess Volkonsky in Petersburg offering to help in every way. If I can only succeed in forming a society like the *Entente Cordiale*, I shall feel I have done useful work.'

Having finished this mammoth task of translation, Rosa felt it was time for her to have a break.

Notes

1. Rosa Newmarch, *The Life and Letters of Peter Ilich Tchaikovsky by Modeste Tchaikovsky*, ed and trans. Rosa Newmarch (London: John Lane The Bodley Head, 1906), pp.vi-vii
2. *Ibid*, ix
3. Richard Aldrich, 'Tschaikowsky and Johannes Brahms', *New York Times*, 31 March 1906.
4. Lawrence Gilman, *Edward MacDowell* (London: John Lane, 1906).
5. Philip Ross Bullock, *Rosa Newmarch and Russian Music in Late Nineteenth and Early Twentieth-Century England* (Farnham, Surrey: Ashgate, 2009), p.107.
6. Vladimir Stasov, *Selected Essays on Music*, trans. Florence Jonas (London: Barrie and Rockliff, 1968), pp.111-2.
7. Olga Novikoff, *Russian Memories* (London: Herbert Jenkins, 1917).

CHAPTER 13: CONNECTING THREADS: BANTOCK, SIBELIUS AND MARY WAKEFIELD

Rosa had been interested in Granville Bantock's music from as early as the 1890s, but she did not really discover the music of Sibelius until the early 1900s. At the time, Sibelius was not well known in Britain as a composer and the only scores of his music available were some of his songs, but he ultimately became one of the great composers of the first half of the twentieth century. By contrast, at the end of the nineteenth century, Granville Bantock (1868-1946) was becoming known both through his own music and as a promoter of music by his English contemporaries. He founded the *New Quarterly Review of Music* in 1893. He succeeded in having his opera *Caedmar* performed at the Olympic Theatre, London in 1892. He worked as a conductor and teacher, succeeding Elgar as Professor of Music at Birmingham in 1908, a post he held until his retirement in 1934. He composed many orchestral and large-scale choral works, inspired by heroic, legendary, or exotic themes. After World War I, changing tastes largely eclipsed Bantock's music, although in recent years, recordings have done much to restore his music from neglect.

28. Granville Bantock

The first work of Bantock's that Rosa heard was his *Helena Variations* composed in 1899. It was a work dedicated to his wife, Helen Schweitzer, whom he married in that year. In the years that followed, Rosa became good friends with Bantock and his wife. She also listened to many of his works and reviewed them for music journals. On 3 October 1903, Henry Wood conducted Bantock's Suite *Russian Scenes*, and ten days later conducted the first performance in England of Sibelius's First Symphony, both at Promenade Concerts at which Rosa was present. Two years earlier, he had performed Sibelius's Suite for Orchestra, *King Christian II*.

In all, Sibelius made five visits to England, the first of which was for five days in December 1905. Earlier in that year, Rosa had found time to attend Ysaÿe's summer school at Godinne sur Meuse. It is not clear from her accounts exactly when she first met Granville Bantock, and most probably they corresponded before meeting, but the first meeting between Rosa, Granville Bantock, and Jean Sibelius is well described, although accounts differ in detail. In 1905, Bantock was conductor of the Liverpool Orchestral Society and wanted to have Sibelius's First Symphony performed. He invited Sibelius to come to Liverpool to conduct it. In March 1905 first Sibelius accepted the invitation but then declined when he was commissioned to write incidental music to Maeterlinck's *Pelléas et Mélisande* for a production at the Swedish Theatre in Helsinki in November 1905. In the event, Bantock conducted it himself. Sibelius made good by coming to England later that same year to conduct his First Symphony and *Finlandia* on 2 December at Liverpool. According to Bantock 'I met Sibelius on his arrival at Victoria Station, London, and as the great man then could speak little English, and my knowledge of Finnish was *nil*, our conversation was limited to a polyglot combination of French and German words. Knowing Rosa Newmarch was a fluent Russian linguist and an accomplished translator I sought her aid, happily not in vain. How well I remember that eventful railway journey from Euston to Liverpool, during which we three were sole occupants of the compartment! I can still recall the pungent odour of those enormous black cigars, which Sibelius produced from a gigantic cigar-case and smoked incessantly. It was due to Rosa Newmarch's sympathetic understanding and tactful interest that this journey became the prelude to subsequent visits paid by Sibelius to England [...]'[1].

Sibelius's biographer, Erik Tawaststjerna, described[2] the meeting, presumably from Sibelius's perspective: 'Coming back on the train from London to Birmingham, Bantock had introduced Sibelius to a lady in her fifties with a somewhat imposing almost masculine bearing. This was Rosa Newmarch, and they were soon engaged in animated conversation in a mixture of French and German. Mrs Newmarch had spent some time in St Petersburg and indeed opened their conversation in fluent Russian, assuming that Sibelius spoke it [...] She generally preferred masculine company to *femmes en bloc* [...]' In Robert Layton's account[3], it was after Sibelius had already conducted his first symphony and *Finlandia* in Birmingham in 1905 that he went with Bantock to London and met Rosa Newmarch on the train.

29. Rosa Newmarch, probably about 1910

Rosa Newmarch described Sibelius's first visit in December 1905 visit somewhat differently[4]:

This time the Bantocks invited me to meet him at their house at Moseley near Birmingham. My fellow-guest proved to be a striking and characteristic example of a man of the North – a Viking type. [...] I was put next to him at dinner with a vague idea that, as nobody knew the language he spoke, a little Russian might come in handy. I had been long enough in Russia and over the Finnish borders to know that the Finns were not too keen to speak the language of their big neighbour, but we soon effected a compromise: a sort of sandwich between French and German, to which, looking over correspondence which has lasted over thirty years, I found to my amusement we always adhered.

After Sibelius's visit to Liverpool in 1905, Bantock wrote to Rosa giving his impressions of the Finnish composer:

> I found Sibelius – unlike other composers – extremely reticent about his own work, and it is not always an easy matter to arrive at the true meaning of his music. We read the score of *En Saga* together in the train on our journey to Liverpool, and it struck me as a picturesque and vigorous work. Sibelius pointed out the final pages (*vide* Clarinet solo) and told me he had a liking for this effect, and thought it one of the most effective phrases, or rather episodes, that he had written.
>
> Above all Sibelius appears to me to be a great symphonic writer, and the Symphony in his hands has recovered the vitality it had almost lost for ever. His two symphonies are so fresh and original that one is forced to accept these obsolete forms as something new. Without doubt he is the greatest living symphonist; he has a message to deliver, and knows how to give it.
>
> The Beloved and Shireem join the singer of songs, the maker of music, the heart-afflicted, the drinker of draughts, the haschish-eater, in greetings and salutary salutations to the authoress of poems, the editress of reviews, the Peri of Papas, and the best of friends[5].

Elsie pointed out that the elaborate greetings in the last paragraph were typical of Granville Bantock's frequent oriental vein adopted in many letters to his friend Rosa Newmarch[5].

Sibelius was well pleased with the reception of his music in Liverpool, but he stayed only two days after the concert before returning home via Paris and Berlin. Thus began a friendship between Rosa and Sibelius that lasted for many years. The language with which they used to communicate is interesting and was inevitably connected with their respective views on Germany and Russia. Particularly after the First World War, Rosa's antipathy to the Germans was very evident as the following quotes from Tawaststjerna show: 'Mrs Newmarch was not one to keep her views to herself, and it is clear from his diary that Sibelius found her hatred of the Germans and the strain of talking French all day onerous.'[6] And, 'He wrote in French, presumably with Aino's [Sibelius's wife] assistance, as he did not wish to expose Mrs Newmarch to the unpleasing prospect of receiving letters in the tongue of the hated *Boches*, though more than a year had passed since the Treaty of Versailles. Even in the future he continued with his imperfect French rather than go back to his fluent and idiomatic German. Rosa's dislike of the Germans had obviously made an enduring impression on him.' Whilst their feelings for Russians and

Germans were very different, they both respected each other's views, realising that they arose from their recent histories of both countries' relations with Germany and Russia. Thus, whilst both of them spoke and understood Russian and German, neither felt they should communicate with each other in these languages except as last a resort and so French was often used. This or course presented no difficulty for Rosa but was harder for Sibelius.

Rosa continued to take a keen interest in the works of both Bantock and Sibelius. The first performance of Bantock's *Omar Khayyam* was at the Birmingham Musical Festival in 1906; Rosa contributed a detailed review of the work to the International Musical Society. In 1908, she wrote the detailed descriptive notes for Bantock's symphony-oratorio, *Christus,* which comprises ten vast sections. The second section of this, *Christ in the Wilderness,* was performed at the Sheffield Musical Union in October 1908. However, a more immediate outcome of Sibelius's conducting at Liverpool in December 1905 was that she was persuaded to give a lecture on Sibelius's music under the auspices of the Concert Goers' Club on 22 February 1906. It was the first lecture to be given on Sibelius in London. It was also a first for the Russian conductor, Vassily Safonov, who offered to take the chair at the meeting, in that it was the first time he had made a speech in English. At the time there were no gramophone recordings of Sibelius's music and the only illustrations of his works were his songs. Rosa was able to call on Miss Grainger Kerr, to illustrate the lecture. There was also an unnamed piano accompanist, both for the songs and also a piano reduction of *Finlandia.* There were no accounts of Sibelius's life and music in English, so the lecture itself was based on information Sibelius had given her, together with the handful of scores of Sibelius's music that were available in England and anything else she was able to acquire. In spite of the paucity of information, Rosa was able to arouse considerable interest in the music of Sibelius, such that Breitkopf and Härtel promptly published her lecture as a thirty-two page booklet entitled *Jean Sibelius, Ein finnländischer Komponist,* together with a list of Sibelius's works.

From Rosa's assessment of the two composers, Bantock and Sibelius, there is little to indicate at this time that she rated one greater than the other, although she did comment on Sibelius: 'Sibelius's music is for the future, when the world begins to tire of the vague or violently coloured music of today with its chromatics and hysterics, and orchestras of 120, and finds it must needs for its health's sake have something with large, definite outlines, sculptural, diatonically sane, rooted in Beethoven not in Wagner.' Given the enormous forces required for many of Bantock's works and the possible Wagnerian influence, this could be foretelling the future reception of his works. Her comments later suggest that she could see 'clear water' between the two composers. In 1912, she wrote with great foresight after hearing Sibelius's violin concerto (1903, revised 1905): 'In fifty years' time your concerto will be as classical as those of Beethoven, Brahms and Tchaikovsky.' And at about the same time, when attempts were being made to persuade Sibelius to compose a work for the Gloucester Festival of 1913, she wrote to him taking a very firm line: 'I have a horror of festival commissions. This is the way we ruin so many of our composers in England […] Elgar is going quickly downhill under the strain of more or less commercial projects; Bantock writes too much – with the result that half of what we hear of his sounds a little facile; does it surprise you to learn that I would not want to see you turned into a composer *en vogue* as happened to poor Dvořák 20 years ago?'[7] As far as Rosa was concerned, in 1913 Sibelius's next work should have been nothing less than his fifth symphony.

Her 1906 lecture had clearly stimulated interest in Sibelius's music such that by 1908 the following list of his works had been performed at Promenade Concerts: Symphony No 1, the violin concerto, the Suite for Orchestra *King Christian II*, the Suite *Swanwhite*, *The Swan of Tuonela*, *En Saga*, *Finlandia*, *The Karelia Suite*, and the Dance Intermezzo No. 2. Granville Bantock also conducted performances of *En Saga*, the *Péllias et Mélisande* Suite, and the Second Symphony.

Sibelius clearly enjoyed the reception he received on his first visit to England and was pleased to be invited back in 1907 to conduct his Third Symphony at a concert of the Royal Philharmonic Society. Richter had given the British première of Sibelius's second symphony in 1905. However, as Karl Ekman described 'the third symphony ripened slowly. The master's incorruptible self-criticism performed its work of selection and improvement.'[8] Its première was not given until 25 September 1907 in Helsinki, thus postponing his visit to London until February 1908. Bantock arranged to meet him on his arrival at Victoria Station, but Sibelius caught an earlier than planned train from Dover. Bantock went to Lyons Corner House in Oxford Circus and, by complete coincidence, he found Sibelius there already with a pot of tea. A few minutes after his arrival, again by coincidence, the band started to play his *Valse Triste*. In their heyday, J. Lyons employed as many as 500 full-time musicians to perform in their corner houses. The Corner House in Oxford Circus might have had as many as twelve players and they performed a varied repertoire from 'The Teddy Bear's Picnic' to 'light classics' such as Brahms' Hungarian Dances[9]. Clearly Sibelius's music was travelling well! In February 1908, his Third Symphony, dedicated to Granville Bantock, was first performed at the Queen's Hall, London. The audience found it difficult on first hearing, as did Rosa, but on studying the work in detail, she gradually came to believe it was a fine work. A number of newspapers wrote in the course of their reviews that Sibelius's themes were derived from Finnish folk music.

In a letter Sibelius wrote to Rosa when he had returned to Jarvenpää, his home near Helsinki, he thanks her for her interest in his music, and in response to a query she made, he states clearly that his symphonies do not have programmes. He also wanted to correct a misunderstanding in a number of reviews of performances of his music, asking: 'I should be glad, Madame, if you would correct a common error. Often I find that my themes are described as folk tunes in the foreign press; so far I have never made use of any themes but those which are absolutely my own. Therefore the thematic material employed in "Finlandia" and "En Saga" is my own invention.' Sibelius had to correct this misunderstanding not only in England but in other countries. As late as 1923, when he conducted concerts of his own works in Rome, in an interview with the critic of *La Tribuna*, Alberto Gasco, he stated: 'I do want to make one point clear: that my music is not folkloric. I have on no occasion made use of Finnish folk melodies. I have admittedly composed melodies in a folk-like style, but they have all been created in my mind, or rather in my heart, as I am a devoted Finn[10].'

For this second visit he stayed at the Langham Hotel and Rosa saw him almost daily, and the more they became acquainted, the more she valued his friendship. At the time, Sibelius was suffering from a painful throat, and on returning home he underwent an unsuccessful operation in Helsinki in May 1908 to remove a tumour. He then went to Berlin on the advice of his doctors to consult with a specialist. For two weeks in June 1908, he underwent a series of throat operations. The doctors in Berlin gave a pessimistic diagnosis, which worried him at the time, although it turned out to be benign and he lived for a further forty-nine years. He was persuaded by Rosa, among others, to give up cigars and alcohol, which he did for seven years.

During this second visit to England, Sibelius met Mary Wakefield (1853-1910) at Rosa's home in Campden Hill Square in 1908. By that time, Rosa and Mary had been close friends for some years. They often met in London and Rosa had also been to her home in Westmorland. From her earliest years, Mary was a talented singer, gave many charity concerts, and sang at the Gloucester Festival. She came from a Quaker family who had acquired their wealth through banking. The wealth was such that it was not necessary for Mary to earn her keep. Her father was happy for her to sing as an amateur, but she was barred by the conventions of the day from pursuing a career as a professional singer, so she poured her love of music into a desire to make music more available to rural communities. She founded and trained a number of choirs in the villages around Kendal and brought them together for the first time in 1885 to take part in a singing competition to raise money for Crosscrake Church. The competition, known as the Association of

Musical Competition Festivals, took hold and within a few years a large choir could be assembled to sing larger works. By the end of the nineteenth century, some 10,000 vocalists and instrumentalists were taking part in the three-day festival held in Kendal. Mary Wakefield herself conducted the festival until 1900 and she also acted as chorus master in chief, going from village to village to rehearse the works performed. By 1904, it was considered that the success of the movement warranted the engagement of Henry Wood and the Queens Hall Orchestra[11].

Although Rosa first met Mary as early as 1877, an occasion that Mary could only vaguely recall, it was not until later, probably about the turn of the century, that they became close friends. In a letter to Rosa dated 11 November 1907, Mary Wakefield says: 'I always feel we have a great deal in common and regret the many years lost when we *might* have been acquainted but such is life and we must make up for them in "what remaineth". They did have much in common, both came from middle-class professional backgrounds, both had a passion for music, and, perhaps most important, both felt they had an overriding mission 'to bring the greatest music to the greatest numbers'. In Rosa's case this was by her writing and lecturing and also promoting the performance of music not previously heard in England. In Mary Wakefield's it was primarily by encouraging singing, particularly choral singing, at the competitive festival that she founded.

A further trait they had in common was one of forming close relationships with other women. Sophie Fuller wrote about its significance in her article 'Devoted Attention: Looking for Lesbian Musicians in Fin-de-Siècle Britain.'[12] In it she drew on Rosa's account of Mary Wakefield's life[13], citing three of her friendships[14]. The first of these is with the songwriter Maude Valérie White (1855-1937), whom Mary met when they were both students at the Royal Academy, and quoting Rosa, 'The intimacy between the two girls ripened apace, and soon we find Miss White a constant visitor at Sedgwick [Mary's parental home].' The second, much later in life, was the writer of fiction and poetry Valentine Munro Ferguson, who shared her Lake District home at Nutwood from 1895. Ferguson suffered from poor health and died in 1897. Mary's sorrow was such that even ten years later she could hardly speak of her. In 1898, she went on a tour of Italy with her friend and neighbour Lady Bective. When she was still feeling the loss of Ferguson, she met Stella Hamilton, with whom she also toured Italy and who came to live at Nutwood in 1903. Whilst it is clear Mary Wakefield had many women friends, the degree of intimacy of the relationships is not clear.

In addition, both had a wide circle of friends and acquaintances in the literary and Arts world. Mary Wakefield was a close friend of Ruskin. In 1894, she edited his collective writings on music[15]. Her friends also included Grieg, Parry and Stanford. By 1904, Rosa was writing articles on the Westmorland Festival, thereby helping to publicise it. Mary Wakefield's letters from 1907 also show that Rosa had already sent Mary part songs by Sibelius that she had translated, encouraging their performance at the Westmorland Festival. This was the year before Sibelius first met Mary in London in 1908. Sibelius says of her: 'She was close on sixty when we became acquainted, and had already retired from the active management of her music festivals, but still exercised a great influence. A very unusual woman, lively and interesting; an acquaintance certainly worth making[16].' Although language was a problem, according to Rosa they met several times, 'and although neither could speak more than a few words of any language that the other understood, they succeeded in understanding something of their mutual opinions and convictions about art[16].'

30. Mary Wakefield in 1904

After Mary Wakefield's early death in 1910, Rosa was invited by her family to write a memoir[13]. She did most of the writing at Eversley, Milnthorpe, the home of Mrs Agnes Argles, Mary's youngest sister. Agnes Argles was closely associated with the festival, acting as both secretary and treasurer. For the 1912 Westmorland Festival, the organising committee decided to rename it the Mary Wakefield Festival in recognition of its founder, and Agnes Argles was elected as president to succeed

Mary. The programme that year included Sibelius's *The Captive Queen*, a ballad for mixed chorus and orchestra, Mozart's Requiem, Bach's Cantata *God's time is the best*, Debussy's *The Blessed Damozel*, and Parry's cantata *Blest Pair of Sirens*. For the Sibelius work, Rosa had translated the Finnish poem by P. Cajander, and she also wrote the programme notes. Another work, *Out of Silence*, was composed by George Rathbone (1874-?) and Gordon Bottomley (1874-1948) especially for the occasion to emphasise Mary Wakefield's contribution to music. Rathbone was an organist and composer of songs and anthems, and Bottomley a poet. The festival continues to this day[17].

Back to February 1909, when Sibelius made his third visit to England, his wife, Aino, asked Rosa to find him some quiet lodgings so that he could work during his stay. She found him accommodation in Kensington kept by three elderly ladies. However, it was initially not quiet enough for him as one of the ladies, knowing that he was a composer, made furtive attempts at playing the 'Moonlight' sonata on her boudoir piano in the room below to express her sympathy with his art. When Sibelius mentioned the problem to Rosa, she persuaded the ladies that Sibelius needed silence, and from then on all was satisfactory. Sibelius actually completed his string quartet *Voces intimae* in March 1909, whilst staying in Kensington; a work he had begun in December 1908. On 13 February 1909, he conducted a performance of *En Saga* and *Finlandia* in the Queen's Hall at an afternoon concert, works that were much more readily appreciated than his Third Symphony of the previous year. The following day, he had lunch with Rosa. Sibelius also spent time at the Newmarchs in Campden Hill Square. He clearly enjoyed his visit to London, commenting that to judge from the audience reaction, and that of the critics, his works had been well received. During his stay, he met Debussy and Vincent d'Indy, who were in London at the time. He was invited to a great number of dinners, which he much enjoyed in spite of not touching alcohol or cigars. He did suffer a cold and became anxious about his throat, which was understandable after the prognosis from the German doctors after the tumour removal. However when Rosa's son, John, examined him, he felt that it did not warrant calling in a specialist.

Sibelius described the reception in his honour on 16 February 1909, at which Rosa was frantically introducing him to the influential members of the aristocracy: 'I was invited to dinner with Lady Wakefield, Lady Burton (formerly Princess of Anhalt) together with Rosa Newmarch, all in full gala dress studded with jewellery. Rosa Newmarch, who is an aristocrat of the purest water, was similarly clad and bore a large diamond on her breast[18].' Rosa also tried to get him to meet Sir Edgar Speyer (1862-1932), the wealthy German-born music lover, who gave very considerable financial support to the Promenade Concerts, in order to sponsor performances of his works, but the strategy came to nothing.

According to Tawaststjerna, before leaving London, Rosa asked Sibelius to sign one of the 'melancholy intimate photographs' that had been taken of him. She wrote eloquently of her feelings towards him: 'I do not want a dedication, or any inscriptions about gratitude or friendship. There is no need for such words between us. My day-to-day life will be the poorer without you, and I indulge the hope that I will see you again in the not too distant future. I feel for you great tendresse, a feeling that is neither shallow nor wanting in propriety. In all situations in life you can count on me – whether you write great and beautiful works (which you will) or whether you do not; whether you are as noble and sagacious as you are now, or have moments of weakness – all this will have no effect on our friendship and I believe you know that[19].'

After Sibelius's visit to London, he left for Paris. Whilst in Paris, he sent Rosa flowers and one pound. The latter was to pay for two latchkeys that he lost, but later found in his pocket. She mentions that he was a 'great loser of small things'; it is also clear from this chapter and subsequent events that she felt that he needed 'managing' when he was away from home without Aino, and that she was the person to do it.

After his return home in 1909, he and his wife pressed Rosa to visit them in Finland. This she did in 1910, combining it with a third visit to Russia.

Notes

1. Granville Bantock, 'Forward' in *Jean Sibelius; A Short Story of a Long Friendship* by Rosa Newmarch (London: Goodwin and Tabb, 1944), p.5.

2. Erik Tawaststjerna, *Sibelius 1904-1914* (London: Faber and Faber, 1986), vol.2, pp.42.

3. Robert Layton, *Sibelius* (London: Dent, 1978), p.39.

4. Rosa Newmarch, *Jean Sibelius: A Short Story of a Long Friendship* (London: Goodwin and Tabb, 1944), pp.8-9.

5. Quoted from Elsie Newmarch's revised version of Rosa Newmarch's biography.

6. Eric Tawaststjerna, *Sibelius, 1914-1957* trans. Robert Layton (London: Faber and Faber, 2008), vol. 3, p.59 and p.186.

7. Tawaststjerna, *Sibelius*, vol. 2, p.221.

8. Karl Ekman, *Jean Sibelius: His Life and Personality* (New York: Tudor Pub. Co., 1938), p.190.

9. Basil Tschaikov, 'The Music Goes Round and Around', http://www.musicweb-international.com/Tschaikov/flyer.htm

10. Tawaststjerna, *Sibelius*, vol.3, p.234.

11. Arthur Jacobs, *Henry J. Wood: Maker of the Proms* (London: Methuen, 1994), p.101.

12. Sophie Fuller, 'Devoted Attention: Looking for Lesbian Musicians in Fin-de-Siècle Britain' in Sophie Fuller and Lloyd Whitesell (eds), *Queer Episodes in Music and Modern Identity* (Urbana: University of Illinois Press, 2002), pp.89-90.

13. Rosa Newmarch, *Mary Wakefield: A Memoir* (Kendal: Atkinson and Pollitt, 1912).

14. Ibid. pp. 22-24 and pp.110-115.

15. Mary Wakefield, *Ruskin on Music* (London: George Allen, 1894).

16. Ekman, *Jean Sibelius*, p.193.

17. The Westmorland Festival Website: http://www.mwwf.co.uk.

18. Tawaststjerna, *Sibelius*, vol. 2, p.105.

19. Tawaststjerna, *Sibelius*, vol.3, p.202.

CHAPTER 14: POETRY

In addition to the huge task of translating Tchaikovsky's Life and Letters, editing the series on *Living Masters of Music* described earlier, and giving several lectures on Russian Music, Rosa Newmarch also published three books of poetry. The first and second of these were collections of her own poems together with some translations from Russian, entitled, respectively *Horæ Amoris*[1] and *Songs to a Singer and Other Verses*[2]. The third was an introductory survey and history of Russian poetry, entitled *Poetry and Progress in Russia*[3].

Rosa Newmarch enjoyed reading poetry from childhood and may have even tried her hand at writing poems in her teens. The collections, *Horæ Amoris* and *Songs to a Singer and Other Verses*, were composed when she was in her twenties and thirties and up until she visited Russia. Her love of music, the visit to Russia, and her meeting and friendship with Bella Simpson are clearly sources of inspiration.

Horæ Amoris

The poems in *Horæ Amoris* (Hours of Love) are grouped in three sections: *In Modo Tristi, Horæ Amoris: A Sonnet Sequence,* and *Verses and Translations*. The overall contents are summarised in an unsigned review in the *Pilot* (16 May 1903, p.476).

Mrs Newmarch's sonnet sequence, which forms the major part of her little book of poems, is an excellent specimen of academic composition. To credit it with the pulse of passionate feeling that beats in the "Love Sonnets of Proteus" [This is a reference to poems by Wilfrid Scawen Blunt, 1840-1922], to quote but one instance would be to view its aim and achievement from a mistaken point of view. The emotions with which it deals are finely and truthfully conceived, but the work as a whole is on a different plane from those in which poets have unlocked the secret treasure of their hearts. The passions of which Mrs Newmarch sings are seen as it were from afar; they are mellowed and softened by an intervening atmosphere of contemplation. They move us by no passionate challenge for sympathy – rather by an appeal to our sense of ordered beauty of design and of the serene perfection of chiselled workmanship.

Two points give individuality to Mrs Newmarch's poems, her love of music and her knowledge of Russian literature; one of the sonnets gives us a masterly interpretation of the feelings engendered by hearing Tschaikowsky's [sic] *Symphonie Pathétique* and another is apparently suggested by a famous passage in *Parsifal*, while *Tatiana* is founded upon an incident in Pushkin, and *Folklore* embodies a beautiful old Slavonic tale. At the end of the volume are several translations from modern Russian poets, all admirable pieces of craftsmanship, of which it is not too high praise to say that they have the ease and freshness of originals.

Most of the poems in the first two sections, *In Modo Tristi* and *Horæ Amoris: a Sonnet Sequence,* are love poems and speak of sadness and longing addressed to a person. Two examples will illustrate this; the first is a sonnet from the first group:

My heart is an untrodden thicket set
With harsh repellent growths of solitude,
Where serried ranks of thorn and brambles rude
And twining ivy weave a close-strung net.
Within its gloom no lovers ever met;
No song-birds build; and in the Spring no brood
Of laughing children on its banks intrude,
Seeking young primrose or March violet.

Yet art thou quite barren, O my heart!
Though none but I may find those hidden dells
The friendly briars close so thick above;
My hands alone the sharp-toothed branches part,
And mine eyes watch those folded flower-bells,
The imperfect blossoms of a hidden love.

The second is the last from the second group and is entitled *Horæ Amoris:*

The day and night make up Love's book of Hours.
Dawn comes, and with the shivering breeze that sighs,
And with the weeping dews and paling skies,
Returns the grief which bore this love of ours.

Noon-tide; the sun in all his solstice powers
Has kissed the parched and amorous earth that lies

125

In rapture throbbing, and with lifted eyes
My passion wakes and blooms like Clytie's flowers.

Sunset; and while I watch the rosy stain
Fade into starless dusk, a cold unrest
Warns me no sunrise brings her back again.
Midnight: long since I saw the tired moon climb
Down by a fleecy pathway to the West.
Good-night to Love for now, and for all time.

In the mid-1890s, Rosa had contacted William Morfill, Professor of Slavonic Studies at Oxford University, at the stage when she started to learn Russian. She contacted him regularly when she needed advice on questions of Russian language and particularly to check her translations. After she returned from her first visit to Russia, they corresponded regularly. When her first set of poems was about to be published, she sent him an advanced copy of the book. Three of the translations, *The Gaffer, The Convicts Song,* and *The Hayfield,* she dedicated to him. He responded in a letter dated 13 December 1902 from his home in Oxford, complimenting her on her sonnet writing but also pointing out that readers would try to 'break into the enclosure of your charmed silence' to try to establish a hidden meaning, apparently alluding to Rosa's relationship with Bella Simpson. The question of the allusion that Morfill refers to, Rosa mentioned in a letter sent three days later to Sir Edward Elgar: 'A friend of mine says my sonnets are as cryptic as your Variations.' This is discussed in more detail by Philip Bullock[4].

Following its publication, *Horæ Amoris* attracted interest from figures in the arts world. Elgar wrote asking permission to set three of her poems for unaccompanied choirs. These were *Death on the Hills, Serenade* and *A Modern Greek Song.* The rather gruesome poem, *Death on the Hills* was Rosa's translation of a Russian poem by Maikov. On receiving permission from Rosa, Elgar wrote, 'Very many thanks for your kind letter and permission to use etc. I will see that the publishers send you one guinea for each of these[5].'

Several lyrics were also set to music by Norman O'Neill (1875-1934), an Irish composer who specialised in works for the theatre and a friend who often visited Rosa at her house in Campden Hill to discuss music. He also set *Death on the Hills* to music, and it was sung by Miss Grainger Kerr at a promenade concert in September 1904[6].

Rosa also received letters from the English critic and poet Theodore Watts-Dunton (1832-1914), noted as the friend and minder of Algernon Charles

Swinburne (1837-1909), whom he rescued from alcoholism. Watts-Dunton also sabotaged the completion of Swinburne's sadomasochistic novel *Lesbia Brandon*. He was a friend of Tennyson and Rossetti and was particularly interested in Romany folklore following in the tradition of George Borrow (1803-1881) and editing Borrow's novels *Lavengro* and *Romany Rye*. In his rather patronising manner, he wrote to Rosa complimenting her on her verse, pointing out that sonnet writing is a rather special art combining compression and sonority, but also 'going to town' with some minor niggles. He described her poem 'Good Friday Magic' as exceedingly good, but commented that 'to some poets it is very distasteful to see the melodious elision in 'the eternal' by cutting off *e* from *the*.' [The line in question is 'Enacts th' eternal Calvary in his heart.']. After commenting incorrectly that Rosa was of Russian extraction, he believed there was a mistake in her translation of the poem 'The Hayfield' by the Russian poet Apollon Nikolayevich Maikov (1821-1897). 'I observe that in one of your translations you use the word "fetlocks" for "pasterns" – a not uncommon mistake to be sure; but very irritating to horsey folk. The fetlock is the tuft of long hair that hangs from the pastern joint or, as some say, from the fetlock joint.'

The verse in question is:

The patient horses, thin and spent,
Half-smothered in their fragrant load,
With drooping ears and fetlock bent
Sleep as they stand beside the road.

In the few days between Watts-Dunton's letter of the 1 January and his second on the 6 January, Rosa Newmarch must have replied making a robust defence of the use of the word 'fetlock', pointing out that Watts-Dunton's own fictitious character Rhona Boswell had used the 'fetlock' apparently incorrectly. In his second letter he made a climb down. 'I am afraid you are right about Rhona Boswell and her misuse of the word "fetlock" for "pastern". There are many of her words and locutions that I would justify if I could. The only female philologist among the Romanies, that I ever knew, was Senfi Lovell; but as you suggest, fetlock has now got the *consensus eruditorum*: it is countenanced in the stable-yard! So I suppose it must pass.'

They continued to correspond and in 1906, Watts Dunton wrote to her: 'I am delighted with your book [probably *The Life and Letters of Tchaikovsky*] and when we next meet we must have a good deal of talk about it.' And then, having evidently mislaid her address, adds: 'On looking in *Who's who* for your address I was astonished at not finding your name there, where so many names are exploited of poets not nearly so worthy of recognition as you. Are you still living at 52 Campden Hill Square?' Rosa did visit him, but it was not until 7 January 1912, by which time they had left Campden Hill Square.

Songs to a Singer and Other Verses

Rosa Newmarch's second book of poems, *Songs to a Singer and Other Verses,* was published in 1906. It contains thirty-one poems in the first section entitled *Songs to a Singer,* five in the second section entitled *Verses* and thirteen in the third section entitled *Fragments from "King Waldemar".* Those in the first section mainly have a song or music related theme, the majority of those in the second section are addressed to a person, and the third section is subtitled 'A Libretto for a Dramatic Symphony based on the *Gurresange* of A.P. Jacobsen (*sic,* presumably Jens Peter Jacobsen, 1847-1885)'.

As with her first book of poems, she sent a copy to Professor Morfill, which he acknowledged in a letter dated 5 June 1906. After thanking her, he says he is very pleased with them and that they show no falling off in the richness and directness of expression. He then lists his favourites and makes the comparison between Rosa and the lesbian Greek poetess, Sappho (*c.*630BC to 570BC). 'You have great lyric power. Sappho would not have been ashamed of some of these pieces –they have the thorough Greek passion.'

In a 1906 music magazine, under the heading 'Books of the Week' there is an unsigned review of *Songs to a Singer, and other Poems,* an abridged version of which is reproduced below.

> This volume of poems is a good deal above the average. "The Song of Dawn" from A.P. Jacobsen, is quite beautiful, and there are very fine phrases in the "Prelude to Today". Indeed, if Miss (*sic*) Newmarch's range was rather wider, she would rank high as a poet, for she writes with fine ease of rhythm and much distinction of phraseology [...] I would gladly have quoted if space had permitted, "The Rose of Song", "New Year's Eve," "The Rest are Dreams," and "In Flood Time." "The Rest are Dreams" is a tender love poem which contains these memorable lines:
>
> > If once in all the years my friend,
> > That I shall only live for you
> > And watch you, careless-handed, spend
> > Your dearest self on aims untrue,
> > And give to others without stint

The faith no zeal of mine may gain.

Poems, to be worth anything, should be worth reading many times. They are not like the ordinary novel, which one reads to see how the plot and characters are worked out, and never touches again unless it be for a prose-poem in a description [...] Poetry is more like a religious work. You value the message because it makes you think and examine yourself. The chief difference is, that a message begins to be poetry when it creates a beautiful effect; judged by this standard, Miss Newmarch has created beauty. [The part of the book for which the writer cared least is the 'Fragments from King Waldemar.]'

A review that considers the confessional aspect of Rosa Newmarch's poems, and raises some issues that Professor Morfill made in this letter to Rosa at the time of publication of her first book, is that entitled 'A New Poetess' by James Douglas in *The Throne* in 1906. A slightly shortened version is given below.

Poetry is the best confessional. It is true that all art is a confessional. The artist can reveal many spiritual secrets in marble and music, in prose and paint. But the finer adventures of the spirit can be disclosed only in the gloaming of rhyme. When the soul brims over into poetry we taste the very spring of life [...]

There is a delicate pleasure in playing eavesdropper to the eavesdropper, in overhearing what the poet has overheard. I have tasted the pleasure while reading 'Songs to a Singer', by Rosa Newmarch. It is curious that women use poetry as a confessional more fearlessly than men. Men generalise their experience, fermenting it into philosophy. Women pour out the pure juice of the grape. Their songs are undistilled; they are filled with the excitement of emotion; emotion is seldom remembered in tranquillity. Perhaps that is why women seldom achieve perfect form in poetry. Mrs. Browning and Christina Rossetti and Mrs. Meynell, at their best achieve the utterance of passion at the expense of verbal beauty. It seems that the imagination in women needs the fire of present experience to fuse it, and that unless the golden ore runs then it runs never. A sonnet such as "Renunciation" could hardly have been written save in an ecstasy of hungry tears.

Mrs Newmarch, to the casual reader, reveals naught. To the attentive listener she whispers a spiritual tragedy. Her temper is rare. She is one of those who see life through the veil of music, and music through the veil of life. The evolution of modern music has made it possible to live one's real life in a paradise of sound, and to disregard the other spiritual languages that men have invented as a clearing-house of dreams. I have no doubt that Mrs Newmarch lives on the other side of life. Her poems prove it. "Rose of Roses" for instance, sings an aspect of love that eludes and evades the proseman: –

Rose of roses! All life's garden
Knows the secret of thy presence,
Like a sweet, soul-healing essence
Breathing love and shedding pardon;
Sweet when noontide's sun has flushed thee,
Sweeter still when rains have crushed thee.

Rose of life, too bright, too tender
For the garden of my spirit,
Desert land that does not merit
Perfume rare and crimson splendour!
Dear in noontide's golden gladness
Dearest in the dusk of sadness.

Few men will fathom that simple song; but many women will say, with a sigh, "How true!" Men are disappointed in love, but women are disappointed with love. Yet out of their very chagrin they drain a diviner joy and their pain becomes a secret rapture. "Mystical Song" compares the soul of the lover to a cloud drawn along a river "out to some distant unconjectured sea."

Too well content with dreams to know
Or reckon with the actual joys of love.

The terrible humility of love, the dreadful heroism of love, the wistfulness of love, the wastefulness of love – all these sad and subtle things ache and throb in these poems. Now and then a mood of ironic bitterness passes over the mood of serene fortitude: –

Forgive me – we are strangers now –
But if sometimes the ghost of old
And murdered love should touch your brow
With lips that are not yet quite cold,
Bid it depart, lest it should bring
A flush of shame, a thrill of fear,

Some warmth from fires still smoldering
Or to your eyes one useless tear.

"Realist to Idealist" is the exceedingly bitter cry of the present caught in the net of the past, the possible strangled by the impossible. "Only dreams and memories last." Men forget their dreams more completely than women. A woman cherishes her dead hope and her buried phantasy for ever. She is more jealous of what a man once was than any fleshly rival. A man may vanquish other rivals: he can never vanquish his former self. What he is can never escape from what he was. In love men are infinitely more fickle than women. Only a woman can vow to "smile when you have wounded her." That is "The Song Unsung". Mrs Newmarch knows that the love of love is the love that hides itself from the loved one; the love that loves unknown to the lover. This is the song that holds a mystery:

"The night is still," it ran, "and thought is free,
And none may read my rapture or my pain,
Since love of soul for soul goes unconfessed,
And cloaks its bitter as it hides its sweet,
Is dear as darkness and as night discreet."

Another strangely lovely poem is "Saint Elizabeth". With its burden, "I cannot live on dreams alone." It is Tannhauser speaking with the voice of Galahad, Tristan with the voice of Dante. It is the cry of love starved by its own chastity, blanched by its own purity, frozen by its own attitude. If it were lower it would be more blest; if it were baser it would be happier: —

But for my daily sin of love
And wasting hungers of the soul,
You have the virtue to reprove,
But not the faith to make me whole.

And for the failing dreams of years,
And for these human hopes that fall
Like frost-slain buds, and for my tears,
You have not any use at all.

But on my life that burns and dies-
A lamp that wanes with each lone night-

You look with pure, unpitying eyes:
God knows, my saint, if you are right!

This is a new voice in poetry, sharply free from facile conventions of phrase, and painfully vibrant with deep spiritual experience. It is the divine stammering of a soul in the confessional of verse.

The third section of *Songs To a Singer and Other Verses*, entitled *Fragments from "King Waldemar"*, is somewhat different from the first and second, in that it is intended as a libretto for a dramatic symphony based on the *Gurresange* of J.P Jacobsen. It consists of thirteen poems. The *Gurresange*, written by Jacobsen in Danish in 1868-9, appeared posthumously in 1886. In 1897, it was translated into German as *Gurrelieder* by the Viennese translator and critic, Robert Franz Arnold (1872-1938). Although Rosa had mastered many languages, she presumably used Arnold's German translation as her source. Prior to her composing the verse *Fragments from "King Waldemar"*, she was presumably unaware that in 1900, Arnold Schoenberg, attracted to Arnold's translation, had begun setting nine of the poems as a piano-accompanied song cycle, which he completed in 1901. However, by that time he had decided to expand it into a massive cantata for a very large orchestra. It was another decade before this was completed and it received its première in 1913, one of Schoenberg's few works to be very well received at its first performance. There is no evidence that Rosa ever met Schoenberg or was particularly sympathetic to the music of the Second Viennese School. None of her six volumes of the Promenade Concert programme notes published as *The Concert-Goer's Library* includes any work by Schoenberg, Berg or Webern, although when Schoenberg's *Five pieces for Orchestra* was first performed at a Promenade Concert in September 1912, and greeted with hisses, she was the Promenade Concert programme writer. However, the six volumes are a selection of the programme notes that she wrote. Schoenberg's *Gurrelieder* was first performed at a Promenade Concert in November 1928, by which time Rosa was no longer programme writer. Rosa's settings of Jacobsen's poems have not been set to music.

Rosa Newmarch also received complimentary comments from Henri Cazalis (1840-1909) in an undated letter from Aix les Bains. Henri Cazalis was both a French Symbolist poet and a physician. He wrote under the pseudonyms of Jean Caselli and Jean Lahor. Three of his poems were set to music by Henri Duparc (1848-1933). The letter is in response to a letter Rosa sent to him that also included a copy of her poems. He comments that her poetry is delightful in what it expresses and he loves the similarities to what he too expresses and loves most willingly. He is also touched by her support, since in France he is generally out of favour, but is received much better abroad[7]. He is also very pleased to see a translation of one of his poems in her *Songs to a Singer and Other Verses*, the poem *Some Night to Come*, so much so that he asks whether she would translate other poems into English, particularly his '*Bréviaire*' (breviary).

Unpublished Verse

There are, in addition to the two published books of poems, thirty other poems; most are not dated, but of those dated one is from 1903, one from 1907, five from 1916, and two from 1917. The first poem, *Dedication,* suggests the collection is dedicated to a person.

Beloved, take the book
I made for you alone.
When in your quiet hours
And tenderer moods you look
Its pages through, condone
Its failings with mine own;
For be it good or bad,
Its records sweet or sad,
Its life proceeds from ours.

Without my skill to write,
These leaves had still been white
And blank as mists at sea.
Without your faith in me,
Without your soul, and my
Great love of all you are,
The book had never been;
Dark as a fallen star
It had been doomed to lie
Unguessed-at and unseen;
Mute as a child still-born,
Who hears no mother-cries;
Whose unwakened eyes
Shall never see the rise
And birthlight of the morn.

Dear, when you read it, think
Not of the poetry,
Writ large in printers' ink
For all the world to see;
But of the hidden word
That you alone have heard.
Seek well the lines among
For lovely things unsaid
And secrets left unsung;
The kiss you gave, the tears I shed-
O friend most dear, most true,
These things are for us two,
And full of mystery!

Two more of the poems within this set also appear to be addressed to the dedicatee and express pain and longing; the first written in Birmingham in October 1916 and the second in Bangor a month later:

Acquiescence

A moment of delight,
An hour of rest with you-
Then back into the fight
Where I have work to do.

A word, a smile, a sigh,
A secret stab of pain
Endured without a cry-
Earth calls me back again.

But every night a dream,
And every morn a prayer,
That when the Twelve Gates gleam
I may behold you there,

To take me by the hand
And lead me safely in,
Or mourn, yet understand,

My unforgiven sin.

So late you came, sweet friend,
Lofe's dusk and curfew bell
Leave me no time to bend
My thoughts to serve you well;

No time to read your heart
In peace inviolate,
Before we drift apart
On racing tides of fate.

Swift vision in the strife,
Dear robe touched in the press-
Beloved, this is life,
And I must acquiesce.

Song of a Tideless Sea

O'er a still sea, a chill sea,
Asleep in a straightened space,
Hover white-winged birds like the mourners
Who salute a dead, grey face.

But a mild gale, a wild gale,
Should it force those narrow straits,
Might roll up tides of new life and warmth
To that pulseless sea that waits.

O hurt soul, my inert soul,
Thou forsaken land-locked sea,
Give thanks for love's tides and winds returned
To flood and freshen thee!

Contemporary View of Horæ Amoris

Although at the time when Rosa Newmarch's collection of poems were first
published they received favourable comment, in the period since she has not
become widely known as a poet. However, there are now signs of renewed interest

in her poetry. 'Women's Studies' has become an academic subject at universities and sexual identities are now openly discussed. Women writers in relation to the sonnet tradition have been discussed in books and articles by Florence Boos (2004)[8], John Holmes (2005)[9] and Natasha Distiller (2008)[10]. Natasha Distiller's book devotes a whole chapter to Rosa Newmarch's poetry, entitled *Queering the Petrarchan Subject: The Poetry of Rosa Newmarch*.

The sonnet was introduced into England by Thomas Wyatt in the early sixteenth century. It was very much in vogue in Elizabethan times, Shakespeare being perhaps the most famous sonneteer of the period, but it went out of fashion with the Restoration. There was a revival in Victorian England with poets like Elizabeth Barrett Browning and Dante Gabriel Rossetti. The Petrarchan sonnet (after the Italian poet Petrarch, 1304-1374) was typically a love poem written by a man expressing longing and desire. Natasha Distiller's book focuses on Petrarchan sonnets by women writers. She describes Newmarch's poems as 'a perfect example of ambiguity of desire in action'. Unlike earlier reviews of Rosa Newmarch's poems, Natasha Distiller analyses a number of them from the *Horæ Amoris* collection in great detail and attempts a much more explicit interpretation of the poems. A brief resumé of three of the sonnets follows. Distiller points out that the poet and the speaker within the poem are not necessarily the same person, and the gender of the speaker may change. The first sonnet is entitled 'Love Among the Ruins' and the first eight lines are given below.

> No radiant cupid is the love of mine,
> To sport with when the summer sky is blue,
> In sheltered bowers of rose and eglantine,
> It is the child of bitterness and rue,
> Born in the wreckage of a fallen shrine
> At sundown, while the night wept tears of dew;
> Upon its birth one star of bale did shine,
> And fed by pity and despair it grew.

Distiller's interpretation is that the 'wreckage of a fallen shrine' is on one level the failed marriage of the poet's beloved, and that the sequence charts how the relationship between the devastated and wronged wife and the poet develops into the poet's desire for the wife. The sonnet questions why this love is so impossible and why it can never deliver happiness.

In sonnet XXI, entitled 'Tatiana', the poet tells of a Russian folktale which prefigures the wife's choice of her husband over her friend. The last two lines are:

And though his pleadings tore her soul in twain,
She chose not love, but duty for her doom.

In sonnet XXXIII, entitled 'The Problem', Distiller interprets this as the poet's reflection once the wife has returned to the husband.

When all is done, what have you been to me?
A vision of uncomforted despair;
A weary child to humour and to bear
Across life's mire; a daily mystery
Of smiles and tears to which I held no key;
A thorn-set rose; a bitter fount; a care
I'd not have changed for all the world holds fair;
And, at last, a gnawing memory.

And through the years, what have I been to you?
A shield upheld a moment in the strife;
A hand upheld a moment in the strife;
A hand to clutch at when you feared to fall;
A song that soothed and passed? Would God I knew
If in the drama of your ruined life
I had in truth played any part at all.

Whilst there is undoubtedly an autobiographical element to these sonnets, they should perhaps not be too literally equated with Rosa Newmarch's own situation.

Poetry and Progress in Russia

When Rosa visited Stasov at the Imperial Library at St Petersburg in 1897, he was concerned that she should not only study Russian music, but the Arts in general, and particularly literature. Rosa did not need much prompting in that respect and soon after she had returned to England, she was giving lectures that included Russian poetry. These lectures, later published[11], were given at the Anglo-Russian Society, the first of which was in 1901, entitled 'Popular Poets of Russia', and was later published in the Proceedings of the Anglo-Russian Literary Society (1901, pp. 19-48). At the lectures, some of Rosa's translations of verses set to music were sung by Olga Wood (wife of Henry Wood) accompanied by Percy Pitt. A few years later she decided to expand these lectures and publish them as a book entitled *Poetry and Progress in Russia*[3], which she dedicated to Stasov, who died in St Petersburg on 23 October 1906. She also composed a poem to him:

> St Vladimir's day
> To V.V. Stasov.
> Vladimir, "World-possessor": name of kings!
> Could they forsee, who chose it in the past,
> How fitly thou shouldst bear it to the last?
> Experience, wisdom, honours, age that brings
> Tried courage and ripe tolerance; all such things
> As make the kingdom of great hearts thou hast.
> And of this wealth thy generous hand broadcast
> On poorer lives a triple largesse flings,
> Most regal in thy gift of sympathy,
> Thy watchful eyes have often marked the birth
> Of genius the dull world was slow to see,
> Proud in all else, in fellowship, dear friend,
> Content with younger hearts to condescend,
> Thou in their homage dost possess the earth.

In her preface, dated Florence, April 1907, she acknowledges help from Professor Morfill and his permission to include several of his translations of the poems that she quotes. On Professor Morfill's recommendation, and prior to completing the book, Rosa Newmarch also sought advice from Professor Louis Legèr, an expert on Russian literature and author of *Russes et Slaves*[12]. She visited him in Paris, attending some of his lectures, *en route* to a holiday in Italy with Bella Simpson (described in the next chapter). The friendly relationship between Professor Morfill and Rosa's family is evident from his letter dated 14 October 1906. The letter encourages her to see Professor Legèr in Paris and explains how to find him, and enquires whether she needs any other contacts in France. It continues: 'Pray accept my very best thanks and carry them to Mr Newmarch for two hares – one received some time ago and the other recently. I have never till this day been able to find out who sent them – I had carefully preserved the addresses and tried to make out whose the writing was, but there was no name of the sender or card or any means of finding out. I thought they probably came at your direction I did not like to ask.'

When Rosa took up Professor Morfill's suggestion of visiting Professor Legèr *en route* to Italy, besides attending a number of his lectures at the Collège de France, she was invited to inspect his private library and go to his Monday 'at homes', where she met many of the other professors at the collège, including those specialising in Slavonic languages. She completed the book in April 1907, reading the proofs whilst on holiday in Italy.

She described the book as a volume of essays rather than a systematic review of Russian poetry, aimed as an introduction rather than a comprehensive account of Russian poetry. Between the time she gave her lectures on Russian poetry in 1901 and the publication of her book, there was an increased awareness in Britain of the struggles in Russia to obtain a constitutional government which resulted in the establishment of the State Duma of the Russian Empire and the Russian Constitution of 1906. This is turn meant that there was an increased interest in Britain in understanding Russian culture, and although the great nineteenth century Russian novelists were well known, there was little awareness of Russian poetry. Although she described the book as an introduction, it is nevertheless quite substantial, amounting to 270 pages. It was a work that gave her immense pleasure and remained one of her most treasured and satisfying pieces of work. The period she described is often known as the Golden Age of Russian Poetry – roughly the first half of the nineteenth century. In it she included the precursors of Pushkin (1799-1837), namely Joukovsky (1783-1852), Krylov (1769-1844), Baratinsky (1800-44), and Kozlov (1799-1840). Then she categorised the later poets as 'The Romantic Poets' and the 'Popular Poets'. The former category included Pushkin and Lermontov (1814-41) and the latter Koltsov (1809-42), Nekrasov (1821-78), Nikitin (1824-61), Khomaniakov (1804-60) and Nadson (1862-87).

The French critic Charles Chassé, after an interview with Rosa, wrote[13]:

It is she who has accomplished for England the work which has made M. de Vogue[14] famous in France. By her book *Poetry and Progress in Russia* Rosa Newmarch has made the English public acquainted with the great Slavonic poets who prepared the way for the Romantic School. With a rare consciousness and power over rhythm she has re-conceived many of their poems in English verse. But the role of interpreter has not been enough for her; for she has also had her song, and the sorrowful cadence of *Horæ Amoris* has revealed to the public a soul which sees life through the curtain of music, and music through the curtain of life.'

Notes

1.   Rosa Newmarch, *Horæ Amoris* (London: Elkin Mathews, 1903).

2.   Rosa Newmarch, *Songs to a Singer and Other Verses* (London: John Lane, The Bodley

Head, 1906).

3. Rosa Newmarch, *Poetry and Progress in Russia* (London: John Lane, The Bodley Head, 1907).

4. Philip Ross Bullock, *Rosa Newmarch and Russian Music in Late Nineteenth and Early Twentieth-Century England* (Farnham, Surrey: Ashgate, 2009) p.119.

5. The Elgar settings (Op.72 and 73) of Rosa Newmarch's verse were recorded by Vernon Handley in 1998. (Elgar Choral Music Hyperion CDA67019).

6. 'Promenade Concerts', *The Times*, 12 Sept. 1904.

7. 'Vos vers sont délicieux et vous comprendrez leur charme pour Jean Lahor puisqu'ils sont un peu frère de ceux qu'ils aiment et chantent et ce qu'il aime et chant le plus volontiers et la musique d'abord qu'il adore aussi, qu'ils sont très musicaux comme il veut que le soient les siens. J'ai été d'autant plus touché par votre sympathie qu'en France d'ordinaire l'on ne me gate pas; la presse du metier à qui jamais je n'ai beaucoup parlé et qui en retour n'a jamais beaucoup parlé de moi. A l'étranger on me fait meilleur accueil et vous me le prouvez encore.'

8. Florence Boos, 'Dante Gabriel Rossetti's Poetic Daughters: Fin de Siècle Woman Poets and the Sonnet', in David Clifford and Laurence Roussillon (eds), *Outsiders Looking In: The Rossettis Then and Now* (London: Anthem, 2004), pp.253-81.

9. Natasha Distiller, 'Queering the Petrarchan Subject: The Poetry of Rosa Newmarch' in *Desire and Gender in the Sonnet Tradition* (Basingstoke, Hampshire: Palgrave MacMillan, 2008), pp.135-153.

10. John Holmes, 'Female Identity in Transition: Gregory, Webster and Newmarch' in *Dante Gabriel Rossetti and Late Victorian Sonnet Sequence: Sexuality, Belief and the Self* (Aldershot: Ashgate, 2005), pp.99-119.

11. Rosa Newmarch, 'The Popular Poets of Russia', *Proceedings of the Anglo-Russian Literary Society*, 30 (February, March and April 1901) 19-48.

12. Louis Legèr, *Russes et Slaves* (Paris: Libraire Hachette et Cie, 1896).

13. Charles Chassé, 'La Musique anglaise moderne: Une interview avec Mrs Rosa Newmarch', *Bulletin Français de la Société Internationale de Musique*, May 1908, pp.556-562.

14. Eugène-Melchior Vicomte de Vogüé, 'Social Life in Russia', *Harpers New Monthly Magazine,* May 1889, vol. 78.

CHAPTER 15: OFFICIAL PROGRAMME WRITER FOR THE PROMENADE CONCERTS

Until about the middle of the eighteenth century, in England concerts were restricted to the nobility, but with the rise of a middle class came the commercialisation of leisure. Concerts were no longer exclusively private performances for the nobility. By Handel's time, the performances of his oratorios were open to those who could afford the subscription. The public were becoming better educated, and thus the demand for programme notes arose. When public concerts began in Edinburgh in the 1840s, John Thomson (1805-1841), the first Reid Professor of Music at Edinburgh University, not only conducted concerts but also wrote 'analytical notes' on the music, thus starting in a scholarly way a feature that has distinguished British concert programmes since. Thomson was succeeded some years later by Sir Donald Tovey (1875-1940), whose style set the standard for these analytical notes. In London, by the 1850s the main venue for classical music concerts at affordable prices was Crystal Palace. Sir George Grove (1820-1900), the Secretary of Crystal Palace, appointed August Manns (1825-1907) as conductor and he transformed what was a military band into a full symphony orchestra, and in 1856, Groves began writing 'analytical notes' for these concerts. From 1858 to the turn of the century, St James's Hall was the rival venue for popular classical concerts with the Monday and Saturday 'Pops' concerts. From 1868, the Philharmonic Society's base was St James's Hall and they introduced detailed annotated programme notes. J. W. Davison*, the music critic of *The Times* (see Chapter 2), contributed programme notes, as did the composer and professor of music at the Royal Academy, G.A. MacFarren (1813-1887).

Thus by the time of the inauguration of the first Promenade concert at the Queen's Hall in August 1895, programme notes were the expectation of audiences of the day. The first programme notes were written by Edgar F. Jacques, a professor of music. According to Henry Wood, 'The programmes, I remember, were printed in single sheet form. They cost the large sum of two pence but contained excellent analytical notes by Edgar Jacques who continued to write them for some years.'[1] However, by the eighth season, Wood wrote: 'We found Edgar Jacques had become slack over the preparation of his analytical notes. Sometimes he kept the scores of novelties until a few hours before the final rehearsal, which gave me no chance to study them properly. Consequently there were often blank spaces where notes should have appeared[1]. This was a dodge of Newman's[2] to "buck up old man Jacques" [he was 52 at the time] as he put it. It had no effect in moving Jacques to more prompt work, and only made him furious.' According to Wood, Newman began paying Percy Pitt (1870-1932), an organist and conductor, a weekly salary to look after Jacques, and any notice Jacques failed to produce, Pitt had to write[1]. Pitt replaced Jacques after 1903, but then he had to be helped by Alfred Kalisch, and they continued until 1907. Alfred Kalisch (1863-1933) originally trained as a barrister, but took up music journalism in 1894 and became a music critic and librettist. Kalisch was said to be efficient but wordy, and with the tone of the programmes becoming tedious and musical examples proliferating Henry Wood, Robert Newman, the manager, and Sir Edgar Speyer, chairman of the Queen's Hall Concert Board, decided it was time for a lighter touch, and who better to provide it than Rosa Newmarch, with a proven record as a writer and who had actively encouraged the introduction of Russian music to a wide audience[3]?

It appears that an informal approach was made to Rosa in 1906. At the time, she was involved in lecturing and literary work, including preparation for the book of essays *Poetry and Progress in Russia*. She wanted to postpone the decision of what would be a major commitment and needed a break from her many commitments, so she decided on a trip abroad for a few months. There seemed to be a window of opportunity for this; her son was now at the clinical stages of his medical training in the hospital, and her daughter, Elsie, had left school and was about to continue her studies at the Sorbonne. She persuaded her husband to make his home with his sisters during her absence, and then the house at Campden Hill Square could be let for the duration of her stay abroad. Bella Simpson would be her travelling companion. She had received an introduction to Louis Legèr at the Collège de France in Paris from Professor Morfill and so would combine a holiday with some further study and writing. Thus, in the autumn of 1906, they set off for Paris and a holiday that would keep them away until the following July. They stayed in an old-fashioned hotel, Hôtel de l'Univers et du Portugal, 10 rue X des Petits Champs, which Rosa described:

Dear old Madame Troulet who keeps the hotel is a French woman of the *ancient regime* – very Catholic and Royalist [...] [The family] are some of the very kindest and best sort of people I have ever come across; so that one says to oneself – 'never mind the old house with the draughty doors and windows Mme Troulet and her daughter are so nice!' The food is really excellent. We have our early breakfast and dinner *en pension* and provide our own lunch and tea. This is quite an understood thing, so there is no concealment about bringing in cold meat, or eggs, milk and bread, or even one's one bottle of wine for midday. As to the house, it is like some old Strand Hôtel. Just before we came Madame put in electric light, but there is neither heating apparatus, nor bathrooms. The upper floors are let to artists and literary people who only now and then come to the downstairs dinner.

Apart from sightseeing, Rosa attended Professor Legèr's lectures on Bohemian Literature and met his colleagues. On what appears to be the same trip, she attended Lamoureux and the Colonne Orchestral Concerts and was frequently at the Schola Cantorum, where she met Vincent D'Indy. He had recently completed a book on his teacher, César Franck, published in 1906. It was later translated into English by Rosa and published in 1910[4]. In a letter to her sister Tiny about this time, she also indicated that she was working on her book and also translations of Sibelius's vocal works. She also saw that Elsie, now in Paris, was settling down well, lodging with their friends, the Errards. Whilst in Paris, she received news of Stasov's death on 23 October 1906.

On 16 January 1907, they moved on to Italy, passing through the St Gotthard tunnel. Rosa remarked on the beauty of the scenery 'Passing through the marvellous blue mists one reads of, but only seen in Turner's pictures, the snow peaks began to gleam out dazzling, and soon we were in a perfect blaze of sunshine.' They arrived in Milan where they stayed a few nights, saw a performance at La Scala of Richard Strauss's *Salome,* and enjoyed the art treasures. Then they moved on to Sestri Levante on the Gulf of Genoa. Here in the peaceful surroundings, Rosa finished the preface to *Poetry and Progress in Russia.* She sent a copy of the preface to Professor Morfill in Oxford and received a reply in which he fully approved it, making only a few minor suggestions. From Sestri Levante they moved on 27 January to Florence, which was to become their base for much of their stay in Italy. Rosa was captivated by Florence and again particularly appreciated the art treasures. And yet there is an enigmatic entry in her notebook that suggests she is not at ease with herself: 'Have been very much interested and impressed here and happier – altho' still perplexed as to the future. Will time show the best and safest way to deal with time's problem of life? I am bitter yet not bitter. That is to say I am a long way from forgetting I do not feel I am meant to go back to former feelings, yet I am not sure if I can keep firm without resentment.' The problem might be tensions in her relationships with her husband and Bella.

Whilst based in Florence during April and May 1907, they also visited San Miniato, Perugia, Assisi, and Sienna. Towards the end of her stay in Florence, for about a week they visited her cousin the Rev. Herbert Jeaffreson, who lived just north of Florence at Fiesole.

John Lane published her book *Poetry and Progress* in Russia on the 5 May and she received a first copy whilst in Florence. Eventually they moved on to Venice in June, where their chief delights were trips by gondola or steamer and the absence of the general bustle and traffic of Florence. This was followed by two nights in Verona, where they met an Irish lady, Miss Elizabeth Johnson, who spent her winters in Italy. They became friends and she joined them on their journey to the Tyrol arriving in Toblach in July. She later became a travelling companion of Rosa on her subsequent trips abroad. In the Tyrol, her son and daughter joined them before Rosa's return to England in July. In a letter Rosa wrote to Elsie in May 1907, she thanked Elsie for offering to go back to the house (Campden Hill Square) first and added, 'I suppose it will be necessary to set up something in the way of new servants. I feel we have had a very nice time and must not mind coming home after all this long holiday.'

Once back home in London, Rosa received a letter dated 5 June from Henry Wood, inviting her to write the programme notes for the concerts at the Queen's Hall. The abridged versions of the letter, given in the book *The Proms: A New History*[3] and in Elsie Newmarch's unpublished biography of her mother, differ slightly in what has been omitted. The letter explains that Henry Wood, Sir Edgar Speyer, and Robert Newman had decided that the programme notes for the Proms required a lighter touch – shorter and without detailed musical analysis, and focused more on musical appreciation. This would be compatible with the audience's requirements. He then suggested that this was something Rosa could do well and makes light of the work it would involve, asking whether she could undertake to supply the notes for the coming season. Omitted from the abridged version[3] is the following: 'Do give the matter your serious consideration, as it would be so nice if you could undertake the work for us, and even if I have not given you enough notice to manage this year's Promenades, which commence on 17 August, perhaps you will let me know whether you can entertain the idea for the 1908 season.' […] 'Please keep all this strictly private, as I do not wish it to get abroad that we are contemplating any change unless you can undertake it.'

In her diary, Rosa described her feelings on accepting the work and the way it developed over the next decade.

I felt a brief hesitation in accepting this new form of work; for I knew it would involve the sacrifice of many of my most cherished literary hopes and plans. I was already in my 50th year and hardly felt with Henry Wood that 'once you get through the first season, it will be child's play'! And it was a relief to me when it was agreed that I should postpone undertaking the work until the season starting 1908. Refreshed in mind and body from a sojourn in Italy I finally decided to take on the job. I never really regretted my decision; and eventually looked back on these analytical notes as one of the most useful and valuable of my musical activities.

It is true that I embarked on this entirely new order of work with some trepidation, for I succeeded a distinguished musician, Percy Pitt, and an equally distinguished critic, Alfred Kalisch. I felt a sense of responsibility not only to a large public, but to my own sex; for I believe I can claim to be the first woman analyst, programmist, annotator, or what you will. Every term for this profession seems equally clumsy. Very soon however, the absorbing interest of the work outweighed its anxieties; although I could never agree with a Victorian neighbour who congratulated me on having found 'such a nice occupation for a lady'. Much as I liked the work, it did not always prove to be of that silken-flowing genteel description which half-a-century ago was still regarded as the prerogative of the 'lady worker'!

After a short time, when Robert Newman – that indefatigable manager – had quite accepted the novel situation of a woman coworker, I was asked to take on the press work, which included the weekly paragraph about forth-coming programmes and new works; but while doing this work, I always stipulated that it should be sent out anonymously – a plan which answered very well; thanks to the co-operation of this idealist manager, I soon learnt what was expected of me, and am sure that for twenty years intercourse was as harmonious as the concerts themselves.

As to Henry Wood, the dedication many years later of the Concert Goers Library volumes to him, proved that our friendship survived a long period of affiliated activity. I always maintained that my close co-operation with him inspired me to put my very best work into the programme notes; and felt what an immense advantage it was to work shoulder to shoulder with a man who had such a profound, almost inexhaustible knowledge of music.

It was hardly possible, however, to expect to supply analytical notes on so large a scale – often considerably over a hundred programmes a year – without enduring a few crumpled rose-leaves; without coming into contact with many varieties of living composers, concert directors, committees and printers; and passing through times of strain, urgency and resultant friction. The ways of the living composer with the programmist, as devious and unexpected as ever were the way of a maid with a man, and may have led me at times to bless the silent and unobtrusive dead.

When first tackling the large repertoire of classical works included in the programmes, my line of thought was 'what the man in the street wants to know when he goes to a concert: a clear definition of classical and modern; the historic sense and power of adjustment to the period; some description of the type of work to be analysed and its frame-work – themes, motives, counter-themes, developments and recapitulation; knowledge of instrumentation and the orchestral groups – strings, brass and percussion. Writing of novelties I made it a principle to avoid criticism of the kind which might in the smallest degree check or cool the enthusiasm of the public who are not yet familiar with it. On the other hand I think the programmist is more justified in pointing out what strikes him, or her, as characteristically beautiful in the work. This may seem one-sided, but in reality it effects the right kind of balance. Most people are capable of some sort of carping criticism for themselves. But to point – with due discrimination – to the things that seem lastingly beautiful in a work can do no harm, and must do good. I think the lack of balanced appreciation has been one of our worst faults as a musical nation. I mention this because, little as I concern myself with the ephemeral criticism which withers during the day or night – according to whether it appears in a morning or evening paper – I have noticed a tendency to fall foul of my programmes because I try to set some details in a poetic rather than a prosaic light.

In a related context, Delius once complained of the fallibility of some critics, to which Rosa put the matter in a nutshell: 'A fine creative work will flourish on paltry criticism as a plant benefits from guano spread on its roots[5].' As part of her philosophy, Rosa pointed out that when writing about novelties, she ' made it a principle to avoid criticism of the kind which might check or cool the enthusiasm of the public.' However, it was only natural that she should warm to some of the novelties more than others. A classic case was when, on 3 September 1912, Henry Wood performed for the first time in England Schoenberg's *Five Orchestral Pieces*. The piece was met with hisses, and Rosa's programme notes may have predisposed the audience to hostility when she wrote: 'Schoenberg's Five Pieces for orchestra – at least as they appear on paper – lead to the conclusion that they are merely experiments in dissonance; protests against all preconceived notions of music and harmony [...]'[6]

During the years up to 1915, in which Sir Edgar Speyer, as the director of the syndicate that took over the financial responsibility of the concerts, nothing was lost in their musical interest and excellence. His policy was to keep the concerts on a high artistic level. He was enthusiastic and enterprising where new composers were concerned, and ready to cooperate even where works did not appeal to him personally. These few extracts from his letters to Rosa show his concern for a high standard, and his appreciation of work done:

> I am sending you a line to tell you how delighted I am with your analytical notes in the programmes. Alike in substance and in style they are admirable, and I am sure they will greatly increase the interest of the public in our musical productions. I greatly appreciate your work which is done with so much ability and so much tact, if I may use such an expression in this connection. I certainly have no objection to your proposed article in *The Musical Times*. In fact I should think, as you do, that the form in which your article is to appear will be a good advertisement for the Queen's Hall Orchestra.
>
> I have not yet risen to the heights of Scriabin, but while there is life there is hope. The performance of Strauss's *Tod und Verklarung* was deeply moving to me; in fact I have never heard it so finely played.

Edgar Speyer certainly took an active personal interest in the building up of the programmes. He was an amateur of cultured and decided tastes, and his wife Leonora (née Leonora von Stosch[7]) was a fine violinist and had performed on the opening night of the Proms in 1900, so that with the high standard of performance and the excellence of the artists engaged, the concerts seemed to reach their zenith during these years. Promenaders first became acquainted with the music of Mahler, Reger, Richard Strauss, and Schoenberg. Other continental schools were not neglected, e.g. Bruneau, Debussy, Vincent d'Indy, and Ravel were introduced to this larger public; many works of Sibelius, some examples of contemporary American music, and compositions by Busoni, Bossi, Sinigaglia, Enesco, Glière, Skryabin, and Stravinsky were all given a hearing.

It was not true that British music languished under the Speyer regime. Amongst many first performances of this period, the names of Bantock, Bax, Frank Bridge, Coleridge-Taylor, Walford Davies, Elgar, Goosens, Roger Quilter, Cyril Scott, William Wallace, and Vaughan Williams spring to mind as men whose works were heard and remained in the repertory. Indeed, looking back to the wide outlook and progressive policy which characterised the period, it was a time of expansion and unostentatious educational value. It was also a period of modernism and, in its comparative freedom from financial anxieties, of productive idealism.

The First World War, and the retirement of Sir Edgar Speyer, unfortunately brought this flourishing period to an end from the board of directors. The concerts were once more in danger of extinction; but in the midst of a social upheaval and at a moment when the expenses of concert giving were going up by leaps and bounds, the firm of Chappell and Co. stepped into the breach. Neither the Symphony nor Promenade Concerts were shorn in any way of their previous musical interest.

Becoming the official programme annotator meant that Rosa was in regular contact with Sir Henry Wood and both they and their families became close friends. In his autobiography, Sir Henry Wood pays tribute to her as a friend and in her official capacity[8]:

> Mrs Newmarch's analytical notes still attract me, for they are not merely a synopsis of the works she treats, but are beautiful specimens of English literature. I owe her something else; she was directly responsible for my interest in Sibelius [...] It is not too much to say that Rosa Newmarch has been a rock upon which I have leaned often enough. She seemed always to understand my troubles, so to speak, at a distance. It has not even been necessary for me to discuss them with her, *for she was always at hand*, with real understanding. In paying her this little tribute, which I do in all sincerity, I can only add that I never witnessed greater devotion in a daughter than in hers – Elsie Newmarch.

Wood's biographer, Arthur Jacobs, observed: 'She also became Wood's valued friend. Although he was generally very formal with most colleagues, she became "Dear Rosa" in his correspondence.'[9] Many years later when Wood separated from his wife Muriel after an unsatisfactory marriage, Mrs Jessie Linton came to live with him. Some friends and colleagues did not approve of what, in those days, was an arrangement not to be publicised. Rosa, knowing and understanding the real problems he had had with Muriel, was one of the first to support him and be openly friendly with Jessie[10].

Whilst Henry Wood was complimentary about Rosa's style of writing, a critical voice claimed, 'her high-pitched literary manner was sometimes maintained to the detriment of factual material', although at the same time acknowledging the positive effects of her enthusiasm in her writings[11].

Providing the notes for the Promenade Concert programmes was a huge task; by 1911, Rosa had written analytical notes for over 700 compositions. Much of her preparatory work on the classical repertoire was done at the British Museum and the London Library, but when analysing works of living composers, she made a point of studying the scores and making contact with the composer, either in person, if possible, or by letter. She had of course met many of the Russian composers, but the breadth of the Promenade Concert programmes meant that she got to know a large number of living composers. One might have thought that this was a full time occupation in itself, but she continued with other writing and other commitments. During the period between her return from Italy in July 1907 and the first promenade concert in August 1908, for which she wrote the notes, she also looked after Sibelius on his second visit to England, on occasions meeting daily at her house. She attended the Sheffield Musical Union's performance of Bantock's *Christ in the Wilderness,* for which she wrote the programme notes. This also included the first performance of Delius's *Sea Drift,* for which she also wrote the notes.

In September 1907 Rosa first met Houston Stewart Chamberlain (1855-1927) at John Lane's house. From then until 1914, a number of discussions took place between Newmarch, Lane, and Chamberlain concerning the possibility of translating Chamberlain's *Das Drama Richard Wagner* and also *Die Grundlagen des neunzehnten Jahrhunderts (The Foundations of the Nineteenth Century).* Rosa advised Lane on the feasibility and potential market for translations. British-born Chamberlain was the son-in-law of Richard Wagner through his second marriage to Wagner's daughter, Eva. He became an important member of the Bayreuth Circle of German nationalist intellectuals and was regarded as their intellectual leader after Wagner's death[12] and was later admired by Hitler as a political thinker[13]. In 1916, he took on German citizenship. Rosa's diary for 1911 indicates that she had booked time in early 1911 to work on the Wagner book. She did start work on this but eventually declined because she wanted Chamberlain to read and approve any translation she made, something he claimed he did not have time for, and also because of what she described as his vexatious criticisms. The book was translated by John Lees and eventually published by John Lane in 1913. The issue is described in detail by Philip Bullock[14].

Rosa attended the first performance of Musorgsky's *Boris Godunov* in Paris on 8 May 1908 with Shaliapin in the title role, and wrote an account of the opera for *The Monthly Musical Record*[15]. She recalled how she met Shaliapin immediately after the performance: 'I remember being led as in a dream through endless and labyrinthine passages behind the scenes of the grand Opera and ushered into Shaliapin's dressing-room. I was still wet-eyed and tremulous after the strain of the last agonising scene of the opera. And there he stood, quite calm and collected, his own undisguised countenance, the beardless and – at the moment – wholly jovial and contented Russian face, beaming at me above the tsarial robes of Boris, whose black beard and crown lay discarded on his dressing-table. It was a shock, but a salutary one; for nothing could have made me realise so forcibly this artist's power of annihilating his personality before stepping on the boards, and resuscitating it in a twinkling of an eye. I felt that I had witnessed the miracle which was a source of wonder to Leonid Andreiev. "How is it possible", he wrote, "that so many personalities, such a plurality of intellects, hearts and emotions can be combined in one man – a peasant hailing from Viatka?"

Whilst in Paris, she was interviewed by the music critic Charles Chassé for an article published in *Bulletin Français de la Société Internationale de Musique*[16]. In the following year, 1909, she again looked after Sibelius during his longer stay in London from February to March, during which he completed his string quartet, *Voces Intimae*. She also translated some of his songs including *Driftwood* Op.17 no.7 and *Autumn Night* Op. 38 no.1.

On 27 March 1909, Vincent D'Indy made his first public appearance in England, conducting at a Queen's Hall Symphony Concert in a programme that included his own *Wallenstein* (three symphonic overtures after Schiller, 1880). For this occasion Rosa wrote for the programme-book, which included a brief account of the composer and his career. By this time, she was also translating from French, D'Indy's biography of César Franck. In the introduction to this translation, she was able to expand on the biographical sketch of D'Indy she had already made for the programme-book. The translation itself was no small undertaking, and the book published by John Lane in 1910 amounted to 286 pages[4].

She also provided the biographies of the Russian composers for the second edition of *Grove's Dictionary of Music and Musicians*. This was published in five volumes between 1904 and 1910 and edited by J.A. Fuller Maitland. These included: Arensky, Balakirev, Borodin, Cui, Dargomyzhsky, Glazunov, Glinka, Ippolitov-Ivanov, Liadov, Lyapunov, Musorgsky, Rimsky Korsakov, Anton Rubinstein, Skryabin, Serov, Taneyev, and Tchaikovsky. Perhaps her fears of having to sacrifice many of her most cherished literary hopes and plans were unfounded.

Notes

1. Henry J. Wood, *My Life in Music* (London: Gollancz, 1938), p.161-2.

2. Robert Newman (1858-1926), manager of the Promenade Concerts from 1895-1926.

3. Jenny Doctor and David Wright, D. *The Proms: a New History* (London:, Thames & Hudson, 2007), p.57.

4. Vincent D'Indy, *César Franck* (Paris: 1906), trans. Rosa Newmarch (London: John Lane, 1910).

5. Myrrha Bantock, *Granville Bantock: a Personal Portrait* (London, Dent, 1972), p.144.

6. David Cox, *The Henry Wood Proms* (London: BBC Publications, 1980), p.62.

7. *Ibid* p.42.

8. Henry J. Wood, *My Life in Music* (London: Gollancz, 1938) p.232.

9. Arthur Jacobs, *Henry J. Wood: Maker of the Proms* (London: Methuen, 1994), p.58.

10. *Ibid* pp.276-7.

11. Nicolas Slominsky, *Baker's Biographical Dictionary of Musicians*, 6th Edn (New York: Schirmer, 1978), p.1230.

12. Alex Ross, *The Rest Is Noise* (London: Fourth Estate, 2008), p.308.

13. Adolph Hitler, *Mein Kampf* (New Dehli: gbd books, 2009) trans. James Murphy, 1939, p.238.

14. Philip Ross Bullock, *Rosa Newmarch and Russian Music in Late Nineteenth and Early Twentieth-Century England* (Farnham, Surrey: Ashgate, 2009), pp.56-8.

15. Rosa Newmarch 'Russian Opera in Paris', *The Monthly Musical Record*, Jul. 1908, pp.147-9.

16. Charles Chassé, 'La Musique anglaise moderne: Une interview avec Mrs Rosa Newmarch', *Bulletin Français de la Société Internationale de Musique* May 1908, pp.556-562.

CHAPTER 16: 1910-1911: VISIT TO RUSSIA AND FINLAND; LEAVING CAMPDEN HILL

By 1910, it was nearly a decade since Rosa had first visited Russia. During that time, she had translated Tchaikovsky's letters, published *Poetry and Progress in Russia,* written several articles on Russian music and composers, and lectured on Russian music. She had also received commissions to translate Russian songs, and she had embarked on translations of the librettos for Musorgsky's *Boris Godunov* and Tchaikovsky's *Queen of Spades.* Now she was anxious to follow up her book on Russian poetry with similar introductions to painting, architecture, and music, and she was always anxious to widen the scope of her own knowledge and interest in that vast country. So, in the spring of 1910, she planned a further visit to Russia, which she spoke of as a 'holiday' although as usual she took work with her. In a letter to her sister, she wrote: 'I have been very busy, for I generally have to cram in so much work before I can take a holiday, that sometimes it hardly seems worth while. Still I am getting to the end of the opera – the English translation of *Boris Godunov* and I think it is now quite settled that I leave for Russia at the end of the month, so as to arrive in Moscow for the Russian Easter if possible.' [Rosa Newmarch's English translation of the libretto for *Boris Godunov* was published by Breitkopf and Härtel in Leipzig, and by Bessel in St Petersburg and Moscow, both in 1910.]

In addition to meeting old friends and hearing new music, she wanted to meet publishers in connection with the translations she was undertaking. Also, after Sibelius's visit to London in 1909, he and his wife, Aino, had pressed Rosa to visit them at their home in Jarvenpää, about twenty miles north of Helsingfors[1]. She had been unable to do so in 1909 but now decided on a combined visit to Russia and Finland. Rosa was by now fifty-two. On this trip, Bella Simpson did not accompany her. Bella was now sixty-four and becoming less mobile; it is possible that she suffered from arthritis so the arduous trip might have been too much for her. Also she wanted to be at home for a nephew's wedding. Rosa was pleased that her friend Elizabeth Johnson had decided to come up from Italy and meet her in Cologne and travel with her to Moscow and St Petersburg. Her letter to her sister continued: 'I keep pretty well, but shall certainly enjoy more fresh air and less sitting at the writing table. Perhaps I will take a riding or walking tour in Finland on the

152

homeward way; the horses there are very strong, since they carried dear old Stasov! His brother is still alive and looking forward to seeing me again.'

Rosa and Elizabeth Johnson left for Russia on 20 April, travelling via Berlin and Warsaw arriving in Moscow in time for the Orthodox Easter Sunday, which in 1910 fell on 1 May (Gregorian Calendar = 17 April Julian Calendar). They stayed for the best part of a week before travelling on to St Petersburg. The visit appears to have been somewhat disappointing compared to Rosa's first visit to Moscow. They joined the crowds outside the Kremlin for the Easter vigil, but after that were both laid up with colds and they also found that during the holiday period a number of things were not functioning, and they were unable to meet the people they had hoped to. They did, however, meet Otto Kling, who happened to be staying at the hotel directly opposite them. Otto Kling was the first manager of Breitkopf and Härtel, the German publishers who opened a London branch in 1892 in Great Marlborough Street. Through her dealings with Breitkopf and Härtel, she and Otto Kling had become great friends. The week's visit is described by Rosa in a letter she sent to the family collectively, from the Hôtel Continental where they were staying.

I will send my news so that it can go on to anyone who is interested in it. First of all it is July weather. I am quite glad to have on all my thin clothes. Then it is the great holiday of the year. Today everything is closed but the Churches, and as I sit looking out on to the great Square, which is called Theatre Square, it is very amusing to watch the groups of holiday-makers passing to and fro [...] We are just opposite the Metropole, I can see Mr Kling's window from mine, and we can almost signal to each other.

I must tell you about last night. It was very interesting, although on the whole I was disappointed with it as a spectacle. At 11p.m. Mr Kling, with 2 Russian gentlemen called for us and we joined in the great string of people making their way into the Kremlin. We were too late to get inside the Square of the Cathedrals, and did not attempt to squeeze into any of them. Indeed I fancy it required some influence to get into the Uspensky as I saw it was roped round. We stood under the Belfry of Ivan Veliky and at midnight it began to ring; first the big bass bell, and then all the church bells in the town chimed in. I believe the Metropolite then comes to the steps of the Uspensky and says "Christus Voskress" (Christ is risen) and everyone begins to say it to his or her neighbour, who answers at once "He is indeed risen". But I must say I heard very little of it around us, nor did I see any exchange of Easter Kisses. I suppose the custom is dying out. There must have been thousands of people in the Kremlin, and at certain gates and corners a great crush. But all so orderly and good-tempered. I saw very few police. A few mounted men at the chief gates to prevent any more people thronging round the Cathedrals. I would not in the least have minded walking the round alone. We saw one of the processions come out of the churches with banners etc, followed by lots of people who had been at the service, carrying lighted candles. There were a few rather feeble fireworks and an artillery salute and then we walked home about 1.a.m [...] Elizabeth and I came back here, and most of the servants being out, brewed ourselves some tea with lemon and ate biscuits. This morning was a great day of tips and congratulations, but two shillings [=10p] judiciously laid out will make many smiling faces here!. The Hôtel has greatly changed and in many respects gone off. The fine Restaurant Bella will remember exists no more. It is like furnished rooms. But the kitchen is *admirable* and the food very decently served in our own room. Like all Russian Hôtels you pay for the rooms separately and fairly stiffly; but then you do as you please, feed in or out, make your own tea, save part of dinner for supper etc, etc. I think I shall stay here till Thursday night so as to hear an opera, Rubinstein's *Demon* or Tchaikovsky's *Mazeppa* before leaving. Besides all the galleries and Kremlin sights are closed till Tuesday.

After explaining that they both caught colds, she finished by saying, 'This holiday [i.e. the Easter holiday] has made this rather a useless visit so far, for I cannot see any of the music people, or hear anything before tomorrow night, if I am well enough.' However, they did manage to see Tchaikovsky's *Mazeppa* and and Glinka's *A Life for the Tsar*.

After about a week in Moscow, they left by train for St Petersburg. Just as they were about to leave their hotel, with the bus waiting at the door to take them to the station, they were offered a two-berth cabin for a Volga trip. Although sorely tempted, they felt they had to keep to their plans, but all night on the train Rosa was regretting they had not taken up the offer. Mr Jurgenson, the publisher, on hearing they were leaving, sent for Rosa in great haste to ask if she would undertake an English translation of Tchaikovsky's opera *Pique-dame* (Queen of Spades).

Otto Kling had also been unwell with flu whilst in Moscow, and they heard the news from Kling's doctor that King Edward had died suddenly. Initially they wondered if it was true or just a rumour, but when they received letters and papers from England, they learned that he had died on 6 May.

Once in St Petersburg, they met Vladimir Stasov's brother Dmitri for lunch and Rosa remarked how like his older brother he now looked. He took them to see his brother's tomb and the monument by the sculptor Ilya Ginsburg in the Alexander Nevsky Cemetery. They also visited the Stasov family home where they met

Ginsburg and many of Rosa's old friends, and also a young composer, Alexander Spendiarov (1871-1928), who studied with Rimsky-Korsakov and had written a memorial cantata to Vladimir Stasov. Rosa went to visit Balakirev, but his housekeeper told her that he was at death's door, so she left flowers and a card. He died a few days later on 29 May. She also met César Cui, who had grown old but was still active, Alexander Glazunov, and the German composer Theodor Albin Findeisen (1881-1936). Whilst in St Petersburg she received part of the proofs of her translation of *Boris Godunov* and learned from Messrs. Bessel that the publishers were in a hurry to publish the German-English edition of *Boris*. By the time she had reached Stockholm she received a letter from the publishers dated 2 June enclosing a cheque for 500 German Marks for the English translation of *Boris Godunov*. Whilst in St Petersburg she wrote to Sibelius about her forthcoming visit to Finland, and received an enthusiastic reply in which he mentions that the weather had been extraordinary and that they should come by late May or early June.

They left St Petersburg on 20 May, having arranged to meet Sibelius at Viborg. Viborg is on the route from St Petersburg to Helsingfors, thirty-eight kilometres south of the present Russian Finnish border, but in 1910 the whole of Finland was part of the Russian Grand Duchy of Finland. From Viborg, Sibelius took them to the Falls of Imatra, about ninety kilometres to the north, later returning to Viborg and catching the train to Helsingfors where they met Sibelius's wife. Much of the visit to Finland is described in Rosa's book '*Jean Sibelius: A Short Story of a Long Friendship*[2] and also in a letters to her daughter Elsie.

From a letter to Elsie, written from The Falls of Imatra about 21 May:

The Falls of Imatra are most beautiful –to be compared with some places in Scotland only much wilder. The Falls are superb and so fascinating that one can sit for hours together watching the terrific flow of water, glorious in the sunlight. The air is keen, but bracing rather than cold. We have a lovely room with a balcony overlooking the Falls where I am now resting. It is curious how one grows so accustomed to the constant roar that makes one drowsy.

Sibelius was delighted to meet us yesterday, and so anxious to do all to make us happy and comfortable. He is looking robust, and seems well and active. Madame Sibelius could not come to meet us as her eldest daughter was not well. Today we drove to another fall lower down the river, where it was very lovely and less terrific. Sibelius and I got into a fisherman's boat and went as close to the rapids as was safe. Elizabeth chose the wiser part and sat on the shore watching us! I am sure there must be endless fishing in the lakes. Later I went out for a while to watch the Sunday peasants, though after Russia they seem very ordinary; good souls, but I am too much of a Slav, as Dmitri Stasov says, not to feel rather disappointed in my first impressions of Finland, coming straight from Russia. This place, though beautiful, has something touristy about it, and I feel it is no more the real Finland than such an hotel at Llandudno would be Wales!

A letter to Elsie from Hôtel Fennia, Helsingfors, Tuesday 24 May 1910:

It seems years since yesterday morning when at breakfast time Sibelius heard that his wife could not conveniently join us at Imatra. I felt sure all along that she was not very keen about it, so I proposed that we should come straight away here and not waste any more money at that expensive hotel. The only decent train however from Viborg to Helsingfors leaves at night, so we profited by the lovely day to drive in two funny little carriages about 3 miles to a place on Lake Saina. It is most beautiful; the Lake they say is nearly 50 miles long and full of charming islands. The woods slope down to the edges, and as the breeze was rather fresh the waves broke on the shore with quite a splash like the sea. The hotel, or rather pension, was so nice. Simple and very cheap. We had for lunch soudak (perch-pike) and a cut from a salmon which had been swimming in the Lake an hour earlier. I would have loved to spend some days there, but our plans had been made, and a wire sent to Mrs Sibelius, so we drove back to the Hôtel at Imatra, packed up our small things and after a cup of tea took train for Viborg at 6 p.m. We had 1½ hours to wait for the (so-called) Petersburg-Helsingfors express. We supped and picked up our trunks, left at Viborg on Friday.

The night was rather tiring, as we did not indulge in the luxury of a sleeping car. Fortunately we secured full length accommodation and slept part of the time. We arrived here at 8. This Hôtel, where they seem to know Sibelius very well is more suited to our tastes and pockets! We have quite a nice room and can go out to meals if we like, and the restaurants here seem numerous and very moderate. It is a very attractive place with pretty gardens, a picturesque harbour, and beautiful outlooks on the sea. I think the air of Finland most wonderfully bracing; one could be knocked up anywhere else with two such days as we have had. We passed Jarvenpää on the railway. It is about 1 hours journey (nothing for Russia and Finland) and there are lots of trains. Mrs S. came at 11 o'clock. She is a very sweet, friendly woman. We all went to lunch together to a pretty restaurant in the Park. The 2 eldest girls are weekly boarders in a school here; but as Eva is not very well yet, she is taking them home tonight and presumably she will call for us with them and we shall go out for a sort of coffee supper at 7. Sibelius caught the 3 o'clock train home, as his head was full of things he wanted to write! We shall see a good deal of them and nothing could be kinder or more affectionate than our welcome. Of course he is very erratic! It is never very dark here now, and the sun sets about 9 I think!

It will be nice to come to anchor here for a week. Then we shall see what we can afford to do. I should like to make a little trip up to the more northern lakes, and Sib. talks of a week's fishing tour, but it is rather vague at present. In the lake near them there is good perch fishing, but no trout I think.

Evidently Sib. is much adored here, and going about with him is like a kind of royal progress through the town. People stand stock still, hats off, while he passes by.

I hope John may have good luck with his exam, but I fear it does not sound very hopeful if he has such a strong competitor. [It seems he was successful because in a later letter she wrote 'Love and congratulations to John; so glad he has got interesting work.']

As I am getting rather tired, I will not attempt to answer all the family news. [...] If you have not already done so, you might find out for me just how my account stands. We must shortly decide our plans. My love to all

Your loving Mother

31. Sibelius and his wife, Aino

During this visit, Rosa was able to meet Sibelius's family, translate some of his songs and also do a certain amount of sightseeing. In her book,[1] Rosa described how they stayed in Helsingfors for several weeks, during which time she got to know Sibelius and Aino and their three daughters, Eva, Ruth and Katarina. Both Eva and Ruth were students, Ruth later making her debut on the stage. She thought Katarina, the youngest, the most remarkable and she really took to her, believing she took after her father, promising to be something of a musician. Katarina clearly had quite a repartee with Rosa and insisted on calling her by her first name rather than any more formal address, even after her parents' scolding, merely answering, '*She* will understand.'

32. The Sibelius family home at Jarvenpää

Sibelius would come to Rosa's hotel in order to translate his songs, as she described:

Our methods were unconventional, but sometimes turned out very successful. I was beginning to know a little Swedish, but of the Finnish texts I knew scarcely a word. Sibelius would come from his house at Jarvenpää to spend an hour or two at Helsingfors. There was in my hotel an ancient square piano lodged in a large and stuffy apartment impregnated with odours of Swedish punch, for it was the reception room for bourgeois weddings and other festivities. Sibelius who was fastidious, often scolded me for my choice of hostelry, but I was exceedingly happy there and preferred economy to luxury. In this rather fusty apartment and on this tinkling piano he would play his songs to me; then suddenly, getting up, he would walk up and down the room and declaim the words in a rough but vivid translation, generally into German. I, catching their meaning, in breathless haste would put them down in English in a sort of impromptu shorthand to be worked up later. Some of them, I believe have kept a little of the spirit infused into them by Sibelius himself.

Besides translating Sibelius's songs, Rosa received parts of the proofs for her translation of *Boris Godunov*. Two instalments arrived by post when she was staying at the hotel in Helsingfors and the final instalment arrived at the post office when they later reached Copenhagen. Besides the urgency to deal with these proofs, she was also anxious because Thomas Beecham had written that he might very likely want her translation of *The Queen of Spades* for the coming season. In the event, *The Queen of Spades* was not given its UK première until 1915 and then in Russian, although by 1910 Jurgenson's had published her English translation. Also, whilst in Helsingfors she received music from the publishing house Apostol.

Whilst in Helsingfors, they took a four-hour steamer trip along the coast eastwards as far as the of town of Borga (Porvo), passing by numerous islands on the way not returning until midnight, but at that time of year it was still light at that time. They also visited Tavastehus (Hämeenlinna), the town where Sibelius was born and about 100 kilometres to the north of Helsingfors. Then, leaving Helsingfors on 8 June, they made their way to Abo (Turku), the historically important old capital of Finland. They visited the old cathedral and castle and went on a boat trip to the island of Runsala, about 2 kilometres to the southwest of Abo. From Abo they started their journey homewards, as Rosa explained:

How I would love to settle in Finland for a month's country life and fishing; it is the natural beauty of the lakes and islands on the coast that attract one rather than the towns, though they are well situated with lovely parks and rivers. It has been a very beautiful tour though quite different to what I expected. For one thing the distances are far greater than they seem when one looks on the map and plans. If we had really made expeditions to wilder and more sporting [i.e. fishing] parts of Finland, we must have given up Stockholm and Copenhagen, and contented ourselves with coming home direct from Helsingfors to Hull by boat; we could have afforded neither time nor money for both joys!

They made their first leg of the journey home by boat from Abo, arriving in Stockholm at 8 a.m., as Rosa described:

Leaving Abo in the afternoon we sat on deck until we passed Mariehamu, the port on the largest of the Aland Islands which lie in the middle of the Gulf of Bothnia. It was then past midnight, and the sunset, round 10 o'clock was most lovely. The water-ways were like millponds and the rocky shores with low-growing fir trees were reflected as distinctly as in a mirror. As we got further from Abo the many summer estates on the islands, each with its own pier, bathing and boating house, grew fewer, and the white sails of yachts and little steam launches – the carriages of the people who live on the islands – became more and more rare. As we reached the open sea, the islands became mere rocks with sparse undergrowth and granite sides worn smooth by the waves; then a few lighthouses, tiny low huts, began to show. Soon the way led back to larger islands, and only once while I was in my berth was I conscious that we might be really at sea. There was not enough movement to be unpleasant, but I just heard the waves lapping the ship. We thought Stockholm very lovely when we came in, though there is a certain sameness in all these northern towns as one approaches them through an archipelago of fir-clad islands.

They stayed in Stockholm at the Hotel Anglais for a few days at the beginning of June 1910. From Stockholm they made their way to Copenhagen. They took berths on a steamer that passed through the East Goth canal and Lake Vettern to Jönköping, a journey of about forty hours. Rosa remarked that in this fine weather it was more pleasant to travel by boat than by train. After staying a few nights in Copenhagen sightseeing and going to at least one concert, they made their way back home. Rosa summed up the holiday: 'It has been a wonderful time, just the holiday and rest I needed in spite of work accomplished too. We have had lovely weather from start to finish; in fact have enjoyed a long perfect summer already, hardly seeing any rain.'

Arriving back at Campden Hill Square in June 1910, Rosa had a considerable amount of work to prepare for the autumn season of promenade concerts at the Queen's Hall. A list of Sir Henry Wood's more important novelties for the 1910 season gives an idea of some of the new analytical notes Rosa had to prepare[3]:

Austin, E.	Variations, Vicar of Bray
Bantock, G.	Three Dramatic Dances; Dante and Beatrice
Bax, A.	In the Faëry Hills
Bryson, E.	Study for Orchestra, Voices
Davies, Walford	Festal Overture: Suite, Parthenia
Elgar, E.	Symphony in E flat, No. 2
Foote, A.	Suite for Strings
Hathaway, J.W.G.	Sketch, Sunshine

Hurlstone, W.Y.	The Magic Mirror
Jervis-Read	Two Night Pieces
Mack, A.	Song of the Shulamite
Martin, Easthope	Eastern Dances
O'Neill, N.	Four Dances from the Blue Bird
Pauer, E.	In der Natur
Pitt, Percy	Serenade
Rogister, J.	Fantasie Concertante for Viola and Orchestra
Sibelius	Romance for Strings
Strauss, R.	Also sprach Zarathustra
Vaughan Williams, R.	Fantasy on English Folksongs

After the promenade season was over, Rosa was at the première of Elgar's violin concerto played by Kreisler on 10 November at the Queen's Hall.

After the stimulus of the further visit to Russia, her ideas for her next two books began to crystallise; the first was a book on Russian Music and the second on Russian painting and architecture. She also had a number of important commitments for the next year. Not only was she writing programme notes for the Queen's Hall, but also for the Sheffield Festival in April, a London festival in May, and the Norwich Festival in October. These involved large choral works including Bach's B minor Mass, the St Matthew Passion, and Mozart's Requiem, as well as a number of smaller orchestral works and chamber music. Her reputation was now such that many provincial concert societies were using her programme notes; these included the Brand Lane Orchestral Concerts in Manchester, the Glasgow Choral and Orchestral Union, and concerts in Huddersfield, Bristol, Leamington, and Newcastle. Even with all this on her plate, Rosa was always ready to support friends, so when in May 1911 Henry Wood's paintings were shown at the Piccadilly Arcade Gallery under the direction of Philip Burne Jones, Rosa helped by writing the annotated catalogue for the exhibition[4]. As Elsie pointed out, Rosa never employed a secretary, although she was fortunate that in later years Elsie willingly took on this role. All the manuscripts she submitted were in her own very clear handwriting.

Whilst in the middle of preparing for the Sheffield and London festivals in 1911, Rosa and the family had to cope with a major upheaval. As Elsie put it, 'Circumstances necessitated their leaving the house in Campden Hill Square, where during the last twenty years she had welcomed many musical and literary friends, and few seasons had gone by without leaving the memory of delightful "musical parties". So in the midst of these preparations and all her other work came the usual upheaval of a move, and during the next twelve months or more life was difficult and unsettled since we had no permanent home again in London until the autumn of 1912. We lived in trunks, half our belongings warehoused; but still Rosa's busy life and work had to go on.'

Although Elsie did not clarify what these circumstances were, it seems most probable they were financially related. Sibelius's biographer, Eric Tawaststjerna, who had access to Sibelius's correspondence, writing about the period 1910-11, stated: 'Mrs Newmarch herself was nothing if not decisive: after her husband had mismanaged their financial affairs, she took them into her own hands[5].' There are a number of occasions in her writings suggesting that she was concerned about financial matters. She never appears extravagant, and when abroad always sought modestly priced-accommodation, which she appears to have preferred. A letter to her husband written a year later suggests that by 1911 she had a controlling say in the family finances.

The family moved out of Campden Hill Square in June 1911. Prior to the move, Rosa had compiled the analytical notes for Bach B minor Mass and the St Matthew Passion, which were both performed at the Sheffield and London Festivals in April and May respectively. She also arranged to translate some Russian songs for the publishers Gutheil, Bessel, and Jurgenson.

Notes

1. Throughout her descriptions of Finland, Rosa uses the Swedish place names.
2. Rosa Newmarch, *Jean Sibelius: A Short Story of a Long Friendship* (London: Goodwin and Tabb, 1944).
3. Henry J. Wood, *My Life in Music* (London: Gollancz, 1938), p.362.
4. Rosa Newmarch, 'The paintings of Sir Henry J. Wood' in 'An Exhibition of Fifty Sketches in Oil by Sir Henry J. Wood (1911), Picadilly Arcade Gallery, London.
5. Eric Tawaststjerna, *Sibelius 1904-1914* (London: Faber and Faber, 1986) trans Robert Layton, vol.2, p.43.

CHAPTER 17: FINDING A NEW HOME

33. The Newmarch's home at Campden Hill Square

From June 1911 until the autumn of 1912 when the family moved out of their house at Campden Hill Square, they had no permanent home, and many of their belongings were stored in a warehouse. For most of this interim period they lived at 155 Goldhurst Terrace in South Hampstead, which they presumably rented. In a letter to her sister Tiny, Rosa explained that Elsie was now working for Henry Wood and liking the secretarial work. According to Pound, Sir Henry Wood suggested that Elsie took over from his wife, Muriel, as secretary; the latter being only interested in his work in so far as it brought in money. Rosa then went on to mention the house and her friend Elizabeth Johnson, who had moved her base in Italy to one in Hampstead[1]:

This house is not bad. I should not choose this road to live in permanently, but I do like this side of London. Elizabeth has now settled in her "den". She has had all her things sent from Italy and Ireland, some beautiful pieces of furniture, and she has had a wonder bed made that turns into a couch by day, she has a tiny dressing cupboard and a bathroom next door, so she can just be as she was in Italy. She is much nearer Hampstead Heath. I went for a walk with her one day. It is really marvellous. On ordinary weekdays it is perfectly quiet, and such miles of it, with views almost like Crowborough!

34. The Newmarch's temporary home in Goldhurst Terrace

By the autumn of 1911, Sibelius, who was then staying in Paris, wrote to her frequently asking her to visit him there. He had completed his Fourth Symphony and its première was given in Helsinki on 3 April 1911. On 21 October 1911 Madame Aino Ackté gave the first performance of his Song with Orchestra *Autumn Night* (*Hostqvall*) at a Queen's Hall Symphony Concert, conducted by Sir Henry Wood. Rosa had met Madame Akte earlier in the year on 24 May, when they had lunch at Pagani's[2] together with Henry Wood, Otto Kling, Granville Bantock and his wife and then again on 30 May, when they had tea with the Bantocks and Otto Kling at Buzzars[3]. Sibelius's Fourth Symphony was to be given its first performance in England at the Birmingham Festival in autumn 1912, and Breitkopf and Härtel wanted her to write an analysis of the symphony for a pamphlet they were to produce. She was also to write the notes for *Autumn Night* and *Valse Romantique*. Earlier in the year, Breitkopf and Härtel issued twelve songs by Rachaninoff and seven by Musorgsky that Rosa had translated from Russian to English. *The Times* commented favourably on her translations, explaining that Rosa was breaking new ground for English singers:

> Russian translations must be good if the songs are to make headway in this country and Mrs Newmarch is well fitted to undertake the task. In almost every case there are few traces of any of the commonplace tags which so often disfigure work of the kind [...] Not only are the verses generally free from such intrusions, but they often have a distinct beauty, and there is a general smoothness which is invaluable in words for songs; for the hearer must not be conscious of the flow of the verse either in itself or in the way it joins hands with the music.'[4]

Breitkopf and Härtel produced a further book of songs by various composers including Balakirev, Arensky, Koenemann, Korestchenko, and Kallinikov for bass voice also translated by Rosa[5].

Her letter to Tiny continued:

> Today Breitkopf and Härtel said they *wanted* me to go [to Paris], so that somebody might see about his [Sibelius's] new works getting corrected and printed – the new symphony for the Birmingham Festival, and something historical which wants an explanation written. If they are going to give me something to do that will pay my expenses, perhaps I *will* go next week. He is so erratic about business and so helpless in all languages but Swedish and Finnish. It would be very nice to see him again and also the Robinsons, but I can't afford to go unless there is a prospect of earning something.

Very soon after the concert on 21 October, and with the Promenade Concert season over, Rosa went over to Paris, staying once again at Mme Troulet's l'Hôtel du Portugal et de l'Univers. She wrote to Elsie soon after her arrival:

> I am writing a line at once to tell you that I have arrived all right, though it was a rough crossing and most of the people were ill. Dear Lady Speyer was on the boat and had her own state cabin, to which she would gladly have invited me, but added 'dear Mrs Newmarch, I know I would be sick all over you!' It was too cold

and wet to be on deck, but I never felt bad for a moment.

I was just getting my luggage through the customs when I felt myself hugged literally, and to my astonishment found Sibelius. He is looking splendidly well, and so delighted to see me – it was well worth coming for the pleasure it has given him.

I have a nice room on the first floor, found a bright wood fire, and everything very cosy. All the old servants are still here and very devoted; Mme T. younger and better than ever, trotting about and waiting on me at dinner. I am glad I came back to the old Hotel.

She went on to explain that it was difficult to get much out of Sibelius about his works and unfortunately he had sent his copy of the Fourth Symphony back to Leipzig, but he 'wired' for it to be sent back. She was anxious to go over the works with him for which she was to write notes, including the Fourth Symphony. Whilst in Paris, she also met the Robinsons.

It is not clear exactly how long Rosa stayed in Paris, except that by the time of Sibelius's 46th birthday on 13 December, she was back in Hampstead. In Paris, Sibelius would work hard each day, and she knew not to ask too much about his composing. Once he had finished, he would come round to Rosa's hotel, and they would go to a café for relaxation. Rosa noticed the very economical way he was living, by contrast with his normally expensive tastes, and was surprised that they walked everywhere, not taking a taxi. Eventually Sibelius revealed that a draft that he was expecting from Helsinki had gone astray and he was temporarily without funds. She reproached him for a lack of comradely feeling that forbade him to borrow from her. The draft eventually arrived, and although Sibelius had now no need to be so economical, he remarked to her one day: 'it is a most curious thing that I lose a gold piece of 25 francs every day of my life! I cannot solve the mystery of it.' Rosa, being very practical, suggested he might have a hole in his pocket. It proved to be so, and although Rosa claimed to be 'no needle-woman', succeeded in mending it.

After returning home, Rosa did receive some material from Sibelius, mostly in Swedish, much of which she was able to use in her programme notes. Of his fourth symphony, Sibelius said: 'It stands out as a protest against the compositions of today. Nothing, absolutely nothing, of the circus about it.'

1912 promised to be another busy year for Rosa; in addition to her Promenade Concert notes for the coming season, she had programme notes for the Westmorland Festival in April and the Birmingham Festival in September. On 3 September, at a Promenade concert Sir Henry Wood conducted the première of

Schoenberg's *Five Orchestral Pieces* Op.16. For this, Rosa wrote the programme note, but it would seem that it was not a work she found easy to describe[6, 7], and the note was not one that she included years later in her *Concert-Goers Library*. She did also attend the second performance of the work sixteen months later, given in a Queen's Hall Symphony concert on 17 January 1914. For the Westmorland Festival she wrote notes for Debusssy's *Blessed Damozel* and Sibelius's *Captive Queen*, a ballad for mixed chorus with orchestra. She was also reading and advising the publishers on manuscripts for potential publication; for John Lane, *The Memoirs of Hedwig von Bismark*, a book already published in German, a book by Myles Birket Foster and some *Critical and Historical Essays* by Edward Macdowell; for Herbert Jenkins, a book on harmony by Churchill Sibley. She was writing a review on *Chauvinism in Music* for the Edinburgh Review[8] and translating Russian songs for a Russian Song Album. She was also asked by Mary Wakefield's relatives to write a memoir for Mary, who had died on 16 September 1910. The eventual memoir ran to 143 pages[9]. She gained much information for this when she stayed at Eversley House, Leasgill, Cumbria, home of Mary's sister, Agnes Arkles.

In *Chauvinism in Music*, she discussed the writings of Hubert Parry, Cecil Forsyth, Edward MacDowell, and Guido Adler in relation to nationalism in music. The article was written at a time when Elgar's music was becoming known on the continent, and England appeared to have a composer of international standing for the first time since the days of Purcell. In Russia, the 'Mighty Five', or *moguchaya kuchka,* were creating a distinct national music aura and asserting themselves over the so-called cosmopolitanism led by Anton Rubinstein. Musicians in both countries had a heightened awareness of the music of their own countries. Rosa considered chauvinism particularly with respect to England and Russia, and at the end of the article also Scandinavian countries, particularly Finland and Sibelius. The article, although very eloquently written, is somewhat verbose by present day standards.

In order to get through all the writing that she was committed to, she decided to spend some weeks in the summer with Elizabeth Johnson at a convent at Merdrignac, Brittany, about forty kilometres west of Rennes, where she found life quiet and restful. Rosa left the house in Goldhurst Terrace on 20 April 1912 and she and Elizabeth set off in early May. The time she spent there is very well described in her letters to Elsie, extracts of which are included below, all sent from the convent at Merdrignac.

Now I am in Brittany; it took ages to get here from Rennes as the little 'goods train' which brings one starts and arrives when it likes. This place has its appeal;

it is not beautiful, but the surroundings are quaint and the house very clean. The food is liberal and as good as in many small pensions, the bread is home-baked and beautiful butter; but of course one could not recommend it to any one fastidious in their requirements.

There is a priest here now, sent specially to lecture on the Gregorian music the Pope has re-instituted in the Church; so I am going to ask to be allowed to attend his instructions! The sisters are hard-working creatures. Unluckily pelting rain has come on today at the moment of the Fête-Dieu processions, putting out the lights on the altars and soaking the poor children in their white frocks. We have all worked like niggers over the 'decors'. I raked up all my past memories of church decorations at Whitnash and elsewhere with splendid results. My monogram for the altar made out of rice on a ground of moss, was pronounced *un si bel effet*. The Convent is certainly not half as stiff and rigorous as I thought it might be; the other day Mother Superior asked me to go into the kitchens and teach the sisters how to make green gooseberry jam! Economical it certainly is! I did not realise how cheap till I came. I paid a month in advance – 75 francs including washing (just £3 then!). In addition I pay 1fr.50 for having breakfast in my room, and extra milk and eggs from the convent dairy in order to try and make up my bill to £1 a week!

In another letter, Rosa suggested Elsie might come and stay with them for a holiday and Rosa could book the room next to her:

If you cared to begin and end your holiday here for a week or ten days I think you might like it and find it would do you good [...] Elizabeth and I have the little kind of enclosed flat the Duke of A's niece is said to have most summers. That is to say we have each one of the 2 big end rooms, the smaller one between us is vacant. We much hope the house will not get full enough to necessitate their letting it, as it would be a nuisance to have anyone at such close quarters. If you thought you would like to come I would take it for you and pay for your board here [...]

If you go to the Bank to pay in anything I wish you could ask them to write down for you what my balance is – apart from *deposit* account; I mean *current* account *only*. I can't help thinking I made a miscalculation, or perhaps they did before, and mixed in the £100 I put on deposit [...]

Give my love to your father.

Well I am unusually late and must make tracks for bed now.

Your loving Mother.

In a later letter:

I am delighted to hear your holiday is fixed and hope you will drop in for the haymaking here. All the Sisters turn out to make hay and it is great fun [...]

I do feel now I am growing older, the need for giving a little more of my time to literary work that will last. The editor of the *Edinburgh* is delighted with my article and will not even let me have it back to revise.

By the time you come, or perhaps before, the "prom" scheme will be ready and perhaps I could do some of the preliminary work here as I want to stay for economy's sake as long as I can.

That reminds me – the *most important* thing of all. Will you pack up that manuscript "The Love Letters of Crabbe" [presumably the poet, George Crabbe], I left with you and send it registered to Herbert Jenkins.

Very busy with letters today. People are finding me out! How is your father?
Your loving Mother.

In a later letter still:

I am sending my list this time. I don't think the things will take up an immense amount of room and I will square up with you for extra luggage, which won't be much if you come here first via St Malo [...]

I am busy writing in the mornings, as I want to take this chance of getting a little more literary work done. I am sorry to miss Aunt Constance, but perhaps I may see her later on. I hope by the time you come the weather will be settled again and I shall give a haymaking tea in your honour. The old ladies will enjoy it

Your affectionate Mother

P.S. I send you a cheque which you can cash and pay these things out of, bring me the rest in English money.

I do not want another whole bottle of whisky as I have some still left, but you can get a bottle of House of Commons 4/s and fill a small bottle or flask, and leave the rest in your father's keeping as if I stay on here till nearer the end of July I might be glad of a further small supply. I hardly ever touch the cider, but on cold nights I sometimes like a tablespoon of whisky last thing.

Whilst staying at the convent, Rosa and Harry had to decide where they were going to live. In two letters Rosa sent to Harry whilst she was staying in Brittany, first she explained her immediate plans on returning to England when she intended to spend about a month with Bella and possibly Elizabeth at Cranleigh, then she went on to the thorny question of where they should live, their financial arrangements, and the various domestic requirements for Bella and herself.

Dear Harry,

I send you Elsie's letter as she may not have had time to write to both of us. The heat has become very intense today although there is generally a nice fresh breeze in my room, I hope she will not get knocked up[10] in Paris. Our plans are now pretty well settled. We leave here on the 25th and go to Dinan on our return journey [...] I want to be in town for one or two nights to see Newman etc, and then join Bella at these rooms near Cranleigh for about a month or five weeks, and if there is a spare room Elizabeth comes too. I wonder if you have come to any conclusion about the future. You said you would be going into office accounts in June and might then know your position more accurately. I have thought things over since I have been here and I have come to the conclusion that I shall not always be able to live at such high mental pressure as I have done during the last year or two. I think the utmost I ought to undertake towards the upkeep of the house should be £100 p.a. and when the time comes that I cannot any longer go on with the strain of Queen's Hall I am not sure that I shall be in a position to go on being self-supporting. However for the next year or so I could do it. In addition to that I have my personal expenses, and although John will be provided for for a time, 6 months soon pass, and he must be seen through his M.D. and M.R.C.P. before he will be able to get any very good foothold in the profession. Elsie seems likely to manage for herself apart from board and lodging, and if Bella returns to us she will probably contribute from £100 to 120. If we all four live together and Elsie and I are engaged as earners, I think it will be difficult to run a house during the winter on one servant nowadays. The question is what are you prepared to contribute? I think it will be better for you to take the house and I will pay my contribution partly to house rent and partly to board. With £200 clear from you I think it would be feasible, in spite of the added expense of living in London. With only £150 I think it would be very close work. The question of Bella is a difficult one. I fear she would be very unhappy left to herself, for it is evident Mrs C. has no intention of joining forces with her. From the pecuniary point of view there is not much catch in her living with us as she makes more work than anyone, and her constant presence necessitates my having a work-room and separate fire. Probably if we settled down in a house on the same terms – but on a more economical scale – as in Campden Hill Square she would not be as tiresome as last year, because I should try to get a cook-general of a better type who would not stand Bella muddling about the kitchen. If she would start on her own initiative I should be glad in many ways; but I am sure she will leave me the onus of what she would call 'turning her out' and I often think left to herself she might drift into the same condition as Fanny Simpson [probably her older sister]. Therefore if we take a house again, which seems inevitable for the next few years, we had better reckon on her joining. If she pays her rent to you as before one source of trouble will be avoided, as she considers it a kind of privilege of friendship to be casual with me in these matters. Rents being equal, I do not think it is a bit more difficult to run a house with 6 bedrooms than with 5 – a box room would make life with Bella a more endurable arrangement as in spite of all I destroyed in the move, I think the only way is to let her hoard in boxes until she departs this life! Perhaps you will write to me on this subject. If we decide that a house is possible we had better try to get settled soon – in September –and save warehousing bill which mounts up – But I want you clearly to realize that a house as a permanent arrangement must depend chiefly on yourself and if you don't feel you can face it again it would be better to say so now.

    Yours R.

A further letter giving her thoughts on the merits of particular houses and some specific requirements followed this letter:

Dear Harry

    I have been thinking a good deal about the houses. I shall be curious to hear about Reg. Park Rd, although in spite of its charming situation I fear it may prove something of a gazebo, and awkwardly planned. I do not think, apart from the delightful situation, that Bella took to Acacia Road. I felt myself there was something not wholesome about that house, and we should have been irritatingly cramped. I still hope that we may come to a decision about Crossfield Rd which seems to me to fulfil almost all my wishes. At the same time I don't want you to take it if you think it will overburden your resources. If we start with 2 servants they can manage that house quite as easily as Acacia. I believe we shall find it a sound healthy abode with plenty of room, light and air. Of course I know £400 is not a great deal to run a house upon, but still when one remembers that it has not to include any wine, pocket-money or educational extras, it ought to do I should think. I am *quite* clear on the point that I am satisfied with the house and consider its advantages outweigh its one drawback of not being quite ideal as to situation.

If you get to negotiations here are a few points.

Are the windows barred downstairs?

The trees must be cut.

What about blinds –were there some?

I should like rather a better grate in whichever room I have upstairs, but I don't expect to get it.

Bella would like first floor back room, and I think this is *much* the best, in case of illness. Also if I have an upstairs library she won't run in and out so much.

My choice of room on top floor must depend on fitting in servants.

Mention that we are willing to keep the drawing room as it is, but the decoration and paper is poor. (It is in very good taste)

Bella wants a handrail to steps, but I do think it is not a necessity. In has

Ever yours

Rosa

These two letters are quite revealing about the domestic arrangements. They suggest that Rosa is very businesslike in their financial arrangements, and that she made a substantial contribution to the costs of running the house, and also at the age of fifty-three she was concerned about keeping up her present workload in the foreseeable future. She also discussed Bella in a very businesslike way, in a tone that suggested the ardour of the welcome of fifteen years previous had somewhat cooled. It might even seem surprising that Bella continued to stay with them for a further sixteen years. Bella was now sixty-five and she appeared less mobile, hence the request for a handrail. She also no longer accompanied Rosa on her trips abroad.

While still at Merdrignac, Rosa completed the Mary Wakefield Memoirs and also the translation of *Prince Igor* and a Russian song album. In addition, she reviewed books for John Lane and Herbert Jenkins. She and Elizabeth returned to London in August.

Notes

1. Reginald Pound, *Sir Henry Wood* (London: Cassell, 1969), p.115.

2. Pagani's Restaurant, Great Portland St was a favourite haunt of Sir Henry Wood's, reckoned to be the best musical meeting place in London, where musicians signed the tablecloths. Later frequented by Philip Heseltine (Peter Warlock), E.J. Moeran, Elizabeth Lutyens, and Alan Rawsthorne. It was bombed during the Second World War.

3. Trevor Bray, *Bantock* (London: Triad Press, 1973).

4. 'Some Russian Songs: Moussorgsky and Rachmaninov', *The Times*, 14 Oct. 1911.

5. 'Some New Songs: English and Russian', *The Times*, 1 Nov. 1913.

6. Philip Ross Bullock, *Rosa Newmarch and Russian Music in Late Nineteenth and Early Twentieth-Century England* (Farnham,Surrey: Ashgate, 2009), p.12.

7. David Cox, *The Henry Wood Proms* (London: BBC, 1980), p.62.

8. Rosa Newmarch, 'Chauvinism in Music', *Edinburgh Review*, Jul. 1912, pp. 95-116.

9. Rosa Newmarch, *Mary Wakefield, a Memoir* (Kendal: Atkinson and Pollitt).

10. Rosa's granddaughter, Renée Bodimeade, assumes that by 'knocked up' Rosa simply meant 'unwell'.

CHAPTER 18: CROSSFIELD ROAD: 1912-1913

Rosa and her husband decided to take the house in Crossfield Road and they finally moved there on 7 October 1912 with Bella Simpson again joining them. A year earlier, Sibelius had expressed his regret that he would not be seeing 52 Campden Hill Square again. Rosa was also depressed about the loss of their previous home. Although 4 Crossfield Rd provided ample accommodation, typical of a four storey Victorian house, it lacked the character of Campden Hill Square, where the houses were built around a square with gardens skilfully laid out by Joshua Flesher Hanson in 1826.

35. The Newmarch's home in Crossfield Rd

Sibelius had been invited to England to concerts at Liverpool, Manchester, Birmingham, Bournemouth, and Cheltenham in the autumn. He wrote to Rosa on 29 August to say how pleased he was to be coming to England, and also that he had been invited to Granville Bantock's country house during the visit. He arrived in London at an inauspicious moment, the morning the Newmarches were about to move and they met Sibelius in 'a carpetless and furniture-blocked passage.' They then travelled down to Birmingham, meeting Bantock at his house at Broad Meadow, with its large garden well away from the traffic. Evenings were spent mostly rehearsing in the Birmingham town hall.

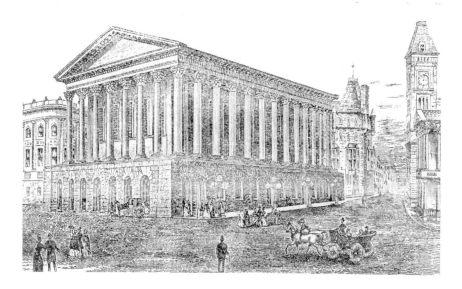

36. Birmingham Town Hall

Rosa was also able to use the Bantocks's library. At one point when she was sitting in a darkish corner of the room, Sibelius entered so engrossed in his thoughts that he did not notice Rosa. She felt he must have had some inspiration, and it was important not to disturb the creative process. She also knew not to ask him about it. He fought shy of analytical notes and it was pointless to consult him on this question, in spite of Rosa having been commissioned by Breitkopf and Härtel to write detailed notes for his Fourth Symphony. At the final rehearsal before the Birmingham performance, she sat next to Delius. Although a very different character, Delius was able to admire the originality of Sibelius's work. Sibelius conducted his Fourth Symphony at the Birmingham Triennial Music Festival on 1 October 1912, sharing the podium with Sir Edward Elgar who conducted the première of his own composition *The Music Makers*. The UK premières of Bantock's *Fifine at the Fair* and of Walford Davies's *The Song of St Francis* were also given at the festival that year. After hearing Sibelius's Fourth Symphony Rosa wrote to her sister Tiny:

I had Sibelius here for the Birmingham Festival. His Symphony is beautiful, but in its idealism quite over the heads of the press at present. I am writing an essay on it which is to be published in German as well as English. Sibelius tells me everything I write is translated into Swedish and Finnish nowadays. It was a joy to see how splendidly he is now ordering and ruling his own life. [He was abstaining from alcohol and cigars at this stage.] When I think what a distracted lunatic he was at times! It makes me believe in the miracle of casting out devils. He is beginning to realise the Moving Fingers behind it all now. I observed a tendency to patronise him this time and commission festival works from him, so I was glad to see him start home for his own country and forest house, where he is quietly doing the most perfectly original and detached work since Brahms – or perhaps since Beethoven – for his ideas are more wholly *ursprünglich* (sic) than Brahms' were.

She felt that one could hardly say that the Fourth Symphony was received with public enthusiasm at its first performance in England, but Sibelius was satisfied with its reception. *The Times* noted after the Birmingham performance that Sibelius was a considerably more significant composer of modern music than *Finlandia* and *En Saga* had led people to believe. After returning home on 30 October, he wrote saying that many artists, including Busoni, had spoken enthusiastically about the Fourth Symphony. Rosa wrote detailed analytical notes for it and Breitkopf and Härtel published these as a fifteen-page booklet. In it Rosa not only analysed the four movements, illustrated with twenty-six musical examples, but she also set the work in its historic context.

Of the other four locations where Sibelius was engaged to conduct, Rosa accompanied him to the second performance given by the Bournemouth Municipal orchestra under their conductor Dan Godfrey. The latter was always enterprising and ambitious in his programmes; but realising the need for ample rehearsal for such a new work, he postponed the performance until the following season. Many friends of Sibelius were present at this performance, including Otto Kling, Granville Bantock, Dr Charles Mclean, and Rosa herself.

As Rosa mentioned, attempts were made to commission him to compose for the Three Choirs Festival at Gloucester in 1913. She was probably pleased when he wrote to her saying, 'I cannot go to Gloucester because I have no new choral work to offer. So far I have no inspiration to write one, and cannot, and will not, force myself. So your opinion has proved quite correct.' Nevertheless, one of his favourite singers, Aino Ackte, sang his *Luonnotar* Op.70 at the Gloucester Festival on 10 September 1913. She also sang the closing scene of

Richard Strauss's *Salome,* for which Rosa produced the analytical notes. The latter was deemed unsuitable for the cathedral, but was performed in the Shire Hall, Gloucester.

Rosa's letter to Tiny continued on a more domestic note, and she appeared concerned about their finances:

> I hear you like the [our] new abode and that it is answering well. We must be *very* careful and see how things work out [...] I find the great increase in servants wages rather a serious item. I pay that, because I do feel that with Elsie and I both earning and so busy it is poor economy to be worn out by the sort of drabs we suffered under last year. I have a very superior house-parlour maid but I don't care for the temporary cook and want a younger and less expensive person.
>
> You will be amused to hear about the Convent. If the world goes too much wrong with me I believe I shall go back to the dear, hardworking, neurotic Sisters. I felt so well at Merdrignac. The air is glorious and the difficulty of spending £1 a week is good for ones health. Thanks to my stay there I was able to give John his five months in Munich.

On 12 November, Rosa had lunch with Lady Bective, whom she had known for some time through Mary Wakefield and the Westmorland Festival. Lady Bective had provided some information for Rosa's memoir on Mary Wakefield, which had been published earlier in the year. The Bective family seat was at Lunefield in Kirby Lonsdale, but they also had a London home at Eaton Place, Belgravia, so while Lady Bective was down in London, this would have been a first opportunity to discuss the memoir since its publication. The following day, Rosa was called to Leamington where her older sister Lily, now sixty-four, was ill.

In spite of her concerns about domestic issues, she still managed to keep up with her writing commissions. A composer she had met in St Petersburg at Stasov's house but about whom she had not written was Skryabin, so when Bernard Pares asked her to contribute an article to the Russian Review, she decided that Skryabin was to be the subject. The School of Russian Studies at Liverpool University was founded in 1907. In 1908, Bernard Pares* (1867-1949) was appointed to the chair of Russian Studies and, in recognition of Rosa's pioneer work for Russian music and art, she was invited to become one of the six founder members of the school. In the years prior to the First World War, public attitudes in Britain towards Russia were changing from one of mild hostility to that of seeing her as an ally, and there was a desire for Russia to replace Germany

177

as a trading partner. There was a need to get to know more about Russia and its culture. As part of this initiative, the School of Russian Studies founded the periodical *Russian Review*, with Pares as editor. In 1912, he invited Rosa to contribute to an early edition, and she suggested the subject *Skryabin and Contemporary Russian Music*. He replied as follows:

> Certainly we will wait until January, but if I may I will definitely book you for that issue. We and our Russian collaborators are anxious that in the Review there should be good contributions from English writers on Russia. That interests the Russians more than their own articles. Consequently I am asking a member of the School to write for each number, and besides that there is always something from our staff here. I think the time, as you suggest, will be a good one because of your book [probably *The Russian Opera* which would soon be published] which I shall much look forward to reading later; and I also agree that it would be very good to have something about the inter-relations between literature and music, which seems to me a good subject.
>
> I hope we are going to keep a high standard with the Review. When I was last in Russia we invited all the leading people we could think of out of the learned world to become contributors. If we once represent the best achievements of Russian thought in English, I don't see how people can be anything but grateful. We have a very good list of subscribers which is growing fast.

Over the next three years, Rosa was to write three articles on Skryabin.[1-3] She also gave lectures on Skryabin's music. In one of her first lectures after returning from her first visit to Russia, she had introduced his music with examples given by the pianist Sandra Droucker (1876-1944). Sandra Droucker was a pianist of note; she was a pupil of Anton Rubinstein and was selected by Welte Mignon to make their piano rolls.

In 1912, Henry Wood had planned to give the first UK performance of Skryabin's *Prometheus, The Poem of Fire* at the Birmingham Festival, but it was found that there was insufficient rehearsal time and he first conducted *Prometheus* at the Queen's Hall on 1 February 1913. Once this date had been fixed and Rosa was to write the programme notes, she realised much homework needed to be done to come to grips with a work by this messianic composer. She corresponded with him and in addition to making a careful study of the score, she felt the need to try to understand his theosophical ideas. It had been hoped that Skryabin himself would come to conduct the performance, or as the soloist in the piano part, but he was prevented by engagements with Mengelberg in Holland. From his letters to Rosa he was evidently grateful to her and to Henry Wood for their interest in his work. A week before the performance of *Prometheus,* Rosa gave a lecture to the Halcyon Club on Skryabin with special emphasis on that work. As a result, one of her audience wrote a letter to the editor of *The Times* suggesting respectfully that in view of the complexity of the work it would be a 'positive boon' if Sir Henry Wood were to give the work twice[4]. This suggestion was adopted by Wood, who played the work twice in the same programme – an experiment that proved, as he himself said in his *Life in Music,* 'quite worth while for very few people left the hall before the repeat of the work.' After the London concert, Ernest Newman wrote[5]:

> Here is music that comes as near as is at present possible to being the pure voice of Nature and the soul themselves [...] the wind that blows through it is a veritable wind of the cosmos itself. The cries of desire and passion and ecstasy are a sort of quintessential sublimation of all the yearning, not merely of humanity, but of all nature, animate and inanimate.

At the lecture on Skryabin and his music that Rosa gave at the Halcyon Club on 21 January 1913, Vassily Safonov (1852-1918) took the chair as he was in London conducting two Royal Philharmonic Society's concerts on the 13 January and 13 March. At the first of these, he conducted works by Schubert, Wagner, Bantock, and Rimsky-Korsakov, and at the second, he gave a first performance in England of Skryabin's First Symphony. Rosa first met Safonov in 1906 when he chaired a meeting at which she gave a lecture on Sibelius. Since then, Safonov had become a regular visitor to England and friend of Rosa's. They had lunch together after his concert. With his background he was well suited to chair her lecture. In his early days he was best known as a pianist, but later became a conductor; the first in modern times not to use a baton. As a professor of piano at the Moscow Conservatory, Skryabin, Medtner, and Lhevine were among his pupils. After being director at the Conservatory in succession to Taneyev, he resigned and conducted the New York Philharmonic from 1906-1909 and regularly visited London. He was one of the first musicians to appreciate Skryabin's talent, although confessing not to understand his musico-theosophy[5]. Rosa wrote detailed programme notes for *Prometheus* in which she discussed the Promethean myth, the theosophical issues, and Skryabin's harmony.

Александръ Скрябинъ.   Alexander Skrjabin

Россійское Музыкальное Издательство. Москва.

37. Aleksandr Skryabin

From 5 October 1912 to 31 January 1913, there was a Second Exhibition of Post-Impressionist Art at the Grafton Galleries, London, the first exhibition having been in 1910. The second exhibition was largely devoted to Russian and English paintings, and at some time during that period, when Skryabin's music was much on Rosa's mind, she visited the exhibition. Among the paintings she was particularly interested in were the three by the Lithuanian painter and composer Mikalojus Konstantinas Čiurlionis (1875-1911) entitled *Rex* (1909), *The Knight* (1909), and *The Mountain* (1906). The English reception to Čiurlionis 's paintings has been described in detail by George Kennaway[7]. She mentioned Čiurlionis briefly in her article *Scriabin and Contemporary Music*[1]: 'Skryabin may have discarded national formulas, but he retains a close kinship to such artists as Bogayevsky and Čiurlionis. Those who have seen in the exhibition a certain picture by the latter, entitled *Rex* the centre of which is occupied by a burning fire, enclosed by circles of shadowy angelic forms, will certainly discern the affinity between the transcendental preoccupations of these two artists, and a resemblance in their illusive and occult methods of expression.' She continued to describe the painting in her book *The Russian Arts*[8]: 'It is a subject such as Skryabin treated musically in his *Prometheus*, and we realise that in this painter's soul sounds and visions are practically interchangeable.

The very complex schemes of design in which the angels, rainbows, procession of stars, and cloud forms, move along hills and valleys, which are not of this planet, is like the working out of some wonderful contrapunctal problem.'

On 18 October 1913 Skryabin's *The Divine Poem* was performed at the Saturday Series of Queen's Hall concerts, then on 14 March 1914, Henry Wood gave a further performance of *Prometheus*. On this occasion, Skryabin came and performed the piano part of *Prometheus* and also his Piano Concerto. The programme notes which Rosa had produced for that concert were approved by Skryabin and were later published in the *The Concert-Goers Library* series[9]. At the time of the concert, Henry Wood said of Skryabin: 'I thought he looked far from well and seemed to be a mass of nerves.' He died a year later in Moscow 14 April 1915. On May 2, Rosa received from Skryabin's friend M. Briantchaninov, who had accompanied the composer on his visit to London, the following telegram:

> Our dearest, greatest Prometheus suddenly passed, through the same lip disease [the lip disease troubled him on his visit to London], having just finished the most wonderfully poetic text, the prologue to the Mystery. We are collecting funds for his children, Ariadna, Julian and Marina; perhaps English friends and admirers could do same. His last words, beginning his painful agony were, clenching his hands: "I must be self-possessed, like Englishmen are." His wonderful death testifies to a terrible mystical fight above us in this war.

Rosa felt that his last words were an eloquent message from Russia to England at a dark time in the First World War, and that they showed clearly and poignantly the high estimation in which Russians held the British character, with its sangfroid, fortitude, and cheerfulness, even in the face of danger and death. She wrote an appraisal of him and his work for the Musical Times[3].

1913 was a busy year for Rosa; she continued assessing potential books for publication by John Lane and Herbert Jenkins, translated a Russian Folksong album[10], prepared a lecture and programme notes on Skryabin, and she was also involved in the organisational aspects of the Finnish choir, Suomen Lauli (The Song of Finland) and their visit to England in June 1913. The choir was formed in 1900 by their conductor Dr Heikki Klementi (1876-1953) initially as a men's choir, but becoming a mixed choir after 1907. They toured Scandanavia and Europe under his leadership from 1901-1925 and came to England in the spring of 1913 to perform three concerts, on 13, 18, and 20 June. Klementi was an enthusiastic collector of Finnish folksongs. At these concerts, they gave a wide selection of part-songs by modern Finnish composers, including Sibelius, Palmgrem, Jarnefelt, and Merikanto. They also sang folksongs and student songs. Although not explicitly stated, one can believably assume that the Sibelius songs were Rosa's translations.

The highlight of the year for Rosa, however, was the first visit of a Russian opera and ballet company to England. When Sir Joseph Beecham, father of Sir Thomas Beecham, brought the Diaghilev Company, with Feodor Shaliapin, to London for a five-week season at the Drury Lane Theatre in June 1913, it was, for Rosa, the fulfilment of a long-cherished hope. Vladimir Stasov first introduced Rosa to Shaliapin in 1897 in St Petersburg. They met on a number of occasions and became friends. Most recently she had seen him perform the part of Boris in *Boris Godunov* in Paris in 1908, visiting him in the dressing room after the performance. For the 1913 visit, the operas performed were *Ivan the Terrible*, *Khovanshchina* and *Boris Godunov*, and the following year, in addition *Prince Igor* was performed, Shaliapin taking the roles of both Galitsky and Konchak.

By 1913, Rosa had made translations of several operas, but she always felt that the British public's first introduction to Russian opera should be through the medium of Russian singers and particularly a Russian chorus. She was commissioned to complete quickly English versions of the librettos of *Khovanshchina* and *Ivan the Terrible* so that they could be on sale during the season[11,12]. The publisher, Belyayev, had also enquired if she would translate Borodin's *Prince Igor* into English. Belyayev had published the full score of the version of *Prince Igor* completed by Rimsky-Korsakov with a Russian libretto in 1888. In Rosa's reply to the publisher, dated 21 November 1913, she names her price as £25 (500 marks) for the translation. Her translation was published in 1914[13]. *The Times* commended her on the translations of Musorgsky's operas: 'For even outside the minority who can read Russian, the majority, who cannot, get some help in the perusal of a translation by seeing how far it has succeeded in distributing the syllables in accordance with the original. In the case of the solos Moussorgsky's method is generally that of one syllable one note, and Mrs Newmarch has been very skilful in the extent to which she has been able to preserve the musical accentuation while writing plain ungarbled English.[14]'

The 1913 visit of the Russian opera and of Shaliapin in particular was a great success with the British public, such that a second tour to London was made in the following year. Shaliapin himself was amazed at the attitude of the British public. According to Borovsky, 'From his very first Russian season in London [1913] he felt the atmosphere of concentrated attention with which the audiences followed everything happening on stage[15]. It seemed that not a single word, not a single intonation was lost. The auditorium's reaction to the smallest artistic detail was immediate and unerring.' Rosa was delighted, as she explained: 'Shaliapin was evidently deeply moved by, and not a little astonished at the enthusiastic welcome accorded to him and his compatriots[16]. He had, of course, been told that we were a cold and phlegmatic race, but he found in our midst such heart-felt warmth and sincerity as he had never before experienced outside Russia.' Stasov had said to Shaliapin many years before: 'Go to England. Play in your own language, they'll understand everything!' In a continuation of the letter of 21 November that Rosa wrote to Belyayev, the publisher, she told of the success of this first London season of Russian opera, particularly on account of the magnificent performances by Shaliapin. She pointed out that the popularity of Russian music had also been helped by Otto Kling who, some years ago, set up the Breitkopf and Härtel office in London and with whom she had been always been happy to work[17]. After Shaliapin's second visit to London, Rosa wrote a short account of the man and his art for the *Musical Times*[18]. In it she described his gifts: 'The greatest of his gifts is not the sensuous beauty of his voice, nor his vocal production, but his re-creative power of imagination. Few actors in our day have possessed in such a degree the sustained force of imagination that makes all he does seem real and inevitable [...] At the same time, though we are disposed to rank one side of Shaliapin's work rather higher than the other, partly because his serious conception of the actor's art is comparatively rare among opera singers, yet we must acknowledge that the balance of his performances is very even; for if he is a superb actor he is also a great singer with "a style that is the man" a singer whose elocution is a thing of joy, and whose tone, timbre, and sense of rhythm are incomparable.'

At the close of Shaliapin's first successful visit to London, Rosa thought she would leave a card for him to bid him goodbye and congratulate him on the final night's triumph, and she often recalled this amusing and unexpected picture of the artist, on one occasion in a letter to her sister-in-law Emily:

His strange little Russian secretary came down to speak to me and having kissed my hands and hem of my coat, much to the amusement of the Hotel-porter, he insisted on my going up to tell his master I was there. Shaliapin sent word that he would be bitterly disappointed not to see me, but he had not made his toilet – should I mind? I said no and went up to find him still in bed, looking like a magnificent amiable statue of Nero, attired in a Russian tunic, cut square at the neck and short sleeves, trimmed with beautiful Russian embroidery. He was just going to have early tea and invited me to join him; so his Tatar servant brought in exquisite China tea, which we sat drinking while we talked for an hour. He had a letter from his little son, and asked me to search on the table for all the other letters he had had from him. Photographs of his children were all around. 'Such good friends of mine,' he said, and it was evident that their doings and their letters formed one of his chief interests of his life. Then we discussed next year's plans, new editions of operas, his throat, which was troublesome, and many other things. Then, after vows of eternal friendship, he kissed my hands and I kissed him on the forehead and both cheeks – the correct farewell kiss between real friends in Russia, which accompanies the real farewell before journeys etc, and is quite proper, because it is generally accompanied by the sign of the cross from right to left. The little Tatar opened all the doors for me in state, and the Secretary accompanied me to the street with more kissing of hands and garments, but in this case I only put my hand on his head, which he afterwards touched with his forehead. All is so oriental, and yet Shaliapin is an impassioned suffragist. Such strange mixtures.

Shaliapin's final performance in 1913 was on 8 July in *Boris Godunov* at which King George V was present. The *Musical Times* declared: 'It was a theatrical and musical sensation without parallel since the coming of Wagner. London was spellbound by the revelation of a new order of vividness in operatic music and operatic acting[18].' Rosa must have felt that the promotion of Russian music that she had worked hard for over at least a decade was well and truly paying off. The second visit in 1914 was no less successful but for Shaliapin it was forever associated with the First World War. On his way back home, he was held up in France as the trains had already stopped running, and he had to return first back to England and then go via Norway, Sweden and Finland. For Rosa, the war polarised her feelings for Russia and against Germany as her writings at the time were to convey.

38. Lily Holcroft Jeaffreson (1848-1913), Rosa's sister

In April, Rosa had been called to Leamington again where her sister Marie-Therese (Lily) was very ill, and on 2 September 1913 she died. Apart from her years of training as a singer at Paris and at the Royal Academy of Music, London, Lily had lived in Leamington throughout her working career as a singing teacher. Like Rosa, she was an excellent linguist.

Notes

1. Rosa Newmarch, 'Scriabin and Contemporary Russian Music', *Russian Review,* Feb. 1913, pp.153-69.

2. Rosa Newmarch, 'Prometheus, the Poem of Fire', *Musical Times* 55, Apr. 1914, pp. 227-31.

3. Rosa Newmarch, 'Alexander Scriabin', *Musical Times* 56, Jun. 1915, pp.329-30.

4. 'Scriabin's Prometheus', *The Times,* 24 Jan. 1913.

5. M.D. Calvocoressi, *A Survey of Russian Music* (London: Penguin Books, 1944), p.86.

6. Rosa Newmarch, 'Wassily Safonoff', *Musical Times,* 1 Jan 1916, pp.9-12.

7. George Kennaway, 'Lithuanian Art and Music Abroad: English Reception of the Work of M.K. Čiurlionis, 1912-39' *The Slavonic and East European Review,* 83 (2005), pp.234-53.

8. Rosa Newmarch, *The Russian Arts* (London: Herbert Jenkins, 1916), pp.271-3.

9. Rosa Newmarch *The Concert-Goers Library* (London: OUP, 1929), vol.2, pp.61-5.

10. Rosa Newmarch, (1915) *Fourteen Russian Folk-Songs with Pianoforte Accompaniment.* selected and trans. (Brighton: J.W. Chester, 1915).

11. Nicolai Rimsky-Korsakov, *Ivan the Terrible,* trans. Rosa Newmarch, (Leipzig: Breitkopf & Härtel, and St Petersburg: Bessel, 1912).

12. Modest Moussorgsky, *Khovanstchina,* trans. Rosa Newmarch (Leipzig: Breitkopf & Härtel, and St Petersburg: Bessel, 1913).

13. Alexander Borodin, *Prince Igor,* trans. Rosa Newmarch (Leipzig: Belaieff, 1914).

14. 'The Season at Drury Lane: Some Russian Operas', *The Times,* 25 May 1914.

15. Victor Borovsky, *Chaliapin: A Critical Biography* (New York: Alfred A. Knopf, 1988), pp.398-9.

16. Rosa Newmarch, *The Russian Opera* (London: Herbert Jenkins, 1914), pp.387-8.

17. 'La popularité de la musique russe est toujours croissante chez nous. Nous devons cela beaucoup à M. Otto Kling, qui a établi, il y a quelques annees, un bureau central chez Breitkopf & Haertel, où je suis toujours prête à co-opérer avec lui. Mais l'éclatant success de l'opera russe, avec M. Shaliapin, à Drury Lane au mois de juin, a beaucoup contribue au progress de ce gout chez nous.'

18. Rosa Newmarch, 'Feodor Ivanovich Shaliapin', *Musical Times,* 1 Jul. 1914, pp.437-40.

CHAPTER 19: THE TRILOGY, THE OUTBREAK OF WAR AND THE FINAL VISIT TO RUSSIA

By 1912, although Rosa had been writing articles, and was the author of several books, she aspired to do more. In a letter to Elsie from Brittany in 1912, she says, 'I do feel now I am growing older [now 55] the need for giving a little more of my time to literary work that will last.' In some ways this comment may seem a little surprising, as she had published a book on Tchaikovsky, two books of poems, *Poetry and Progress in Russia,* a short biography of Henry Wood, and a memoir on Mary Wakefield. However, much of her time must have been taken up with programme notes, writing short articles for music journals, and also reading manuscripts by other authors to assess for publishers. A number of her books, although substantial, were translations, e.g. the biographies of Brahms and César Franck, the life and letters of Tchaikovsky, the book on Borodin and Liszt, and also the librettos for *Boris Godunov, Khovanshchina*, and *The Queen of Spades.* She was about to embark on two books covering a wide range of Russian culture. The first, entitled *The Russian Opera,* was to cover opera from its earliest beginning to what was then the present day. The second, entitled *The Russian Arts,* was very wide ranging and included architecture, iconography, painting, sacred art and sculpture. These, together with her *Poetry and Progress in Russia* published in 1907, she regarded as making up a trilogy. There was also a further, less substantial book, published later. It was a collection of Russian religious writings about which Rosa wrote a commentary, entitled *The Devout Russian. The Russian Opera* (1914), *The Russian Arts* (1916), and *The Devout Russian* (1918) were all published by Herbert Jenkins.

Up to 1912, several of her books were published by the Bodley Head (John Lane Ltd), and she had come to know both John Lane and his manager, Herbert Jenkins, well, but around 1910, Herbert Jenkins took the decision to set up on his own as a publisher. Elsie Newmarch takes up the story:

> Herbert Jenkins had many years experience with John Lane, but was not always in agreement with the latter's decisions which he, as manager, had nevertheless to carry out. It was a venture, however, on which he hesitated to embark, and I think it was to some extent Rosa Newmarch's friendly interest and sympathy in his ideals which finally decided him to take the plunge; for throughout his

correspondence with her during the next few years he often expresses his gratitude for her help, and his wish to have the opportunity to reciprocate. 'I value very much the advice you give about the purity of books,' he wrote, 'and I endorse every work that you write. I hope we have to do a lot more work together yet, and I shall soon see your name in my list.' Like John Lane, he seems also to have found her an ideal publisher's reader, always taking into consideration, not only the literary value of a manuscript, but also the commercial side which those inside the ring know to be most important. 'Nothing that I can say can convey to you how deeply I feel all your kindness to me during that rather trying period,' he wrote having made his final decision. 'Such comradeship as you showed is a thing to be paid in spirit, and someday I may have an opportunity of showing how much I value your friendship.' The feeling was, I am sure, mutual, for she appreciated his ability and judgement; and in 1911 when she had to meet a crisis in her own affairs, both personal and professional, his kindly and thoughtful advice was equally valued –though he felt sure her own well-balanced judgement would certainly guide her to take the right course.'

The letters from Herbert Jenkins to Rosa dated 1912 refer to a trying period in his life and his gratitude for her kindness. By November 1913, referring to the trying period, he wrote that he was in danger of becoming bitter, because of the attitude of some who had every reason to stand loyally by him. Later in the same letter, referring to Rosa's problems, he wrote: 'I am firmly of the opinion that you will look back gratefully upon the present crisis in your own affairs […] If you stay you will have a better defined position; if you go it will be to find something more congenial and more profitable.' Herbert Jenkins's trying period may relate to setting up on his own as a publisher, Rosa's could relate to a number of things, some of which might have be interrelated. Leaving Campden Hill Square was something Rosa was very reluctant to do, but almost certainly financial circumstances dictated the move. Before re-establishing their home in Crossfield Road, there was the question of whether Bella should rejoin them. Also, as already quoted Rosa stated in a letter to Harry in 1912: 'I shall not always be able to live at such high mental pressure as I have been doing the last year or two. I think the utmost I ought to undertake towards the upkeep of the house should be £100 p.a. and when the time comes that I cannot any longer go on with the strain of Queen's Hall I am not sure that I shall be in a position to go on being self-supporting.' Herbert Jenkins's reference to whether Rosa stayed to have a 'better defined position' may relate to her contractual arrangements with the Queen's Hall.

Soon after Herbert Jenkins had set up as a publisher, he wrote an article which was entitled 'Mr Jenkins Explains What he Considers His Duties' for the *New York*

Times Review of Books, in which he explained the role of a publisher[1].

> I am one of the first to realise that the publisher is a business man. He must be possessed of a species of double-action brain. He must be shrewd in affairs and far-seeing in literary matters. He must remember that the early productions of Shelley were almost beneath contempt, and he must apply the knowledge to every manuscript that passes through his hands [...] Those who urge that a publisher need only be a business man, a seller of books his authors write, forget that there is the prejudice of the author to be considered. He likes to feel his publisher has a knowledge of letters and can talk something more than sales, musical though the word may sound to his eager ear. It is true that a publisher employs "readers" to act as literary brains; but he must always be there to decide. The "reader" tells him what the manuscript is about, whether or not an author can write, what he considers its chances of success. It is then that the publisher comes in. He must decide for himself what are its chances. I myself have just accepted a novel that a "reader" utterly damned as impossible of achieving any sort of success. I have done so because I am not in agreement with his judgement.

Herbert Jenkins's views were important, as Rosa was both a "reader" and author, and her books were for what might be described as a specialised market.

Herbert Jenkins was immediately successful with several popular works including his own witty and amusing series of *Bindle* novels, which sold well and established him financially, so that he could embark on more ambitious literary, if less remunerative, publications. Although Herbert Jenkins died in 1923, the firm thrived as a small publishing house until 1964 when it combined with another publisher, becoming Barrie and Jenkins. That was subsequently taken over by Hutchinson, which in turn merged with Century and later Random House.

It is not clear when Rosa began writing *The Russian Opera*, but she had given much thought to Russian opera over the previous decade. She had given a series of lectures to the Musical Association of London between 1900 and 1905; each of these lectures was followed by a discussion. The lectures, including discussion, were published by the Musical Association as five papers totalling seventy pages. These covered the period from Glinka's *The Life for the Tsar* in 1836 to Rimsky-Korsakov's opera *The Tsar's Bride* in 1899. She had seen the French première of *Boris Godunov* in 1908 and also the 1913 visit of Russian Opera to London and had translated the librettos for three Russian operas. She also wrote an article on Musorgsky's operas for the *Musical Times*[2]. Her book was to be a synthesis of her thoughts and previous writings on the subject. She was anxious to complete it so that it could be available for the 1914 visit of Russian Opera to London. It covered a more extended period than she gave in the lectures to the Musical Association and included two chapters devoted to the period before 1836, chapters on the foundation of the nationalist school of composers and also the period 1900-1910. In her preface, she described her aims: 'In view of the extended interest now felt in Russian opera, drama and ballet, it has been thought worth while to offer to the public this outline of the development of a genuine national opera, from the history of which we have much to learn in this country, both as regards things to be attempted and those to be shunned. Too much technical analysis has been intentionally avoided in this volume.' Rosa was keen to pass on her enthusiasm for Russian culture and the Russian people.

Herbert Jenkins was delighted when she accepted his proposal to publish the book, hoping that it might be the first of a series of books on Russian culture in all its aspects. On 23 March, he wrote to her enthusing over the cover design. 'I am sending you some cover designs for *The Russian Opera*. Your name, of course, will be added later. The general impression in the office is that this is the most wonderful cover that we have done, and it is only appropriate that it should enclose your book.' Nowadays, with the technology available, the cover design might not seem so striking, but at a time when most books simply had covers of a uniform colour, this seemed quite novel. So much so that it was repeated on Rosa's next book in the series on Russian arts.

39. Herbert Jenkins's cover design

The Russian Opera ran to 403 pages and was dedicated to Feodor Ivanovich Shaliapin in Memory of Our Dear Friend Vladimir Vassilievich Stasov. It was published on 14 May 1914, just in time for Sir Joseph Beecham's second season of opera and ballet. Rosa sent a copy to her friend the singer Ffrangcon Davies, who replied saying: 'It was indeed good of you to think of sending me your new book. I have already read a good deal of it and find it most interesting. There is a strong warm pulse in every page, and it cannot fail to interest and educate the people on the subject.' But perhaps more importantly, the book was favourably received by the critics. At the time when *The Russian Opera* was published, a book on an overlapping subject was also published, entitled *A History of Russian Music* by M. Montagu-Nathan. Both books were reviewed in the *New York Times Review of Books* on 1 November 1914[3]. Rosa's compared favourably with that of Montagu-Nathan's as this extract shows:

Mrs Newmarch's thoroughly competent presentation of the history of this operatic music is welcome. She has long been known as one of the musical writers in English most familiar with the subject at first hand, and her previous books have acquired authority. There has been a good deal written about the work of the modern Russian school of music, but the earliest beginnings and later developments of that school have received much consideration. Mrs Newmarch confines herself to the operatic literature, but her study takes her back to the dawn of music in Russia, to the music of the primitive Slavs, the "gleemen", the Biblical plays, the early ballet, and the first public theatre in Russia in 1703. The first Russian operas were for the most part echoes of contemporary Italian art, and indeed, were mostly composed by imported Italian musicians. There seems to be some uncertainty as to the first Russian national opera, but before the end of the eighteenth century numerous operas had been produced by native Russians. It is interesting to find one of them by Fomin, called "The Americans", the Americans being red Indians. In many of these operas native folk songs were used, but they were crowded out by the increasing cosmopolitanism of Russian society till Glinka came to sound the national note more clearly and to establish the real starting point of the Russian school of later times.

There are chapters there on Dargomijsky, Rubinstein, Balakireff, and his circle of the "five" so often spoken of, besides himself, Moussorgsky, Borodin, Cui and Rimsky Korsakoff – and of these there are many interesting personal details. There is a chapter of course on Tschaikovsky, and the more recent and most recent composers, as well as the leading operatic artists of the present time, receiving attention. Mrs Newmarch's plan includes the analysis and description of the most important operatic works of the Russian school. Her book on the whole affords a valuable addition to our knowledge of musical development that has been described rather fragmentarily hitherto.

Mr Montagu Nathan undertook at about the same time to fill the same gap, but his book does not enter into a study of the earlier period. He begins with Glinka and his immediate predecessors and traverses from this period much the same ground as Mrs Newmarch, but he writes with something less of authority, with less confidence in the use of original sources, and with apparently the necessity of resorting to translations and other second-hand information that Mrs Newmarch has no need of [...]

The review in *The Times* generally welcomed the book for its wide-ranging coverage and complimented her on the musicianship and intuitive sympathy which her writing shows. Her views were much influenced by those of Stasov. A slightly critical note questions what appears to be a dual purpose, in that Rosa began to write a history and ended by writing a guide to Russian operas[4]. In 1972, a new edition of *The Russian Opera* was published[5]; this predates the adoption of 'print on demand' publication methods and must be a measure of the continued use of the book, over sixty years after it was first published.

The excitement of the second visit of the Russian Opera and the publication of Rosa's book *The Russian Opera* in the summer of 1914 could not hide the political events in Europe. As early as 1911, in a letter Rosa wrote to her sister Tiny, she was aware of developing tensions when she mentions the visit of Dr von Hase of Breitkopf and Härtel to London: 'He says there is such a danger of war between Germany and England. The Germans are so set on it. He, of course, is not of the rabid anti-English set.' After the assassination of the Archduke Franz Ferdinand of Austria on 28 June 1914, it was just over a month before the Kaiser declared war on Russia and, after Germany invaded Belgium, Britain declared war on Germany. As mentioned in the previous chapter, by the time Shaliapin returned home to Russia after the Russian Opera visit, he had to make an extensive detour because of the hostilities. But in spite of the outbreak of war, it was apparent that some entertainment would be needed, so the Promenade Concerts, and later in the year the Symphony and Sunday Concerts at Queen's Hall, were continued with a few adjustments to the programmes. Henry Wood had admitted a small number of women to the Queen's Hall Orchestra (discussed in Chapter 27). Thus, while continuing with her heavy workload of writing, Rosa was anxious to do what she could for the war effort. Her son, John, joined the navy as a surgeon very soon after the start of the war and her daughter, Elsie, was a nursing sister of St John's V.A.D

(Voluntary Aid Detachment). One of her brothers, Charles, now in his late seventies, also a good linguist, took up a post in Gibralter as censor, and her husband, Harry, joined a Batallion of the County of London Volunteer Regiment. In a letter to her sister-in-law Emily, Rosa wrote: 'Harry is often out drilling with "Gawds' Rejected".'

Rosa turned her energies immediately to furthering the knowledge and understanding through their arts of those who were to be our allies. At that time, British attitudes towards tsarist Russia were often extremely negative, despite the Anglo-Russian entente of 1907, since the country was still widely seen as a backward land ruled over by an autocratic government. The outbreak of war meant that Russia became a vital ally for Britain in the struggle with the central powers. Its presence in the allied coalition nevertheless made it difficult to present the conflict as a fight for liberty and democracy against Prussian militarism[6]. To improve the public's general understanding, Rosa was soon lecturing to widely differing audiences: schools and colleges and private clubs and societies in London, the suburbs, and the provinces. Her lectures seemed to appeal to both young and old, and her happy knack of humour and insight made all she had to say alive and interesting, as well as instructive. As an old colleague wrote: 'Her life-long work in pointing out the wonders of Russian music is well known. Her lectures are so full of emotional appreciation and broad erudition that the audience leaves them full of new thoughts and echoes of that broad comprehension which has made her so infallible a judge and critic of music. It is not given to us all to travel and obtain foreign knowledge first-hand; but Mrs Newmarch brings Russia very close to us, and we must give her thanks for a most valuable store of information.'

Her lectures were often illustrated by songs performed by Miss Grainger Kerr and sometimes Miss Olga Haley, also by slides of Russian people, their life and surroundings. The latter would have been quite an innovation at the time. She also wrote to Dmitri Stasov explaining how glad she was that Russia was an ally and explained that her son was a surgeon in the navy and her daughter was working in a hospital. She also told him how she was lecturing about the Russian people to improve understanding between allies.

Within six months of the publication of *The Russian Opera*, Rosa was contemplating her next book. Herbert Jenkins was encouraged by its sales, including some to Japan, especially at a time when the war was high in most people's minds, and by November 1914 he was discussing ideas with Rosa for another book on Russia. He wrote: 'At the present moment of course the form of the book is more or less nebulous. It will settle itself probably as you go along. Personally I think somewhere about sixty-thousand words, in which should be given an historical impression of the Russian people, so that men of culture shall not be able to ask each other, "Is there a Russian literature? Is there a Russian art?" and the like. I think the published price ought to be not more than 2/– net (= 10p, but based on the Retail Price Index equivalent to about £7), in which case we could pay a royalty of ten per cent (10%).' Rosa responded by sending him chapter headings for a book that might be entitled *Russia* or *A Short History of Russia*. Of the seven proposed chapters, five trace Russian history from earliest times to the present day, and there is also a chapter on Art and Literature and one on Trade and Industry.

Rosa and Herbert Jenkins went on discussing the scope of a book on Russian history and its people, but a letter from him to Rosa dated 28 December 1914 suggests there may have been additional factors that had to be taken into account, such as competition from two other authors. Stephen Graham* was probably the lesser worry of the two. Born in 1884, he was a freelance journalist and was in the Altai Mountains, Russia at the start of the war. His articles appeared in *The Times* and he went on to write a book, *Changing Russia,* which was published by John Lane in 1915. Sonia Elizabeth Howe's writings posed a more serious threat. She published four books between 1915 and 1917: *A Thousand Years of Russian History* (1915), *The False Dmitri: A Russian Romance and Tragedy: Described by British Eye Witnesses 1604-1612* (1916), *Some Russian Heroes, Saints and Sinners, Legendary and Historical* (1916), and *Real Russians* (1917). In spite of the assurances Herbert Jenkins gave in the letter, there would appear to be a clear overlap between Rosa's proposed book and *A Thousand Years of Russian History.* This is even more evident from the preface to Sonia Howe's book, written from her home at St Luke's Vicarage, Finchley in May 1915: 'I dedicate this book to the bright hope of a closer alliance based on better mutual understanding between two mighty nations to both of which I belong – the one by birth, the other by marriage.'

Rosa felt that any book on such a wide field as she had proposed should not be undertaken in a hurry. It would require thorough research at the British Museum, The London Library, and elsewhere. In Herbert Jenkins's letter to Rosa in late December 1914, he wrote: 'I think it would be better to arrive at Russian Art via 'The Russian People'. However, Rosa had been contemplating a book on Russian arts ever since she visited Stasov in the Imperial Library at St Petersburg in 1897, and she had already done a considerable amount of work on it; it now appears that she decided that completion of this book should be the priority rather than a more general book on the history of the Russian people, including their art. By April 1915, she must have made substantial progress on this because in the postscript of a letter from Herbert Jenkins, he wrote: 'I have just received an order from Dutton's [American publisher and agent] for 100 of *The Russian Opera* and also for 500 of

The Russian Arts. I know you will be delighted.' However, an unexpected turn of events delayed completion of *The Russian Arts*. It came about through her friendship with Otto Kling, the London manager of the music publishers Breitkopf and Härtel. With the onset of war, German firms were seen as enemy firms. Otto Kling was completely out of sympathy with German belligerency, having lived in London since about 1890 and being of mixed parentage. Otto Kling's father, Henri-Adrien-Louis Kling (1842-1918), was the son of a German father and a French mother. He was a musician, writer, and composer. At the time of the First World War, he was living in Geneva. In 1915, Otto Kling, with Rosa's support, became the proprietor of the music publishers J & W Chester. Two letters that Rosa wrote to her sister Tiny in the spring of 1915 explain her plans and her feelings about the war and are quoted below:

> I have something to tell you that may surprise you, and I hope will not alarm you, for there is no occasion for it. Mr and Mrs Kling are going to Russia next month and want me to go with them. The business is rather important and will repay the journey in a short time. At first everybody exclaimed, but the Russian Consul here, Baron Heyking says it is perfectly safe. One route is kept strictly open and patrolled for the mails. It is a daily service and mine swept and escorted like the Channel service. He says he has issued hundreds of passports since Xmas and all has gone smoothly. Old Mr Safonov [conductor] tells me he has crossed 3 times since the war! When I asked Baron Heyking if he considered it too risky to take my daughter, he said – of course not. I should let any of my people go. The wife of the Norwegian Minister goes to and fro and all our diplomatic people.
>
> So, unless anything new occurs Elsie and I will go about the middle of May with Mr and Mrs Kling. He is a good sailor and traveller. We expect to be away 6 weeks and to get home in good time for summer plans. It will be interesting Baron H. says "you'll be received with open arms, and I'll give you a letter of introduction that will take you anywhere." But of course we are not going near the fighting.
>
> Bella is in Birmingham for a few days. Sharp [family pet] very poorly with an abscess and tooth which Pope cannot take out in her present condition. Elsie is at the Military Hosp. this week and finds she gets a good deal of work, as she now has a reputation for steadiness and nerve.

The purpose of the trip was part musical and part a political goodwill trip. For Rosa it was an opportunity to keep in touch with friends and also collect further material with which to complete her book *The Russian Arts* and to acquire new material for what was to be her last book on Russia, namely *The Devout Russian*. This first letter to Tiny was followed by a second shortly after:

I write to tell you that Mr Kling and I have decided to postpone our departure for the present. Cork still declares the Norwegian mail steamers are safe, but I do not think just at the present moment the Germans can be trusted to behave decently even to neutral ships. The "Lusitania" business [sunk on 1 May 1915] is too ghastly and has finished up the last vestige of feeling left in this country for Germany. In fact Mr Kling's chief reason for putting off going to Russia is that he has determined no longer to be associated even indirectly with Breitkopf and Härtel. Today he has given orders to have their name crossed from the shop and will put their affairs into the hands of the Public Trustee. All this will take a little time and in the interval things may happen to make the sea-journey safer. I wish they would confiscate all German property in England. Our government is a disgrace in its supine attitude to them over here.

We do miss dear little Sharp. Pope at first thought it was teeth, but when the bleeding at the mouth got so bad he came to the conclusion it was internal haemorrhage, probably from a growth on the liver. After his man – a very nice retired coachman – had sat up with her for some hours and found she could no longer take any beef-tea, they laid a little chloroformed pad under her head and she just fell asleep. We have buried her in the backgarden and Elizabeth bought some brown and yellow pansies –"just like Sharp" she said, and planted them on her grave. We are making all kinds of domestic upheavals. Marie is going back to France, she has grown rather intolerable, and it is well she should depart. Bella is going to take baths at Droitwich.

Ever yours affectionately, Rosa.

Tiny was her only sister by then still living in Leamington. She was rather an invalid and looked forward to going away with Rosa's family in the summer, so the letters were partly to reassure her. Herbert Jenkins was somewhat concerned about her making the trip, saying: 'I do not like the thought of your bobbing up and down in the sea exchanging pleasantries in German with the commander of an enemy submarine!'

Rosa, Elsie, and Mr and Mrs King embarked at Newcastle on 28 May 1915 on the *S.S.Haakon VII* bound for Bergen on the first leg of their journey to Russia. There are at least two accounts of the trip, the first by Elsie in the unpublished biography of her mother in which she also quotes from Rosa's diary, and the second by Otto Kling, published in the first issue of *The Chesterian*[7]. Otto Kling became the proprietor of the House of J & W Chester[8]. There is also Rosa's version of events described in her book on Sibelius[9], and also some interesting comments by Tawaststjerna[10] on the visit to Sibelius en route. The account of the journey itself that follows is that of Otto Kling, with additions from the other sources.

A Voyage to Russia in War Time

I think it will be considered that it needed some little courage to undertake a business trip to Russia in these days of submarines and aircraft. However, it had to be done; so on May the 28th, in the year of grace (?) 1915, was a fateful day selected for what proved to be by far the most memorable as well as the most exciting trip of my life. I think it is not altogether unfitting that I should inaugurate the first issue of *The Chesterian* with a short account of my journey to Russia, and I hope that, especially under the exceptional circumstances, the account – consisting of short extracts from my diary – for which no literary claim is made, may not prove without interest to my readers.

On May the 28th, in company with my friend, Mrs Rosa Newmarch (the well-known authority on Russian music and art in general), her daughter and my wife, I left London for Newcastle where we embarked on the S.S. "Haakon VII" for Bergen. It will be remembered that the "Haakon VII" has been held up several times by enemy submarines, and that on one occasion the mails on board destined for England and France were intercepted and sunk by the pirates. The "Haakon VII" left at midnight for Bergen and before leaving all passengers are subjected to much cross-examination, giving a little taste of future delights in store. The journey to Bergen proved uneventful; the North Sea was not in its best humour [Elsie described it: Everyone seemed to be ill and we did not attempt to leave our berths: I think our remedies helped, but I doubt whether anything would have really made us comfortable in such a tossing] and we were greatly relieved to enter calm waters at Stavanger, where the boat picked up the mail. After a journey of 48 hours we sighted and landed at Bergen. The charm of Bergen lies in its individuality. It is a homely, quaint, romantic town with an attractive residential district framed by surrounding heights. The evening of our arrival, Mrs Newmarch took us to her friend, Madame Grieg [wife of the composer Edvard Grieg], to the beautiful residence at Troldhougen which was reached by motor car. Madame Grieg received us in hospitable fashion, and altogether our short visit proved a delightful one. [Elsie: 'I think we almost brought her and her sister out of their beds; but their delight at such unexpected visitors and news from England, was beyond all doubt. Doors were at once opened, tea was made, and we sat talking long into the night. It was a very great pleasure to Rosa Newmarch to see these two dear people again.'] The next day we left Bergen for Christiana [Oslo]. The journey is a perfect delight from start to finish. The picture presented by the fjords and the surrounding mountains is not easily reproduced. In the 12 hours' journey, you seem to travel through the four seasons of the year, namely – Summer, Autumn, Winter (for, for about three hours you find yourself among ice and snow), and Spring. We stopped at Finsen, where the hero of the South Pole, the late Captain Scott, used to train his dogs, and where a monument has been erected in his memory. Christiana was reached in the evening. It is an old-fashioned city of great interest and surrounded by pine-clad hills and the gleaming fjord, alive with shipping, affords a very fine view. After having paid visits to my colleagues, we left for Stockholm, a bright handsome prosperous city. Here I began my business and called on several well-known publishers; here I met Armas Järnefelt [Sibelius's brother-in-law, whom Rosa also met] whose delightful Præludium and Berceuse, published by my house, are well-known to the British public. Järnefelt is the Conductor at the Stockholm Opera House. A man of great charm and individuality, as his music shows. At Stockholm we also had the pleasure of meeting the great Swedish composer Emil Sjögren [1853-1918], with whom we had a very illuminating conversation on matters musical. [According to Sibelius's biographer, Tawaststjerna, in Stockholm they were received courteously but not warmly[10]. Sweden maintained neutrality in the First World War, but prior to 1916 the government was pro-German.] We left Stockholm for our long journey to the north of Sweden, Karungi [...] [The Gulf of Finland was too heavily mined to admit a safe crossing and they had to travel by land.] We reached Boden in Sweden in gorgeous weather and midnight sun, and we had the unique pleasure of picnicking in broad daylight at 11.30pm. Karungi!! You may search the map in vain for this interesting spot, for the simple reason it is a war baby-city. It is near the Swedish frontier and is being built of wooden huts, which are springing up like mushrooms and to which pretentious names have been given, such as Grand Hotel, etc. [The present day population appears to be less than 300.] There is no railway to take us to Haparanda the terminus before crossing the river "Tornea" which separates Sweden and Finland, so we had to take a motor and Haparanda (about 30 miles) was reached after an exciting journey, the roads being in shocking condition. [Rosa's account: All sorts of strange vehicles were waiting about at the terminus to pick up passengers and take them on to the frontier town of Tornia. There were horse vehicles, one or two carriages drawn by reindeer, and a few motorcars which looked like the cast-offs from many garages[9]. Here my Russian came in useful in securing one of the latter. I remember it had a large gaping hole in the floor, a veritable pitfall to be avoided in getting into and out, and that our luggage such as it amounted to was tied on to the equipage with worn bits of string. A very Rosinante[11] among motorcars, it sufficed to get us to the station at Tornia.'] The Tornia is a beautiful river, much bigger than the Thames, and, unlike the latter, of beautiful deep blue. We cross into Finland by means of wooden foot-bridges and here Customs and Passport examination take place. We get a first glimpse of the stalwart Russian soldiers who scrutinise severely your passport. The town of Tornia is small but interesting, with its little one-storey wooden houses, primitive and painted white. You begin to feel you are entering a new country, breathing a new atmosphere. We now leave for Petrograd, via Helsingfors. The journey is very long and trying and this is mostly due to the execrable train service. We change at Rihimaki for Helsingfors. A pleasant interlude is afforded us by the sight of our old friend Jan Sibelius who, with his wife, is waiting for us at his country place, Jarvenpaa. [Tawaststjerna[10], quoting Rosa Newmarch, contrasts their reception in Finland with that in Sweden: 'In Finland, however, their welcome was altogether different. Sibelius and Aino went to meet them in Helsinki, and took them out to Järvenpää: Sibelius and his family received us with all their usual warmth and hospitality'.] [...] Next day was spent visiting the music publishers at Helsingfors (who have brought to light the works of the new Finnish School – Sibelius, Palmgren, Melartin, Kuula, Merikanto, etc) and subsequently lunching with Sibelius on the gay Esplanade to the sound of a very capable military band, conducted by the well-known Apostol, who is also a music publisher. We afterwards made a tour in an automobile through splendid Finland scenery. The trip wound up agreeably with a dance to Finnish Folk-Tunes played by one of these wonderful Finnish Brass Bands [...] An imposing spectacle was a number of Russian Dreadnoughts guarding the Gulf, and the war is further brought home to you by the number of wounded seen on the balconies of the "Lazarets" and in the streets. [Rosa's comment: 'So far Jarvenpää was the same peaceful country district that I had known of yore. Madame Sibelius was little changed since I had visited her in 1910, but in the meantime her elder daughters had grown up and married. My particular friend Katarina was at school, and the younger ones playing about in the garden. Our visit was short, for I was anxious to push on to Russia; but it was a happy interlude in a period when friends were so widely divided.' Nevertheless, it appears from Tawaststjerna's account that Rosa found time to air her views on the political situation[10]: 'Mrs Newmarch was not one to keep her views to herself, and it is clear from his diary that Sibelius found her hatred of the Germans and the strain of talking French onerous. He did not involve himself with the delicate question of German-Russian hostilities, for his perspective was of course very different. On the whole, however, with his English sympathies he had little difficulty in understanding Mrs Newmarch's point of view.']

Leaving Helsinkfors at mid-day, we arrived at midnight at Petrograd and were very thankful we were, after a journey which may be described as more or less a tribulation, as although Finland belongs to Russia, the laws are totally different and another strict customs examination and searching of passports is the penalty one has to pay before entering Holy Russia. In Finland you may indulge in beer, wine, and spirits, in Russia alcoholism of every kind is denied, and you must be satisfied with tea, mineral waters or kvas. [The Tsar's Prohibition Decree came into force on 1 August 1914.] But what a difference it has made to the Russian people! The old calendar being still in force in Russia, we find ourselves 13 days younger.

They arrived in Russia on 8 June (new calendar) after arduous travelling since the 28 May. Rosa, now fifty-eight, appears to have coped with the journey and was eagerly anticipating meeting old friends. At this point, the narrative is compiled by Elsie from from Rosa's diaries.

We arrived in Petrograd late last night (8 June), as a long and minute examination holds everyone up at the frontier. Thanks to my letters of recommendation I got through with little delay. This is a large hotel just off the Nevsky Prospekt and exactly opposite to the dear old Library with its many happy memories.

We had a very good time at Helsinkfors, though I do not of course admire the attitude of the Finns; it seems to me quite parochially narrow-minded to think of one's own small grievances at a time like this. [It seems more than a small grievance that Finland is subsumed into Russia!] Sibelius is all right, and knowing I love Russia he would never say a word to hurt my feelings; besides I feel sure his sympathies are on the right side.

Here we are living in a whirl! We have dined and spent the evening as of old with the Dmitri Stasovs. They were on the point of departure for their country house, and far from expecting English visitors in war time. Nevertheless they were determined to have one more musical evening for my benefit 'as in the good old times'. Preparations for flitting were temporarily suspended; their long suite of spacious rooms, so ideal for music, were not inappropriately shrouded in white covers, and the big chandeliers swathed in dark-coloured tarlatan. They were all there, older but well; Dmitri and his dear sweet wife, their married daughter and her husband, Mme Natalie Pirarovova and Marie, now very old but quite well; the sculptor Ginsburg and some young men, pupils of Balakirev, Liapunov, black-bearded, with dark and eager eyes – altogether a striking personality – was our chief musician. His playing, though it had plenty of power and a rich quality of tone, was more akin to the art of Liszt than to the crushingly vigorous and tempestuously passionate style of Anton Rubinstein. Liapunov was the best exponent of his own music, and also of Balakirev's. Afterwards we ate supper in the spirit of subdued gaiety, and were careful to look away when, in defiance of the strict temperance laws, one small glass of wine was poured out for our octogenarian and ailing host. The rest of us drank fruit kvas and feigned that it was an exhilarating beverage. Liapunov discussed with me the possibility of coming to London to introduce his first Piano Concerto.

This afternoon Mr Kling and I visited Rimsky-Korsakov's widow, also the son and his wife, and tomorrow I go with Mrs Stasov to see the newly erected monument to Mily Balakirev, and to take a wreath to dear old Vladimir Stasov's grave. There are a good many ghosts here now, but they are all kindly and much-loved ghosts, and one likes to feel them around one.

I have just seen Shaliapin who was off to Moscow; we shall meet again later as he wants me to spend some days in his country home at Jaroslav.

It is difficult to get definite news here. People seem rather depressed by the gradual falling back of the army; but personally I attach very little importance to the loss of Premsyl. By and by I think they will make good again, although perhaps in a different direction. The opening of the Dardanelles would have a splendid effect morally and materially. Of course the immediate effect of poison gases upon soldiers so simple-minded as these dear Russians must have been ghastly. They are brave and stand any amount of legitimate hammering, but to such unsophisticated minds wholesale poisoning must appear most uncanny and alarming. There is foolish talk as there is at home; but sensible people all believe there can be but one end to the war – the ultimate overthrow of Germany.

I must confess I came to Russia consumed with curiosity to see how the Russians were accepting the discipline of the temperance movement. The Tsar's prescript forbidding the sale of alcohol throughout the Empire was announced on 1 August 1914, simultaneously with the order for mobilisation, when the passionate enthusiasm of the people for a war which they instinctively felt to be holy inclined them to ungrudging self-sacrifice. But how were they playing the game? Were they enduring this restriction on their self-indulgence merely as a necessary evil growing out of war? Did they protest openly or in secret? Were wage-earning classes sulky, and was there much exercise of ingenuity in order to evade the rigour of the law? Any secret doubts I may have felt before I left England were soon swept away by a wave of enthusiasm for the courage and sweet reasonableness of the people.

For the severity with which the enactment was carried out and its impartial application to all classes, I was hardly prepared. The day after my arrival I lunched at the well-known Café de Paris with Otto Kling and his wife. Otto inquired 'What wine will you take?' 'Excuse me, sir,' said the head-waiter, 'there is no wine served in Russia now.' And it took us some moments to realise that this throng of prosperous business men, Government officials, and military officers, discussing their food all around us, had nothing stronger on their tables than kvass, lemonade, or a bottle of Caucasian mineral water. Of course, it cannot be denied that the law presses harder on the poor than on the well-to-do, because the latter have a greater variety of temperance drinks open to them

The deepest impression made on me was in Kazan Cathedral, where I stood among the wounded soldiers brought there by detachments of Red Cross sisters. Very few of those who had lost a limb or were lame accepted the offer of a seat which deprived them of full view of the celebration. They brought home to me the cruelty and wickedness of war so keenly that I felt the tears running down my cheeks as I shared the service with them. They literally worship, these men, bowing their broken bodies before God's altar. Who can say that their worship is a mere formality? Let them stand among them as I have done, and see the rapt expression on their faces, and the wonderful change that comes over them as they listen to the beautiful music. Their religion may not have any link with intellectualism, but it is of the heart. Again when the long string of collectors come round with their plates, how eager every man is to drop his copeks into this or that receptacle. And copeks mean a real offering from these poor soldiers – a cigarette or two the less, or an orange coveted from the baskets temptingly piled up at the street corners, or a pocketful of sunflower seeds.

Rosa also reported that the musical activities in the city appeared not to be affected by the war with plans for the forthcoming season well underway. The most striking thing she noticed in this area was the music of the military bands and soldiers singing in the streets; not an hour went by without some regiment passing her window. Otto Kling's account gave more details of the musicians they met in St Petersburg. They met the composer and conductor Alexander Tcherepnin (1899-1977) at his house, together with a number of well-known artists. They also met a number of composers who formed the managing committee of the music publisher

M.P. Belyayev when they visited the publishing house. These included Glazunov Nikolai Artzibushev (1858-1937), a composer and music editor who, after the revolution, went to Paris in charge of the Belyayev publishing office and the Latvian composer and teacher Joseph Wihtol (1863-1948), who, after 1919, returned to Latvia to found the Latvian National Conservatoire. They were suitably impressed with Belyayev's old office, the hallowed meeting place of so many great Russian Masters, describing it as a veritable temple, upon the walls of which were portraits of Belyayev, Rimsky-Korsakov, Glazunov, and Lyadov. At the time of their visit, the opera house was closed, and so they were unable to meet Albert Coates (1882-1953) or Alexander Ziloti (1863-1945), both of who were away on holiday. They attended three lecture recitals on Skryabin. At one, the music writer Vyacheslav Karatygin (1875-1925) spoke in Russian for one hour without a break. Otto Kling, who was quite modest about his knowledge of Russian, was greatly relieved when the pianist Mr Baravski sat down to play all the Preludes by Skryabin. One can only surmise that Rosa would not have been disconcerted by an hour's Russian. Whilst in St Petersburg, she met the sculptor Ilya Ginsburg and also Madame Olga Novikoff.

From St Petersburg they travelled on to Moscow, a tiring overnight journey in a crowded train, but nevertheless Rosa was thrilled to see Moscow again. One shortage she noticed: by then it was virtually impossible to get postcards or photographs she was hoping to obtain to use for her books or slides for talks. They had planned to go on to Kiev but were invited to Shaliapin's country house in Yaroslav and they went there instead.

Her diary continued:

> During the early months of the war death took heavy toll from Russian musical circles, especially in Moscow. First A.M. Kerzin, who had done much to encourage a taste for music among the masses; then the admirable artist Grjimaly, a Czech by descent, who had taught the violin at the Conservatoire since 1869, and was invited to Moscow by Nicholas Rubinstein as assistant to Laub. The premature death of Scriabin followed in April this year, and Moscow hardly recovered from this painful shock when the familiar and respected figure of Serge Taneiev was taken from the scene. Russians know how to honour their dead, and no one who was present at Taneiev's burial service will easily forget the impressive nature of the scene [23 June 1915]. The Conservatoire was already closed and many professors had already left for their holidays; but the little parish church of St. John the Baptist, in the Arbatskaya quarter, could hardly contain all who came to pay their last respects to the Director of the Conservatoire. Those who could

not find standing-room around the bier, which was completely hidden under a huge pyramid of palm-wreaths and flowers, waited patiently in the courtyard of the Church, with sun beating fiercely upon them until the long musical service was over. The music – Tchaikovsky's Liturgy of St John Chrysostom – although perhaps a little sentimental for our taste, was exquisitely sung by the Archangelsky Choir, and the whole congregation visibly moved. At the end of the Liturgy friendly hands bore the coffin to the composer's house a short distance away, where another farewell service was held. The mourners followed on foot, a long procession; most of them having in mind a longer and sadder cortège which a few weeks previously had escorted Scriabin to the grave: sadder because Taneiev, though not an old man, had apparently said his say, whereas Scriabin died with his most arresting message still upon his lips, at the moment when his spiritual enthusiasm and lofty optimism were most precious to his country. His widow was perhaps the most touching and pathetic figure in the cortège following Taneiev's coffin, and every step must have recalled to her the grievous pilgrimage made a short while before when Taneiev himself walked by her side, sharing in the universal regret for a loss that left not only her life, but the life of the whole world the poorer.

One thing the war may be expected to do for Russian music is strengthen still further the conscious expression of the national spirit in this art. There will not of course be a return to the exclusive national outlook of Balakirev's school: an exclusiveness which had its uses at a time when German influence threatened to possess the whole world of music in Russia. That danger has passed. New departures there must be, or the old national ideal would become a stagnant and unprofitable thing; but some recent unimportant movements, imitative of certain extreme and morbid tendencies in Western art, will certainly be swept away before the rolling fires of the war, and we may soon find Russia developing a healthier and simpler musical art, with a strong motive behind it (I use the word religious in its widest sense). Scriabin was alive to this tendency, but he frames the thought in the language of his chosen philosophy: "these upheavals, in shaking the souls of men, open them to the reception of the ideas hidden behind the outward happenings. The circle is complete, and the stage of the journey is finished: something has been attained; the creative idea has made one more impression on matter. We are living through just such a period of upheaval, and in my eyes it is an indication that once again an idea has matured and is eager to be incarnated" [...]

Itlar, Yaroslav District

On leaving Moscow my lot was cast for a time among a merry party of young people, particularly jubilant because 'Papa' was taking a long promised month's holiday in their midst, a rare occurrence in the strenuous life of Feodor Shaliapin. On his picturesque property in the district of Yaroslav, the great actor-singer reverts to type and seems at one with the people from whom he originally sprang. It would be difficult to imagine a jollier holiday life than that led by the young Shaliapins, five in number, their tutor, governess and guests during the summer months in the large log-house, with its spacious verandahs, standing in a clearing among the forests with a charming vista of a crystal-clear river winding through the flowery meads that slope up gradually to a further stretch of dark and wild woodlands.

Let me say at once and for all that Shaliapin in the role of *père-de-famille* is just as convincing as in any other part. At Itlar all the occupants live the life that suited them best; the voices of the children came from the stable-yard, or the meadows by the riverside, but the grown-up folk generally wait for the cool of the evening to take our walk in the woods. No one thinks of disturbing the host until he is inclined for our society. He sits there reading and musing, with Karlash, the white English bull-dog on one side, and Boulka, the black French bull-dog, on the other. But his attire is as beautiful as anything he ever wears on the stage: a dressing-gown of some oriental silk the colour of the pine forests in spring. Alas, the tragic history of that green silk garment! At Itlar there was a boat and bathing stage. The boat manned by the children had a playful habit of turning turtle at unexpected moments. It had already precipitated my daughter and one of the children into mid-stream. Fortunately they swam like fish. I had saved myself from similar fate by stepping over the side and wading ashore. Shaliapin was wickedly amused when he saw us, dripping and depressed objects, creeping in at the back door of the house. But Ate for once was on the side of her own sex. The bathing stage needed mending, but the carpenter – like all carpenters eastern or western – had replied day after day, *Seichass, seichass* (directly, directly) and had done nothing. So one perfect summer evening, when the master of the house had finished bathing and put on fine linen and a lovely green robe, the planks rebelled under his weight and back he went into the water. The green garment was reduced to a long strip of dank water-weed, and our eyes never privileged to envy its loveliness again. Sorrow for its ruin tempered our vengeful exultation, and these dipping episodes were tactfully forgotten on both sides.

Those were quiet and happy days! A fictitious peace and happiness was ours perhaps, for the war was going none too well on the eastern front, and the spirit of revolution was trying its wings. But the front was 600 miles away and the revolution a half-fledged thing of terror; but the family were by no means indifferent to the struggles and sufferings of their fellow countrymen. During the winter Shaliapin had frequently visited the front, and was continually singing for the benefit of the wounded and homeless; while in both Petrograd and Moscow he maintained small hospitals for the wounded and convalescent. Itlar was far removed from any town or large village, and even beyond the reach of newspapers, so that the people used to come up to his house to hear Shaliapin read the latest war news to them from the verandah.

At the end of June, they began their return journey home, first returning to St Petersburg and then largely taking the same route by which they came. In Finland they took the opportunity to visit Rachmaninoff, who spent the summer at Ravanti in Finland. At Bergen they happened to meet Delius and his wife. Their crossing of the North Sea on the Norwegian steamer *Iris* was without incident although they came across the floating wreckage of the Russian boat *Anna*, which had been torpedoed by a German submarine about an hour before their passage and they were relieved to arrive at Newcastle safe and sound, after a trip that none of them would have wanted to miss.

Sometime after returning from what was to be her last trip of two months in Russia, Rosa composed two poems; the first capturing her feelings towards Russia and published in *The Times* in 1916.

To Russia (1916)

To thee the hard-pressed nations lift their eyes,
Land of vast potencies, land of my heart;
Whilst thou, unflinching, dost fulfil thy part
As in the past: *unstinted sacrifice*.
But when peace comes, shall we once more misprise
Thy purpose? Use thee as a genial mart,
Yet still suspect? Or bid old doubts depart,
And let thy spirit teach us, and be wise?

Ah, come what may, thy future shall be great;
Strong, sober, lit by faith inviolate,
Moving to Godward ends; and though I die
Ere thy meridian, I am reconciled
If but one Russian, passing where I lie,
Should say: 'She loved us poor, assiol'd, reviled.'

In the second, an unpublished poem written on her fifty-ninth birthday on the 18 December 1916, she reflects on her age, especially in relation to the war.

Si Viellesse Pouvait

Too old to do canteen work,
Too old to be a nurse,
But not too old to hate to shirk,-
Years are a woman's curse!
Too old to guide a ploughshare straight,
Or drive a pair-horse van:
Lord, if I could reincarnate
I'd pray to be a man!

No use to bear a rifle,
Or steer a Red Cross car,
To charge where gases stifle,
Or die where Russians are.
I've given to a British ship
My all – my only son:
Lord, if I do reincarnate,
Make me an Amazon.

Nevertheless, she used her skills as a writer and lecturer to inform the general public of our new found ally in Russia.

Notes

1. 'The Publisher; Mr Jenkins Explains What He Considers His Duties', *New York Times Review of Books*, 28 Jul. 1912.

2. Rosa Newmarch, 'Moussorgsky's Operas', *Musical Times*, 1 Jul. 1913, pp. 433-40.

3. 'Russian Music: Two Histories of a Subject of Increasing Interest, *New York Times,* 1 November 1914.

4. 'The Russian Opera: A History and a Guide', *The Times*, 29 May 1914.

5. Rosa Newmarch, (1972) *The Russian Opera* (Westport, Conn: Greenwood Press, 1972).

6. Michael Hughes, 'Searching for the Soul of Russia: British Perceptions of Russia during the First World War', *20th Century British History*, 20/2 (2009), 198-226.

7. Otto Kling, 'A Voyage to Russia in War Time', *The Chesterian*, November 1915.

8. *The Chesterian* was published from 1915-1961 by J & W Chester, an English firm of music publishers founded in Brighton in 1874, transferred to London in 1915, specialising in Russian and contemporary foreign composers.

9. Rosa Newmarch, *Sibelius: A Short Story of a Long Friendship* (London: Goodwin & Tabb, 1944), p.37.

10. Eric Tawaststjerna, *Sibelius, 1914-1957* trans. Robert Layton (London: Faber and Faber, 2008), vol. 3, p.59.

11. The name of Don Quixote's horse.

CHAPTER 20: RUSSIA: FROM GREATER COMPREHENSION TO GREATER APPREHENSION, 1914-1918

During the First World War, there was inevitably a sharpening of public attitudes towards those countries that became allies of the British, and those that became enemies. Several events were organised to promote a better understanding of the Russian nation and conversely there was a reluctance to show any sympathy for Germany and its culture. Furthering a better understanding of the Russian nation was pursued on a number of levels that included writers, such as Stephen Graham* and J.W. Mackail*, musicians, politicians and religious leaders, and has been described in detail by Michael Hughes[1]. When Rosa returned from Russia, with her sympathies for the Russian people more heightened than ever, she was anxious to promote a better understanding of Russia to the public at large. This she did by her lectures and writings. *The Times* published regularly and *gratis* an extensive Russian Supplement or Russian Section[2]. In one such issue on 25 March 1916, the supplement included an article by Rosa entitled 'Russian Soldier Songs: Chants and Regimental Ditties'. In it she described the character of a number of Russian marching songs and translated a number of them. She suggested that some of the marching tunes might be commended 'to our own Tommies' but at the same time recognised the difficulty of the adaptation of suitable words. Nevertheless, she ended the article, which was also reproduced in *The Chesterian* in May 1916, suggesting 'An interchange of tunes would be distinctly to the advantage of our Army, and this, I hope may be effected by the twopenny booklet of "Russian Songs for British Soldiers" published by Messrs J. & W. Chester.' At the bottom of the article there is an advert: *NOW READY* Russian Songs for British Soldiers, English words by Rosa Newmarch. Price 2d. net.

In the spring of 1916, she gave lectures at Camberley, at Roedean School, and to the Irish Literary Society. It was probably on her visit to Roedean School that she met the headmistress Miss Annie T. Weston and discussed jointly producing books of graded musical exercises based on Russian music, which were published by J & W. Chester in 1917[3].

In another article written to endear the Russian people to the British public, Rosa explained the positive effect that the Tsar's Prohibition Decree had had on the life of the nation. In the article, 'The Greatest Victory in the War', she compared the decree with that of the emancipation of the serfs: 'I say without hesitation that the emancipation of the serfs in 1861 was not a greater boon for Russia than the emancipation of the peasants from the tyranny of vodka in 1915[4].' Rosa fulfilled many requests to lecture not only on her own special subjects of Russian music and art, but also on many aspects of the country's life. She went from universities to colleges and schools, to the Y.M.C.A. and soldiers' camps, to clubs and Women's Institutes. She even addressed a Temperance Meeting on 'Prohibition in Russia' at the Free Trade Hall, Manchester on 19 October 1915. She found the prospect of speaking in that vast hall a little alarming, especially to a temperance gathering; but a friendly member gave her a few kindly words about the acoustics of the hall, and all went well. By this time, she had acquired a reputation as a speaker on Russian affairs, so it was perhaps not surprising that she was invited to a two-week meeting at Cambridge University, from 2 to 14 August 1916, devoted to the discussion of many aspects of Russian life – political, scientific, and the arts.

A number of Russian speakers were invited to the meeting and the text of their lectures was published the following year by Cambridge University Press as a book entitled *Russian Realities and Problems*, edited by J.D. Duff. The speakers included Professor P.N. Milyoukov, who spoke on 'The Representative System in Russia' and 'Balkan Politics', Petr Struve, Professor of Political Economy at Moscow University on 'Economic Prospects of the Russian Empire', Harold Williams on 'The Nationalities of Russia', Roman Dmowski on 'Poland, Old and New', and Professor Alexandr Lappo-Danilovsky on 'The Development of Science and Learning in Russia'. The inaugural address was by Lord Robert Cecil. Rosa's lecture was on 'Russian Iconography and Modern Painting', and the preparations for this fitted in well with what she had written in her book *The Russian Arts*, published in June of the same year. According to the *Cambridge News*, Rosa's lecture attracted a very large audience and 'was illuminated by many beautiful lantern slides showing the best of the paintings of the most famous Russian artists[5].' She also gave an informal talk on 'Russian Women'. She enjoyed her stay at Newham College, but what she enjoyed most was visiting King's College Chapel, where her friend Dr Mann played her own choice of Bach fugues for voluntaries.

Many events were organised with the aim of furthering mutual understanding and sympathy between Russia and England. Various musicians, with the support of J and W Chester Ltd, formed a Russian Music Committee; its aim was to encourage the performance of Russian music in the United Kingdom and likewise reciprocity in encouraging English music to be performed in Russia. The committee had a distinguished membership drawn from England and Russia. The Russian members included Cesar Cui, Glazunov, Rachmaninoff, Safonoff, Arteiboneheff from Belyayev publishers and Madame Novikoff*, and the English members were Granville Bantock, Sir Joseph Beecham, Dan Godfrey, Robin Legge, Dr Charles McLean, Sir Donald Mackenzie Wallace, Sir Henry Wood, and Rosa Newmarch. *The Times* correspondent, whilst lauding its aims, was somewhat sceptical about what it might achieve, given the difficulty of all its members ever meeting[6]. However, Granville Bantock, as a member of this committee, was largely responsible for organising the Russian Week held in the autumn of 1916 from 23 to 28 October in Birmingham. Shortly before the Russian Week, a chair in Russian had been established at the university. It was therefore opportune to organise such an event, to which Rosa was invited.

The Russian Week provided a feast of Russian culture in four sections: an exhibition of Russian Art and Handicraft, Lectures on Russia, Concerts of Russian music and Russian plays. C Nabokoff, Councillor of the Russian Embassy, opened the art exhibition. During the week, seven concerts were organised, mainly of chamber music performed by local musicians. The ambitious choice of music was selected from a wide range of Russian composers, including Borodin, Tchaikovsky, Cui, Balakirev, Rachmaninoff, Rimsky-Korsakov, Glinka, Arensky, Medtner, Prokofiev, Glazunov, Musorgsky, Rebikoff, Taneyev, Kalinnikof, Skryabin, Glière, and Gretchaninov. The Russian plays by Griboyedof (1795-1829), Tolstoy (1828-1910), Chekov (1860-1904), and Evreinov (b. 1879) were performed in English translations at the Birmingham Repertory Theatre. Experts in various aspects of Russia and its people gave the lectures. These included E.A. Brayley Hodgetts (1859-1932) of the London Chamber of Commerce on 'Russia after the War', Dr Hagberg Wright (1862-1940), one of the most distinguished librarians of the London Library, on 'The Social Life of Russia', Ayler Maude (1858-1938), who had lived in Russia and translated many works by Tolstoy, on 'The Literature of Russia', Alan Lethbridge, author of the book *The New Russia from the White Sea to the Siberian Stepps*, on 'The Romance of the Russian North', and Rosa Newmarch, who lectured on 'The Art of Russia'. The distinguished physicist and first principal of the University of Birmingham, Sir Oliver Lodge (1851-1940), gave readings from Russian authors. Rosa particularly enjoyed the week, highlights of which were her conversations with C. Nabokoff, Councillor of the Russian Embassy, and Sir Oliver Lodge. To the latter she sent a copy of her *Poetry and Progress in Russia*, which he gratefully acknowledged.

From Birmingham, at the end of 1916, Rosa went to Bangor to give a lecture. She stayed with Sir Harry Reichel (1856-1931), the first principal of the University College of North Wales, and his sister. She had a few days respite there and was shown around by a young history professor. She found Bangor a delightful place: 'the sunset, and then the moonlight on the Menai Straits, the lighthouses, the snow on the distant mountains – it was all enchanting.'

1917 was to be another busy year for Rosa. A Russian Exhibition, in aid of the Anglo-Russian Hospital, was organised by the Russian Society to take place at the Grafton Galleries, Bond St, London[7]. The Russian Society was formed in 1916 to further better knowledge of the language and of Russian history and culture. Its inaugural AGM was held in March 1916. Meetings were generally held in the House of Commons, and the committee, including Stephen Graham*, Sir Samuel Hoare, Brayley Hodgetts, Mme Olga Novikoff* and Dr Hagberg Wright, all having strong connections with Russia, was chaired by James Lowther, M.P., speaker of the House of Commons. The society organised Russian language classes in London, Manchester, Glasgow, and South Wales and was also able to supply the government at short notice with interpreters for the army. Rosa was invited to serve on the committee of the Russian Society but declined because she felt that by having a musical branch of the Russian Society it was treading on the toes of her Russian Music Committee, as she spelt out in a letter to Dr Hagberg Wright dated 26 March 1916: 'I am less likely than ever to go on upon the Committee of the Russian Society seeing that it is obviously making an effort to cut the ground from under the feet of my committee. But as I feel I shall probably have to thrash the matter out on the grounds of the R.M.C [Russian Music Committee] which, with its strong committee and fine list of musical members both English and Russian, I am not inclined to hand over to the Russian Society, I think it is best for me to repudiate this suggestion.' [It was incorrectly reported in the *Morning Post* on 25 March 1916 that Rosa was a member of the Russian Society's committee.]

The exhibition was held from the beginning of April until the end of May, under the patronage of the King and Queen and Queen Alexandra. It was organised by Lady Muriel Paget* with a committee of expert advisors. There were several sections illustrating phases of Russia's intellectual and cultural life, and opportunities for commercial development between the two countries were not overlooked. Baron Heyking, the Russian Consulate General, was in charge of the commercial information bureau. Rosa and Dr Hagberg Wright of the London Library were in charge of the sections on literature and education. There were also collections of costumes and peasant industries, icons and church vestments, and stands devoted to pictorial and decorative art; whilst on the floor below, music was performed under the direction of Sir Thomas Beecham.

From Rosa's account to her sister Tiny, it appears that the organising committee worked together for a period of about six weeks, which was quite arduous. Early in

1917, before the start of the exhibition, Rosa visited Mrs Birkbeck at her home in order to go through her husband's collection of icons and make a selection for the forthcoming exhibition. She wrote:

> I have been spending a few days with Mrs Birkbeck widow of W G Birkbeck* who worked so hard for the union of the Russian and Anglican churches. [...] Mrs Birkbeck was a Gurney and lives near Norwich and singularly enough she is a tremendous High Church woman. We got on pretty well, having Russia and the Orthodox Church as medium. She is a particularly well-bred woman, rather a terror to her neighbours, I believe, because of a lingering streak of Quakerish reserve. Some day, if time ever permits, I hope to catalogue her husband's library! Next week [16 to 20 April 1917] I go for a few days to the Colmans (they are of mustard fame) –the bosom of nonconformity! This rather shocks Mrs Birkbeck, and her parting injunction to me was: 'I hope you will make them good church-women!' At Mrs Birkbeck's I deciphered about 30 ancient Slavonic inscriptions. But at the Colmans' I mean to rest.

A brief account of the exhibition, which opened on 24 April, was reported in the *British Journal of Nursing*[8].

> The Russian Exhibition held during the past week at the Grafton Gallery, in aid of the Anglo Russian Hospital, was a very interesting one: and there were many and beautiful exhibits. The surgical appliance section had to fall back on the dressings that were destined for the Russian Hospitals, as those that were on their way to the Exhibition from Russia went to the bottom of the sea with a torpedoed vessel. There was a large collection of sacred icons, many of which had an historical as well as artistic value. Embroidery, silver, lovely enamel jewelry, and priests' vestments were among the exhibits. There was a large case of dolls dressed in the costumes of Russians of various ranks, amongst which was a domestic nurse holding a baby. The nurse wore a costume of a beautiful and most becoming rose colour and held the baby, which was done up in a sort of satin and lace parcel. A most interesting collection of war photographs hung around the room where tea served Russian fashion in glasses with sliced lemon, was distributed by ladies in the costume of the country. Those who wore the heavily ornamented coifs with strings of pearls and long gauze veils represented princesses in Court dress. The young girls wore costumes of pale blue with caps of the same colour ornamented with swans down and silver tassels. At intervals in the theatre there were examples given of Russian dances.

Rosa described how she felt in the run-up to the exhibition in a letter to her sister Tiny:

This blessed Russian Exhibition is going to be very hard work. The musical people have fallen out already! I am afraid I shall have a tiresome and thankless task there; but the book and art sections will work well and smoothly. We have good people on them. When we have had our first general committee meeting on Wednesday I shall get a better idea of how tied I am going to be. Six weeks is really not time enough for all there is to do. [...] Lady Muriel Paget who is very nice herself and easy to work with, has been away for a month's rest. I really want a spring tailor made, but I was so dreadfully disappointed with the rough commonplace grey suit Summers made me last year that I don't feel much like going to them for something good. I shall have to be so much en evidence at the Grafton Galleries, I want something useful, yet a little smart. All my blouses happen to be green, so I must have one or two black or black and white things for spring.

After the exhibition was over, Rosa wrote letters to both Tiny and sister-in-law Emily, explaining how she felt it went:

I am getting dreadfully into arrears with my letter writing, but this exhibition takes so much of my time and energy! [...] However it has pleasant moments. I sometimes meet people I haven't seen for years. Then killing things happen, as when a lady stood in ecstasies before the cash registering machine and said: "How Russian!" Then seeing a life of Tolstoy standing on top of it, she added "it must be Tolstoy's typing machine!"

One of the more interesting features of the Exhibition was the duty of showing people round. It fell to my lot to attend on Queen Alexandra (she apparently heard all I said for she never called in anyone to interpret), the Speaker (very dull), Lord Carnock, previously our Ambassador at Petrograd, and many others, including lots of Russian soldiers. But Smuts [Jan Smuts, 1870-1950, South African leader and philosopher] interested me more than anyone else. He made a fine speech. He is not a typical Boer, but every inch a soldier and leader. When I said to him that as regards Russia, I could only describe myself as "a reactionary democrat" he gave me a piercing glance, grasped my hand and said: "then may I say, Good luck go with you and your work". I hear he has many enemies among the baser kind of radicals.

Three months before the exhibition, Tsar Nicholas II abdicated following the Russian Revolution in February 1917. He and his family were imprisoned in various locations, finally at the Ipatiev House in Yekaterinburg. A year after the exhibition came the tragic report of the assassination of the whole family on the night of 16/17 July 1918. Rosa described how the truth of this was at first thought almost unbelievable. But when a few days later the sad news was confirmed, a memorial service was held in the Russian Orthodox Chapel in Welbeck Street. The service was attended by King George and Queen Mary. Rosa said afterwards that when King George, probably in Russian uniform, passed down the aisle of the little chapel, it was almost impossible to believe that it was not the Tsar himself. It was with a shock that Rosa recalled the incredulous fact that they were all there to mourn the death of Tsar Nicholas II. All were deeply moved by the fine liturgy sung most beautifully by the deep-toned voices of the priests and unaccompanied choir.

After the busy time of the Russian Exhibition, Rosa was looking forward to the summer holidays with the family at Highcliffe-on-sea, Dorset, but her various comments in letters to the family show that finances appeared to be tight. To Tiny she wrote:

I am having some correspondence with Miss Sayle about her little cottage at Highcliffe on Sea. She has a lot of people after it. For July she asks £2.12.6, for August £4.4.0 and £2.20 for the whole of September. Now the question is would £4.4.0, which does not include servant, be too much for us this year? I have written to ask her how many bedrooms. I fear only 3, which means that we could not all be there at once. It is quite a tiny house, but everything is now so expensive, and the place is certainly nice with its mixture of sea and country. It is rather long for you to wait till September. Send me a line by return with your views as to securing it for August. If we share 3 at a time it would I suppose work out at about £2.10 each a week including servant, food etc. She will not let it I think except by the month.

They did take the cottage for the month of July. Later in the same letter:

Elsie has just bought a wonderful gas oven with part of her war bonus. It is called the "Duck" stove and it seems to me we shall be able to cook our dinner in the drawing room if we are left servantless. Wonderfully neat and clean and attaches to any burner.

Rosa began her book *The Devout Russian* after her return from Russia in 1915, completing it in the early days of the revolution, and Herbert Jenkins published it in 1918. Its rather lengthy subtitle is 'A book of thoughts and counsels gathered from the Saints and Father of the Eastern Church and Modern Russian Authors'. It was aimed at helping the British public understand Russia and its people; in this case, focusing on spirituality. It comprises three sections. There is a long introduction in which Rosa outlined the history of the Russian Orthodox Church and listed the differences in dogma and practices between the Eastern and Western Churches. With the worrying news of the Russian Revolution, she wondered anxiously how it would affect religious practice. 'Writing at a moment when all the old landmarks of faith and custom are being thrown down with bewildering rapidity, when the whole country is dazed by an orgy of discussion, and "the soil of common life is too hot to tread upon," we may pause to ask ourselves whether such thoughts as are gathered together in this volume can ever have any meaning for Russia again.' The main body of the book is an anthology of Russian spiritual thought, including quotations from such writers as Philaret Metropolitan of Moscow, St Tikhon Zadonsky, Jacob Archbishop of Nijny-Novgorod, St Dmitri of Rostov, and some Eastern writers such as, St Chrysostom, St Basil the Great, St John Damascene, and others. Those included not only ecclesiastical figures, but also writers such as Dostoyevsky, Gogol, Pushkin, and Turgenev. The concluding third of the book contains brief biographies of the authors of these extracts. Much of the material she collected whilst in Russia, but she also had discussions with Archdeacon Wilberforce.

For many years, Rosa had been a regular member of the congregation of St John's Church, Westminster, where Archdeacon Basil Wilberforce* was rector. She found his sermons a source of strength, and all through these busy working years she turned continually to his published works for spiritual thought and guidance. While in Russia, she had written several letters to him concerning the religious aspects there, knowing that he too was attracted to the Greek Orthodox Church and its many common aspects with the Western Anglican churches. This exchange of letters may in part have been the stimulus to write *The Devout Russian*. From her first visit to Russia, the deep significance of the Russian Church to its people had been very evident to her; she felt that no history of the Russian people would be complete that did not give a full account of the Eastern Orthodox Church, its influence with the masses and their faith in it. So when she was in Russia in 1915, as well as the churches she visited several monasteries, including the Choudov in the Kremlin in Moscow and the Troitska-Serghievskaya, founded in early 1340 by St Sergius. Here she met the men who taught and supplied the demands of the reading folk and monks who, with lively and sympathetic interest, were most willing to help her in her quest for devotional literature.

Rosa received two short letters from Archdeacon Wilberforce in August 1915. In the first, he wrote: 'You write so admirably I think you would write a book – I hope you did not mind my quoting you in the pulpit! The Germans are getting heavily punished in the assault on Warsaw, but of course they will get it. Very sincerely, Basil Wilberforce.' In the second, he thanked her for sending her book and then went on to explain that he was having heart trouble and had been prescribed digitalis. It is not clear which book was sent but it predated the publication of *The Devout Russian*. Wilberforce preached what was his last sermon on 16 April 1916 and he died on 13 May1916 before her book was complete, but its dedication to him, to which he had agreed, remained and read:

> To one who now watches the Russians
> from the other side
> I dedicate this book in thought
> because it reflects
> The teaching of his "Angel"

When the book was published in 1918, Rosa sent copies to various ministers of the church, who might have a special interest in the subject and also to Basil Wilberforce's wife, Emily. William Temple (1881-1944), many years later to become Archbishop of Canterbury, replied thanking her, commenting that the quotations were interesting and beautiful. William Willcox Perrin, Bishop of Willesden, also wrote saying what a delightful book it was. Bishop Herbert Bury (1861-1933) wrote: 'How very kind of you to send me this book. I shall greatly value it, and particularly for the inscription. I do long to be a true friend to that great people for I believe that they will show themselves worthy of true friendship which does not think so much of what it has to get as of what it has to give. Things too, at last, are beginning to look full of promise of light after darkness. I don't know whether you ever get to my Church of St Peter's Vere Street – though I am to be away myself for the next three Sundays – but we always have some friends of Russia here, and intercessions for Russia at the early service. Believe me to be, sincerely yours Herbert Bury Bishop.'

Herbert Bury was Bishop of Northern and Central Europe during the First World War. He visited Russia and Central Asia and the POW camp at Ruhleben (ten kilometres from Berlin) working to improve conditions for British prisoners of war in Germany. He wrote a number of books as the result of these visits: *Russian Life*

Today (1915), *Russia from Within* (1927), *Here and now in the war area* (1916), and *My visit to Ruhleben* (1917).

Although for some years Rosa was a regular member at St John's Church, Westminster, she was not a believer in the conventional sense of the word. She explained to Sibelius that she felt 'we carry within us a part of that divine and indefinable life which we recognise everywhere and without which the whole world would be cold and barren[9].' Also, in both letters to her sister-in-law Emily in 1919[10], after her sister's death in a cycling accident, and to Aline O'Neill in 1934[9], after her husband's death, she alludes to her belief in an afterlife. She also expressed her admiration for agnosticism[9].

The Devout Russian was just one of a number of writing projects that Rosa was working on during the war years. When in 1913 and 1914 the Russian Opera Company came to London to perform Russian operas, the excitement was comparable to the first appearance of Wagner's *Ring*, especially with the appearance of Shaliapin. Four years later, in June 1917, *Boris Godunov* was first performed in English using Rosa's translation of the libretto with some adaptations by Paul England[11]. Then in the autumn of 1917, Rosa was back in Birmingham for the Birmingham Festival Choral Society. On 22 November, there was a first performance in England of *Requiem for the Fallen Heroes of the Allied Armies* by a composer little known today, Alexander Dmitrievich Kastalsky (1856-1926), and Rosa had been called upon to write the detailed programme notes. In September, she was correcting proofs of the book *The Fall of the Romanofs* by the author of *Russian Court Memoirs* (believed to be the Polish princess Catherine Radziwill, 1858-1941) and reporting on a book by Petr Dolgorukov, probably with a view to translating it into English, both for Herbert Jenkins.

40. Rosa's sister Tiny (left) and sister-in-law Emily (right)

In spite of having many different commitments, Rosa generally found time to write letters to friends and family at fairly regular intervals, both when she was at home and also on her travels abroad. Apart from her son, and daughter, the most regular recipients were her youngest sister, Tiny (Caroline Georgina), and her oldest sister-in-law, Emily Newmarch. Emily was the oldest in a family of eight girls and two boys, and she lived to the age of ninety-three (1842-1935). The letters Rosa wrote during the war years, apart from describing her various Russian-related activities, also touched on a number of family matters. One of her concerns was her older sister Sophie, now in her early seventies and in poor health. She lived in a house alone but had a nurse sleep in, as a temporary arrangement. Bella was also now in poor health, suffering from sciatica and only able to go out in fine weather. Elsie's work in the hospital meant that she was away much of the day and thus not at hand. As Rosa puts it: 'I have no doubt that it is better and healthier for Elsie to lead her own life, but it does leave me with a tremendous amount to do single handed. I have not even a messenger in these days, but have to see to taking all my letters and parcels to the post etc. Bella is not able to do much – at any rate in bad weather it is less risky for me to go out than for her.'

Her husband was in a volunteer regiment and she refers to him out drilling and visiting a camp in York: 'H. away in York this week. He looks very smart in his new Khaki, and I presented him with a fine regulation overcoat for guard duty.'

Their son, John, joined the Royal Navy shortly after the outbreak of war. Apart from the obvious dangers of war that anyone in the services faced, she was concerned that his skills were being wasted as he was doing 'mere routine service work and losing opportunities.' When writing to Emily, Rosa gave John's address for mail as 'Temporary-Surgeon John Newmarch, R.N., H.M.S. "Sapphire" c/o G.P.O.' In May 1915, *H.M.S. Sapphire* was sent to Brindisi under the terms of the agreement that brought the Italians into the war, remaining there into 1916. That year she was transferred to the East Indies station, remaining there until the end of the war. Rosa explained: 'John writes fairly often. He goes backwards and forwards between Brindisi and Malta [...] He says the heat is rather terrific, but the bathing heavenly. The ship is rather a crock and behaves wildly on the smallest provocation; but I fancy he has got used to that now. He has a fairly good cabin, but I fear no professional work. Such a waste of a specialist!' His frustration with his duties is explained further in another letter: 'I am rather sorry for John. He is certainly wasted where he is, doing mere routine service work and rusting as regards the scientific side of things. Also he is losing many fine opportunities here. His friend and patron Sir Frederick Hewitt* is obliged to retire, and I had always felt that would be a very important moment in John's career. He says one cannot imagine a more mechanical existence than that of a service doctor, and the worst crime one can commit is to show zeal or do a trifle more than anyone else!' Rosa reported on the various air raids they experienced, including one on her birthday, 18 December, but this did not appear to provoke her alarm, but rather heightened her fury with the Germans.

The war inevitably caused general public suspicion of all of those of German origin. Since 1902, the promotion of the Promenade Concerts had been by the Queen's Hall Orchestra Ltd, financed by Sir Edgar Speyer. He was born in New York, although of German extraction. According to his brother Edward Speyer, Sir Edgar had spent £4000 on the concerts each year. With the onset of the war, he was attacked by the newspapers and eventually he wrote to the Prime Minister, Herbert Asquith, offering to resign his baronetcy and privy councillorship. Although not accepted, Speyer was sensitive to public feeling, especially as he did range himself on the German side in contrast, for example, to Otto Kling. Speyer and his family left for America, and the publishing firm of Chappell took over the Queen's Hall leasehold.

The opening night of the promenade concerts in 1914 was on the 15 August, eleven days after Britain's declaration of war. Richard Strauss had been dropped from the opening night, and Monday nights had previously become traditional Wagner nights, but on the 17 August, this was replaced by a selection of French, Russian, and British music. However, after what might be described as an initial 'wobble', the normal diet of programming resumed, and Robert Newman, the manager, put out a statement: 'With regard to the future, the Directors hope – with the broadminded co-operation of their audience – to carry through as nearly as possible the original scheme of the Concerts as set out in their Prospectus.'

In 1931, William Boosey, chairman of Chappell & Co, published a book, *Fifty Years of Music*, and this was reviewed in the *Monthly Musical Record*. The reviewer commented, with surprise, at the account of the termination of Sir Edgar's tenancy of Queen's Hall. The paragraph ran:

Messrs Chappell and Co. were very soon awake to the fact that, in spite of the war, Sir Edgar Speyer's programmes were aggressively German – in fact, contained nothing but German music. Messrs. Chappell came to the conclusion that under war conditions such a position could not be tolerated. They therefore gave Sir Edgar notice that his tenancy must be terminated.

The editor of the *Monthly Music Record*, Richard Capell, felt there must be a misrepresentation of the facts, and so he asked Rosa, whom he felt would be able to set the record straight. Rosa made a very full reply of the events as she recalled them:

I am not surprised that in your review of William Boosey's *Fifty Years of Music* you call attention to the author's statement that 'in spite of the war, Sir Edgar Speyer's programmes were aggressively German – in fact *nothing but German music* (the italics are mine). This allegation is an unnecessary blot on the pages of a book which has otherwise all the qualities of bonhomie, racy humour, and inside knowledge of the musical world, combined with a charm of personal touch, such as one would expect in a book by Mr Boosey. Messrs. Chappell's action in taking over the Queen's Hall concerts at a very risky crisis in their history was, no doubt, dictated to a great extent by patriot feeling. This, I believe, was understood and appreciated in 1915, so now there is no need for the gibe about German music.

With regard to the Promenade Concerts in 1914: War was declared on August 4 and on the first Monday of the season [Aug. 17] for only one time in the history of these concerts the usual Wagner concert did not take place. By the following Monday the temper of the public and of the leases of the hall having been gauged, the Wagner nights were resumed and continued as before. They were always largely patronized by 'Khaki'. One possibly controversial item was omitted from the Wagnerian repertory – I believe, at my suggestion. Sir Edgar Speyer thought this move illogical; but after hearing my point of view he accepted it.

The absurdity and impossibility of cutting out the great classics – Bach, Beethoven, Brahms and others – was acknowledged from the beginning. Where else could material have been found from which to make up a series of sixty-one programmes? But in the scheme for 1914 there will be found side by side with these 'German' geniuses the names of Elgar, Bantock, Vaughan Williams, Rutland Boughton, Walford Davies, Goossens and O'Neill. Continental music was represented by César Franck, Bruneau, Saint-Saëns, Debussy, Dukas and Ravel, Dvořák, Sibelius, Mussorgsky, and all the Russian school. The only reproach possible against this policy was with regard to the retention in the programme of two or three works by Richard Strauss. I cannot remember who was responsible for the plentiful sprinkling of National Anthems in the scheme of 1914. Musically speaking, they were not always calculated to draw the Allies together in bonds of fraternal affection. The same policy was followed in the Symphony Concerts of that year.

Pass on to 1915, when Messrs Chappell had taken over the orchestra and the services of Sir Henry Wood as conductor. Do we find a radical change in the style of the programmes? Not at all. The name of Richard Strauss was dropped for a time, but the world classics, German or otherwise, kept their places in the Promenade and Symphony Concerts; Wagner and Beethoven still filled the hall on their accustomed nights. And here let me pay Mr Boosey the highest compliment as guardian of the public taste; he, a sincere and enthusiastic admirer of light music and of the ballad, had the wisdom and tolerance to let the public have what it wanted in the way of music. If Sir Edgar Speyer's programmes were *not* entirely given over to German music, neither were Mr William Boosey's concerts wholly run in the interests of British composers.

At the present moment when so many of our professional musicians appear to have eaten the 'insane root' and are babbling about the exclusion of foreigners, and against imported music as though it were tallow, jute or sugar, a comparison between these two men who ruled the destinies of the Queen's Hall Concerts in turn, affords an interesting lesson. Sir Edgar Speyer, a cultivated dilettante, stood for the widest international policy; Mr Boosey, the astute man of business and the champion of light opera and the English ballad, looked at music from a totally different standpoint. Yet both had to accept the fact that we are a level-headed, fair-minded and, on the whole, friendly folk, and both had to sacrifice some personal predilections for the sake of the public taste. We shall not easily become disloyal to English music, but our public will not submit for long to have its face dipped in the stagnant waters of chauvinism. Have we not reason to be grateful to both Sir Edgar Speyer and Mr Boosey?

Rosa Newmarch Jan 12, 1932

Understandably, Rosa's attitude to German culture was very different from her attitude to German businesses in Britain and the German military. In a letter to her sister Tiny in 1915, after discussing air raids she continues: 'To think after all these months that we have not yet built up enough aeroplanes to retaliate! It is a dreadful business and to think that England once so safe has let herself be duped by these pigs.' And in an earlier letter to Tiny: 'I wish they would confiscate all German property in England. Our government is a disgrace in its supine attitude to them over here.'

Nevertheless, Rosa was a loyal supporter of Sir Edgar Speyer. Speyer was a naturalised British subject, but in 1921 his naturalisation was revoked, as was that of his family, and he was taken off the list of privy councillors in 1921. He strenuously denied being disloyal to Britain and felt he was being politically persecuted. He lived the rest of his life in America and died in 1932. Rosa sent a message of sympathy to his widow, Leonora Speyer, and received the following reply: 'I greatly appreciate your kind message and the warm and friendly sympathy of the thought in sending it to me. It brought so many happy memories to mind, and revived the old friendship between you and my beloved husband and me. I shall always treasure it and hope that some day I shall have the real pleasure of seeing you again. My husband was so loved – letters and telegrams pour in – all who knew him honoured and understood his fineness and his goodness. I who knew him best, the most. In the midst of my loneliness and desolation I am lifted to great heights by the thought of the thirty years happiness I have known in his love. Thanking you again, I am, dear Mrs Newmarch, always sincerely your friend, Leonora Speyer.'

To the great relief of the nation, the Armistice was signed on 11 November, 1918, and on the following day, Rosa attended the great Thanksgiving Service held in St Paul's Cathedral. But though there was much rejoicing that the war was at an end, the future of Russia was still an unsolved problem. One of her last lectures in the cause was given at King's College, London University, in the following week on 18 November. She had been invited to lecture on Russian music by the School of Slavonic Languages. With her strong views on music as a living force – a link between nations – she suggested that music should play its part in the League of Nations: 'The world needed healing and it would be a pity if we neglected the finest healing power in the world, in the reconstruction work before us. Music was the tongue of emotions, and the feelings rather than the intellects of other nations should be understood. Russian Literature and Art reveal deep feeling and a great national soul; a nation with soul and capacity for deep feeling could surely not go under.'

After the revolution in Russia and during the early post-war years, members of the Anglo-Russian movement for greater reciprocity were puzzled by news of events there and for a time uncertain of the policy to follow. The School of Slavonic and East European Studies at the University of London began life as the School of Slavonic Studies, Kings' College in 1915 under the guidance of Sir Bernard Pares*. In 1932, the school became a self-governing department of the University of London. Rosa wrote to Sir Bernard Pares in 1919 about the suggested policy of the Anglo-Russian movement. He replied saying in effect that the situation in Russia was somewhat fluid, that the policy of the movement would have to take into account the 'present disastrous position', then adding 'I particularly hope we shall be able to have your cooperation in the School of Slavonic Studies. At present we are still at the organising stage, but as soon as we get to publication it will be essential to us to have such help as yours if you can give it. The more things go wrong the more I am convinced that we shall find the right, though the hardest, solution to our difficulties in building up a voluntary association of English people knowing, and willing to work for Russia.'

Rosa was clearly despondent about all changes brought about by the Russian Revolution and was pleased to be able to write about the visit of Nicholas Roerich (1874-1947) to London in 1920. Roerich was a well-known Russian painter and writer, a friend of Stasov, and married to Musorgsky's niece. Thomas Beecham had invited him to undertake the designs for a performance of *Prince Igor* staged in 1918 and so his work was known in England. After suffering pneumonia, he convalesced in Finland at the outset of the revolution and realised it would be unsafe for him to return to Russia. He was invited to exhibit in Stockholm and then in London. In an article entitled 'Roerich's Art' for the magazine *The Quest* (April 1920), Rosa wrote: 'We are indeed the gainers by his exile for I venture to predict that his forthcoming Exhibition at the Goupil Galleries (London) will prove a revelation of a new and strangely beautiful art. Moreover it will help to keep before us that aspect of the Russian soul which we are in danger of forgetting at the present time. Since Roerich is, above all, the interpreter of ancient spiritual traditions and lingering memories from the myths of Northern Russia; since he is the painter of the many-coloured land – of what service could he have been to that government of astute fools who have said in their heart; "There is no God". Therefore no vision; no Divine Mind, therefore no ordered activity; only the fevered and confused machinations of the Dictatorship of the Proletariat. Such a regime would have no profitable use for Roerich.' She went on to speak of Roerich's art as interpreted by Leonid Andreiev, whose last literary effort was made on behalf of his friend. The writer died shortly afterwards from heart disease aggravated by grief at the condition of his country. The close spiritual kinship between the painter and the writer, in her view, gave an intimate penetrative value to Andreiev's analysis of Roerich's work.

By the time of this exhibition, Rosa probably realised that she was unlikely to be able to visit Russia again, but there were new challenges on the horizon.

Notes

1. Michael Hughes, 'Searching for the Soul of Russia: British Perceptions of Russia during the First World War', *Twentieth Century British History*, 20, (2009): pp.198-226.

2. James Muckle, 'Russian in the University Curriculum: A Case-study of the Impact of the First World War on Language Study in Higher Education in Britain', *History of Education* (2006), pp.1-22.

3. Anne Weston and Rosa Newmarch, *Introduction to the study of Russian Music, Educational Series of Russian Music in Six Progressive Books*, 6 vols. (London: J & W Chester, 1917).

4. Rosa Newmarch, 'The Greatest Victory in the War', *Mothers in Council*, Oct. (1916), pp216-221.

5. 'Russian Art. Mrs Newmarch on Iconography and Modern Painting', *Cambridge Daily News* 8 Aug., 1916.

6. 'A Guide to Russian Music: New Committee's Work', *The Times*, 5 Feb. (1916).

7. Announcement in *Lady's Pictorial*, 6 Jan. 1917, p.5.

8. *British Journal of Nursing*, 12 May (1917), p.325.

9. See Philip Bullock, *Rosa Newmarch and Russian Music in Late Nineteenth and Early Twentieth-Century England* (Farnham, Surrey: Ashgate Publishing, 2009), p.92 for further discussion and references.

10. See Chapter 22 for Rosa's letter after the death of her sister-in-law Alice.

11. 'Boris Godounow: Its Performance', *The Times*, 2 June (1917).

CHAPTER 21: CZECHOSLOVAKIA BECKONS

Rosa's interest in the Slav nations widened as a result of chance meetings. While on a few days visit to her sister in Leamington, she met two Serbian men, who had somehow arrived in England. On their behalf she visited the Serbian legation, where she had already been in touch with the Serbian Red Cross. Always keen to learn a new language, she arranged for a young Serbian soldier to give her lessons. She described this in a letter to Tiny: 'I am waiting for my Serbian to come and give me a lesson. If I am going to work for the Serbian Red Cross it will be very useful to know it better. I have a young man on hand now who has fought for 6 years on end, since the first Balkan war. He had first appeared in opera at Belgrade, and now he has left off further service in order to take up his musical studies here in England. He has a pretty tenor voice, but is still suffering from the shivers and aches of malaria.' With his help, Rosa translated an album of Yugoslav popular songs, collected from Bosnian, Herzgovinian, and Serbian groups, by C. P. Manojlovic, which was published in 1920[1].

Another chance meeting in 1917, again in Leamington, began her interest in Czechoslovakia. On a journey from Leamington, a train full of troops drew up alongside her train – not an unusual sight during the war years, but she noticed they were dressed in an assortment of strange uniforms and apparently talking excitedly in a Slavonic language. She spoke to them from her window in Russian, and they told her they had come from Russia and Siberia and were on their way to France but asked where they were. However, before they could exchange further explanations, the train moved off, and she was left with the meagre knowledge that they were Slavs who had fled the Austro-Hungarian armies, escaped into Russia earlier in the war and there formed the Jan Hus regiment. At the time, she knew little of the aspirations of Czechs and Slovaks for independence from the Austro-Hungarian Empire, but as her interest was sufficiently roused, she got in touch with the small committee already working in London under Thomas Masaryk's guidance. Thomas Masaryk* was a member of the Realist party in the Austro-Hungarian parliament, an advocate for Czechoslovak independence, and as such had to flee the country. From London, he strove for support for Czechoslovak independence. With the help of this committee and a few British sympathisers, including Dr G. Hagberg Wright, librarian of the London Library, they were able to welcome these exiled allies who were awaiting transfer to France, where they were to be re-equipped and would serve with the French army. The Czechoslovak National Council had already been established, with its headquarters in Paris led by Dr Eduard Beneš.

Some weeks later, while staying in Winchester, where these exiles were in camp with other foreign troops, Rosa met a contingent coming down the high street to the cathedral, headed by a banner of Jan Hus – a black banner with the red chalice in the centre – and singing *Kde domov můj?* ("Where Is My Homeland?"), a song later to be adopted as the Czechoslovak National Anthem. It was a Sunday morning and these men, visibly moved at the sight of the historic cathedral, decided to attend the service. The great west doors were opened to receive them, and reverently they entered, filling more than half the nave. The banner of Jan Hus and the red and white flag of a free Bohemia were carried in with them and rested for a while near the chantry. At the close of the service, the men rose and sang with great fervour as they left the cathedral. Many of them may have been members of famous choral societies, for their tone was warm and round, the ensemble precise, the feeling touching without being exaggerated. Rosa found it a moving experience, especially when they sang the venerable Hussite War Hymn *Kdož jsú Boží bojovníci* ("Ye Warriors of God").

This chance meeting brought back memories of days spent with her friend William Morfill in his library at Oxford, when he took down from his shelves the works of Jan Kollar*, of the Abbé Josef Dobrovsky*, and of František Palacký*, as frequently as he might those of Pushkin. It awoke again the echoes of a fresh and delightful folk music, and Rosa returned to London, determined to find out more about the Czechs and Slovaks and their culture. These contingents soon left the country to join other forces in France, but she remained in touch with Vladimir Nosek, representative of the National Council in London. From him it was possible to learn much more of the history and aspirations of the Czechs, Moravians, and Slovaks, and Rosa was drawn to further study of their folk music and national composers.

However, not only was she keen to learn more about the music of Czechoslovakia, but she was also anxious to maintain her friendship with Sibelius, with whom she had not been in contact since her return from visiting Russia and Finland in 1915. She wrote to him on New Year's eve 1918 assuring him that her friendship had remained wholly undiminished during the hostilities that had engulfed their countries: 'Until recently there seemed little point and possibly some element of risk in making contact with you. I have no idea how much you have suffered during these terrible events' […] The Promenade concerts and symphony concerts under Sir Henry Wood had continued in spite of German air attacks and power cuts and, according to Rosa, Wagner's music exercised a specially magnetic effect on Zeppelins and aeroplanes. Sir Thomas Beecham's surmise about the Zeppelins was somewhat different, saying that the Zeppelins will drive people into the Albert Hall not only as a musical resort but also as a shelter from the bombs[2]! Rosa's letter to Sibelius continued: 'Now it seems to me that we have an insatiable thirst for music. I want to see you here as soon as it is possible for you to undertake the journey. You know, when all is weighed in the balance, we English have our good qualities, and we are always prepared to give old friends a warm reception[3].' Sibelius replied saying how pleased he was to hear from her, that he was glad her family had not suffered during the war, that his family were well, and that he had been composing several works including a symphony although he had not been able to publish anything[4].

Rosa commented that this was the only letter Sibelius ever wrote to her in English, and the English was so fluent that she suspected his wife, Aino, must have helped him. It was only later that she learnt something of the family's suffering during the early months of the revolution and of Sibelius's narrow escape from being shot by the disaffected Russian soldery[4].

Soon after the declaration of peace, it was decided to hold a Czechoslovak musical festival in London to commemorate the foundation of the Republic of Czechoslovakia. Dr Stephan Osuský* was already established as minister at the legation here, and with his help, Rosa was doing useful 'propaganda' work for their music in this country. Whatever trials the Czechoslovaks had been through in their country during the war, they had managed to keep their musical life alive, and were able to send over the excellent orchestra of the National Opera House in Prague with conductor Karel Kovařovic and the famous male voice choirs – the Prague Choral Society of Teachers with their conductor Professor Franz Spilka and the Moravian Choral Society of Teachers, the well-known artists, including the soprano Emmy Destinn*, the violinist and composer Jaroslav Kocián*, and the Bohemian Quartet – over 200 artists in all. The festival, held at Queen's Hall and Wigmore Hall, ran from 26 May to 4 June 1919. It opened with an informal afternoon at Æolian Hall on 25 May, and as an old friend of the Slavs, Rosa was asked to say a few opening words of greeting and explanation. She also wrote the programme notes for the concerts. In all there were five concerts in the period of ten days. They included works by Dvořák and Smetana, opening with Smetana's symphonic poem Šarka, followed by Vltava. Ostrčil's *Christmas Legend* with words by the poet Jaroslav Vrchlichy was included, and Jaroslav Kocián played Dvořák's violin concerto. Madame Destinová sang "Vendulka's Lullaby" from Smetana's opera *The Kiss* and an aria from Dvořák's *Rusalka*. The last concert was sold out, and the choirs sang farewell at Victoria Station. Rosa judged the whole visit a great success[5].

Rosa described this festival as the most thrilling choral experience in London since the visit of the Finnish Suomen Laula choir in 1913. The members of the two Czech choirs were all drawn from one group of the population – the teachers in the state schools of Bohemia were men determined to keep alive the language and literature of their race and to carry the folk music far beyond the boundaries of their native land. Their unflagging physical and mental energy was astonishing, for when in London, after a full morning's sightseeing and a strenuous Queen's Hall Concert, they returned to their hotel and volunteered to sing a whole repertory of songs for Rosa's benefit.

At the close of the festival, Rosa was invited to visit the new Republic, and she and Elsie travelled back with some of the musicians. Prague was hardly ready to receive visitors, and only a few of the advance guard of Bohemia's sympathisers and well-wishers were invited to take this early opportunity of visiting the capital. She already knew something of the early history of Bohemia, a subject she had often discussed with Professor Morfill, before either of them had contemplated Czechoslovak independence.

Notes

1. C.P. Manojlovitch, *Jugoslovenske narodne pesme* (Jugoslav popular songs) trans. Rosa Newmarch, (1920).

2. Charles Reid, *Thomas Beecham: An Independent Biography* (London: Gollancz, 1961), pp. 157-8.

3. . Eric Tawaststjerna, *Sibelius, 1914-1957* trans. Robert Layton (London: Faber and Faber, 2008), vol. 3, pp. 143-4.

4. Rosa Newmarch, *Jean Sibelius: A Short Story of a Long Friendship* (London: Goodwin and Tabb, 1944), p.39.

5. Rosa Newmarch, (1919) 'The Czechoslovak Music Festival', *Musical Times* 60 (1919), 1 Jul., pp.334-6.

CHAPTER 22: ELSIE NEWMARCH'S ACCOUNT OF THE VISITS TO CZECHOSLOVAKIA IN 1919 AND 1920

Elsie Newmarch was Rosa's travelling companion throughout her visit to Czechoslovakia in July 1919 and gave her account of the visit.

We journeyed from Paris to Prague in brilliant June sunshine. Except for the presence of a few French officers, active middle-aged and much decorated veterans, going to join the Czechoslovak army which was still defending the frontier from Hungarian Bolsheviks, nothing between Paris and Buchs reminded us of the titanic struggle of the last five years. We must have passed through some war stricken areas during the night, and at Buchs, on the Swiss-Austrian border, we entered Austrian territory. Children waved to the train with sweet impartiality, but we were conscious of a certain atmosphere of repressed unfriendliness. At Innsbruck the Italian Carabinieri, armed and beplumed, lounging in pairs up and down the platform, brought home to us for the first time some of the territorial changes wrought by the War. Once across the Czechoslovak border a smiling country and warm welcome greeted us everywhere. The breezy open uplands seemed wonderfully well cultivated considering how long all the work had been carried out by women, children and a few aged men. The peasant women were busy in the hay fields, looking like patches of field flowers in their blue and red cotton skirts, kilted over striped petticoats, with white or red kerchiefs on their heads. Doubtless a nearer view would have disclosed little but picturesque rags, for even the commonest dress materials were scarcely to be purchased at that time, and only at ruinous prices. On the hill slopes rustled a healthy, upstanding but light harvest. Besides the absence of male labourers in the field, the shortage of horses and livestock made a painful impression. The work was being done almost entirely by poor little pairs of oxen, or even by the last surviving weary little cows that were left over from the former fine dairy herds. Less land in pasturage and more in corn, added to the ruthless requisitions of Germany during the war, had caused a milk famine in Bohemia. Generally speaking there was a great shortage of foodstuffs, for, until later in the year, the rural districts had not much to offer to the towns. A friend told us that during the winter every balcony and backyard in Prague was turned into a miniature farmyard – a goose in a cage outside the sitting room window of a fourth-floor flat was no unusual sight. The geese, resenting their restricted quarters, thrust forth their heads and hissed long enough to save a hundred Capitols.

The people of Czechoslovakia were touchingly grateful for the presence of English folk among them in the critical moment of their liberation. They could not do enough for us, and materially they had so little to spare. Cheery as the people were at the roadside stations where we got out to talk to them, the underlying exhaustion and poverty of the population soon became apparent. The children caused one a pang, for they were the chief sufferers. Anaemia, tuberculosis, defective sight and rickets – must these always be the aftermath of war for the young generation for whom no sacrifice has seemed too great.

In Prague, life has kept, at least externally, something of its old gaiety. 'Youth will be served' and demanded some of its former characteristic enjoyments. Late on a hot June afternoon one would have supposed Prague to be inhabited by a race of water sprites. Looking towards the old Karluv Bridge from the quayside, the shallow water above the weir was alive with human bodies glistening pink and white in the sunlight; in the distance they looked like a drifting mass of petals dancing and floating on the surface of the Vltava.

But the true, spiritual life of the city centred in its music. Throughout the anguish of war, the Národní divadlo (National Theatre) – the beautiful national opera house which stands out against the green slopes of the Petrin Hill across the river – had been the sanctuary of the anxious and suffering population of Prague. Here during our first week in Prague we heard Smetana's *Libuša* [20 June], *The Bartered Bride* [25 June, matinée performance] and *The Two Widows* [26 June]; Kovařovic's *Psohlavci-The Dogheads* [25 June, evening] and *The Old Bleaching House* [28 June], and Janáček's *Jenůfa* [1 July]. At the head of a long list of singers and actors associated with the National Theatre stood that great artist and patriot, Emmy Destinn*. In addition the National Opera was blessed under Karel Kovařovic* with what is after all, more essential to the life of opera than the possession of a few stars – a choice of experienced well-trained singers, accustomed to an interchange of parts, who can always be relied upon for a good average interpretation of whatever works may be put into the week's repertory. Rosa also visited the Méstka divadla (Municipal Theatre), where opera was given under the direction of Otakar Ostrčil, later to succeed Karel Kovařovic at the National Theatre. Opera was also a regular institution in Brno, Plzen, and other provincial towns, as well as in Bratislava.

We arrived just in time to be present at the annual summer concert of the Prague Conservatoire, in the beautiful hall of the Rudolfinum. It was in its way an historical event, for the Rudolfinum was soon to become the Parliament House, and probably never again would the stately room echo to the sounds of music. [The Rudolfinum opened in 1885. The Czech Philharmonic Orchestra first performed there in 1896. From 1919-1938 and 1945-6 it was the seat of the Czechoslovak Parliament, but since 1946 it has been the home of the Czech Philharmonic Orchestra.] The Conservatoire had always ranked high among music schools of the continent, for the Czechs have shown a genius for pedagogy. It was then undergoing a complete re-organisation under its gifted director, Vitězslav Novák*, and Professor Franz Spilka. Many traces of oppressive Teutonic tradition were being swept away, and the Conservatoire aimed to fulfil the functions of a sound but independent and progressive school. Rosa only feared, in the first year of the Republic, that, with all its musical attractions, the artistic life of Prague, like its social life in general, might be in danger of suffering from overcrowding. Over emulation tended to develop into a fever of activity that achieves nothing of the very highest order. Indeed, she found the music that was emanating from the quieter provincial districts, held more of the vitality and promise for the future than the products of the city.

Unfortunately during the busy days in Prague came the news of the sudden death of her youngest sister-in-law, Alice Newmarch, the result of an accident while cycling. When Rosa received the news on 27 June, she wrote to her sister-in-law, Emily, likening life to a symphony: 'Harry's letter with its overwhelmingly sad news came as a great shock to us here. It seems too terrible to be anything but a bad dream. Elsie felt it very much. So do I. But at her age such sudden passages from life to death are still inexplicable; whereas for me they appear like the movements of a symphony: – exposition – more or less development, sometimes as in this case ending in an abrupt chord – and then a reprise the meaning of which we do not fully understand.'

Our first feeling was that we should return home, but on reflection this seemed hardly justified. Rosa's reception had been something so unexpected, so much had been planned beforehand by these dear good folk, that she felt they would have regarded her return as a catastrophe. So she carried out the programme, which included a tour through Moravia and Slovakia. A sudden crisis in the Cabinet prevented the Minister of Education from accompanying her as he had intended, but he sent one of his secretaries, a very interesting and charming person – and incidentally one of the leading poets of the day – Petr Křička* to prepare the way.

We left for Brno on 2 July 1919, visiting the caves at Macouka and the Vesna School. Brno proved to be the second great musical centre in Czechoslovakia, for she found there a musical life pulsating as strongly as in any European town; music schools were full of promising students, the choral societies had a wide reputation, and there was an excellent opera. But the central figure of all this activity was Leoš Janáček, one of the most powerful and original creative geniuses – not merely of Czechoslovakia, but in all Europe at the moment. Before meeting him personally, Rosa had formed this opinion, and already pronounced it at home; in her eyes his opera *Jeji Pastorkyna* (Jenůfa) was the most remarkable psychological music drama since Musorgsky's *Boris Godunov*. And when she heard *Kát'a Kabanová* she felt it reached a still higher level of psychological insight and dramatic concentration, and she was convinced, and rightly so, as events have shown, that such works must eventually make a triumphant progress round the whole music-loving world.

She left Brno with regret, and was seen off by her large family of adopted sons – the Moravian Teachers' Choir –for a further tour. Accompanied by Karel Kovařovic and his wife, Petr Křička and Mr Maneš (patriot founder of the Vesna Schools) we travelled to Hradište where there was a remarkably interesting ethnological museum, arranged by the enthusiastic curator, Mr František Kretz (1859-1929), who showed us round his amazing collection of embroideries, pottery and other peasant industries. Not only was he the founder of the ethnographic museum he was also a poet and organist. He did for Moravia what her old friend Vladimir Stasov had done for Russia for the preservation of peasant industries. From here we drove to Velehrad on 5 July, where pilgrimages of some 50,000 peasants in national dress come in from the surrounding country to celebrate the festival of St. Cyril and St. Methodius in the monastry there. At Olomouc on 6 July they saw another performance of Kovařovic's *Psohlavci-(The Dogheads)*.

Travelling through much of the country it seemed to Rosa that this new Republic had a splendid future: her art, her splendid scenery, her health resorts would certainly attract visitors; the warm-heartedness and charm of her people were perhaps the strongest of her assets. But there was much to be done before the country could take the place due to her among the nations; a vast work of propaganda abroad, of reconstruction and improvement at home. Everything had to be made over anew and on national models, which required continuous industry, determination and level-headedness. The Czechoslovaks had many of these qualities and with gradual emancipation from the German influences which they had been forced to imbibe, she felt they would acquire the rest. They had a splendid, steady stout-hearted leader in their President, who was already greatly admired and respected abroad. In her enthusiasm Rosa longed to stay in the country in some capacity, and said so one day. 'What would you like to be?' asked her friends, 'a secretary in the Ministry of Education?' No, she did not aspire to anything so grand, she would have liked to advise the Minister of Health on a new type of dust-cart, and have a finger in the pie of organising some of the watering places unknown abroad and as yet not up to the standard of British, French and American ideals of comfort! A very humble fly on the wheel, which should turn for future prosperity of the Republic!

But she had to return to her own country, and considered herself fortunate that in the furtherance of the Czechoslovak cause in England her small share was concerned with the interests of its music; of all the branches of special propaganda, in her view it was the 'pick of the basket'. Music overcomes the language difficulty; it speaks without dissimulation or ambiguity, direct from the heart of one nation to the heart of another, better than any diplomatic language, and if treated on a wide enough basis should induce sympathy and silence bitterness. Literature must follow more slowly in the wake of music. We already had an excellent Professor of the Czech language and literature in the School of Slavonic Languages at London University, though the study of Czech might well deter all but the bravest; and Dr Seton Watson's well-formed and authentic lectures on the history of Bohemia, at King's College, were steadily rousing interest among students.

During her visit she had met many members of the first government including Dr Karel Kramař, Gustav Haberman, Dr Eduard Beneš* and Antonín Svehla*; but it was not until she returned to Prague on 7 July 1919 from Moravia that she came to know personally Thomas Masaryk, leader of the entire movement for freedom. She retained a vivid memory of the meeting, when he invited her to an interview at the Hradčany, which was then being prepared as his official residence. On the day arranged she went alone to visit the President, with no formal invitation, merely receiving a friendly warning that the President liked expected guests to arrive punctually. When she got out of the car two sentries guarding the door of the Palace gave her a moment of trepidation lest her entrance should be questioned. But no doorkeeper inquired the reason for her presence, and she mounted the flight of steps alone, feeling that this was a delightfully informal entrance to a palace. Rosa described the interview some years later:

'It was as still as the Palace of the Sleeping Beauty, but I knew very well that the presiding genius of the place was very wide-awake indeed. I passed from the vestibule into a room where an official was the first to challenge my right of way. In halting Czech I said that I had received an invitation to visit "Pana Presidenta".

He was then living at his country house at Lany and came up daily by car to his work at the Hrad, and the official explained to me that the President had not yet arrived from the country. I was ushered into one of the stately rooms of the Palace; it was hung with pictures of navel battles and set me thinking of Shakespeare's "Bohemia by the Sea". While waiting I crossed to one of the long windows and looked out. Down below in the shady garden enclosed by the crenulated citadel walls some men were remaking the gravel paths round a picturesque old stone fountain. But it was the panorama spread before me that riveted my attention, and as I stood mentally comparing it with other superb vistas – Moscow from the terrace of the Kremlin, Florence from the Piazzale Michelangelo, Paris from Montmartre – I heard the President's automobile coming into the courtyard, precisely on the stroke of 11.30. Almost immediately the Secretary came to fetch me. For an instant the whole history of the Bohemian struggle for freedom poured through my mind like the dying visions of a drowning man. And now she was free, and had her own government, and the President of the free Republic of Czechoslovakia occupied the venerable and venerated Hradčany, and I was on the point of meeting him. I did not feel at all like words as I entered a smaller reception room and found myself face to face with Thomas Masaryk.

I had been told that Masaryk was a self-made man, son of a coachman in Slovakia. His appearance completely belied the idea of rusticity. He was quite an intellectual type – the professor not the peasant. His manner was quiet, dignified and refined. Seated at a writing-desk that was thickly bestrewn with letters and documents, he rose and, pulling an armchair forward, motioned me to sit in it. I could see the play of his very impressive intellectual visage while we were talking. What was the conversation about? Well, I feel rather ashamed to recall how purely personal and egotistical it was, from my point of view. In a few moments I felt sufficiently at ease to talk about matters which lay nearest my heart. He was so sincere, and the motto which he adopted for his country's use "Truth shall prevail" reigned always in his mind and speech. He inquired about several matters of interest to him: what things had impressed me most in Czechoslovakia, the success of the recent Music Festival in London, etc. We went on to speak of his people's musical gifts, but I do not think he shared my enthusiastic belief in the art as a method of bringing nations together. At any rate he listened with an indulgent, but slightly sceptical smile when I pointed out how much music had done to cement the bonds of sympathy and tolerance between England and Russia. The mention of Russian Art caused him to switch from perfect colloquial English to equally pure and fluent Russian, in which language he spoke to me of one of his finest books *The Spirit of Russia*[1]. After touching on other topics, I came away with the impression that I had *chattered* a good deal to one of the wisest men in European politics, who had given me the opportunity of meeting him at a moment when he was overwhelmed with the cares of state involved by a change of cabinet. I remembered the profound insight, the sympathetic, almost affectionate, advisory spirit and lofty patriotism of the letters which only two days before he had addressed to the new, and the retiring, ministers. Once or twice in the course of this first meeting the President spoke of the lack of completeness in his official residence. But this un-preparedness only threw into stronger light the ever-readiness of this wonderful man for my situation or unaccustomed surroundings, leaving me with the impression that true power requires no rehearsal to enhance its impressiveness. It was no princeling of a German house who entertained us on many occasions later at the Hrad, but a man endowed with the highest qualities of leadership.'

Rosa and Elsie appear to have packed a lot into a comparatively short visit, returning to England in mid July as Rosa described in a letter to Emily: 'At 4pm we had everything on the platform, waiting for seats in the military train, when the French officer in command announced that in consequence of so many staff officers having permission to travel to Paris for the 14 July fête, no civilians could be accommodated on the train. So now we cannot start homewards before tomorrow, Sunday. But I thought I would write to you and post the letter from Paris [...] I intend only remaining in Paris long enough to rest a night or so and get the English visa for my return via Boulogne and call on the Czechoslovak Minister in Paris as I am taking some things through with me.'

After staying a night in Paris, they returned home. Ten days later, Rosa visited her friends the Colmans at Carrow Abbey, Norwich, and then in August she received the news of the death of her eldest sister, Sophie, at Southsea. The autumn of 1919 was the 25th season of Promenade Concerts and Rosa compiled a souvenir brochure commemorating this anniversary. In it she described the history of the Proms from 1895 to 1919 and compiled a complete list of all the new works which received their first English or London performances.

Czechoslovak music was very much in the forefront of her activities before she visited Prague again the following year. The Bohemian String Quartet had performed in the summer at the 1919 Czechoslovak Festival in London, and at the end of October they returned, giving a concert at the Wigmore Hall, as *The Times* correspondent described: 'Considering the amount of interest which their vividly picturesque performances aroused then their reappearance should have brought a larger audience. Indeed it was not until Mrs Newmarch had come forward and had told the audience that this concert coincided with the first anniversary of the Czecho-Slovak declaration of independence from Austrian rule that the temperature rose above the ordinary tepid level of the average concert audience[2].' Although a relatively small intervention, this is a good example of how Rosa could size up a situation and put herself in control. In December, she attended a lecture by Seton Watson and a meeting of the Czechoslovak Committee. In January 1920, she first met the Danish singer Mischa-Léon, who was later to perform Janáček's *Diary of One Who Disappeared*. In February, she wrote articles on Czech Opera[3], the painter Roerich[4], and Purcell's *Fairy Queen*[5].

In 1920, the first Sokol Festival to be held since the establishment of the Republic took place. It was attended by over 500,000 people, including the Czechoslovak President. There were various types of competitions held over five days, and the march *Into the New Life* composed by Josef Suk was heard for the first time. The Sokol (Czech for 'falcon') is a youth movement similar to a scouting movement and was established in the nineteenth century. A party of English journalists, writers and musicians were invited to Prague for the event. The occasion was Rosa's second visit to Prague, and it brought many opportunities for meeting once more members of the Czechoslovak government: Dr Eduard Beneš, then Minister of Foreign Affairs, Dr Prokop Drtina* and Mr Gustav Haberman, Minister of Education. The latter was a remarkable self-made man who spoke five languages and since the foundation of the Republic had already opened nearly 3,000 schools throughout the country. Dr Karel Kramář (1860-1937), a Czech politician, was the country's first prime minister from 1918 until he resigned in June 1919. Rosa knew him to be a great Slavophile, working before the war with Thomas Masaryk for the Czechoslovak causes as leader of the young Czechoslovak party in the Austro-Hungarian Parliament. He took her one day with him to the laying of the foundation stone of the Masaryk Homes by the President in one of the poorer quarters of the town. They were in the car following the President's, so that she saw the great ovation he received from his people. During the festival, she also saw a good deal more of President Masaryk. He received all the guests at the castle and gave a large garden party in the grounds of the Belvedere, the former royal family's summer palace. Indeed it was a most enjoyable visit and particularly interesting for her to see the progress made in every direction since the previous year. At an evening gathering in the impressive Spanish Hall of the Hrad, with its long mirrors and sparkling chandeliers, they had the pleasure of hearing the Bohemian Quartet in a programme of national music – Smetana's Quartet *From My Life* and some Dvořák. Rosa was much amused when, on taking leave of the President, who had evidently not forgotten her views firmly expressed at their first meeting on 'music as the finest form of propaganda', he remarked with a smile: 'Now, have I done right? Are you satisfied with the efforts of my fine boys?'

On subsequent visits, she found life generally improving. Food became more plentiful; veal was the chief meat, varied by pigeon, goose, and sometimes beef, vegetables were excellent, and there was plenty of good butter, with milk and cream no longer scarce. The opera house seemed changed for her after the death of Karel Kovařovic in December 1920, and his lifelong colleague and director, Gustav Schmoranz, was ailing too. Theirs had been a wonderful cooperation and friendship over some twenty years – not unlike the partnership of Henry Wood and Robert Newman. [Gustav Schmoranz continued as director until 1922.]

The concerts in the Smetana Hall, conducted by Václav Talich*, offered much of interest to Rosa, and going one day to the rehearsal of the Philharmonic Society's orchestra, she met the violinist Jaroslav Kocián*, who introduced her to Talich, whose musical vitality she admired. He was a great patriot too, and when he was in England recording just before World War II, she was impressed by his determination to return to his country and his orchestra, to carry on, whatever the future might hold for them.

As time went on, the Czech publishing house Hudebni Matice was anxious to issue English editions and English catalogues of their publications and Rosa spent many hours translating titles of operas and songs for the printers. Many Czechs were learning English, but when it came to translating and writing literary English, the language was as much a problem to them as theirs to us. She translated some of Vitězslav Novák's songs for a new Czech album, and his knowledge of English was very good, so he appreciated the difficulties of translation and was pleased with what she had achieved.

After her 1919 and 1920 visits, Rosa made several more visits to Czechoslovakia, her last visit being in 1937, her eightieth year.

Notes

1. Thomas Masaryk, *The Spirit of Russia* (London: Allen & Unwin, 1919).

2. 'Music: London Chamber Concert Society', *The Times*, 29 Oct. 1919.

3. Rosa Newmarch, (1920) 'Opera in Czecho-Slovakia', *The New Europe*, 14 (1920), pp.162-7.

4. Rosa Newmarch, 'Roerich's Art', *The Quest*, Apr. 1920.

5. Rosa Newmarch, (1920) 'Purcell's Fairy Queen at Cambridge', *The Chesterian*, Mar. 1920, Series no.6 pp.161-4.

CHAPTER 23: SIBELIUS'S RETURN

By 1920, Rosa was no longer solely responsible for the programme notes for the Proms. From 1908 to 1918, she had written the programme notes single-handed, but in 1919, she asked the thirty-year-old Eric Blom to assist her with the notes, a task that was shared until 1926. Eric Blom generally wrote the notes for the more contemporary music. It was now three years since she had completed her most recent book on a Russian theme, and she appears not to have committed herself to further major works at this stage. Nevertheless, she continued to write articles with great regularity and by 1920 she had made the two visits to Czechoslovakia, a country that appears to have been supplanting her interest in Russia now it was no longer possible for her to travel there, and contact with old friends had become difficult. She had begun learning Czech, and although she had always found picking up languages easy, it could not have been quite so easy as she became older. At the age of sixty-two, and with many achievements behind her, she might have contemplated resting on her laurels. That was not her style, however, and in the next decade she achieved as much for Czech music and musicians as she had previously done for Russia. In addition, she was anxious to re-establish close contact with Sibelius. She very much appreciated his music and realised well before many of the critics and the music-loving public that he would become recognised as one of the great composers of the twentieth century. Much of the information on Sibelius's next visit to England has been drawn from Rosa's account, published in 1939[1], and Tawaststjerna's biography of Sibelius[2]. Tawaststjerna was given unrestricted access to Sibelius's papers, letters, and diaries by the family and he worked on the five-volume biography from 1960-1988.

After her second visit to Czechoslovakia in 1920, Rosa went on to Geneva to recuperate. She left Prague on 6 July 1920, stayed a night in Strasbourg in order to see the cathedral, then stayed one night in Basel before arriving in Geneva. She stayed at the Hôtel Beau-Séjour at Champel, Geneva, a noted hydropathic centre, where writers such as Joseph Conrad, André Gide, Guy de Maupassant, and the Swiss philosopher and poet Henri Frédéric Amiel had taken the waters. At Geneva, she met Otto and Mrs Kling, and there Elizabeth Johnson, with whom she had travelled on an earlier visit to Russia, joined her, and Elsie left for home. From Geneva, she wrote to Sibelius on 17 July, saying: 'Have heard that a new symphony was ready [...] I continue to work but with not quite the same energy as before. I am already sixty-two and am beginning to feel signs of my age. But they say I haven't changed much[3].' In her letter, she also passed on an invitation from Robert Newman, manager of the Queen's Hall Orchestra, asking if Sibelius would conduct one of his compositions on 12 February 1921, and if so, what would be his fee.

None of Sibelius's symphonies were performed at Promenade Concerts during the war because they would have generated fees for 'enemy publishers', although *Valse Triste* and *Finlandia* were not banned as they came under a different publishing arrangement[4]. On 5 August, Rosa returned home in time for the start of the Proms on 13 August.

In the period immediately after the World War I, both the Finnish and German marks had become substantially devalued and this meant Sibelius's earnings from the royalties on his music, particularly his major works, had been drastically reduced, and he was left in financially straightened circumstances. Early in 1920, Sibelius had been offered the post of Professor of Composition at the Eastman School of Music in America with a salary of $20,000, at much the same time as the invitation to conduct the Queen's Hall Orchestra. Sibelius replied to Rosa in a mixture of French and English, knowing her feelings about the Germans, saying that he would very much like to conduct his new symphony (his fifth) and any other of his new compositions which would occupy from forty to fifty minutes, suggesting a fee as much as £150 because of the very high travel costs the journey would entail.

It was then arranged that he should come early in the following year, 1921. Understanding the high cost of travel, and in order to augment Sibelius's fee, Robert Newman arranged for four appearances at the Queen's Hall. In the meantime, Rosa wrote to Sibelius again asking for a list of his more recent works that would be new to English audiences. After some delay, he replied: 'You know how idle I am!' and then proceeded to send a list which included *The Oceanides* Op.73, his Fifth Symphony Op. 82, Incidental music to Hofmannsthal's Everyman Op.83, and the cantatas Op. 92, 93 and 95[5]. However, he was reticent about giving details of the Fifth Symphony, writing: 'Later on I will write and tell you about the symphonic works that are occupying me at the moment. This is all I can say at present about my pieces, and there is no expert on my music to whom I could turn for help. What are the prospects for my three concerts in February?' Since Rosa would be writing the programme notes, his reply was for her exasperating and she wrote again on 15 November 1920: 'It is not enough just to send a list of compositions [...]What we need, dear friend, is your Fifth Symphony[6]. Even Henry Wood has asked me to write to you about this, as he cannot be expected to learn your work at the last minute, as if it were a Haydn symphony.' The Fourth

Symphony did not present the same problem, as Henry Wood had conducted a performance with the Queen's Hall Orchestra the previous year.

Less than a month before Sibelius set off from Helsinki to England on 31 January 1921, he also telegraphed Klingenberg, the Rector of the Eastman School of Music, saying *Yes* to the offer of the professorship at the agreed sum of $20,000. Sibelius arrived in England on 7 February 1921 after an exhausting journey but felt pleased that on arrival the immigration officer knew who he was[7]. He had dinner with Marcus Tollet from the Finnish legation that night and the following day had lunch at the Langham Hotel with Rosa, whom he was delighted to see again. He received a telegram from the Eastman School indicating that he should start there in October. Rosa was totally against him going to America and she made this plain to him. She had enormous admiration for Sibelius as a composer, but she felt, particularly when he was away from home, that he needed looking after, especially in his wife's absence. From a number of incidents, this was even more apparent on this trip than on his previous visits. Some years earlier when he had been asked to write something for the Three Choirs Festival in Gloucester in 1913, Rosa had strongly advised him against it. She was convinced that time would tell that he was one of the great composers of his day and she felt strongly that he should compose what inspired him and avoid potboilers and commissions, although realising that they brought in much needed cash. So she saw going to America as a teacher of composition as an even worse distraction as she made clear both to him during his visit and later to his wife by letter.

Three days after his arrival, on 10 February, Rosa arranged a reception for him at Claridges and, knowing how absentminded he was, she sent him a reminder: 'Don't forget to be at Claridges tomorrow, otherwise it will be Hamlet without the Prince of Denmark. Ask the nice Mr Blom (Eric Blom) to take you. Bantock and Henry Wood will be there.' Saturday 12 February was set for his first concert with the Queen's Hall Orchestra in which he conducted his Fifth Symphony. Henry Wood had rehearsed the symphony beforehand on the Friday 11th and on the following morning. After the concert, in which Sibelius was called back to take five bows, he felt that it had been a great success. He also commented that Bantock and Rosa looked after him very well but made such a fuss of him before the concert that he felt worn out afterwards. In between concerts, there was much wining and dining. On previous visits, Sir Henry Wood had found the wining and dining particularly difficult to manage with the combination of Sibelius and Busoni, as they were apt to wander off, regardless of time[7].

On the 13th, Sir Hugh Allen invited him to lunch at the Royal College of Music, where he conducted a student performance of *En Saga*. Then on the 15th, as Sibelius had expressed a wish to see Shakespeare country, he and Rosa travelled to Leamington, where Rosa had ordered a carriage and a pair of sound horses, which they both felt would be more comfortable than travelling by car, which in those days were less comfortable[8]. Sibelius was impressed with the countryside, especially the trees, which were much more sparse in his own country. In the evening, he and Rosa took the dinner train from Leamington to London. On Wednesday 16th, they travelled to Bournemouth, where Sibelius conducted his Third Symphony, *En Saga*, and *Valse triste*. No sooner was that was over but they were back on the train to London, where Sibelius rehearsed with the New Queen's Hall Orchestra. After another visit to the Royal College of Music, on Sunday 20th Rosa, Bantock and Sibelius took the train to Birmingham, where Bantock had prepared a long programme that included his Third Symphony, *Finlandia, En Saga, Valse triste, Valse lyrique*, and the slow movement of his Violin Concerto. There was only time for one rehearsal. Sibelius and Rosa stayed with the Bantocks whilst in Birmingham. On Monday evening (21st), they went to a concert of Bantock's songs, Sibelius sitting next to Mrs Bantock and Rosa. Mrs Bantock was hard of hearing, but with Rosa Sibelius could converse easily. Rosa remarked that they 'spent several days with the Bantocks[8].'

They arrived in Birmingham on 20th and left for Oxford on 23rd, where Sir Hugh Allen had invited them. They met him in his rooms at New College, where they spent the afternoon meeting a select group of musicians. Rosa felt that Sibelius, whose English was not very fluent, had difficulty in fully entering into the conversation with his usual zest. In the evening, he was a guest at New College high table, whilst Rosa was barred from the all male preserve, but 'a pleasant solitary meal' was served for her in Sir Hugh's college rooms. Sibelius expressed the wish to hear the organ in New College Chapel. The organist, Sir William Harris (1883-1973), took him to the organ loft where he played a Bach Chorale, which Sibelius seemed to enjoy. According to Elsie Newmarch, Sir William was somewhat disturbed that Sibelius continued smoking 'the inevitable cigar' during the visit to the organ loft. The 24th was reserved for sightseeing at Oxford before they returned to London ready for his next concert on Saturday 26th at the Queen's Hall. At the rehearsal before the concert, Rosa sat next to Busoni while they watched Sibelius rehearse his Fourth Symphony. She remembered Busoni's lively conversation, although by this time he was quite ill; he was thin and gaunt. Inflation of the German currency had eroded his resources, and this forced him to perform and tour much more than he would have done otherwise. At the concert, Busoni's performance of a Mozart piano concerto was clearly preferred by the audience to Sibelius's symphony.

Rosa greatly admired Sibelius's music and was interested to know how the younger generation reacted to these unfamiliar works. After Sibelius had conducted his Fourth Symphony, she wrote: 'I was glad, therefore, to overhear two trenchantly conflicting verdicts [...] The First Voice testified that the music had cast a spell over the hearer; that every phrase suggested some unfamiliar beauty, some germinal thought or emotion; finally this Voice expressed a longing to hear the whole work repeated at once. The Second Voice proclaimed in accents of equal sincerity a wish that Jean Sibelius and his music might enjoy a long period of repose in his own remote fatherland [...] Only music which is really strong and original can divide the general vote so sharply. The customary mild criticism based upon reminiscence was inaudible[9].'

On Saturday 26th, Sibelius conducted a further concert at the Queen's Hall, which included *The Oceanides,* some numbers from the *King Christian II* Suite, and *Valse lyrique.* The following day, he and Rosa travelled to Manchester, where on Saturday 5 March he conducted *Valse triste* and *Finlandia* in the Free Trade Hall and Henry Wood conducted the other works on the programme. Then in the evening, they returned on the night express to London in time for his farewell concert in London on 6 March, in which he conducted *The Swan of Tuonela, Festivo* from the *Scènes historique,* and *Finlandia.* Monday 7th was a quiet day according to Rosa's diary, and on Tuesday 8th Rosa took him for a farewell visit to the Royal College of Music, and in the evening dinner at Henry Wood's house.

Eric Blom felt Sibelius was being rushed off his feet without any time to himself. He gave eight concerts in all in London and the provinces in the space less than a month in addition to receptions, dinners, meeting the musical establishment, and sightseeing. However, it must have been equally exhausting for Rosa, for not only did she travel with him to most of the concerts and sightseeing occasions, but she was always anxious because of his absentmindedness that he might not turn up at expected times. Perhaps not surprisingly, after looking after Sibelius for a month, she and Elsie went for a few days' break at Eastbourne from the 8 to 12 April.

Before Sibelius left for home, Rosa drafted all his thank you letters to conductors, impresarios, and orchestras; they were then typed at the Finnish legation and Sibelius only had to sign them[7]. In one such letter he thanked Sir Henry Wood for the insight he and the New Queen's Hall Orchestra had shown, particularly in the performances of his Fourth and Fifth Symphonies, and hoped he might have the honour of conducting the orchestra in the future.

Some years later, Wood was disappointed that after such a warm letter, Sibelius appeared to favour Beecham as his London interpreter[10].

Towards the end of Sibelius's visit, on 7 March, Rosa used her most eloquent pleading to dissuade him from the American offer: 'You know I have long waited for your great breakthrough here, and am now more than ever certain that it will come. But I beg you not to squander your energies in teaching young Americans harmony and orchestration *à la* Sibelius. They can find all that by studying your works. You are a composer, not a pedagogue; possibly the greatest creative musician of our times – and certainly one of the noblest and most individual. *That is your mission. Au diable les dollars!* Spend the summer in Järvenpää; don't smoke too many Corona cigars, for the sake of your finances; don't drink too often (on the advice of your Leibarzt Mme Rosa Newmarch), and compose your Sixth (on the Almighty's command). This will give your life real meaning. You do not have the right to freely dispose of those years that remain to you, which most certainly do not belong to young Americans. And don't give up your musical autographs without making sure about your future royalties[7].'

Sibelius had been worrying as to whether he had made the right decision in agreeing the contract with Klingenberg, and Rosa's pleading finally convinced him. He telegraphed Klingenberg before leaving London: 'WILL COME TO AMERICA ONLY AS CONDUCTOR AND NOT THIS YEAR'. By the time Klingenberg's telegrammed reply, 'TERRIBLE FOR ME', reached London, Sibelius had already set sail for home[7].

Rosa was not one to let things rest and Tawaststjerna goes on to explain that in order to reinforce her message, she gave Sibelius a note, dated 6 March, to give to his wife Aino on his return. Apart from reporting on how the visit had gone, she added[7]: 'I hope that your husband does not go to America. I cannot imagine him as a professor or giving lessons. I do not believe that his nerves would survive such a life for as long as a year. Of course, there is always the question of money, but what is the point of money if the consequence is *un homme fini*. I have seen so many artists ruined by America: Dvořák, Safonov and others. Life is far too hectic and inartistic. Sibelius is a creative artist, possibly the greatest who remains in our world. I am horrified at the thought of him squandering those years he has left to him on teaching. A concert tour is another matter. I am certain he will be re-engaged here for the next season [...] He is fifty-five now, a critical age in a man's life, and he would have no one to look after him in America.' Tawaststjerna suggests that the reference to 'a critical age' may reflect a further concern of Rosa's[7]. Whilst in London, Sibelius had been seen in the company of the twenty-five year old pianist Harriet Cohen. By 1921, Harriet Cohen was very much a rising star. She had performed the première of Bax's *Symphonic Variations* at a Promenade Concert in 1920, for which Rosa wrote the programme note. Rosa made a point of consulting living composers wherever possible before writing a programme note, and therefore almost certainly consulted Bax. By 1921, Bax had left his wife and family for Harriet Cohen, and it would seem very likely that Rosa was aware of this. During her lifetime, Harriet had relationships and friendships with many men of varying ages[11]. By 1921, she was friendly with the writer Bernard Shaw. If Rosa was concerned, it might be that at this 'critical age' Sibelius might become distracted from his life's work as a composer.

Harriet clearly impressed him after a chance meeting at Pagani's restaurant. Sibelius was dining with the music critic Edwin Evans and at a table nearby, Harriet Cohen was with some young people. Edwin Evans, who had taken an interest in Harriet's career, introduced her to Sibelius. She said she knew a number of his orchestral scores, but Sibelius sounded sceptical. There was a piano in one of the banqueting rooms, where she was able to confound him by playing *En saga* by heart. Sibelius was clearly moved, and from further discussion it was clear that she appreciated the complexities of his Fifth Symphony as few at the time did. She often included his piano music in her recitals. She and Sibelius spent time together both during this visit and in subsequent meetings, including one with Bax in the early 1930s. This not only worried Rosa but also, according to Robert Layton, occasioned displeasure at Ainola (the family home), where Harriet was never received[12]. This is at variance with Tawaststjerna's statement: 'A year before his [Sibelius's] death she visited him at Ainola[13].' Harriet's enthusiasm for Sibelius as a composer and person did not diminish over the years.

When Sibelius embarked at Newcastle for Bergen on 10 March 1921, there was every expectation, after such a successful visit, that he would return to England to conduct, but although his music gained increasing popularity worldwide, he never returned to England, nor met Henry Wood, Granville Bantock, or Rosa Newmarch again. This was not for lack of invitations. Rosa continued to correspond though not as frequently in later years, and Sibelius was not an enthusiastic letter writer. A few months after his visit in the summer of 1921, he sent his Op. 98 *Suite mignonne* to Chappell & Co, who at first refused to take it, but later changed their minds. Tawaststjerna suggests that it was under pressure from Rosa Newmarch that Chappell & Co paid £200 for it[7]. Various factors contributed to him not returning to England. In 1922, his brother died and Sibelius was deeply distressed. With increasing age he found the journey arduous and his wife had suffered for many years from rheumatism and was reluctant to take long train journeys. In all he had made five visits to England, in 1905, 1907, 1909, 1912, and 1921. On each occasion, Rosa spent much time looking after him. She also visited him in Paris in 1911 and Finland in 1915.

In 1924, she received an invitation to his daughter Katerina's wedding, and in 1927, there is even the suggestion in his letter from Paris that he might visit her. He also explained that he had written his Seventh Symphony and the symphonic poem *Tapiola*[14]. In a later letter, dated March 1930, Sibelius suggests a meeting in Karlsbad. In Rosa's account, she simply states: 'The meeting in Karlsbad foreshadowed in this letter never actually took place.' By then she was seventy-two and suffering from diabetes and probably reluctant to travel herself.

Notes

1. Rosa Newmarch, *Jean Sibelius: A Short Story of a Long Friendship* (London: Goodwin & Tabb, 1944).

2. Eric Tawaststjerna, *Sibelius, 1914-1957* trans. Robert Layton (London: Faber and Faber, 2008), vol. 3.

3. Ibid. p.185.

4. Arthur Jacobs, *Henry J. Wood: Maker of the Proms* (London: Methuen, 1994), p.150.

5. Rosa Newmarch, *Jean Sibelius: A Short Story of a Long Friendship*, p.40.

6. Tawaststjerna, *Sibelius*, vol.3, p.192.

7. Ibid. pp.196-213.

8. Rosa Newmarch, *Jean Sibelius: A Short Story of a Long Friendship*, p.42-3.

9. Rosa Newmarch, 'Sibelius', *The Chesterian*, Series No 14, Apr. 1921, pp.417-421.

10. Jacobs, *Henry J. Wood: Maker of the Proms*, p.169.

11. Helen Fry, (2008) *Music and Men: The Life and Loves of Harriet Cohen* (Stroud, Gloucestershire: The History Press, 2008).

12. Robert Layton, *Sibelius* (London: Dent, 1978), p.55.

13. Tawaststjerna, *Sibelius* vol 3, p.205.

14. Rosa Newmarch, *Jean Sibelius: A Short Story of a Long Friendship*, p.45-7.

CHAPTER 24: THE YEARS 1922 TO 1925:
MEETING LEOŠ JANÁČEK

After her first visit to Czechoslovakia in 1919, Rosa visited Czechoslovakia in the spring almost every year for the next few years. Although Czech music was her main musical interest in that period, she continued to take a great interest in a wide range of music, writing programme notes for various festivals, reviewing concerts for *The Times*, and meeting musicians in England. Only five days after Sibelius's departure, she was in Liverpool for the first British performance of Rachmaninoff's *The Bells* on 15 March, for which she wrote the programme notes. Three days earlier, she was at her grandson Michael's christening at St Stephen's Haverstock Hill. In April, she had a short holiday with Elsie at Eastbourne. On returning, she attended a recital by the pianist Frederic Lamond (1868-1948) and later entertained him and his wife at her home. On 9 June, there was a Skryabin Sonata Recital at the Wigmore Hall by pupils of George Woodhouse. Five of Skryabin's piano sonatas were played, for which she provided the programme notes. In her diary, she commented that in September, presumably while staying near Cromer, Norfolk, she walked six to seven miles to the Roman encampment at Sheringham, proving her fitness at the age of sixty-four. In October, the young Finnish pianist Toivo Ilmari Hannikainen* arrived in London and she was involved in looking after him. He performed Rachmaninoff's Piano Concerto No. 1 at the Proms on 18 October. Also in October 1921, Shaliapin had been invited to the United States, and he stopped over in London for a week, giving a solo recital in the Albert Hall and making his first post-war recording with HMV. During the week, he visited Rosa at her home in Crossfield Road, as her daughter Elsie described:

> By 1921 London was welcoming old friends to the concert platform again. One of the first to come was Shaliapin, whom Rosa Newmarch had not seen since our visit to his country home Itlar in 1915. She was delighted to welcome him again at our house, where he could sit and talk of his art, his work and affairs in Russia. At that time the singer Herbert Heyner* was living next door to us and often put on records of Shaliapin in his roles of Boris Godounov and Ivan the Terrible, parts he was then studying himself; Shaliapin was very amused to sit in our small garden listening to himself on the gramophone. But most of all Rosa

Newmarch was interested to hear what he had to say of Russia; she felt he was by no means a communist at heart, though he had stayed on in the country partly for family reasons, and partly perhaps because he had been made a revolutionary hero, and still gave his art to his people. He seemed, however, to be very happy to be in England again, and was just as friendly and affectionate to his 'Batoushka', as he always liked to call her.

The English public were now to hear him only as a concert artist, but found him equally arresting. When in 1913 London awakened to the one superb aspect of his art – the operatic – few thought of him as a concert singer, and we had no conception of his attraction in a miscellaneous programme. But in this respect Rosa Newmarch thought of Shaliapin as almost unique; undoubtedly it was as an interpreter of songs that he had won his immense popularity in his own country. For every ten Russians who had the privilege of hearing him in opera, a hundred adored him as the singer of Moussorgsky's *Song of the Flea*, or Glinka's *The Midnight Review*. In his recitals side by side with Beethoven, Schubert, Brahms and Grieg, he made a practice of giving his compatriots a proportion of songs they could readily understand; songs that touched them directly and filled the spirit with patience or rebellion, bitterness, despair or heroism as the case may be. He drew all classes in Russia to his feet. There was a story, current during the war, that when he visited a small country town to sing for the funds of the Red Cross, the prices of entrance being prohibitive to the masses, they determined by hook or by crook to hear their favourite, and settled the question by removing part of the roof of the hall, and so got their concert for nothing.

Rosa also gave her account of Shaliapin's visit in a letter to her sister Tiny in the autumn of 1921:

I seem to have been as busy as in the height of the season! There have been so many foreign friends in London. The conductor Nedbal* from Prague, and now young Hannikainen* from Helsingfors for whom I got an engagement at the Proms.

Yesterday Shaliapin came and spent about 2 hours here. He looks old, but splendidly well, not at all starved. I was very much interested to hear what he had to say about Russia. I don't think he is a Bolshie, but of course he has to live there and make the best of it. He stayed too long to escape besides I think they made a fuss of him and I expect he thought he would be a kind of revolutionary hero. He is a funny mixture of vanity and charm and greatness, with a good deal of the peasants money-making instinct. However he was just as affectionate and nice personally as when we parted, and seemed pleased to see Elsie and I (*sic*) again.

Many of her musical activities at the time were Czech related. In April, the Ševčik-Lhotsky Quartet performed in London for the second time and Rosa attended the reception for them at the Czechoslovak Legation. In May 1921, Rosa met the Danish tenor Mischa-Léon*, who was giving a recital with Fanny Davies*, and later was to sing to accompany Rosa's lectures on Czech composers. In June, she met Dr Alois Kolisek*, a priest and long standing friend of Janáček, who from 1919 taught theology in Bratislava, and she accompanied him to Cambridge where he gave a lecture. In July, she dined with Baron Heyking, the Russian Consul General and his wife, and later that month had lunch with Otto Kling and Dr Bramberger from the Ministry of Education in Prague. She came to know many significant figures of the Czechoslovak establishment who visited London at the time.

In January 1922, she and Elsie went down to Sidmouth where they both caught 'flu; she wrote to Tiny after she had recovered to describe her next Czech commitment:

I promised before I had 'flu' to help Fanny Davies with this entertainment of the Czech Quartet given by the Music Club. I promised to speak the address of welcome and there would have been great disappointment if I had failed. But I managed to get through and don't feel any the worse [...] Poor Fanny D. had arranged a lovely programme of music, but it was rather spoilt because her beloved Suk [2nd violin] wasn't well enough to come, and Herold [viola] had to stay and nurse him so only 2 of the Quartet came. I was interested to meet Jan Masaryk, the President's son, who was in America when I was in Prague. He said he was always hearing about me at home as the one foreigner who speaks the language of the Czech hearts. I said I hoped his father gave me a good character because I dearly loved him. He said "God bless you for that. He is a dear old man, and we all want you back again."

They did not have to wait long; on 1 April, Rosa and Elsie left for Prague via Paris. Whilst in Paris, they met her friends Mabel and Mary Robinson and also the Czechoslovak diplomat Dr Štefan Osuský* (1889-1973) and Dr Vojtech Mastny (1874-1954), the Czechoslovak Minister in London. Dr Mastny was later to become the Czechoslovak Minister to Berlin, and in 1938 was sent as the Czechoslovak representative to the fateful Munich Conference, where the Gestapo detained him and his colleague. Having met Rosa and Elsie in Paris, he accompanied them to

Prague. They arrived in Prague on 5 April and stayed at their usual hotel, the Hotel Paříž, where they were to attend the Competition Choral Festival, as Rosa was to serve as one of the judges[1]. Among the competitors was the Moravian Teachers' Choir from Brno. Janáček was also there for the festival.

Contact between Rosa and Janáček was made initially indirectly. Janáček wrote to Professor Chudoba* in London asking him to invite Rosa to Brno between the 20th and 29th of April; this would enable her to see the performance of *Kat'a Kabanová* on 20th and also the opera *Beatrice* by the Moravian composer Neumann on the 28th. Professor Chudoba then wrote to Rosa from his home in Surbiton on 7 April, relaying Janáček invitation and asking whether Rosa was still in Prague as Janáček hadn't seen her[2]. Janáček also wrote to Rosa directly on 12 April[3] repeating the invitation to see both operas and the musical life in Brno. He finished by saying: 'We should wait for you in Brno on 20 at noon when the express train is due.' Janáček's letter is a brief typed letter in English. It is assumed that since he did not know English, this was translated for him. This was why he wrote the earlier letter to Professor Chudoba, who could relay his message in English. Rosa replied from the Hotel Paříž on 13 April saying how delighted she would be to visit Brno again, having had happy memories of her 1919 visit[4]. She explained that she was a great admirer of his works and considered *Jenůfa* one of the most remarkable of all modern music dramas. She also mentioned that she would be giving two lectures on Czechoslovakian operas at London University in June and that the second would concentrate on modern Czech composers. She asked if he would reserve rooms in a hotel for her and Elsie and indicated they would stay until the 29 April.

On the same day, Rosa also wrote to Bella Simpson from the Hotel Paříž:

Dearest Bella,

I will begin a letter to you tonight because I foresee that writing will soon become more of a difficulty. The letter you sent me on from Prof. Chudoba arrived this morning at the same time as one from Leoš Janáček inviting me to Brno on the 20th till the 29th. They have evidently organized a kind of municipal reception for me which will coincide with the production of several new Moravian operas, including his own "Káta Kabanová". From there we shall very likely go on to Bratislava for a few days as it is more than half-way there. But I am not sure yet. This week end there is a big Competition Festival here, at which many provincial choirs compete, and it will bring many musicians to Prague including Janáček himself and Kolisek, so we can then settle things more definitely. I shall leave a good deal of our baggage here and come back to fetch it for a day or two on our homeward way. I daresay I shall be able to send an address in Brno, but at any rate I can arrange with the porters here to send everything on to me.

Today has been warmer, but Tuesday took the cake in the way of beastly weather. Elsie and I both caught colds and went to bed feeling very seedy. Two aspirins and bed till midday seem to have staved mine off, but Elsie has come out in a regular blow-nose cold. The contrast between the heated halls and banks and restaurants (as in Russia) and the outside cold is trying, and one longs for warmer weather. I must say it *is* milder today. The English Singers had an enthusiastic reception last night. They are being charming, if a little monotonous. But everyone says they sounded tired last night. They were very pleased to see me and we had supper together. I am glad you are getting on comfortably. Mrs R. is a comfort. Give my love to cat and kitten. The man's [her husband's] letter with the cards arrived; but please remind him that foreign postage is now 3^d not 2½.

The letter continued:

Good Friday

Today summer seems to have come at last! After wearing my furs daily, today I could wear my summer black coat and skirt. Tonight Fanny [Fanny Davies] and I have asked the Phil. Conductor Talich to a quiet meal. People don't pay much attention apparently to Good Friday. Tomorrow I shall go to the Emmaus Church to hear the music in the evening. We are very much engaged one way or another. I seem to have one visitor after another. *Yesterday* the Director of "Hudebny Matice", the new publishing society, for 3 hours; such dreadful muddles as they are making! They are such innocents. *Today* a young Russian Prof. came to tell me all about the new Russ. University. Novák came today and it is evident from what he says that this opera-festival in Brno has been arranged entirely for me. I expect I am a municipal guest. At the opera here Ostrčil is not popular and only does two works of a clique, and as Schmoranz resigned last week on account of health; they can't get their works done for me here, so they think they will have a special show of new things in Brno. It will be very interesting, though strenuous. With much love, hoping you are enjoying this weather too.

Ever yours affectionate

Rosa Newmarch

Perhaps you will send this round.

Do not forget some more visiting cards for Mother [added in pencil in Elsie's handwriting]

On the day before Rosa wrote to Bella Simpson, 12th of April 1922, she also wrote to her sister Tiny. Much of the information overlaps with that in her letter to Bella, although there is additional information that is quoted in the following extract:

We went out to tea with the poet Křička, who travelled with us in 1919, and lunched at the Brit.Leg. on Monday [11 April] and met an interesting military attaché from Warsaw and the Brit. Consul from Bratislava. Lady Clerk [wife of Sir George Russell Clerk , British Consul General to Czechoslovakia from 1921-6] was not able to put in an appearance as she had only come from London the day before and was knocked up by the journey. However, we went to tea with her yesterday, their house (the old Palace of the Thun family) is lovely; but their garden is so backward. Quite extraordinary. [The British Embassy in Prague is situated in the Thun Palace on Malá Strana] They say we shall find it better and greener when we go South to Bratislava [...] The opera is very much gone down since Kovařovic's death, and people seem to prefer the concerts now. [Rosa visited Kovařovic's grave on 11 April] [...] I have been invited to go to Brno to hear some national opera and as we can take it on the way to Bratislava I think it would be interesting. I have been there before, it is the town where they gave us such a reception, Elsie and I, in 1919 ...

We are very well fed and for us living is cheap. The veal is always good, and we vary it with pigeon, or roast goose, beef occasionally, nice vegetables and very good butter and cream and one can hire a nice closed motor car, like a private one, and do a lot for 10/s [=50p]. So life is really rather luxurious for the money than otherwise [...]

We are just going to post this so I must stop now. Having kind and amusing Fanny Davies on the floor below makes it very friendly and nice. We look in on each other in spare moments, and Elsie "maids" her a little before she goes out to play – which is very necessary.

With much love, Rosa

On 20 April 1922, Rosa and Elsie arrived in Brno where they met Janáček. The visit from the 20th to 29th is well decribed by Zdenka Fischmann[2] and by John Tyrrell[3], who quote from Rosa's diary and also from that of Marie Stejskal, Janáček's housekeeper. Rosa and Elsie met at Janáček 's house on several occasions before travelling on to Bratislava. A friend of Janáček 's, Miss Valerie Joklová, was also present to help with interpretation. Rosa's comment in her diary was 'supped with Janáček – wonderful man'; she clearly rated the visit a success. It was an opportunity to use her linguistic skills. To Janáček she spoke in Russian, to his wife, Zdenka Janácková, she spoke in German to his housekeeper, Marie Stejskal, she spoke in Czech, and presumably she spoke to Elsie in English. In her diary, Marie said Rosa spoke Czech 'and I must say pretty well.' Elsie commented that Valerie Joklová spoke 'fair English'. The only linguistic problem appeared to have been that Zdenka had difficulty in understanding Rosa, and there Valerie Joklová's help was needed. Marie expressed surprise that Rosa smoked, to which she laughed saying that the only non-smoking Englishwoman was her daughter.

Whilst in Brno, they were able to see *Kát'a Kabanová* on 20 April, at the time the only production in the world. Rosa received a copy of the newly published score, which Janáček had specially solicited for her from Universal Edition. On 22 April, she was able to see *Jenůfa* at the Brno Theatre together with the Czechoslovak Ambassador to Denmark. According to John Tyrrell, she was also able to hear the première of Janáček's violin sonata played by František Kudláček (violin) and Jaroslav Kvapil (piano) on 24 April, although she did not mention it in her diary[7]. She also heard the Moravian singers' concert on the 23rd and Fibich's opera *Šarka* on the 26th. She attended a reception at the Anglo-American club on the 26th and on the 27th visited the Children's Country Homes at Tihov Orphanage. Although not travelling to Bratislava until 30 April, it is not clear whether she saw the performance, or the rehearsal of the performance, of Neumann's opera *Beatrice* on the 28th. Chudoba's letter indicated the performance was on the 28th whereas Rosa's diary notes indicate a rehearsal on the 28th.

41. Dr Alois Kolísek

Rosa and Elsie travelled with Dr Alois Kolísek to Bratislava on 30 April. During their short stay there, a reception was laid on for them on 1 May, at which they met important politicians and musicians. Rosa had a meeting with Ferdinand Juriga and Emil Stodola. Ferdinand Juriga (1874-1950) was a Catholic priest who became one of six members of the Slovak People's Party, who sat in the Hungarian Parliament before Czechoslovak independence. He was secretary of the Party. Emil Stodola (1862-1945) was the president of the Slovak National Party.

On the evening of their arrival, they attended a performance of Smetana's *Dalibor*. They visited the children's hospital and the memorial to Milan Štefánik (1880-1919), the Slovak politician, diplomat, and astronomer. Dr Kolísek arranged a steamer trip along the Danube to Vienna, where they stayed for a couple of days seeing a performance of Mozart's *Don Giovanni* on their first night. The following day, they visited Schönbrun, where they heard a performance of Lehar's *The Merry Widow*. They returned to Bratislava on 6 May and had tea with Dr Kolísek in his rooms in the Cathedral Close before they returned to Brno on the 7th and then back to Prague on 9 May. They stayed in Prague for a further four days before returning home on 13 May. Whilst in Prague they saw the composer Vitězslav Novák, Czech writer and editor of Hudební Matice, Otakar Nebuška (1875-1952), Lady Clerk, and President Masaryk. It seems likely that it was on this occasion that Rosa agreed with Nebuška to make English translations of some of Janáček's *Twenty-Six Folk Ballads*. Uncharacteristically of Rosa, she never made these translations, and the ballads were not published in Czech until 1950[8].

Soon after returning home, Rosa gave two lectures on the Music of Czechoslovakia at the School of Slavonic Studies, King's College London on the 2 and 16 June. After giving them, she wanted to repeat them at a more public venue so that Czech music could receive greater publicity in England. She wrote to Janáček on 25 July explaining this to him[9]. This letter was the only letter she wrote to him in French, thinking it would be easier for him. Subsequently she wrote to him in English and he wrote to her in Czech. In the letter, she explained that her second lecture included much about his music and she was having Mischa-Léon sing *The Diary of One Who Disappeared*. It would be the first performance in England. She went on to explain her choice of Mischa-Léon. He was a Jewish-born Danish tenor who spoke French, English, German, and Dutch, and she felt because of his background he would not have the 'stiffness' of English singers. Rosa explained that she wanted it sung in Czech and not German and that Mischa-Léon wanted to come to see Janáček in order to perfect the style and pronunciation. After he visited Janáček in September, Janáček wrote to Rosa on 22 September indicating his satisfaction with Mischa-Léon as a singer[10].

The two lectures she duly repeated at the Wigmore Hall on the 20 and 27 October. Tickets for the Wigmore Hall lectures were 5/ 9 d and 3/6d. The first lecture covered Czech Music before the nineteenth century – The Renaissance of the National Spirit – The Story of Národny divadlo (National Theatre) – The

Founders of the Modern National School: Smetana, Dvořák, Fibich –The Cult of Melodrama – Dvořák's Musical Descendants: Vitězslav Novák and Josef Suk. The second lecture covered Progress of Music under the Republic – New Musical Centres – The Chief Pupils of Fibich: K. Kovařovic and Josef B. Foerster – The Ultimate Development of Folk-style – Slovak Song and Moravian Music Drama – Leoš Janáček. The musical illustrations accompanying the lectures were performed by the singers Tonči Urbankova and Mischa-Léon and piano solos by Fanny Davies. The singers were accompanied by Frederick Kiddle and Harold Craxton. After the first of the two lectures, *The Times* reported that 'the whole occasion was calculated to inspire the wish for more intimate knowledge of an art which, in spite of the Boheniam Quartet and other artists, has not been fully explored by English musicians'[11].

After the performance, she reported to Janáček in a letter dated 28 October. She explained: 'I cannot say truthfully the *Diary* was a success in the common sense of the word,' but she goes on to say, that she saw people moved to tears although not all understood the psychology of the work, but they all felt they had heard something original and personal. She said how well Mischa-Léon performed the part. Then she went on to make scathing remarks about the press, whom she said dislike her because she is in a powerful position writing programme notes for the Queen's Hall. She says: 'The Press are a stupid narrow-minded self-opinionated Chauvinist lot of men.' She ends by saying: 'You are one of the great *ursprünglich* [original] creative artists in Europe.' The report in the *Morning Post* on 28 October gave a balanced account of the performance and explained that Mrs Newmarch had provided a translation of the text and background information which greatly helped the audience's appreciation of the work. The Czechoslovak Minister Dr Mastny, who chaired the proceedings, complemented Rosa on bringing Janáček's music to a wider audience.

It was after Rosa's visit to Czechoslovakia in 1922 that she began to compile material for her book *The Music of Czechoslovakia*, which was eventually published posthumously in 1942. She had already written about Dvořák, Suk, and Novák and was now revising what she had previously written about Janáček. She was also invited to contribute an article entitled *Moravian Music Drama* to the first volume of the *Slavonic Review* published in 1922. The article, favourably commented on by *The Times*, was entirely devoted to Janáček, explaining his 'late flowering' as a composer and his development of speech melody in his compositions[12].

Rosa's musical activities in 1923 were dominated by her visit to Czechoslovakia in the spring and the Promenade Concerts in the autumn. She visited Czechoslovakia from 24 March until 27 April and, as her diary shows, the month was filled with concerts, visiting friends and musicians, and renewing acquaintances. She attended a concert on the day of her arrival, and on the following day she attended a concert at which Josef Suk was soloist. In the evening, she had supper with Josef Suk, Vitĕzslav Novák, Boleslav Vomáčka (1887-1965) and friends. On the following day, she called on the widow of Karel Kovařovic. On Good Friday, 30 March she visited the Tyn Church and the Emmaus Monastery. She saw Smetana's Opera *Hubicka* (The Kiss) and an opera by Ostrčil. She had lunch with Sir George and Lady Clerk and also met the English Singers at Sir George's residence at the Thun Palace. On 9 April, she attended the rehearsal of the *Cantata of the Last Great Things of Man* by Ladislav Vycpálek (1882-1969) and a cantata by Jaroslav Křička (1882-1969), most probably *Temptation in the Desert* performed by the Hlahol Choir. On 11 April, she was given a private performance of Janáček's *Pohádka* (Fairy Tale) by Julius Junek (1873-1927), cello, and Růžena Nebušková (piano) at Nebuška's house. She also met Lubvik Kuba (1863-1956), a Czech landscape painter and musician, and Jan Branberger (1877-1952), the administrative director of the Prague Conservatory, and renewed her acquaintance with Alois Kolísek.

On 23 March, Rosa wrote to Janáček from her hotel, saying that she was in Prague and she must come to Brno and see Janáček for a few days possibly the week beginning 8 April[13]. She said that he must get Miss Joklová to translate this letter. In response, she received the briefest of notes, dated 7 April from Janáček mentioning two concerts, one on 10 April in the Municipal Theatre at which works of František Hradil, Gustav Homola and Pavel Haas (pupils of Janáček) were to be performed, and the second on 21 April at which the Prague Teachers' Choir would sing his *The 70000*[14]. He asked whether she had heard Mrs Nebušková and Junek perform his *Pohádka* and told her that Miss Joklová was not yet in Brno.

On 12 April, Rosa wrote a long letter to Bella Simpson giving the flavour of the visit, the reception she was receiving and an amusing account of meeting Bishop Gore.

My dear Bella

It is not easy to write much now as I am in full swing of all kinds of business and pleasure. But I have half an hour this morning, as I am waiting to take Bishop Gore up to Žižkov to see the Russian Archimandrite Savatije. I offered to go as interpreter, but am rather hoping a young Russian lady may accompany us, as though I feel equal to ordinary conversation, or even aesthetic discussions, I don't know about ecclesiastical dissertations!

It has been so far a very eventful week, and it is difficult to know where to begin our tale. On Tuesday, Morfova [the teacher and concert singer Christina Morfova, 1889-1936] sent me flowers and tickets to hear Prokopova [Ludmilla Prokopová, 1888-1959?] as "Madame Butterfly". You know how I loathe it; but I am bound to say that "Properpoker", as someone called her, is a fine actress, and has a good voice. I am going to see Morfova today. Yesterday I was at the Nebuška's, where we were just an intimate party of 8 or 9, and made music: Janáček's 'cello Sonata played by Mrs Nebuška and a fairly good 'cellist; and Karel's Violin Sonata [Rudolf Karel 1880-1945, violin sonata in D, 1912] – very good stuff indeed – played by Hoffman [Karel Hoffman, 1872-1936] and Roman Vesely, who is also a fine pianist. Then I took a cab with a "rychle Uharský Kon" (A quick Hungarian horse) as his owner called him, and arrived very late at the concert of the Prague Teachers' Union [...]

Altogether my visit this year seems to have evoked even more enthusiasm than in 1919. The newspapers have treated me rather like a Cabinet Crisis or a Murder. But it is rather odd that so far I have had no communication whatever from the Hrad. I know that generally Masaryk has left me till my last week, and also that he was away at Easter, but the old Chancellor here occasionally forgets to send on cards to Lány and that makes it awkward.

I cannot tell you half what I have done, but must reserve a good deal for my return. We now leave for Brno on Saturday morning [...] I feel *very well*, and everyone thinks me very energetic for my age. I am not sure which day next week we shall return here, but it ought not to be later than Saturday 21st, because the Umělecka Beseda (Society of Arts) is preparing a large reception for me on Sunday or Monday. After that culminating event I think I had better retire gracefully from the scene. It is really summer-warm today.

I began the day by escorting Bishop Gore in hot sunshine to the heights of Žižkov where dwells the Pravoslav Archbishop in two squalid little rooms. *I* had hoped to get some news of Russia, and I don't quite know what Bishop Gore wanted; nor, I think, did he know himself. But the new Archbishop Savatije was a dull amiable type of pope who turned on a tepid flow of inane talk, mostly about elementary facts of Church history which I am sure Bishop Gore knew in his deacon's days. Until I really had to intervene and explain that the Anglican "sviastchenik" [transliterated here] was a very "умный челове" [in Cyrillic here] learned man. After enduring this for 20 minutes we made our bows. For a long time Bishop Gore refused absolutely to believe I had introduced him to the Orthodox Archbishop and thought it was the Deacon and he on his side kept saying in Russian "do you tell me this is an Anglican Bishop?" In point of clothes, the Russian had it. The only really funny incident was when I insisted on Bishop Gore taking the seat of honour behind the table, and he carelessly lent back against a rickety shelf and brought down on his head a large crucifix and an assortment of sham Dresden shepherdesses! The Russian Archbishop and I behaved with commendable gravity, but I am afraid that *he* perhaps regarded it as an ill-omen. The poor Bishop looked more miserable than usual. But afterwards, at lunch, I was relieved to find that he really had been wanting to laugh too. This is my first and last attempt to promote the union of the Eastern and Western Churches.

How is Snip, dear little soul? This is not a country for cats. They mostly live in cellars and are scared of human beings. I am going to preach a crusade in their favour. But of course living up 5 or 6 flights of stone stairs makes the domestic puss impossible as an inmate. The climbing one does! Not a lift except in hotels. Morfova lives an *quatrième*, and how she gets there, and what prevents her rolling from top to bottom of the house when she is there is more than I can say; for she is *quite globular* on close inspection (Morfova with her pet canary sitting on her head). 🐦 I am so glad to hear your cough is almost gone. Thank the Man [Rosa's 🐦 husband] for his, received today (Thursday) and my love to dear Elisabeth. Please send this around. I think you may as well continue to write here, but in case of anything the address at Brno is enclosed. Ever yours affectly Rosa Newmarch.

42. Karel Hoffman

Rosa and Elsie travelled down to Brno on 15 April and returned to Prague on 19 April. This visit was not as fruitful as the 1922 visit. She did meet Janáček on the

18th, but she missed both concerts that he mentioned in his note of 7 April. On the 16th, she went to Prostějov, about sixty kilometres northeast of Brno, to hear a performance of Vitězslav Novák's cantata *Svatební Košile* (The Wedding Shirt, based on a text by Erben). On returning to Prague, she went to a conservatoire concert, saw an opera by Ostrčil, met Novák again and returned home on 27 April.

Once back at home, Rosa got back into her routine straightaway. At the beginning of May, she reviewed a book for Herbert Jenkins entitled *Memories of Russia 1916-1919* by Princess Paley. 'Princess Paley' was the title given to Olga Valerianovna Karnovich (1866-1929), Countess von Hohenfelsen, by Nicolas II of Russia. In her diary, Rosa noted that she called into Herbert Jenkins's office in early May, and that on 8 May, Jenkins died. The book in question was published by Herbert Jenkins Ltd. in 1924. In August, she discussed with Oxford University Press a possible book on Tchaikovsky, and in November, met Dr Arthur Somervell, the editor of OUP's series *The Musical Pilgrim*. However, she never wrote a book on Tchaikovsky, and it seems likely that her colleague Eric Blom did so in her stead. His book *Tchaikovsky's Orchestral Works* was published in that series in 1927. It may have been then that she anticipated a more important commitment with the third edition of *Grove's Music Dictionary* in the offing. In December 1923, she published an article on letters so far unpublished that she had received from Balakirev between 1902 and 1906[15]. Balakirev wrote to her in Russian and she translated the letters into English.

After her return from Czechoslovakia, there was one exchange of letters between Rosa and Janáček in 1923[16]. Janáček, wondering why he had not heard from her, wrote on 13 August, beginning: 'Are you so angry with Brno that you do not remember it even with one little word?' He then continued to tell her that he was searching for a libretto for a new opera and mentioned Karel Čapek's *The Makropoulis Case*. He also mentioned problems he was having with the publishers, Universal Edition. Rosa replied to his letter on 4 October explaining that she was not at all angry with him, but that she had been away from London and then had the pressure of work, as she was involved in four different concert series at the Queen's Hall. She then said: 'So it was business, not *böse*-ness [*böse* = displeased, German] that prevented me writing.' She told him that his *Šumařovo dítě* (Fiddler's child) was to be performed in London on 3 May 1924. She suggested H.G. Wells as a possible source of an opera libretto, expressed her wish to see him in England the following spring, telling him to get Valerie Joklová to translate the letter, and asked him to write to her in Czech as she could now understand it quite well. She added a postscript to the letter: 'Elsie sends her love. She has not tasted wine since that memorable night.' Besides the exchange of letters, Janáček sent her two postcards, the first to Prague on 22 April and the second to London on 30 December, both from Brno. In the first, he informed her that his *Čtveřice mužských sborů* (Four Male-Voice Choruses) was published in Czech by Mojmir Urbánek and also in German, but he did not know where, and it was without his permission. In the second, he asked if she had a translation of his *Diary of One who Disappeared* and sent her greetings for the new year[17].

The rest of her diary for 1923 is filled with concerts she attended, lectures she gave, the Promenade concert season, and various people she met for dinner. She attended a Czech Society Committee meeting on 16 October, in preparation for President Masaryk visit on 21 October, and on 22 of October, the Czech Society gave a reception for the President.

For Rosa, 1924 followed her usual pattern of a visit to Czechoslovakia in the spring and the Promenade Concert season in the autumn interspersed with other concerts and meetings. The Promenade Concert season was also followed that year with the Norwich Festival. However, 1924 was special in that there were anniversaries to celebrate: in Prague the centenary of the birth of Smetana (1824-1884) and in the autumn the 30th anniversary season of Promenade Concerts, celebrated by the first visit of royalty.

Rosa and Elsie arrived earlier in Prague on 28 February; Rosa was commissioned as *The Times*' correspondent[18] to cover the Smetana celebrations, as she described:

Smetana's posthumous influence grew ever stronger in Bohemia. The nearer the country approached to the hour of liberation and the possibilities of return to its ancient glory, prophesied by Smetana in his epic opera *Libuša*, the more fervent grew the cult of his music. With the proclamation of the Republic in 1918 enthusiasm reached a climax; and the Smetana centenary celebrated all over the country in the spring of 1924 showed that his popularity had not waned in the hearts of his people.

All through the month of March commemorative concerts of Smetana's music were given, and in April the entire series of his operas, with new scenery and dresses, were presented at the National Theatre. In order that every class might share in this national commemoration of their beloved musician, free concerts were organised on a similar basis for students, workmen and soldiers. I can think of no other country where the memory of an individual musician has been so generally and cordially honoured; we can hardly imagine our own people thrilled collectively by a Purcell or Sullivan

Festival; even the memory of Shakespeare would scarcely suffice to produce such a universal thrill. Since Tyrtaeus rallied the courage of the Spartans and led them to victory with his songs, has any musician played so great a part in the rehabilitation of a race as the composer of the opera *Libuše* and the Symphonic Poem *My Fatherland* did in the destiny of Bohemia. The occasion had an almost epic significance for the Czechoslovak nation. The opening ceremony of the Festival was in the National Opera House, when addresses were given by the Chairman of the Centenary Committee, Fr Taborsky, the Chairman of the National Assembly, the Minister of Education, a representative of the Government, and Professor J.B. Foerster representing Czech musicians. But the chief interest centred round the oration delivered by Professor Zdeněk Nejedlý, who made Smetana and his music the subject of a life-long study.

President Masaryk attended many of the concerts, and invited me to his box; sending a car to fetch me from the Hotel he received me in his private room behind the auditorium of the Smetana Hall. Dr Alice, his daughter, was unable to come, but I was glad to have the opportunity of meeting her substitute, Madame Beneš, wife of the Prime Minister, a charming woman whom I was to know well in later years. During the interval we went back into the anti-room, where we talked of politics, books and music; the President was always an interesting companion, simple and dignified, but with a great sense of humour too!

H. C. Colles*, an eminent British music scholar, had been appointed to revise a third edition Grove's *Dictionary of Music and Musicians*. Colles had asked Rosa to oversee the articles on Czech, Moravian, and Slovak composers. Rosa felt that circumstances had so long confounded the art of Bohemia with that of South Germany and Slovakia with that of Hungary, denying them each a separate existence, that she felt that to make this fact clear was an act of historical restitution. She was therefore very glad when Colles asked her to be involved in the process. It was decided that some of these articles should be contributed by authoritative writers from Czechoslovakia and most of these were to be translated by Rosa, so whilst in Prague, she took the opportunity to discuss these proposed articles with Vitěszlav Novák, a leading Czech composer, and Otakar Šourek, a Czech writer on music and biographer of Dvořák.

43. Petr and Jaroslav Křička

[Inscribed: *A notre chère mere anglaise, Madame Rosa Newmarch, 1927 Jaroslav*]

On 28 February, Rosa met Petr and Jaroslav Křička for dinner. She first met the poet Petr Křička on her 1919 visit to Prague when he escorted her on her journey through Czechoslovakia (see Chapter 22). She also became good friends with his brother, the composer and teacher Jaroslav (1882-1969), as is evident from the photograph. On 20 March, Rosa and Elsie were invited to a party at the President's residence.

Janáček wrote on 5 March to Rosa in Prague explaining that *Jenůfa* was being performed in Berlin on 15 March and that if he went, he would leave for Berlin on 11 March. He also asked whether she would like to go and finished by saying he expected they would meet in Brno. Janáček also put her in touch with Max Brod. Whilst in Prague, there was a suggestion about a possible English translation of Brod's biography of Janáček[19]. Rosa did pay a short visit to Brno on 1 April, meeting Janáček and also Alois Kolísek, but she comments in her diary that little was going on in Brno.

After returning home in early April, she went to a party given by the Finnish envoy, Ossian Donner, on 8 April, and a week later met Dr Vojtech Mastny of the Czechoslovak legation. On 6 May, she attended a reception at the Czechoslovak legation and had lunch with the Czech pianist Jan Heřman. At the beginning of

August, she was on holiday at Bacton-on-Sea, Norfolk before the start of the Proms season on 9 August. For the 1924 season, unusually there were no new works performed[20], and so Rosa's already prepared analytical notes could be used. The highlight of the thirtieth season was the visit of the King and Queen to the Proms on Wednesday 15 October, three nights before the 'Last Night'; it has been well described elsewhere.[21,22] The format of the Prom stayed as it had done for many years. The King had asked for Elgar's Overture *Cockaigne*, 'O Star of Eve' from *Tannhäuser*, and Wood's *Fantasia on British Sea-Songs,* and these formed part of the programme which also included two movements from Beethoven's violin concerto played by Jelly d'Aranyi, and Frank Bridge's suite *The Sea*. The programme was conducted by Sir Henry Wood, Frank Bridge, and Sir Edward Elgar. There was no royal box at the Queen's Hall; it had been removed a while back as it was taking up too much room in the Grand Circle. Instead, a whole block of seats to the left of the platform was reserved for the Royal Party. The King congratulated the three conductors during the interval and Wood's twelve year-old daughter, Tania, presented a bouquet. The King clearly enjoyed the concert as an extract of his diary reveals: 'At 8.00 we went to the Promenade at Queen's Hall, such a good orchestra conducted by Sir Henry Wood. House very full, they gave us a great reception and sang the National Anthem at the end.' Wood saw the King again at the end of the concert, and the latter commented that he found *Rule Britannia* 'a jolly good tune' and better than *The Red Flag*. Jacobs points out that it was a topical remark as it was the year of Britain's first short-lived Labour Government[22]. After the concert, Rosa wrote to Tiny describing events:

Dearest Tiny

The great event went off very well. The Hall was full and the King and Queen had a tremendous reception. But people, though quite well behaved, did all the usual "Prom" things, so their majesties saw us as usual, and were a good deal amused. They read their programmes, especially the King, who really seemed to *study* his – and tore it out of its watered-silk cover and apparently folded it up to put in his pocket! Tania presented the Queen with a bouquet in the lobby and I believe Muriel [Wood's second wife] was presented to them; otherwise they received no ladies, only three conductors during the interval. I was not sorry, for I feel that if ever I *was* presented to the King and Queen I should prefer it to be socially, not on an occasion of this kind. Everybody enjoyed it and I shouldn't be surprised if they came again – if the concerts go on, but I sometimes wonder. We were very lucky in having a nice dry night. The next excitement will be Norwich I expect! I am not sorry for a week or so of peace in between. But I think we shall enjoy it, especially Elsie. The Colmans are giving a lunch, and a tea for the Orchestra, and a tremendous big squash at Carrow Abbey. I am afraid in the pressure of writing and telephoning I quite forgot Miss Louisa's birthday. Please give her my love and tell her how busy I was.

I am glad you enjoyed those sunny days. It is dull and grey now, but quite nice for moving about. On Tuesday I sat a long while in Belsize Avenue and was overhot in the sun. I was interested in the paper. I will send this off now. I saw Mr Newman this afternoon, he said the King and Queen were really charming and as they were leaving they made quite a long stop at the door to say they thanked everybody and the King said "we really *did* enjoy our evening". With much love,

Yours ever affect

Rosa

Shortly after the Prom season was over, Rosa was off to Norwich for the rehearsals for the Norwich Festival, which took place from 27 October until 1 November. The Norwich Festival has a long history. Occasional festivals were held from 1770 to 1817, and then triennially until the First World War. The festival scheduled for 1914 was postponed and the series was not revived until 1924. So the resumption of the festival after thirteen years was important in re-establishing the tradition. Major works that year included Mendelssohn's *Elijah*, Beethoven's *Mass in D*, Bach's *St John Passion*, Verdi's *Requiem*, and Vaughan Williams's *Sea Symphony*, all performed by the New Queen's Hall Orchestra. Sir Henry Wood was the principal conductor from 1908 until 1930. Frank Bridge's suite *The Sea* was again performed and conducted by the composer as at the Promenade Concert on 16 October. The ten-year-old Benjamin Britten and commented: '…heard Frank Bridge conduct his suite *The Sea* and was knocked sideways.' Bridge became Britten's mentor in his early years. The programme notes for *The Sea* used at both concerts were written by Rosa[23], who mentioned in her letter that the Coleman's were entertaining the orchestra to lunch at Carrow Abbey. Many distinguished musicians were entertained there including Sir Edward Elgar.

The most notable event in 1925 for Rosa was her annual visit to Czechoslovakia. She went in May as *The Times'* correspondent to cover the International Music Festival in Prague from 15 to 20 May. Earlier in the year, she had read in a Czech newspaper about Sibelius's success in Copenhagen and his invitation to attend the Three Choirs Festival in Gloucester. She wrote to Sibelius on 9 March congratulating him on his success but explained that it was too early to fix a date for a new concert of his works in London. Much as she would like to see him at the Queen's Hall, things were not working out well for the orchestra under Chappell & Co management, and it seemed symphony concerts were somewhat out of favour, possibly the expansion of broadcasting was partly to blame[24]. Chappell & Co were losing money on sponsoring the Proms by this time, and it reached a crisis point just over a year later.

The *Musical Times* reported in September 1925: 'The biggest blow to the Festival [The Gloucester festival] was the fact that Jean Sibelius was due to have had his *Seventh* and final *Symphony* given its British première – however he had been unable to complete it on time[25].' The author of this article lamented the fact that this meant the festival 'lost' its only connection with the modern music of the continent! This statement is surprising since Sibelius's Seventh Symphony was completed in March 1924[26].

Madame Olga Novikoff, who had been a great supporter of Rosa's efforts to see Russian music played in England, died on 21 April and Rosa attended her funeral on 27 April. On 26 April, she wrote to Janáček explaining that she would be in Prague on 10 May, as *The Times'* correspondent at the festival and that she was studying *The Cunning Little Vixen* and hoped to see him there at the rehearsal. She left London on 9 May and stayed in her usual hotel on arriving in Prague. She went to three orchestral concerts on the 15, 17 and 19 May and saw *The Cunning Little Vixen* under Ostrčil on 18 May. At the second of these orchestral concerts, Vaughan Williams's *Pastoral Symphony* was performed. Vaughan Williams was in Prague at the time and he also saw the performance of *The Cunning Little Vixen* and is said to have liked it[27]. Rosa wrote three reports for *The Times*, in the third of which she reported on the last of the orchestral concerts and Janáček's opera. Two works she was particularly impressed by and thought they should be performed in England were Rudolf Karel's *Dämon* and Vycpálek's cantata *Four Last Things of Man*. Of *The Cunning Little Vixen* she reported that the orchestration was brilliant and sure and is generally complimentary about the opera. However, she did not seem 'bowled over' as she was on first seeing *Jenůfa*, but this seems to be on account of its strangeness compared to other operas.

A week after the opera, she visited the small town of Roudnice nad Labem about fifty kilometres north of Prague, on 25 May. The town is dominated by the castle of the old Bohemian Lobkowicz family. Joseph Franz Maximillian Lobkowicz was one of Beethoven's patrons. There she met the librarian Dr Blažek who showed her the scores of Beethoven's *In Questa Tomba Oscura* for voice and orchestra and Marcello's *Psalms*. She had most probably heard Shaliapin sing *In Questa Tomba Oscura* in one of his London recitals. The following day, she had lunch with Zdeněk Nejedlý (1878-1962) in Prague. Nejedlý was an eminent and controversial musicologist and later a politician. In 1903, he published his *History of*

Czech Music. Rosa, by this time, had started to collect information for her book *Music of Czechoslovakia,* which was published nearly twenty years later, and presumably saw him as a useful source of information. In 1921, Nejedlý joined the Communist Party and in the 1948 government was appointed First Minister of Education and Culture.

On the 28th, she attended a Mahler concert before returning home via Karlovy Vary (Karlsbad). This was the first of several visits she was to pay to the spa town of Karlovy Vary, where the waters are reputed to be good for metabolic and digestive complaints. As Elsie said: 'She found renewed health and energy in this health resort.' She arrived there on the 2nd and returned home on 26 June. In her later years, Rosa suffered from diabetes, but it was not until May 1930 that she first took insulin. Later in the summer, she spent time on holiday in Norfolk.

Notes

1. John Tyrrell, *Janáček: Year of a Life* (London: Faber and Faber, 2007), vol. 2. p.430.

2. Zdenka E. Fischmann, *Janáček-Newmarch Correspondence* (Rockville, Maryland: Kabel Publishers, 1986), p.43.

3. Ibid. pp.45-6.

4. Ibid. pp.46-7.

5. Ibid. pp.47-8.

6. John Tyrrell, *Janáček: Year of a Life* (London: Faber and Faber, 2007) pp.429-31.

7. Ibid. pp.430-1.

8. Ibid. p.399.

9. Zdenka E. Fischmann, *Janáček-Newmarch Correspondence*, pp.50-1.

10 Ibid. p.55.

11.'Lectures and Meetings: Wigmore Hall', *The Times,* 10 Oct. 1922.

12. 'The Slavonic Review', *The Times,* 29 Dec. 1922.

13. Zdenka E. Fischmann, *Janáček-Newmarch Correspondence*, p.71

14. Ibid. p.72

15. Rosa Newmarch, 'Some Unpublished Letters of Balakirev' *The Chesterian,* Dec. 1923, pp.73-7.

16. Zdenka E. Fischmann, *Janáček-Newmarch Correspondence*, pp. 73-4 and 76-7.

17. Sotheby's Music Catalogue, London, 22 May 2003, p.55.

18. 'The Smetana Centenary' and 'The Choirs of Czechoslovakia', *The Times,* 8 and 22 Mar. 1924.

19. Zdenka E. Fischmann, *Janáček-Newmarch Correspondence*, pp.78-9.

20. David Cox, *The Henry Wood Proms* (London: BBC Publications, 1980), p.272.

21. Ibid. p.72-4.

22. Arthur Jacobs, *Henry J. Wood: Maker of the Proms* (London: Methuen, 1994), pp.200-1.

23. Rosa Newmarch, *The Concert-Goers Library* (London: OUP, 1933), vol 3, pp.15-8.

24. Eric Tawaststjerna, *Sibelius, 1914-1957* trans. Robert Layton (London: Faber and Faber, 2008), vol. 3, p.258.

25. Unsigned article, *Musical Times,* 66, Jul. 1925, p. 838.

26. Robert Layton, *Sibelius* (London: Dent, 1965), p.166.

27. Tyrrell, *Janáček,* vol 2, p.599.

CHAPTER 25: THE YEAR 1926: JANÁČEK'S VISIT AND NEWMAN'S DEATH.

For the first five months of 1926, Rosa was very much occupied with making arrangements for Janáček 's visit to London. Nevertheless, she was able to find time to write her first article for the *Radio Times* which had been established in repsonse to a newspaper boycott of listing radio programmes. The first issue of the *Radio Times* was on 28 September 1923. Her first article was entitled "A Master of Russian Folk Music: A Study of Rimsky-Korsakov[1]."

Janáček's visit is described in detail by Tyrrell[2] and also in Fischmann's *Janáček Newmarch Correspondance*[3]. By this time, Rosa Newmarch had vast experience of organising events and people, but even with all that experience, it must have been an anxious time for her. She was now in her sixty-eighth year and still maintaining a high workload. Her health was not as good as in earlier years. She had begun going to the health resort at Karlovy Vary, and in the run up to Janáček's visit, she took a week off at Eastbourne in February to recuperate. In addition, although there is no mention of this in her accounts, it seems very probable from letters that her husband was probably beginning to suffer from the early stages of what is now known as senile dementia and Bella, still living with them, was immobile upstairs. She was also concerned about her son, who was suffering from tuberculosis, which was to continue to dog him in the years to come. She was very used to dealing with the foibles of temperamental musicians, and in this respect Janáček must has given her some uneasy moments, but at the same time he did appreciate the efforts she was making on his behalf. She had clearly staked much on this visit. From Janáček's letter it appears that she had also paid some of the expenses from her own pocket[4].

During the period from the end of January until late April 1926, Rosa wrote eight letters to Janáček and he replied with six to her. These give a good account of the arrangements prior to his visit. In the first letter, dated 29 January, Rosa explained that she had suggested to the Czechoslovak legation that Janáček should visit London[5]. She hoped he would bring his wife, Zdenka, and then went on to suggest a programme for a concert of his works. Opera would not be possible, and she suggested his first string quartet, the suite *Mládí* (Youth), and his violin sonata. She explained that Mischa-Léon was in America and so a performance of *The Diary of One Who Disappeared* would not be possible. She also suggested he might see

Oxford and Stratford. She and Elsie would look after him and make sure he was comfortable, but because her house was small, she used the Czech word, *domek,* she would put him up in a quiet hotel and she felt sure that the minister, Dr Masaryk (son of the President), would take an interest in his visit. In Janáček's reply, he and Zdenka are very happy to be invited but he was disappointed that Rosa was suggesting only 'trifles' to be performed. He says: 'I am not refusing – I will wait, there is plenty of time[6].' Rosa explained that there was no national or state opera house in England and that an opera at this stage would not be possible. She then drew the analogy with Debussy, where his string quartet and *L'Après-Midi d'un Faune* were played several times in England before his opera *Pélleas et Mélisande* was performed, and that said it was necessary to start with small beginnings. She was obviously worried that Janáček was hesitant and that he did not realise that it took time in England to get these things organised. She wrote: 'It is not, dear Mistr, a long time to April-May' and then repeats the message in Czech: '*Do dubna května ne je tak daleko.'* She then used a similar analogy to the one she had used years before with Sibelius, 'neither can I play Hamlet with the part of Hamlet left out[7].'

On 15 February, Janáček accepted the invitation and asked whether his *Concertina for piano* might be added to the programme. Mrs Ilona Kurzová-Štěpánová played it from memory in Brno and Prague and it was well received. Rosa, who was resting at Eastbourne, wrote that she was delighted he had accepted, she had engaged the Wigmore Hall and the best wind players, together with the pianist Fanny Davies, but was doubtful about the *Concertino*. Janáček explained that it only lasted fifteen minutes, and suggested *The Fairy Tale* for cello and piano might also be included in the programme; that English artists would be acceptable although he would have liked Mrs Ilona Kurzová-Štěpánová. He added that he would not be bringing his wife as he wanted to take in everything while in England and she would be a distraction, instead he would be bringing a young musician as an interpreter (eventually this was Jan Mikota, his second choice). Tyrrell suggests that not bringing his wife is puzzling as they were in a 'good phase' with each other and when she had travelled with him to Venice, she had been an asset[8].

Rosa responded that the programme was excellent, assured him that he would be met off the boat, and asked how many performers were required, i.e. whether some of the parts were doubled. He was not to be put off, as he would soon be receiving an official invitation, as that was how things were done in England[9]. Janáček had obviously been studying the maps and noticed that Crossfield Road was some distance from the Thames, which he very much wanted to see. He still worried that only 'trifles' were going to be performed, that he did not want too many social events, and would he need to bring tails as well as a dinner jacket? Rosa responded that he would need both;

tails were needed for the minister's reception, and he should bring his 'nice tweed suit' for everyday. He would be able to see the Thames, as his hotel would be much nearer the Thames than her house at Crossfield Road. She answered him that second class rail was very good, but said he should take a private cabin for the long sea-crossing at a cost of 15/5d (= 77½p, but based on the Retail Price Index, about £35). Rosa herself was a 'good sailor' but Elsie was not, but she found that if Elsie were kept warm and lay down in the cabin, she avoided sea-sickness; she advised Janáček to do likewise.[10]

Janáček's letter of 10 April must have set alarm bells ringing for Rosa. He complained that two clouds had descended. The first was haggling with the Czechoslovak Ministry, who initially agreed to give him £150 (equivalent to 24,600 crowns in 2007) and then reduced it to 14,000 crowns. The second was that he had had 'flu' and this had left him unable to hear in his left ear. He wrote: 'Thus it seems to me that you will give the concert without me.' This was followed by a flurry of three letters from Rosa, two on 15 April and one on 18 April. These gave further details about the arrangements and instructions that he should follow, such as: 'Be sure to keep warm on board of the boat. Even if you do not feel seasick, people easily take a chill walking about on deck. Lie down, and keep well covered up for most of the journey' and 'Travel in a warm overcoat and bring a lighter, for the weather in May is changeable, sometimes warm, sometimes rather cold[11].' Tyrrell suggests, in relation to all these detailed arrangements, that 'Like Janáček in his attitude to Kamila [Stösslová], Mrs Newmarch was turning into a possessive fusser[12].' This is very true, and in many ways comparable to the way she looked after Sibelius, particularly on his 1921 trip. However, one should not overlook her genuine concern to make as sure as she possibly could that the trip was an enjoyable and rewarding trip for Janáček. This is evident in little touches, for example, in her letter of 18 April, she mentioned that there were one or two Czech-speaking waiters at the Langham Hotel where he would be staying. She must have been greatly relieved to receive his final letter on 21 April, which began: 'Well the clouds disappeared. I will go for sure[…] But [as to] expenses for me and Mr Mikota – that is my worry. You already have enough on your shoulders […] I look forward to the rehearsal. To our happy meeting. Yours very truly, Drph Leoš Janáček. (After Janáček received an honorary doctorate, he liked to use his new title.) Even Janáček's handwriting shows his excitement about the visit. Finally she sent him a cable to Brno, which read: 'Please don't disappoint us all well arranged many friends expect you. Newmarch[13].'

Janáček set off for Prague on 27 April and before leaving, wrote to Kamila and his sister, Josefa. In both letters it is clear he regards it as a long journey with the possibility of misfortune, such that he might not return. Although travelling with Mikota, who spoke dubious English, the Czechoslovak legation in London also provided him with good interpreters. The sea trip went well and he was not seasick, perhaps heeding Rosa's advice. Elsie met him at Folkstone expecting the seventy-one-year old to be tired after a long journey, but as she commented: 'He was his usual energetic self, full of interest and vigour and enjoyed a dinner on the way to London and wanted to know all about the programme and arrangements for the visit.' At London, he was met by the welcoming party, which included the Czechoslovak Minister, Jan Masaryk, and his staff members, members of the Czech community in London, and, of course, Rosa herself. The official programme started the next day, Friday 30 April, with a reception at Claridge's, where Rosa had gathered various dignitaries and artists and friends of Janáček. Later he was driven to see the changing of the guard, Big Ben, the Houses of Parliament, and Westminster Abbey. In the Commons there was a lively session as it was immediately before the General Strike. On Saturday 1 May, an article Rosa had written about Janáček's visit, 'A Czechoslovak Composer: Janáček in England', was published in *The Times*. The same day, there were rehearsals in the morning at Adila Fachiri's house and in the afternoon at H. C. Colles's house. In the morning, his violin sonata was rehearsed and he considered Adila Fachiri, Joachim's great niece, played beautifully, but was less taken with Fanny Davies. May be appearances also coloured matters, with Adila a lively thirty-seven-year old, but Fanny Davies now an elderly sixty-five-year old.

44. Rosa Newmarch, Fanny Davies, Janáček, and Adila Fachiri

In the afternoon, Janáček's *Fairy Tales* was rehearsed, and that was followed by a trip on the Thames, and in the evening dinner with Henry Wood, Lady Wood, Rosa, and Elsie at Les Gobelins, Heddon Street (off Regents Street). The following day, the First String Quartet, *Mládí*, and the Concertino were rehearsed at the Czechoslovak legation. Janáček felt the London Wind Quintet played excellently, the Woodhouse Quartet played correctly, though coldly, but he was very dissatisfied with Fanny Davies in the Concertino. According to Mikota, Fanny Davies misunderstood the music and played it in the romantic style of Schubert instead of the modern spirit of Janáček. After an unsuccessful attempt to contact Ilona Kurzová-Štěpánová as a replacement, it was decided to drop it from the programme. After lunch at the legation, Janáček, together with Rosa, Elsie, and the bass Herbert Heyner, went to Henry and Muriel Wood's country home, Appletree Farm in Chorleywood. Janáček was delighted to be there, as is clear from his notebook entry: 'Living there as in a fairy tale.' Janáček and Henry Wood were photographed in the garden.

At seven that evening, Janáček was driven back to London for a reception by the Czechoslovak community at the Czechoslovak Club, where he enjoyed the food, and the proceedings were mainly in Czech. He responded to the official speeches of welcome with a speech about how being in London seemed like a fairy tale, about Czechs' place in the world, and it included a tribute to Rosa: 'Well now! Who invited me here? Was it a Czech? No it was Mrs Newmarch. That means, someone belonging to a completely different nation. However she has something in common with our country after all. She likes it. She likes its music. And she rather took a liking to my music so she was able to publicise it well. I am astonished how much good one person can do. Believe me sometimes entire organizations do not manage what she has done. She can do a lot for us on 'London soil' [sic]. May it please God that she live for a long time.' At 10.30pm, Janáček returned to the hotel 'not even tired', as he reported to Zdenka.

45. Sir Henry Wood and Janáček at Appletree Farm

Monday 3 May was spent sightseeing, with a visit to the London Zoo, where

271

Janáček took down the animal noises at Monkey Hill and the plaintive cry of the walrus as it clambered out of the water. Lunch was with Lady Muriel Paget*, whom Rosa knew on account of her Russian connections. In the afternoon, Mr Hanč, the legation's press secretary, took him on a bus and on the Underground, on what turned out to be the last day before public transport came to a halt with the General Strike. The next day, he was the guest at the Royal Academy of Music, where the director, Dr John McEwen, had invited him to lunch. Among the others present was Henry Wood, whom by now Janáček was getting to know and like. Wood had already performed Janáček's *Fiddler's Child* in 1924 and was to conduct the English premières of the Sinfonietta, *Taras Bulba*, the *Lachian Dances*, and the *Glagolitic Mass*. In the evening, there was a dinner party that included Jan Masaryk, Rosa, Adila Fachiri and her husband, the bass singer Herbert Heyner, Mr and Mrs Courtauld, and Dr Císař from the Czechoslovak legation. The Courtaulds, who were great supporters of the arts, appeared to Janáček to be promising a production of *Jenůfa* at Covent Garden in 1927. However, later in September, Rosa had to write to Janáček to explain the problems she was encountering in realising this plan and a production at Covent Garden in the near future would not be possible. According to Elsie, Rosa even worked on translating the librettos of *Kat'a Kabanova*, *The Cunning Little Vixen*, and *The Makropoulous Affair* in the hope that these operas might be performed in Covent Garden sometime in the future.

In the evening, there was a reception organised by the School of Slavonic Studies, King's College and the Czech Society of Great Britain. This included a short concert given by a boys' choir, and Herbert Heyner sang some solo songs, including two of Janáček's *Silesian Songs* in Rosa's translation. There was a speech by Seton-Watson on cultural relations between Great Britain and Czechoslovakia and an improvised reply by Janáček, translated by Dr Císař. Plans to have a further rehearsal on the day before the concert were largely abandoned because of the General Strike. The concert took place at 3pm on 6 May at the Wigmore Hall. Because there was no public transport on the day, there was not a capacity audience and the works to be performed were announced by the manager as no programmes were printed. There were no reviews of the concert the following day. The oboist, Leon Goosens, performing in *Mládí*, had a three-hour walk in order to get to the concert. From Eric Blom's account in the *Manchester Guardian* nearly a fortnight later, and also Mikota's account, it seems the audience was enthusiastic; there was endless applause after the string quartet and Janáček appeared on the podium to acknowledge it; the audience even applauded each movement of Fachiri's performance of the violin sonata. *Mládí* was described as fresh and original.

After the concert, because of the lack of transport, Janáček moved out from his hotel and stayed at Jan Masaryk's house for the remainder of his stay. The trip to Oxford also had to be abandoned. According to Janáček, 'they might stop the car. Already today they shouted at the person who was driving us', and there was the worry as to how he would get back home. However, a train manned by volunteers set off from London to Folkstone on Saturday 8 May and saw Janáček and Mikota on the first leg of their journey to Prague. A crowd of well-wishers saw them off at the station.

46. Janáček's Departure from London, May 1926.
Rosa Newmarch holding the bouquet, Elsie immediately to her left

Janáček's fortnight visit to England was the climax of much work and preparation for Rosa. She was present to oversee the whole of the week's events. She probably had mixed feelings after the visit; pleased that she had managed the first visit of a major Czech composer since Dvořák's last visit to England in 1896 and pleased that Janáček obviously appreciated all she had done. It was unfortunate that the General Strike meant that some planned events were curtailed and that there might otherwise have been a larger audience. She would obviously have liked to have had a wider selection of his works performed. Once Janáček had returned home, he wrote to her on 14 May: 'My first letter after my arrival here belongs to you. You had planned everything with an able hand, and with energy you brought it up to the point where victory can be sensed. But we shall exclaim hurrah [only] when Jenůfa begins to sing that she knows the love God is content with[14].'

Between May and September 1926, there were four letters from Janáček to Rosa and three from Rosa to Janáček, from which much can be discerned about Rosa's movements in that five months[15]. On the day of Janáček's departure from

London, Rosa's step-nephew, Jack, who had been ill for some time, died of pneumonia. [Although Rosa refers to him as her step-nephew, he was strictly speaking her step-grandson. Her son John married Gwendoline Stephens, whose eldest child by her first marriage was Jack.] He was only eighteen and his mother, who was in a nursing home at the time, was distraught. Rosa went to Leamington, where she helped her through the worst of her distress. She came back to London on 2 June. She had been invited to the Sokol Festival at the end of June as a reporter. In a letter dated 23 June, she says she is leaving for Prague. However, it seems, from a comment in Janáček's letter, that she was also paying another of her now regular visits to the health resort at Karlovy Vary *en route*. She was in Prague on 5 July, where she was invited to a lunch given by the Mayor of Prague at the Municipal House of Prague (Obecní dům hlavního města Prahy) given in honour of foreign delegates. Whilst in Prague, the Czechoslovak Artists Union conferred honorary membership on her in recognition of her work on behalf of Czechoslovak music, especially for making it known in England. It is a distinction given to few foreigners; previously honoured foreigners included the playwright Pirandello and the French sculptor Bourdell[16]. Elsie believed there had been a wish on the part of her friends in Prague to make her a member of the Order of the White Lion; but since the services she rendered were not of personal service to the President or of an official nature, nor had she ever been the recipient of any order in her own country, this was not possible.

She was back in London by 25 July. It seems she did not see Janáček whilst in Prague, nor have time to visit him at Hukvaldy, and she missed the Prague performance of his Sinfonietta. In Janáček's letter to her on 8 September, he told her that he was dedicating Sinfonietta to her and the committee that invited him to London. Prior to that, on 4 September, Rosa had to give him the disappointing news that *Jenůfa* would not be staged at Covent Garden in 1927. Mrs Courtauld explained to Rosa that the losses from the Opera House in 1925 and 1926 meant that they could only afford to stage one new opera in the 1927 season, and it had to be one that could be assured to attract the British public. Although Mrs Courtauld felt *Jenůfa* was a more interesting work, for box office reasons, Puccini's *Turandot* had to be the new opera for the next season. Rosa tried to soften the blow by explaining that she did not despair of getting *Jenůfa* performed in the future, and that Henry Wood was performing *Taras Bulba* in October and she was doing her best to get *Mládí* performed again soon.

The thirty-second Promenade concert season opened on 14 August and lasted until 16 October 1926. Rosa continued, with Eric Blom, to provide the analytical notes. In all previous seasons, Robert Newman, founder and manager for thirty-two years, had not missed a single evening, until 1926. The programme for the last night included a note which began: 'The familiar presence of Mr Robert Newman, the popular founder and manager of the Promenade Concerts, has been greatly missed at Queen's Hall during the last few weeks. In all thirty-two years since the first inauguration of the 'Proms' Mr Newman has never before been absent for a single evening. His assiduous attention to business and to the service of the music public are too well known to need comment. In answer to many kind enquiries we regret to say that Mr Newman is still too seriously indisposed to be here this evening, but he will no doubt have the thoughts and the sympathy of his many friends present among the audience of the Promenade Concerts.'

Robert Newman died on 4 November 1926. On Sunday 7 November, Rosa wrote to her sister-in-law Emily:

My dear Emily,

I write a few lines to wish you good health and happiness, for there *is* a considerable amount of happiness due to one as one gets older, although it may not be in the least what one anticipated. I am afraid our (Elsie's) card sounded rather careless the other day, but we have been and still are, so distracted with things, mostly troublous. The choir [the Prague Teachers' Choir] took up much of my time and on Wednesday I had to accompany them and speak at considerable length, first at the Central Hall Westminster, and then at the National Union of Teachers. Both places were overheated, and I got home at 10.30, very tired, and developed a bad cold and some temperature. I stayed in bed 2 days, and would have been glad to take longer, but I dragged myself down on the Monday evening, because I was afraid Elsie would knock up. Bella makes no progress in walking and is still upstairs and needs constant waiting on. Then on Thursday [4 November] about 10.30 p.m. Mrs Newman rang me up with the news for which we have been all more or less waiting – that her husband had just passed away. It immediately involved me in a great deal of work; press notices, alterations in yesterdays' programme, an obituary notice[17], and incessant telephone calls. Tomorrow I must attend the funeral at 1 o.c. and even after that I shall be very busy, because it is our intention to turn his personal concert which he had organised for Dec 4, into a benefit Concert for his widow and children. For this it will be necessary to interest the Press, and as he was a man who did everything himself, his two sons and the clerk in his office have not much *savoir faire*, being all young things.

Tomorrow as you know is also Bella's birthday [82nd] and she sends you greetings. I am somewhat troubled about her, she seems to have 'settled down' to the situation more than I like. If you are free on Wednesday, would you come to tea? Mrs Ommanney comes to have tea with Bella a good many days in the week, but I think she is not likely to be here that day. I am afraid that is the only day I can count on this week.

> With love from us all
> Yours affectly
> Rosa Newmarch

Henry Wood's arrangement of Chopin's Funeral March was played in Robert Newman's memory at the Queen's Hall concert on 6 November, just as previously it had been played as an *in memoriam* tribute to Joachim, Grieg, and Sarasate. The funeral was on Monday 7 November, and Rosa wrote to Tiny on the following day describing it:

Dearest Tiny,

Thanks for your letter this morning. I did get to the funeral with the Woods. It would have been very impressive but for the dreadful weather which played havoc with the beautiful wreaths. After the family, Henry and I, followed by 30 or 40 members of the orchestra, were I suppose the chief mourners. But there were many other people of the musical world, singers, agents and pressmen. The clergyman wisely cut the service at the grave as short as possible, and gave more in the chapel. It *did* slash down. But thanks to galoshes, gaiters and a big coat I kept dry. Lunch was waiting for us at the Woods and we took hot drinks, and I do not feel any worse today. Personally I can stand wet better than a cutting wind. Henry and I had a long talk about the Queen's Hall. We both feel very much in the dark as to the future. Perhaps we shall just carry on as we are until the present season ends in April; but I am sure Boosey cannot carry on without a manager and they are few and far between. Newman was very experienced and tactful, and knew his Press and public. Also he was a strong minded man and perfectly honest. Such people are not picked up everyday of the week. But for the moment, I expect there will not be anyone appointed, which means that they will refer to me for lots of things. The young folk, in fact all of them, are frightened of Willie Boosey. I don't mind him because he is always courteous to me and if he wasn't I should resign at once. In fact I think the future problematical, because if I did not like the new manager I should *not* go on. But for the moment I should like to see everything through, as far as I can help. After Mr Newman's benefit concert on Dec. 4 there will be no more concerts until Jan. 8, so I think I had better wait and come to you on or about Dec. 6 when I shall be free of all these bothers and the weather may happen to be just as good as now. I can do some of my Christmas shopping in Leamington, which is always a help, and all being well I can stay a few days longer than I could now.

Last night I bribed Bella with a glass of champagne to come down to her birthday dinner! It was a very slow process and she had to rest on the stairs, but she got *up* better, and now she realizes that she *can* do it, and none the worse, she will try to move more everyday. Tomorrow she is to begin massage. Probably it will be a week or ten days before we get her out for a little drive. Once she gets down to meals there will not be so much for Elsie to do [...] With love, yrs ever R.N.

During the year, Rosa also managed time to make more notes in preparation for her book of music of Czechoslovakia. At the end of 1926, the future arrangements for the Proms were being discussed, but for Rosa and Henry Wood, the outlook was uncertain.

Notes

1. Rosa Newmarch, 'A Master of Russian Folk Music: A Study of Rimsky-Korsakov', *Radio Times*, 19 Mar. 1926, p.582.

2. John Tyrell, *Janáček: Years of a Life* (London: Faber and Faber, 2007), vol.2, ch. 26.

3. Zdenka E. Fischmann, *Janáček-Newmarch Correspondence* (Rockville, Maryland: Kabel Publishers, 1986).

4. Ibid. p.102.

5. Ibid. pp.87-8.

6. Ibid. pp.89-90.

7. Ibid. pp.91-2.

8. Tyrrell, *Janáček*, vol.2, p.601.

9. Fischmann, *Janáček-Newmarch Correspondence,* pp.96-8.

10. Ibid. pp.100-1.

11. Ibid. pp.102-8.

12. Tyrrell, *Janáček*, vol.2, p.595.

13. Fischmann, *Janáček-Newmarch Correspondence*, p.110.

14. Ibid. p.131-2.

15. Fischmann, *Janáček-Newmarch*, pp.131-144.

16. 'The Artists Union of Prague', *Musical Times*, 1 Jul. 1926, p.650.

17. Obituary to Robert Newman (unsigned, presumably by Rosa Newmarch), *Musical Times* 67, 1 Dec. 1926, p.1134.

CHAPTER 26: THREE SCORE YEARS AND TEN

There was much change in Rosa's circumstances in 1927. The year began with a period of uncertainty about the future of the Queen's Hall concerts following the death of Robert Newman. The Proms, since their inception, had been fortunate in having a succession of financial backers, initially the London throat specialist Dr Cathcart, followed by Sir Edgar Speyer, and most recently Chappell & Co. The Proms had been running at a loss for some time; the loss increasing each year. Before his death, Robert Newman had confided to Percy Scholes (then music critic for the BBC) that he wished to see an arrangement between the BBC and Chappell & Co that would ensure their future. William Boosey, then managing director of Chappell & Co believed that broadcasting would spell the end of concert-giving, and on 7 March it was publicly announced that Chappell & Co would no longer support the Promenade and Symphony concerts at the Queen's Hall. Three days before, on the 4 March 1927, Rosa wrote to Tiny from her home in Crossfield Road:

Dearest Tiny,

Your letter and generous present was most welcome and comforting this morning! Yesterday Henry [Wood] came in to see me with Chappell's letters and the not unexpected news that they were chucking all the concerts after March. I had not said anything to you as I thought by the time I saw you I should know definitely. Naturally we should not be human if we did not feel it very much. Henry has done 33 years work at Queen's Hall and I 20! Of course I think *his* services will not be lost. The B.B.C. or a syndicate will in all probability offer him a position. But perhaps *I* shall not go on under the new arrangements. I am not going to worry. I shall be 70 in December and perhaps it is time to take a backseat! Meanwhile it is very consoling dear to feel that somebody thinks of me. So many things have happened since the beginning of the year. We can have a chat when I come. Let us hope for fine weather! Influenza is better here, but I hope we shan't get it in Manchester! However one would never go anywhere if we waited for it to disappear. I expect our letters crossed.

With much love, Rosa.

Negotiations between the BBC and Chappell & Co went on for months, but by

May 1927, the BBC was able to announce that it had reached an agreement with Chappell & Co that a six-week series of Promenade Concerts at the Queen's Hall would take place starting on 13 August. The BBC continued with Sir Henry Wood as conductor. Rosa decided to reduce some of her regular commitments in order to have a more relaxed life and also to complete some literary works that she had begun. Eric Blom, who had assisted her and was by now making a name in musical journalism and as a music critic, also decided not to continue with the programme notes. At the request of Henry Wood and the BBC, she continued to supply her existing programme notes for the Promenade Concerts until the time of her death in 1940.

Earlier, on 28 February, Rosa wrote to Janáček telling him that she was studying *The Makropoulis Case* and thanking him for dedicating his Sinfonietta to her. She explained that she was waiting to know about the future of the Queen's Hall concerts and that she was planning to go to Prague *en route* to Karlovy Vary. The latter visit to the health resort she needed to 'renew youth and strength'. The timing of the visit is given in a later letter dated 6 March, in which she explained that H.C. Colles and his wife were going to Vienna for the Beethoven Festival and would like to return via Prague, especially if there was a Janáček opera to see during their visit[1]. She was timing her visit to Prague also to meet Colles and his wife. Janáček explained that there would not be any performances of his operas in April in Czechoslovakia, but *Jenůfa* was to be performed in Berlin at that time. Rosa visited Karlovy Vary, staying at the Hotel Savoy in April, and then went on to meet Colles and his wife in Prague before returning home. On 12 July, the BBC broadcast Stravinsky's *L'Histoire du Soldat* from the Arts Theatre Club, London, in Rosa 's English translation.

Later in July, shortly after the family began what was to be a six-week summer holiday at a cottage in Porlock, Somerset, tragedy struck. Four days after their arrival, Rosa's husband, Harry, who was a keen fisherman, decided to go off for a walk, taking his rods with him. He did not return in the evening and the family were concerned and began looking for him but without success, so a larger search party was called, including a police constable, to make a wider search. Eventually Harry was found dead in Copper Wood, an unfrequented spot on Exmoor, about two miles from Oare. Because he was missing and a search party was required, his death was reported rather dramatically in the newspapers. *The Times* described that he was found lying face downwards over a bank with his head in a little stream at the bottom of a deep combe or gully, thickly over grown with bracken[2]. His body was put on a hurdle (sled) and taken through rough moorland undergrowth to the nearest road and then on to Oare to await an inquest. In the *Daily Express* on 3

August, on the front page the heading was 'Doone Valley Tragedy – Husband of Noted Writer Found Dead – Body in a Wood', and a detailed account followed, including: 'The missing man had been found dead about twelve or fourteen hours, and appeared to have broken his neck by falling down the bank while in an exhausted condition [...] Mr Newmarch left the house on Saturday to walk the ten miles to the Doone Valley. Night came and he did not return. More than a hundred people have been hunting since Saturday over every square yard of the bare countryside where it was thought Mr Newmarch might have wandered.'

Rosa wrote to her sister-in-law Emily explaining the circumstances:

Thursday [1927 pencilled in by Elsie, and probably 4th August 1927]

Pilly Green Lodge

Porlock

Dearest Emily

Thanks you for yours this morning. It is not nearly so dreadful as it looks in the papers. Poor dear Harry was (for him) quite cheerful on Saturday when he trudged off with his fishing rod. But you know I have thought him steadily failing lately, and at times his mental condition made him *quite oblivious* of physical disabilities. He habitually overestimated his powers of walking and taking constant restless exercise. He was not easily "managed", and indeed one could not forever be saying: "Harry you shall not", and "you must" and lately reasoning and persuasion were of very little avail. His end was instantaneous, dear Emily. Elsie and I searched all we could, but it needed a number of active men to go over the comparatively small circuit in which he was wandering. He must have passed through some phase of forgetfulness, or aberration, with a fixed idea in his mind.

He is resting in a most beautiful old farm about 12 miles away. I was with him yesterday. He looks quite peaceful, not a sign of injury, fear or distress. Not quite like Harry, but the face of a man completely at rest. The good people have given up their parlour for him to lie in. John and Elsie and I all spent some time there yesterday. We took up some flowers and I asked the Rector here to come with us and we had a short service in the room. The Rector read that psalm "The Lord is my Shepherd", so marvellously suited to the last hours of his life. As soon as the inquest is over and we hope that may be today (but the Coroner lives rather far away) I have arranged for him to be transported by motor. Kenyon's people will receive him (just opposite St Mary Abbots) and they are preparing Frank's grave which Harry said to me once that he had bought and would be available. We should go home by train and all meet at Kenyon's, we hope at 11 *a.m. on Saturday*. All depends now on the arrival of the coroner.

Dearest Emily, when I compare what has happened with what *might* have been, I feel we must thank that all-wise Father-Spirit who sees when we have had enough. If he had been brought home alive all life must have been changed for him and us. Instead of merely superseding him in a few trifling things like carving, buying his clothes etc. John says we should have felt the necessity of constantly watching and thwarting him. Instead of which there is a dignity and beauty in just breathing one's last in a heavenly spot, without pain, and I feel sure without apprehension. His was not the excitable restless mind which topples over; but there was a gradually increasing confusion and apathy which those who lived in very close contact with him noticed day by day. Even John did not know as Elsie and I did how odd and lost he was at times. And Bella has often said to me lately "I don't think the Man is always responsible."

He had the liberty to the last and passed away literally walking into lovely spaces to nature.

Yours affect *Rosa*

Later:

P.S. Everything is now fixed for *Monday* at about 2 o^c. John will call for you and take you to Kenyon's. But he says will you go to tea, as arranged, on Saturday and he will be there and tell you all about the final arrangements? I may perhaps see you before Monday I cannot say now when I shall get home exactly. The newspaper reports are some of them quite garbled. Of course he was not on a walking-tour – had unfortunately no rucksack with him – and was not near a stream. So you need not feel any distress about such details.

[The church referred to is most likely St Mary Abbots, Kensington.]

The inquest was held on 4 August and the *Daily Express* reported on the 5th with the headline: 'Aged Man's Lonely Death – Inquest on Victim of Exmoor Tragedy'. It then managed to link the death with the fictional shooting of Lorna Doone. 'A verdict of "Accidental death" was returned at the inquest held at Oareford Farm on Henry Charles Newmarch aged seventy-two, surveyor and land agent of Crossfield-road, Hampstead, who was found dead on Tuesday in a small stream near Oare Church, where Lorna Doone was shot at her marriage ceremony.' Evidence was given by John Newmarch, who said that his father had aged considerably but that he walked ten miles every day, to and from his office. Rosa explained that he left with his fishing rod, took notes from a map before leaving but took no food. She judged that he had overestimated his physical powers. The farmer at Cloud Farm saw him walk through his yard on Monday looking tired and weary and said that Harry told him that he was going to Porlock. The doctor who examined the body suggested that he had been walking in bemused condition without food, had fallen over the bank of the stream and broken his neck, which would have caused instant death. From Rosa's description, it seems most likely that Harry was suffering from what would now be described as some form of dementia and may have lost his way.

Janáček wrote to Rosa on 31 October, after he had a chance meeting with the Czechoslovak diplomat Dr Císař, at which he told him of Harry's death: 'I did not find words for the fate that bestows so cruelly. Accept heartfelt sympathy from me and my wife. And accept the coincidence! The same evening when I was at home talking about the death of your husband, my wife also fainted and almost killed herself in the fall! One never knows where the black moment waits for him[3].'

The last week in October, Rosa attended the Triennial Norwich Festival; Sir Henry Wood conducted most of the programme, although Frank Bridge conducted the première of his symphonic poem *Enter Spring* on the 27th. Together with Eric Blom, Rosa wrote some of the programme notes, including those for Parry's *Jerusalem* and Bantock's *Omar Khayyám*, performed on the 28th. Whilst at Norwich she stayed as usual with her friends the Misses Colman at Carrow Abbey.

After her seventieth birthday in December, Rosa showed little sign of any slackening in her schedule, and her diary for 1928 shows she was involved in a wide variety of activities, including about three months abroad. By now she had evolved a regular pattern of activities, which included an annual visit to Prague, coupled with a trip to the health resort at Karlovy Vary. She was invariably present at any concert involving musicians visiting from Russia or Eastern Europe and the associated receptions. In 1928 these included a reception for the Czech soprano Jarmilla Novotná (1907-1994) in January, a concert given by the soprano Emmy Destinn*, whom Rosa had met a number of times previously, a concert conducted by Václav Talich (1883-1961) and a recital by the Russian the virtuoso pianist and composer Nicolai Medtner (1880-1951) both in February, and a first performance in England of Vycpálek's cantata *The Last Things of Man* in Liverpool in March[4], for which Rosa provided both a translation and programme notes . 1928 (technically 1927) saw the publication of the third edition of *Grove's Dictionary of Music and Musicians*, edited by H. C. Colles, in which Rosa had contributed both as an author and translator. Rosa had been a member of the Society of Women Musicians, founded in 1911, for some time, and in 1928 she addressed the annual meeting.

Part of her winding down was an extended holiday in Italy prior to her visit to

Prague in May. Rosa and Elsie left home towards the end of March, travelling via Paris, where they stayed a night meeting her friends the Robinsons before leaving for Italy on 26 March. They arrived in Frascati, a town twenty kilometres southeast of Rome, where they stayed until 10 April with Rosa's niece Annie. Rosa described life with her niece:

> Very glad to be here with Annie and the family. The weather is far from ideal; bright sunshine for a couple of days was followed by a thunderstorm, and the cold winds last night turned to a gale from the sea, which one can see clearly from the roof of the house. This is really a delightful situation in summer, high and exposed, but the house is the roomy, stone-built Italian type needs central heating to be comfortable in this chilly weather. Valentino's dear old aunt carries a charcoal-burning *scaldino* – a sort of brazier – round with her! I have a beautiful room with lovely views over the Campagna, but just now a cold grey mist lies heavily over the plains: it looks more like a northern sea than the 'sunny plains of Italy'.
>
> Annie and her husband seem always busy, working like peasants to keep the place going and productive. He is most kind, delightful and easy-going, and never seems to want anyone to pay him for anything! Living is very Italian, heaps of macaroni, greens and rice – all cooked with oil and garlic – not quite the diet for a diabetic! Still eggs are plentiful though meat is scarce. The children are attractive and interesting: Pietro a medical student, a dear steady hard-working fellow, rather shy and studious; Romola, whom we knew of course in England, very charming, vivacious and affectionate and the youngest Carlo, an original and delightful boy still at school. Paulo, the second son is away studying to be a veterinary surgeon. One has to laugh at the confusion and happy-go-lucky life on the downstairs floor, where chickens, dogs, cats, even a pet crow, and up to the moment of my arrival, a monkey, all wander in and out of the kitchen. It is not easy to explore Rome from here, but we have made some excursions into the hills and visited Verulam and the interesting old 'villas' in the neighbourhood.

They moved on to Rome on 11 April, staying just over a fortnight. Apart from sightseeing, they had tea with the Fuller Maitlands [The music scholar John Fuller Maitland, 1856-1936, was editor-in-chief of the second edition of Grove], saw Dr Mastny, by then the Czechoslovak Minister in Rome, and his family, and Rosa was particularly delighted to meet her old friends Mary Duclaux and her sister Mabel Robinson. Rosa described her visit to Rome and Florence:

Rome

We spent long mornings at St Peter's, and after a rest went forth again to the Spanish Steps, the Piazza del Populo, and to the galleries. After calling on the composer Respighi, I went on to the Coliseum, which is really one of the most impressive things I have seen yet. We arrived as the sun was getting low, the rays slanting through the many arches. It is so vast, big enough to escape the crowds of tourists! Rome is very noisy, and perhaps much gayer than Florence; but to my mind less lovely. The sculpture is finer here, but the pictures are certainly more interesting in Florence. A Papal Mass and a visit to the Vatican were memorable events, but I must tell you about them later.

Today is a popular Festival, the Birthday of Rome. The Square and streets will be illuminated at night. We look out from our hotel window on the crowds of holiday makers – fascists in their black shirts parading in the Square just beyond us. Pietro has just been in to see us; he is studying at the University and has to join the 'black shirts' – rather against his inclinations I gather! The parks and gardens are growing green at last, and the Judas trees make a lovely effect with their rich mauve flowers among the dark green.

Florence

Back after twenty years and in many ways [I] find the place very unchanged; it certainly is a lovely town with lots to see, yet less overwhelming than Rome. On the other hand it always had the fault of very few squares and gardens to rest in and contemplate its beauties, and unless one goes out of the town into the hills. The place is a mass of English folk, elderly maidens, clerics and families, and in the hotel and elsewhere one never hears a word of anything but English. Such a contrast to our Roman *albergo* which was almost unknown to our countryfolk. Mary and Mabel are still here, staying with Violet Paget. Her villa is several miles out of the town, and they are enjoying the quiet of the garden and the evening drives. They find Violet Paget very much changed, far from strong and highly nervous; the latter partly because she has become so deaf that talking with people is an exhausting strain to her. Another contemporary friend of girlhood days in Leamington, is also in Florence – Nora Maude (née Young), and it is many years since we four all met together.

Yesterday Elsie and I found a trip being organised to San Geminiano and Sienna, and being very anxious for Elsie to have a glimpse of these places, we decided to try it. We went in a small, well-protected motor char-à-banc, and [there] were only seven or eight people. Leaving about nine o'clock we arrived in good time at the wonderful old hill town perched up and bristling with thirteen ancient watch-towers. We had an hour to look round San Geminiano, then lunch and on to Sienna. Of course here one can spend days, but still three hours gave us time to see the beautiful cathedral and general lie of the town. It was a very pleasant and happy day, and I was delighted that Elsie had these glimpses of places I knew well from former visits.

We are having the usual Italian weather, not altogether ideal; blazing sun at one hour and chilly winds, or close sirocco ones the next. Today we have had a thunderstorm, so I have not lost much by staying in – with inflamed mosquito bites and raging tooth-ache! I certainly think Rome with its large open spaces is healthier than Florence; at least in May one should be somewhere up the hills, rather than in this town of narrow, picturesque, but often smelly little streets. They exist in Rome too, but one can avoid them, whereas here they lead everywhere. But it *is* lovely! Every time I come over one of the bridges I stand to gaze at the lovely view of the next, with the hill of San Miniato and the cypress trees in the background. I am glad to see it all again, and I think Elsie has enjoyed it too.

Vernon Lee* has gone to Assisi; she seems very nervous and almost a recluse these days. Mabel is amusing about her, but I am sure at times she is the same clever and original Vernon as in old days. She has kindly lent them her car while she is away so today we have been up the Fiesole and shown Elsie the old Roman amphitheatre and the Cathedral. We passed my cousin Herbert and Edie's dear old home, where I spent many happy days in 1908; but the present owners are quite strangers so we did not go in, but only peeped through the garden. Perhaps it would have been sad to go in and find it all changed and possibly *nouveau riche* in possession.

On 11 May, they travelled on to Venice and then on to Prague on 18 May. They were only in Prague for four days, but that enabled Rosa to visit the music publisher Hudebne Matice and meet Karel Hoffmeister and Vitězslav Novák. The Czech music critic and musicologist Otakar Šourek published in Czech *Život a dílo Antonía Dvořáka* (The Life and Works of Antonín Dvořák) in four volumes (1916, 1917, 1930, and 1933). An abridged version was subsequently translated into German in 1935, but not into English until 1941. Rosa felt that in order to encourage further interest in Czech music in England there should be a biography of Dvořák in English. She felt it was too big an undertaking to translate Šourek's multiple volume work and believed a translation of Karel Hoffmeister's shorter German biography of Dvořák would be useful for English music lovers, perhaps to prepare the way for a translation of Šourek's work later. She must have discussed her proposal with

Hoffmeister during this visit because by August 1928, John Lane of Bodley Head Ltd had agreed a contract with her. John Lane's director, B.W.Willett, wrote to her on 24 August: 'I am glad to tell you that we are willing to do Dvorak on the terms suggested by you, namely £25 payable on publication on account of a ten per cent royalty in England and a ten per cent on the net proceeds in the United States. We could not very well publish the book in the Masters of Music series as these volumes are only 3/6 and that is too cheap. We propose to do it at 5/-.' By February 1929, Willett wrote again sending the promised cheque and the book was published in 1929[5].

After four days in Prague, they left for the health resort of Karlovy Vary and returned home to Crossfield Road on 15 June. In August, her sister-in-law Ella Newmarch died and four days later, on 12 August, she learned of the death of Janáček. She wrote an obituary for Janáček for the September/October issue of *The Chesterian*. On 3 December 1928, she sent a postcard from London to Mrs Zdenka Janáček, which read, 'With kindest remembrances, from Rosa Newmarch and Elsie Newmarch.' Then added below on the postcard, written in Czech, the words: 'Today we gave a memorial performance of Janáček's folksongs at Scotus Viator' and it was signed Dr A Kolísek[6]. [Scotus Viator refers to Professor Seton Watson, presumably at his house.]

After her husband's death Rosa and Elsie planned to move from Crossfield Road, as Elsie explained: 'My mother and I decided to move to a flat; it was with great regret that Bella Simpson, who had lived with us and been a constant companion for nearly forty years, left us to join her widowed sister. Fortunately they took a flat not very far from ours, so that there were few days when the old friends failed to meet and still enjoy their mutual interests in music.' They moved in March 1929 to a flat in Belsize Park. The flat Bella and her sister lived in was at 41B Abbey Rd, Hampstead, less than a mile away. Now, having moved from a house to a flat, and with fewer commitments than in previous years, Rosa hoped to have a little more leisure time. Nevertheless, she was re-elected in 1929 to the presidency of the Society of Women Musicians for a third year, described in the next chapter, and Oxford University Press brought out the first volume of *The Concert-Goers Library* in 1928; it was followed by the second in 1929, the third in 1933, preceded by the fourth in 1932, the fifth in 1938, and finally the sixth seven years after her death. The analytical notes were selected for the most part from the Symphony, Sunday and Promenade Concerts performed by the Queen's Hall Orchestra, together with some written for the Liverpool Philharmonic Society, the Choral and Orchestral Union of Glasgow and the Sheffield and Norwich Music Festivals. In the preface to volume five, it stated: 'It may be possible to follow the classical selections with a volume dealing entirely with modern composers.' However, when the sixth volume was published posthumously in 1948, it was entirely devoted to great choral works. All the volumes were dedicated to Sir Henry Wood and have been reprinted a number of times in response to demand.

Rosa was invited to Henry Wood's sixtieth birthday celebration on 3 March 1929 at the Royal Academy of Music. Later in the year, he was able to spring on her a pleasant surprise, as Elsie described:

> For some years past Rosa Newmarch had only possessed an upright Blüthner piano, which she had seldom had time to play for sheer pleasure but which had served her well for all purposes connected with her work. Now in her new home she hoped for more leisure to enjoy her own and other's music, and there being a good music room in the flat she decided to exchange her upright for a small boudoir grand. She spoke of this to Henry Wood one day, and asked him to keep it in mind if he heard of one available. Out of this grew a wonderful presentation which she describes in a letter to her sister: 'Yesterday was perhaps one of the most wonderful and exciting days of my life! I had a vague idea that Henry was trying to hear of an extra nice piano for me for the new flat. But when he asked me to meet him at Blüthners at 5 o'clock yesterday, I was not at all prepared to be shown into one of their reception rooms, where lots of chairs were ranged round the loveliest brand new Blüthner grand I ever saw. It appears that he, Harry Colles and other musical colleagues and friends laid their heads together and agreed that I ought to have a testimonial! This is the result, and such a wonderful list of contributors: orchestral players, colleagues and friends in the musical world, publishing firms and many others: and even some old personal friends (let into the secret apparently by Elsie). Now I am proud possessor of the most beautiful Blüthner that money can buy, with two music stools and an electric lamp! As soon as I come home I am to spend the rest of the money on a wireless set, a gramophone and records that I like. The whole thing was kept a profound secret from me. Myra Hess cabled from America apparently that she would be back in time for the 'ceremony', and after the presentation she christened the piano with a delightful short recital.'

The piano presentation at Blüthners was on 6 June 1929. The list of over 130 contributors is a veritable 'Who's Who' of musicians of the day and is given in Appendix 2. Shortly after this presentation, Rosa made her now annual visit to Karlovy Vary, travelling via Bruges and Antwerp. She was back at home in the flat for a house-warming party, at which the pianist Balbina Brainina played for her.

Then in July, the 'official' presentation of the piano at her home took place, and it was at this latter event that Myra Hess played.

1929 marked the twenty-fifth anniversary of the death of Antonín Dvořák. There was a festival in Prague to commemorate his death with a number of musical events from 20 March to 22 May. It is not clear whether Rosa was in Prague for any of these events. Rosa was still very much in demand as an expert on Russian music and earlier in the year, when the BBC was putting on two broadcasts of Rimsky-Korsakov's *Le Coq d'Or,* she was asked to contribute an article for the *Radio Times* entitled 'What to Listen for in Russian Music[7].'

Notes

1. Zdenka E. Fischmann, *Janáček-Newmarch Correspondence* (Rockville, Maryland: Kabel Publishers, 1986), pp.133-9.

2. 'Death of Mr. H. C. Newmarch', *The Times*, 3 Aug. 1927.

3. Fischmann, *Janáček-Newmarch Correspondence*, p.150.

4. Rosa Newmarch, (1942) *Music of Czechoslovakia* (London: OUP, 1942), p.231.

5. Karel Hoffmeister, Karel (1929) *Antonín Dvořák*, trans. and ed. Rosa Newmarch (London: John Lane, 1928).

6. Fischmann, *Janáček-Newmarch Correspondence*, pp.160-2.

7. Rosa Newmarch, 'What to listen for in Russian Music', *Radio Times*, 25 Jan. 1929, p.194.

CHAPTER 27: PRESIDENT OF THE SOCIETY OF WOMEN MUSICIANS

According to Elsie Newmarch's account: 'In 1929 she [Rosa Newmarch] was invited to be President of the Society of Women Musicians, for the following year. This she agreed to do and was elected in succession to her old friend Mrs Norman O'Neill, and was happy to have the help of Dame Myra Hess as Vice-President for the year.' However, this is not quite consistent with the society's archives, as Philip Bullock described[1]. She was president for three successive years – 1927-1930. For the year 1927-8, Mrs Norman O'Neill was vice-president and chairman; Dame Ethel Smyth, hon. vice-president; Mrs Dorothy Erhard, hon. secretary; Miss Marion Scott, hon. treasurer and Sydney C. Scott, hon. solicitor. The society was founded in 1911 for the mutual cooperation between women composers and performers in response to the limited professional opportunities for women musicians at the time. The idea for forming the society came from Marion Scott (1877-1953), a gifted violinist, later to become a musicologist, and she drew in her friends the singer Gertrude Eaton (1863 – ?) and the composer Katherine Eggar (1874-1961)[2].

The first meeting was held on 11 July 1911 at the Women's Institute, 92 Victoria Street, and was attended by over 150 people. The founding women and their provisional council made it clear that the society had no political agenda and was open to men, thereby countering any criticism of exclusivity. The businessman Walter Cobbett (1847-1937) was the first benefactor and the composer Ivor Gurney was one of twenty men to join in the first year. The composer-singer Liza Lehmann (1862-1918) became the first president, and she was succeeded by Emily Daymond (1912-3), Cécile Chaminade (1913-4), Katherine Eggar (1914-5), Marion Scott (1915-6), and Gertrude Eaton (1916-7). The post of vice-president was largely honorary and has been held by Myra Hess, Nadia Boulanger, Imogen Holst, Elisabeth Lutyens, Elizabeth Maconchy, and Fanny Waterman. The society continued to exist until 1972 when it was disbanded. By 1920, the society had outgrown the premises in Victoria Street and moved to 74 Grosvenor Street.

According to the society's archives, during her period of office, Rosa set an example by her attendance at council meetings, offered practical help and showed great interest in its activities. She felt that her final year as president was somewhat uneventful although the society achieved the legal status of a corporation during the year. In her 1929 presidential address, she dealt with the burning question at the time – the threat against women's progress in the music profession.[3] She began by tracing the history of women's fluctuating participation in musical activity. Assyrian and Egyptian pictorial art suggested that women worked side by side with men as instrumentalists, but she suggested that by the eleventh century women had become listeners rather than participants, citing the rites of the church excluding women from participation, and that there were no female troubadours. However, in Tudor England, playing the lute or virginal became a part of a lady's education. In 1883, the Royal College of Music opened with Sir George Grove as Director[4]. It started with twenty-one foundation students, ten of whom were girls. Women students were welcomed on the same terms as men. The teaching staff of thirty-one appointed by Grove included Jenny Lind-Goldschmidt, Arabella Goddard, Eliza Mazzucato and Madge Kendall[5]. However, in Victorian times, few women were becoming professional musicians, and this was largely due to the snobbish disapproval that girls encountered in family and social circles. (Mary Wakefield's experience is a good case in point.) 'The *average* woman left her musical studies either to marry or take the humblest jobs in her profession. Music teaching in all large girls schools was at that time mostly in the hands of fearsome "Fräuleins", which I expect, tended to keep us from becoming a music-loving nation. English girls got some of the poorer posts. For them, too, the dustiest of organ lofts in small towns and the harmonium stools of chapels. Women became skilled not indeed in the art of music so much as in the art of taking back places with sweet and uncomplaining smiles[3].'

Elsie's account of Rosa's address continued:

During the war years a small number of competent women players had been admitted by Sir Henry Wood to the New Queen's Hall Orchestra. 'Some of us shook our heads,' she said, 'I was among their number. The fact that nothing lamentable happened in consequence of their co-operation is perhaps the best justification of this open door policy. The women naturally and simply made good. They showed themselves punctual, and musically alert as any crude male instrumentalists who make up the padding of the orchestra. They helped through ten glorious educative years of the Promenade Concerts: the years which popularised Bach, Haydn and Brahms. Suddenly our musical *petit maîtres*, with their abnormally acute ears and infallible flair for tone-quality, tell us that the weakness brought about the participation of women was audible to them almost before they entered the concert room. 'Where' they ask, 'have fled the full rich tone, the steadiness, the passion, the exhilarating, virile noise of the old wholly masculine orchestra?' Vanished, gone for ever, extinguished by the presence of eight or ten women distributed among the strings! I think too highly of a good male orchestra to believe that its tone can be weakened, its fine edge blunted, by mingling even a dozen picked women players in its ranks. There can be no doubt in the minds of unprejudiced listeners that women players blend as admirably with male instrumentalists in the orchestra as in chamber music. Yet, at this actual moment when the possibility of forming a permanent national orchestra is being discussed, it is pertinent to ask whether this door is to be kept open for women or not. May they indeed retain the places they have won, and not have to return to an early Victorian acquiescence. If we permit it to be decided for us that we belong musically to an inferior class of workers, the gains of recent years may be lost. But do not let us drift back into apathy; it will be our own fault if ever again we become listeners, listeners-in, only.

As Philip Bullock points out, Rosa's recollection of Wood's decision is faulty, since women had begun playing in the Queen's Hall Orchestra in the autumn of 1913; when auditioned, they had equalled or surpassed men players[6]. When the BBC announced the formation of its symphony orchestra in the late 1920s, women were determined to be included. Rosa wrote to Sir John Reith, director of the BBC, in October 1928 explaining the society's concern that the new National Orchestra of the BBC contained no women members and asked consent for him to receive a deputation from the council of the Society of Women Musicians to put their point of view[7]. A delegation that included Rosa, Marion Scott, Katherine Eggar, and Dorothy Erhard met representatives of the BBC on 14 November 1928. By reason and diplomacy they convinced Percy Pitt, BBC Music Director from 1922-1930, that the conductor Adrian Boult (BBC Music Director from 1930) should hear all applicants from behind a screen and judge them on their merits, not dismiss them because of their gender. As a result, an increasing number of contracts went to women.

Elsie's account continued:

On the subject of women composers she was equally broadminded and confident. 'The question of women's creative power has its bright side also'; she continues. 'Not every male student turns out a Beethoven, a Wagner, a Richard Strauss. Let the world show equal tolerance to women who are beginning to lift their heads above the vast undergrowth of musical composition. I do not believe women lack inspiration. But self-expression has become a much more complicated thing than in the spring-tide of human social life, when Deborah and Judith burst into heart-thrilling improvisation. Only recently have women felt themselves technically the equals of men, and at present are perhaps obsessed with the idea of presenting their thoughts and emotions in masculine forms and by masculine methods. But I can conceive of a time when a woman creative musician of the first order may suddenly burst upon the world. Her music will enable the full expression of a woman's soul and emotions; her womanhood will condition her way of thinking and style of expression. The quality of her work will be clearly distinguished from man's work, permeated with a peculiar originality, a peculiar passion, rare and exclusive tenderness that will be wholly feminine. Some may think that I am talking rubbish; but I am persuaded that women will never set the Thames on fire by hitching their boats on to the crafts that are manned by the opposite sex with a view to their own special conflagrations. Let them design and steer their own fire ships. My advice is – start out ambitious, a size or two too large; aim at something really big. Don't remain a megalomaniac, but cultivate as you go the kind of dignified philosophy which – when you have found out what you really are fit for – will enable you to do it competently and without whimpering.'

She admired much of the work of Dame Ethel Smyth, whom she knew well for many years. She was one of the composers who usually supplied her own analytical notes for works performed, but in a short biographical note we find Rosa quoting Tchaikovsky's appraisal of this composer, in his Diary of 1883, as 'one of the few women composers who may be seriously reckoned among the workers in this sphere of music. She gives promise of a serious and talented career.' A prognostication which Rosa evidently felt had been more than fulfilled in succeeding years.

Whilst Rosa's address to the Society of Women Musicians showed that she was concerned that women had the same opportunities in the world of music as men, she did not appear strident in support women's rights. The final year of her presidency coincided with the year of the general election in which women aged twenty-one to twenty-nine were able to vote after the Equal Franchise Act of 1928. Women aged thirty and over had been granted the vote in 1918. The suffragette movement began in 1903. There is no mention of women's suffrage in Rosa's autobiography, and although she does mention other political issues in her letters to her sister Tiny and her sister-in-law Emily, she does not refer to women's suffrage.

In his chapter on 'Women and Society', Philip Bullock has an excellent analysis of the position and opportunities open to women, particularly in the arts and literature in the late nineteenth and early twentieth century, and with respect to

Rosa Newmarch in particular[8]. From his writing and a number of points described in the previous chapters of this book, one gains the impression that Rosa strove a middle path in the sense that pushed at the boundaries of what was considered acceptable for women in late Victorian times but at the same time, although clear and decisive in defending her own position, did so with decorum, working within the system rather than creating a strong backlash. A number of points illustrate the factors that determined her attitude. From her childhood and youth, parental attitudes were important. Her literary ambitions at an early age clearly were greatly helped by her mother's encouragement. Her father was a strong advocate for wider education for all; this is evident in his strong support for the campaign for implementation of the Public Libraries Act, which would enable the public to have free access to books. However, when Rosa expressed an interest in medicine, both he and one of his sons made it clear that medicine was not an option for women. At the time when Rosa grew up, daughters of upper middle-class families were no longer tied to a wholly domestic life and music and linguistic skills were desirable accomplishments for women. Since Rosa was brought up bilingual and music was important in their household, these factors may have helped her determine her career path. Journalism and writing were activities that could be pursued from home and combined with normal domestic life, unlike a career as a professional singer, to which her sister might have aspired. Within the acceptable norms of the day, she had a self-confidence that enabled her to visit Russia and subsequently introduce herself to Henry Wood on her return.

Most of her early writings were translations, and at that time the translator was not always acknowledged and was often hardly conspicuous. In a few of the translations Rosa carried out she is not acknowledged, but in most she is. Often she included a significant amount of her own original material as the translator's preface, and this also ensured that she was identified. Her translations are mostly dedicated to males, e.g. Henry Wood, Vladimir Stasov, Sergei Taneyev, Feodor Shaliapin, Basil Wilberforce, and President Masaryk, but this is not always so. *Tchaikovsky, his Life and Works* is dedicated to both Henry Wood and his wife, and *Mary Wakefield: A Memoir* is dedicated to 'All Singers and Workers in the Musical Competition festivals, Past, Present and to Come'. At the time her books were published, there were few obvious female dedicatees. Of the three ways in which she could sign herself, Mrs Henry Newmarch, Mrs Rosa Newmarch, or Rosa Newmarch, she chose the last and most radical. Since she did not begin writing before she married, she was always known by her married name. Her designation contrasts with her friend and chairman of the Society of Women Musicians, the pianist, formerly Adine Rückert, who was known as Mrs Norman O'Neill after her marriage.

In other matters, as Philip Bullock points out, she guarded the copyright of her work, e.g. for reprinting her programme notes from *The Concert-goers Library*, and insisted on equal payment when she took over from a male predecessor in writing the notes for the Sunday Concert Society[6]. He also sees her feminism being 'palpably expressed' in a letter to Herbert Jenkins in January 1909 to request payment for her work: 'In spite of your special note my cheque has not turned up yet. I should really be glad to have it, but possibly it slipped your memory, so I write to you personally. I shall come with a banner: "Cheques for Women" and chain myself to some office table.' This contrasts somewhat with a quote from a much later letter from Herbert Jenkins to Rosa Newmarch, dated 23 March 1917, suggesting almost the converse: 'I am very pleased indeed that you should be always on the look-out for me in the way you are; but please will you be on the look-out for yourself and send in your account. How exciting it must be for you to have a publisher demanding an account. I see you have attached a ridiculous memorandum to your letter demanding three guineas. I decline absolutely to pay you any such sum. You were very helpful in the matter of Petrograd and you have been helpful in many other ways. If you do not increase that account to ten guineas then you may put me in the hands of the Authors' Society!' Perhaps Herbert Jenkins had learned from previous experience. It is interesting to note that when she began writing analytical notes for the Proms, Robert Newman asked her to do the press work which included the weekly paragraphs about forthcoming programmes and new works; she agreed to this provided her authorship remained anonymous.

On financial matters, she felt her husband had been mismanaging their affairs for sometime before things came to a head and they had to leave Campden Hill Square in June 1911[9]. By then, she had achieved a measure of financial independence. As early as the autumn of 1906, when she decided to go with Bella Simpson to France and Italy until July 1907, she was able to park her husband with his sister so that the house at Campden Hill Square could be let while she was away. By 1912, in her letter to her husband from Brittany, she seemed to be almost directing him in their choice of a new home and showed her independence by suggesting he bought the house and she paid him rent. (See Chapter 17).

An aspect of her feminism was how she looked after Sibelius and later Janáček during their visits to England; in both cases she felt they needed to be managed whilst away from home. She was unlike her near contemporary Dame Ethel Smyth who also succeeded in a 'man's world'. Ethel Smyth became a friend of Emmeline Pankhurst, the founder of the British Women's Suffrage Movement. In 1912, she herself was arrested and imprisoned for her efforts toward securing the women's right to vote. She served two months in Holloway Prison for smashing the windows of a cabinet minister's house. She composed *The March of the Women* in 1911 and it was premièred by a chorus of suffragettes at a fundraising rally at the Albert Hall on 23 March 1911. Rosa, by contrast, although supportive of women's suffrage, adopted a much more moderate attitude.

When Henry Wood left his wife Muriel to live with Jessie Linton (discussed in Chapter 28), Rosa was quick to recognise and accept the liaison, very much taking Wood's side rather than Muriel's[10]. By contrast, Ethel Smyth's initial reaction to the news was that desertion of a devoted wife by her husband was despicable[11].

One further clue to Rosa's attitude pointed out by her granddaughter Renée is that whereas her grandson Michael's christening is mentioned in her diary, an event at which she was present, and also his entrance to Aldenham School in 1934, neither the christening, nor schooling of her granddaughters, Helen and Renée, are mentioned. Rosa's attitudes were both progressive and traditional.

Notes

1. Philip Ross Bullock, *Rosa Newmarch and Russian Music in Late Nineteenth and Early Twentieth-Century England* (Farnham, Surrey: Ashgate, 2009), p.115.

2. 'Marion Scott and the Society of Women Musicians' http://www.musicweb-international.com/Scott/Scott_Women.htm

3. Rosa Newmarch, 'Women's Musical Activities', *Time and Tide*, 4 Jan. 1929, pp.19-20.

4. Eric Blom, *Music in England* (West Drayton, Middlesex: Penguin Books, 1947), p.220.

5. Percy M. Young, *George Grove, 1820-1900* (London: Macmillan, 1980) p.168.

6. Bullock, *Rosa Newmarch*, p.117.

7. Ibid. p.118.

8. Ibid. pp. 99-136.

9. Ibid. p.13.

10. Arthur Jacobs, *Henry J. Wood: Maker of the Proms* (London: Methuen, 1994), p.276.

11. Ibid. p.272.

CHAPTER 28: RETIREMENT TO THE COUNTRY

1930 saw Rosa and Elsie living in their flat in Belsize Park and in spite of health problems, the coming year saw little reduction in Rosa's writing and social activities. She also had encouraging signs that two of the composers whom she had worked hard to promote, namely Sibelius and Janáček, were both receiving more performances of their works in England. Just after the New Year, Harry Colles visited them, spending the night there on his way back from Italy. Then on 16 January, Basil Cameron conducted the Royal Philharmonic Orchestra in a performance of Sibelius's Fourth Symphony. Just over a month later, Rosa travelled to Hastings for the Third Annual Musical Festival of the Hastings Municipal Orchestra, where on the 25th, Henry Wood conducted a concert and the following day, Basil Cameron conducted Sibelius's Prelude to *The Tempest* Op.109 and the tone poem *Night Ride and Sunrise* Op.55. Prior to these concerts, Cameron had written to Sibelius in September 1929 telling him that he had been invited to conduct the Fourth Symphony at the Queen's Hall in January and that he would very much like to visit him to go through the score, as he was naturally anxious to give the best possible performance of the work[1]. He also pointed out to Sibelius that he 'had the pleasure of playing violin in the Queen's Hall Orchestra under his [Sibelius's] direction' in 1909. The visit to Helsinki was a great success and Cameron invited Sibelius to conduct at the Hastings Festival in February. At first Sibelius accepted but then had cold feet. Rosa was very impressed with both performances by Cameron and was undoubtedly delighted that there was now another Sibelius enthusiast conductor, other than Henry Wood. She wrote to Sibelius enthusing about both performances, and he replied to her on 10 March 1930. He was pleased to hear about the performances of his works and had a wish to come to England although not in 1930, but he hoped to see her at Karlsbad in the summer[2]. Although she was in Karlsbad in June, she did not meet him.

In January 1930, Sir Henry Wood began a new series of 'miniature symphony concerts' at the London Coliseum, each of them forty-five minutes, as part of a thrice-daily variety programme. The London Coliseum had opened in 1904 as a People's Palace of Entertainment under the management of the impresario Sir Oswald Stoll, and these concerts were a new venture aimed at encouraging a wider audience to concerts of 'classical music'. Rosa, who wrote the programme notes, reported that 'the vast Coliseum public readily adapted themselves to what evidently appealed to them as the cardinal event of the programme. Not less than 5,000 people must have attended those daily concerts, and it would be interesting to know the sum of fresh converts to fine music made by this daring and novel venture[3].' Rosa considered how public taste changed like the ebb and flow of tides in an article entitled *Tide-Dials in Musical Life*[4]. She discussed the Richter Concerts in the late 19th century, then the advent of Promenade Concerts and later the possible impact of broadcasting and of the gramophone. Her views are interesting in comparison with the present day musical scene:

Those who were already in the swim of musical life in 1895, will remember that the inauguration of the "Proms" caused a violent commotion in the "tide-rip" of musical life. During the first years of their progress they disturbed all that was stagnant or self-complacent in our musical world. Venerable institutions believed their foundations to be shaking. Venerable highbrows and critics administered Canute-like rebukes to the encroachments of these advancing waves. How subversive to convention to hear music in an upright posture. How derogatory to art to have a refreshment bar in the background. Above all who could put confidence in this young British Siegfried, brandishing a new sword Needful, who ventured on a passage of arms with the Wotan of old tradition and Teutonic culture? The upshot was the same in Queen's Hall as in Erda's cave: "Pass, I cannot prevent thee." The Promenade Concerts, accounted subversive in their first years, gained in force and stability and continued at their appointed season to irrigate wildernesses of musical ignorance.

More revolutionary, and weighted with incalculable promise for the future of music, are those ninth waves which have more recently swept across our musical life: the gramophone and the wireless. The former a homely and obedient servant, laying at our feet everything we need, and nothing we do not want; re-echoing our best-loved music, and much that is also new, as often as we care to hear it, and leaving no shadow of excuse for ignorance of its inner beauty. The other a rapidly developing, and still somewhat unruly giant; sometimes kind to music, sometimes brutal; rarely like the gramophone a solace, but often a stimulant; now booming the transient and trivial vulgarities of life in our ears; now making us participate in the noblest and most thrilling events of contemporary history. Here are tidal forces that will require new dial-figures daily if we are to take accurate account of the velocity and range of their activity.

Rosa had been suffering from mild diabetes for some time, but in early May she saw a specialist, Dr Graham, and he prescribed insulin, something not available to her father when he had similar symptoms. Five days later, she had an operation on a parotid gland (salivary gland), presumably to remove a swelling. On 31 May, she went to Chorleywood, returning to the flat at Belsize Park on 11 June she had tea with Mabel Robinson and Mary Duclaux. The purpose of the visit to Chorleywood may have been to view a site for a house which they would later they build. On 12 June, she set out for her regular visit to the health resort of Karlovy Vary.

In September, her son, John, now a practicing doctor and married with a family of three children, became unwell and was taken to St George's Hospital London where he was found to be suffering from tuberculosis. He became ill again in November; tuberculosis was to dog him in the years to come. In December, Rosa took him to Torquay where they stayed for Christmas. But in spite of worries about her own and John's health, she managed to continue many of her activities. She went to a number of concerts, but perhaps her most important musical event in the autumn was the Norwich Triennial Festival.

From the time when Rosa first heard *Jenůfa* in Prague in 1919, she realised that Janáček was perhaps one of the most original composers of the twentieth century and she was determined that his work should be performed and appreciated in England. After his visit to London in 1926 she continued to champion him. So in 1930 she managed to persuade Henry Wood to put on a performance of his *Glagolitic Mass* at the Norwich Triennial Music Festival. Henry Wood needed little persuasion and was always keen to put on new works. This year's Norwich Festival was no exception. In addition to Janáček's *Glagolitic Mass*, Bliss's *Morning Heroes* and Vaughan Williams's *Job* were performed in 1930. For this event Rosa made a translation of the *Glagolitic Mass*, no easy task as it was written in Old Slavonic. In order to try to ensure as good a performance of a very unusual work, she gave a lecture in April in Norwich to the chorus that would be singing in the performance, so that they were well versed in the background. The mass was performed on 23 October. In spite of all the effort, it seemed, for the majority of the audience, that this was a work well ahead of its time and totally different from what they might expect in a mass. Also, although being sung in English might have helped the audience understand it, the characteristic sounds of the original language were lost[5]. Nowadays it is almost invariably sung in the original language. The following year Rosa wrote an article entitled 'New Works in Czechoslovakia[6]', almost entirely devoted to Janáček's compositions; this was aimed at keeping up the 'Janáček profile' in the English musical world.

At some stage around 1930, according to Elsie, Rosa felt that she still had two books to be written. For some time she had been collecting material for *The Music of Czechoslovakia* and she also wanted to write her autobiography. For the book on Czechoslovak music there was much new material concerning the younger generation of composers emerging and it was not until the days of the Munich Crisis and the break-up of the Republic that she felt it expedient to terminate the contemporary section with a view to publication. The book was eventually published posthumously in 1942. With the autobiography, she had only reached the early 1900s when she died. In order to have time free of other distractions, Rosa decided to move from London to the country. They opted to build a bungalow at Chorleywood, not far from the home of Sir Henry Wood. The timescale of the building is not completely clear, but it appears that Rosa and Elsie started to visit the site in 1930 and between then and 12 June 1933, when they completely settled into the bungalow, they had a number of temporary moves. In the spring of 1932, they left the flat in Belsize Park, letting it to Turkish Embassy tenants, and stayed at the bungalow at Chorleywood, where Rosa worked on a translation of Smetana's *Bartered Bride*. In June, they returned briefly to Belsize Park before going on their annual trip to Czechoslovakia. In November 1932, they gave up the flat at Belsize Park and spent the rest of 1932 in Leamington, presumably at Rosa's sister's. At the beginning of 1933, they moved back to London, first staying for a few weeks at the Woods' house in Elsworthy Road while Sir Henry and Muriel Wood were away on a holiday in Costa Rica and Trinidad[7]. Then they moved to a flat in Hamilton Terrace before returning to their bungalow in Chorleywood.

After the performance of the *Glagolitic Mass* at Norwich, the next modern Czech choral work that Rosa wanted to see performed in England was the Moravian composer Ladislav Vycpalek's cantata *The Last Things of Man*, a work with which she had been impressed when she saw it performed in Prague. Sir Henry Wood agreed to perform it at a Liverpool Philharmonic Concert in February 1931, for which Rosa provided the translation. The soloists were Elsie Suddaby, soprano, and Roy Henderson, baritone.

During the summer of 1931, when Rosa and Elsie Newmarch went to inspect their bungalow under construction, they called in on the Woods, who were occupying their garden bungalow whilst Appletree farm was being redecorated. By this time, there was tension between Henry and Muriel, as Elsie recalled. When Muriel Wood appeared, Rosa asked after Sir Henry. Muriel replied saying that he had lumbago and could not eat. Rosa offered to take him in a cup of tea and on approaching the bedroom saw a notice on the door which read: 'Enter Not – Wild Beast Within.' She found Sir Henry in a high fever, very ill. He was diagnosed as having pneumonia and skilled medical attention was required for him to recover in time for the 1931 Proms season[8]. Four years later, Sir Henry left his wife Muriel.

In both 1930 and 1932, Rosa and Elsie visited Czechoslovakia, where apart from the musical interest, Rosa also went for her regular visit to the health resort at Karlovy Vary. In 1932, they left for Prague on 28 June. According to a postcard Rosa sent to Bella Simpson, they stayed at the Hotel Splendid and whilst there they met Jaroslav Křička. They travelled on to Brno, staying at the Hotel Passage, and in a second postcard to Bella, Rosa said what a wonderful time they were having, although they were sad to see so many friends missing. They visited Mme Janáček and the widow of the painter Ondrušek, and also made a pilgrimage to Hostyn, where Alois Kolísek (1868-1931) was buried. Elsie described the visit to Hostyn:

Monsignor Kolísek's tragic death in 1931, from food poisoning on the return journey to Lourdes, brought the loss of a delightful friend. On Rosa Newmarch's return to Moravia in 1932 she was anxious to visit the Monastry Church where Monsignor Kolísek was buried. On arrival in Brno she was fortunate in finding his brother Abbé Karel Kolísek just returned from Dublin; so with the generous loan of an official car we were able to make our pilgrimage to Hostyn, the small monastery on the hillside. It happened to be the festival of the Virgin Mary, to whom the church of St. Hostyn was dedicated; so all the way along we met parties of pilgrims in their national dresses, some on foot, others driving at ease in their light wooden carts – for the peasants in this then prosperous agricultural district of Hanak were well-to-do and often owned magnificent horses. Our chauffeur drove us up the steep and difficult road to the very top of the hill, through delicious smelling fir woods, to the church served by a small community of Jesuit priests. Attached to the monastery was a small, beautifully kept burial-ground, overlooking the mountains and valleys, reserved entirely for this special order of which the Monsignor was a member.

On our way down we visited the village of Bystriče where, after lunching at the inn, we went to see Madame Ondrušek, widow of a well-known Moravian painter. Her husband had visited London a few years previously, and Rosa Newmarch had pleasant memories of accompanying him to several of our picture galleries. She was grieved to find that he too had departed this life only a few months earlier. His wife, a charming, simple woman, showed us some of her husband's work including an excellent, life-like portrait of President Masaryk intended to be presented to the city of Brno. We felt greatly in love with the old house and its large, cool studio in the garden, with exquisite views over the woods and hills.

From there they returned to Prague and then on to Karlovy Vary before returning home.

Rosa was clearly taken by Hostyn, to the extent that she decided to name their new bungalow at Chorleywood 'St Hostyns'.

47. St Hostyns, Chorleywood

Notes

1. Eric Tawaststjerna, *Sibelius, 1914-1957* trans. Robert Layton (London: Faber and Faber, 2008), vol. 3. p.297.

2. Rosa Newmarch, *Jean Sibelius: A Short Story of a Long Friendship* (London: Goodwin & Tabb, Ltd., 1944), pp.46-7.

3. Reginald Pound, *Sir Henry Wood* (London: Cassell, 1969), p.166.

4. Rosa Newmarch, 'Tide-Dials in Musical Life', *The Chesterian*, April/May 1930, pp.182-5.

5. Arthur Jacobs, (1994) *Henry J. Wood: Maker of the Proms* (London: Methuen, 1994), pp. 230-1.

6. Rosa Newmarch, 'New Works in Czechoslovakia', *The Chesterian*, July 1931, Vol. XII No 96.

7. Jacobs, *Henry Wood*, p.240.

8. Pound, *Sir Henry Wood*, p.167-8.

CHAPTER 29: THE FINAL YEARS

By the mid-1930s, Rosa was in her late seventies and so was inevitably unable to continue her activities at the pace she had been accustomed to. She had been suffering from diabetes for some time and had become much less mobile and somewhat overweight. Her eyesight began to fail, obviously a great handicap for writing and proofreading. In addition, she was worried about her son's health. He had been suffering from tuberculosis, and for considerable periods was too ill to work. In November 1932 and also in 1934, he went to Madiera to try to recuperate. The family – his wife, a son, two daughters and two stepdaughters – lived in Worthing and Rosa paid them periodic visits. Rosa was very fortunate in having a devoted daughter in Elsie. She travelled with her on her visits to Worthing, where they stayed in a local hotel. Ill health was to remain with John for the rest of his life and he was only to survive Rosa by seven years.

Rosa was very much saddened by the plight of Czechoslovakia. In the early part of the twentieth century, she was unable to keep up her connections with Russia after the Revolution and then enthusiastically turned her interest to the newly formed state of Czechoslovakia. Now she was to live to see it overrun by the Nazis. Unlike with Russia, where she never came in contact with political figures, in Czechoslovakia she met and became good friends with many of the political leaders including both Presidents Masaryk and Beneš. She made her last visit to Czechoslovakia in 1937, spent a busy week in Prague meeting many friends and attending musical events, and then travelled on to Karlovy Vary, where in past years she had found renewed health and energy. The efforts that she had made to promote Czechoslovak music for nearly twenty years were much appreciated as is evident from the birthday tribute to her on the occasion of her eightieth birthday in December 1937 from her friends in the Society of Arts in Czechoslovakia (Umělecká beseda):

> The world-wide name of the English writer, Rosa Newmarch, is familiar to us; to nearly all Czechoslovak musicians she has been known for many years for her propaganda work for our music in England; for her translation of Smetana's opera *The Bartered Bride* and of many songs and choruses; for her work in connection with the Czechoslovak section of the 1928 edition of *Grove's*

Dictionary of Music and Musicians, and also for her work in organizing Leoš Janáček's visit to England in 1926, when many of his chamber-music works were given for the first time in London at a concert specially arranged by her. To attain all this, and much more, she has maintained a vital and continuous contact with Prague during the last years.

Less well known perhaps are the outstanding personal qualities of this exceptional, sympathetic, gracious and lovable lady. We who know her well, love and admire her more today for these qualities which contrast so strikingly with her youthful freshness, her vivacity, energy and continued activity in her eightieth year. She still works, travels, and with vital energy penetrates all that is new and of value in art, with that thoroughness she has brought to all her studies.

During the first Czechoslovak Music Festival in England in 1919 she did much to make known our music and greatly helped to the success of these concerts. Shortly afterwards she made her first visit to this country, and having heard and seen our Prague musical life, in spite of the travel discomforts of those early days of the Republic, she toured Moravia and parts of Slovakia accompanied by the conductor Karel Kovařovic and his wife, and the poet Petr Křička, who then held a post in the Ministry of Education and acted as interpreter. Not confining herself to music, she visited the beautiful stalactite caves at Macocha, took part in the Festival of St. Cyril and St. Methodius at Velehrad, seeing the national life of the country and studying the various peasant arts, songs and dances; delighting one and all with her indefatigable interest in and grasp of everything she saw. In Brno she made the acquaintance of Leoš Janáček, whose music was of special interest to her, and here began her close and intimate knowledge of his works. The late Monsignor Kolísek was another friend of this visit, and that well-known and admirable interpreter of Slovak songs, brought her into contact also with the contemporary school of Slovak composers.

Nor must we forget how cordially she was received by our 'president Liberator', and these two dignified personalities in the President's box in the Smetana Hall on the occasion of the Smetana Festival, presented an unforgettable picture.

Rosa Newmarch, who has acquired a great affection for our music as for our country, is as unbiased as she is searching, though always loyal to her point of view. Since the days of Dvořák our music has had its admirers in England, but there is a difference between appreciation and friendship, between friendship and love. No one has done more to foster this interest in our music, to deepen the knowledge and love, than Rosa Newmarch, and to her we are deeply grateful especially at this time when true friendship means so much to us.

So we, her many devoted friends, her so-called 'sons' in Czechoslovakia, send her all our thanks; from one and all goes forth to this rare and cherished friend of our art our heartiest wishes for her eightieth birthday, for health and happiness for many years to come.

Her special interest in Janáček's music led her to translate librettos for *Kát'a Kabanová*, *The Cunning Little Vixen*, and *The Makropulous Affair* into English in the hope that they would be performed in England. However, that was not realised in her lifetime, but she did have the satisfaction of seeing Sadler's Wells Opera Company perform Smetana's *The Bartered Bride* in 1934 in her English translation[1]. It is regarded as a good translation, although the language in places is now regarded as rather quaint. It was used as the basis for a revised version produced by Eric Crozier and Joan Cross in 1948[2]. In June 1935, the BBC broadcast a performance of Janáček's *Glagolitic Mass* in Rosa's translation with the BBC chorus, choral master Leslie Woodgate, and the BBC Orchestra conducted by Sir Henry Wood. The soloists were Laella Finneberg, Doris Owens, Walter Widdop, and Stanley Riley.

Over a period of many years, Rosa had been very supportive of Sir Henry Wood, as he makes clear in his autobiography: 'It is not too much to say that Rosa Newmarch has been a rock upon which I have leaned often enough. She seemed always to understand my troubles, so to speak, at a distance. It has not been even necessary for me to discuss them with her, *for she was always at hand*, with real understanding. In paying this tribute, which I do in all sincerity, I can only add that I have never witnessed greater devotion in a daughter than in hers – Elsie Newmarch[3].' When Sir Henry Wood left his wife Muriel, having a good insight into their domestic situation, Rosa was quick to recognise his new liaison and wrote a very warm and tactful letter to Mrs Jessie Linton on 11 April 1935 accepting an invitation for dinner with Henry and Jessie and signing 'Yours sincerely and gratefully.' Rosa had never been on very cordial terms with Muriel and was obviously pleased to see Sir Henry in much better spirits now he was with Jessie[4]. In his autobiography, Sir Henry Wood also states of Rosa: 'Even though she has passed her eight-first birthday she can still hold her own at a dinner-table with most amusing conversation and sparkling repartee[5].' Just over a year earlier, she made a speech at a dinner given by Sir Henry Wood for members of his orchestra at the Langham Hotel on 26 September 1937:

Ladies and gentlemen – among whom I recognize with pleasure many colleagues from the old Queen's Hall Orchestra – we cannot leave this table without thanking our host for his hospitality, and drinking to his health and continued prosperity. Anything like a set speech would be out of place at a friendly gathering such as we have enjoyed tonight. Nobody present – except perhaps Dr Cathcart – could I believe dispute with me the honour of being Sir Henry's oldest friend; and he will not grudge me the privilege of saying a few words tonight.

Of course I can remember 'little Henry J. Wood' pulling himself – not I think entirely unaided – on to his organ stool at the Fisheries Exhibition in 1883. But our real friendship began on a late autumn morning in 1897, when I had just returned from my first musical tour of Russia. I brought a few scores by Glinka, Moussorgsky and Rimsky-Korsakov – then much unknown to the general public in England. I wanted the 'Prom' audience to enjoy what I had been enjoying myself in Moscow and St. Petersburg. On the doorstep of his flat in Langham Place I collided with a vivacious, tremendously energetic young man – the conductor himself. Heaven knows how long we discussed music on the pavement. Well, I took those precious scores to Henry Wood not because I was particularly infatuated with his conducting, or because I had any axe to grind myself – it was many years before I had any official connection with Queen's Hall – but because I already knew that he had the spirit of youth which is the true spirit of real propaganda: he already *thought for the future*. He still has it.

Sir Henry was then 27 – I needn't confess my age – it will soon be forty years since that day when we set up a friendship which has never suffered a break or been clouded by a quarrel…Yes, one, we disagreed over the *tempo* in *Tannhäuser*! It is worthwhile having to live to be a very old woman if one can boast of one long and perfect relationship in life.

All those years I have watched Sir Henry's career moving from *strength*: and these are the points of which I would ask you to take note.

A true friend to *orchestral* music which was not our strongest point at the end of the last century.

He has not tied himself to narrow specialism – not a one-man conductor (Tchaikovsky, Wagner, and splendid Bach, British music, etc).

And he has given women their first chance of taking an honourable place in first class orchestras.

Ladies and gentlemen, I must not detain you any longer: it has been whispered in my ear that in the next room a first rate conjurer is waiting to entertain us, but before we leave do not let us forget to pay honour to the Conjurer who sits beside me: the man who conjured away the old, undeserved reproach that England is not a musical Nation.

During the last eight years of her life Rosa's publication rate slowed. From 1933-1940, she published nine translations; these included the libretto for *The Bartered Bride*, five works by Vaclav Divina, one by Tcherepnin, Rimsky-Korsakov, Handel, and Lishin[6]. She also wrote obituaries for Josef Suk and the singer Leonid Sobinov and short articles on Sir Henry Wood and Alexander Glazunov. The fifth volume of her *Concert-Goers Library* was issued in 1938[7], all five volumes were favourably reviewed, and in 1937, the Australian Broadcasting Commission asked permission to use her notes for their orchestral concerts in Sydney, Melbourne, Brisbane and other cities, then being conducted by Sir Malcolm Sargent. Her analytical notes were often reused when there were repeat performances of works. For example, Rachmaninoff's *The Bells* was first performed in England in 1921 at Liverpool, and when a performance was given at the Sheffield Festival in 1936, Rosa's notes were again used.

The three books she worked on during this time were a book on Sibelius, *Music of Czechoslovakia*, and her autobiography. She had begun collecting material for *Music of Czechoslovakia* since the early 1920s and by 1922 she had written the parts on Suk, Novák, and Dvořák. She had also written on Janáček but needed to extend her original chapter to take account of his more recent compositions. Of the three books mentioned, this was the one that required most research and was published by Oxford University Press in 1942, two years after her death. In it the editor thanks English and Czechoslovak friends who helped in the revision of the author's posthumous work. The book on Sibelius entitled *Jean Sibelius: A Short Story of a Long Friendship* is based on Rosa's recollections of Sibelius from the time she first met him in 1905; she began working on it in 1931. In addition, the book contains a general note on Sibelius's seven symphonies, which occupies approximately one third of the book. Much of this is an expansion of the programme notes that Rosa had already written for concert programmes that included his symphonies. After Sibelius's last visit to England in 1921, Rosa and Sibelius corresponded sporadically.

In 1932, Arnold Bax and Harriet Cohen visited Sibelius in Helsinki, as Harriet Cohen described: 'Arnold and I had the gayest meeting with Sibelius at an outside restaurant sitting in the sun where I took their photographs, together and separately. We laughed and ate and drank, and the two composers, who liked each other on sight, got on famously. I remember noting how their talk veered round continually to history – a subject in which they were both interested. When the shadows lengthened we went to another favourite haunt of his, the Hotel Kemp and we talked about literature, art and even world politics for hours. During the twenty-four hours we were together, Sibelius smoked ten cigars, and I too. We drank four magnums of champagne between us[8].' So much for Rosa's earlier advice to Sibelius! Harriet Cohen sent Rosa a postcard postmarked 5 July 1932, care of Sir Henry Wood, relaying Sibelius's description of Newmarch as '*une femme inoubliable*', expressing her assent, and giving a breathless account of the 'divine time' spent with Sibelius and Bax, signed Harriet/Jean Sibelius/Arnold Bax/Our united loves to Sir Henry[9]. Surely Rosa would have envied them. Rosa wrote to Sibelius in 1935 on the occasion of his seventieth birthday and received a very warm reply, which begins: 'You can hardly imagine the joy that your welcome letter brought to me. It was like a tender memory of old and precious days, which were so precious to me and, thanks to you, of so much importance to my music[10]. From May 29 to 4 June, there was a Sibelius Concert Festival in London which Rosa attended.

She completed writing the book on Sibelius sometime in 1938 and negotiated a contract with the American publishers C.C. Birchard Co. of Boston, Massachusetts. The publishers accepted the manuscript in October 1938 and were keen to have an introduction by Sir Granville Bantock, since it was through him that Rosa first met Sibelius in 1905 and Bantock was well known in America so they felt it would boost sales. At the time, Bantock was in Australia and there was a little delay in contacting him although once contacted he was very willing to write the introduction. In a brief draft reply that Rosa wrote to the publishers in November 1938, she expresses one of her concerns at the time: 'I thank you for your letter. I have not yet received a contract from Mr David Stevens and cannot expect before Xmas as I know what a busy time it is. Less impatient for contract than for proofs as on account of eye trouble glad to get proofs while can still see them. For this reason asked Granville to send preface direct to you.' [This is from her handwritten draft.] Rosa had wanted Chester Ltd to be the agents to promote her book in the UK, but C.C. Birchard were already negotiating with Goodwin and Tabb as their London agents. It was Tabb and Goodwin who reprinted it in 1944. All the correspondence from C.C. Birchard between October 1938 and July 1939 is addressed to Rosa at 53 Circus Mansions, London NW8, her home at the time. One month after the outbreak of war there is a final letter dated 2 October 1939 from David Stevens to Rosa at Kingsway Hotel, Worthing, which strikes a gloomy note. He thanks her for her letter and is glad she has taken the precaution of moving out of London, and expresses general concern about the war, which would undoubtedly affect the prospects of sales in Europe. He concludes by saying that they will do their best to promote the book's sale and hopes she will be reasonably immune from trouble away from London.

Earlier in 1939, the last of her sisters, Caroline (Tiny), to whom she was closest, died.

Rosa lived to see the Sibelius book published; the *Music of Czechoslovakia* was so very near completion that friends were able to finish it, but with her autobiography, begun in 1934, she had only covered just over half her lifetime. She sent a draft of the early parts of her autobiography to her friend and author Esther Wood, who commented in a letter dated 2 February 1934 that she had made a very promising beginning to the opening chapters. She also suggested that she should include a chapter on the circle of friends she knew who came to Leamington Road Villas, where she lived when first married. These included the Robinsons, the Wilsons, Arthur Strong, Franklin Clive, and Vernon Lee.

By 1940, Rosa's eyesight was very poor, Elsie had to administer her regular injections of insulin and her mobility was somewhat limited, so on visits to her son's family in Worthing, Elsie would have to help her out of the taxi. It was on such a visit in April 1940 when she and Elsie were staying at Percival's Hotel, Worthing that she died.

Notes

1. Bedřich Smetana, *Bartered Bride: A Comic Opera in Three Acts*, libretto by K. Sabina, trans. Rosa Newmarch (London: Boosey and Hawkes, 1934).

2. Timothy Cheek, *The Bartered Bride: Performance Guide with Translation and Pronunciation* (Maryland: Scarecrow Press, 2010), pp.278-9.

3. Henry Wood, *My Life in Music* (London: Gollancz, 1938), p.232.

4. Arthur Jacobs, *Henry J. Wood: Maker of the Proms* (London: Methuen, 1994), pp.276-7.

5. Wood, *My Life in Music*, p.231.

6. Philip Ross Bullock, *Rosa Newmarch and Russian Music in Late Nineteenth and Early Twentieth-Century England* (Farnham,Surrey: Ashgate, 2009), pp.163-4.

7. Rosa Newmarch, *The Concert-Goer's Library of Descriptive Notes*, vol. 5 (London: Oxford University Press, 1938).

8. Harriet Cohen, *A Bundle of Time* (London: Faber and Faber, 1969), pp.206-9.

9. Sotheby's Music Catalogue, 22 May 2003, p.118.

10. Rosa Newmarch, *Jean Sibelius A Short Story of a Long Friendship* (London: Goodwin and Tabb, 1944), pp.47-8.

EPILOGUE

After Rosa Newmarch's death on 9 April 1940, there were obituaries in *The Times* on 12 April and in the May issue of the *Musical Times*. Both highlight her role as a programme writer for the Proms and many other concerts. The pianist Frederic Lamond, whom she had known for many years, wrote to Elsie: 'I feel I have lost a very dear friend, a high and noble spirit. Her love and understanding for the music of Tchaikovsky, Dvořák and Sibelius; her deep appreciation of the Slavic literature of Russia and Czechoslovakia, made her a unique personality in England. Indeed I have never met any musician or author who had that intuitive feeling for the Slav Muse to such a remarkable degree; and I am proud to have had the privilege of knowing her and calling her my friend.' However, it is in the role of programme writer for the Proms that she is perhaps best remembered today. She developed a new style of programme note that most suited the concert-going public and for the first three decades of the twentieth century was the most highly regarded woman writer on music[1]. From a much larger number of programme notes, over 350 were selected and published in six volumes as *The Concert-goers Library* between 1928 and 1948.

At the outset of her career as a music writer, and after writing two major books on Tchaikovsky, she probably planned to continue writing in the same vein. So when the opportunity arose to write the analytical notes for the Proms, she needed time to think whether to accept the offer, which would undoubtedly distract her from this plan. Later, she showed no regrets at having taken on this role, one very much in keeping with her mission to bring classical music to a wider public. It also brought her very much into the public domain, and with it further possibilities. Her other associated missions were to see that both Russian and Czechoslovak music became more widely performed in England. Her authority on Russian and Czechoslovak music is evident from the major contributions she made to the second and third editions of *Grove's Dictionary of Music and Musicians*, contributing many articles on Russian composers in the former and Czech and Slovak composers in the latter. A major asset to much of her writings and her extensive travels was her linguistic ability; she could speak French, German, Russian, Czech, and, to a lesser extent, other European languages.

She became very widely known in musical circles, particularly as a result of her writings. When she was presented with a Blüthner piano in 1929, there were over 130 contributors including friends and musicians. She was a great friend of Sibelius and had the foresight to see that he would become one of the greatest composers of the twentieth century long before this was widely recognised. Her comment on his violin concerto bears this out (see Chapter 13). An aspect of her career not mentioned in *The Times* obituary is her poetry, largely neglected until recently. Her poems are not often found in anthologies of poetry, but since the beginning of the twenty-first century, a number of articles have appeared on her poetry and a new edition of her collected poems has been produced[2].

In the years after Rosa's death, Elsie devoted much of her time acting as her executrix and was concerned to keep her legacy alive. At the height of the Second World War, the country's focus was very much on the war effort, and music, concerts, and publishing were accorded lower priorities. In spite of this, Rosa's *Music of Czechoslovakia* was published in 1944, but her autobiography was less than half finished, and Elsie required time to decide how it might be completed. She continued living in the flat at Circus Mansions until the mid-1950s when she moved to Windsor. One of her first concerns was to see that many of Rosa's extensive collection of books and her lantern slides should be placed where they would be of most use. She donated many of her books on Russian subjects to the School of Slavonic Studies at London University, books on Czechoslovakia to the Beneš Institute, and her opera scores to the Sadler's Wells library. She donated the lantern slides to the Russian Refugees Community in the United Kingdom.

Elsie took a particular interest in performances of works her mother might have been associated with. She wrote to the BBC on 28 February 1944 after they had broadcast one of Janáček's works, explaining that she had enjoyed the performance and enclosing Rosa's English translation of the text. She received a reply from Alec Robertson saying that he had wished he had known of Rosa's excellent translation because the one they used 'did not always feel as if it belonged to the music.' In another letter from the BBC in February 1952, they wrote to ask permission to use Rosa's translation of Tchaikovsky's *Queen of Spades* for a projected seventy minute televised broadcast, indicating their usual fee of 10/ – per minute for the first 15 minutes and 7/6d per minute thereafter, to which Elsie agreed, although it is not clear that the broadcast materialised. Elsie also agreed to a request from the Gramophone Co. Ltd to use Rosa's translation of an aria from the *Queen of Spades*. This was to be sung by Joan Hammond and recorded for which the company would pay 2⅝d per record.

Rafael Kubelík was Director of Covent Garden Opera from 1955 to 1958. During his tenure, he conducted a performance of *Jenůfa*, which Elsie particularly enjoyed, and she wrote to tell him so. She received a gratifying reply in which he praised Rosa's efforts in bringing Janáček's music to the attention of the English public and said that he very much hoped that other Janáček operas would by staged in England.

In general when dealing with requests concerning copyrights etc for Rosa's work, Elsie's replies were helpful and precise, but at the same time, she was careful to protect Rosa's legacy, as the following request illustrates. In 1958, she was asked by the editor of *Music and Musicians*, on behalf of the editor of *Soviet Music*, if she could provide a photograph of her mother to accompany an article. Her response was that she did not know the magazine *Soviet Music* and before consenting she would need to learn more of the author and if possible see a translation of the article, as lending the photograph would suggest approval of the contents. The editor of *Music and Musicians* replied that asking for a copy of the article would be discourteous as *Soviet Music* was a highly regarded magazine and that in his thirty years of music journalism he has never received such a request. Elsie's reply was that in view of his response, the matter was closed. By contrast, when she received a request in 1968 for copies of three letters from Rosa to Skryabin from the Director of J & W Chester Ltd, who was acting on behalf of the Director of the Central State Museum of Musical Culture in Moscow, she was happy to oblige.

Whilst Elsie was cautious about lending out material when she was uncertain of its potential use, she was very generous when she was confident it was going into the right hands. In 1948, Leoš Firkušný (brother of the pianist Rudolf Firkušný) and his wife, Růžena Hořáková, came to England, supported by the British Council, to give a series of lectures on Czech music. At some point on this visit, they met Elsie and realised they had many interests in common. Knowing that Leoš was a well-known music scholar, Elsie offered him a collection of letters between Janáček and Rosa which would enable him to do further research. Sadly, Leoš died suddenly in 1950 before he had an opportunity to use the letters. Some years later, in 1963, Růžena Horáková met the musicologist Zdenka Fischmann and was anxious for the letters to be used since they were important historical documents. Zdenka Fischmann contacted Elsie asking permission to publish the letters in translation with suitable commentary. Elsie readily agreed, but there were further delays before Zdenka made a full analysis of the letters, which were finally published in 1986. A more detailed account can be found in Zdenka Fischmann's book[3].

After the war, Elsie decided that she should attempt to complete Rosa's autobiography, based on letters and documents and on Elsie's recollections, since she had been her travelling companion and effectively her secretary for many years. In a letter to Sibelius in September 1945, she wrote that she hoped that some day it would be possible to publish her mother's memoirs. However, three years later, in a letter to Jessie Wood, she explained that completing the memoirs was proving stressful because of the difficulty of keeping apart Rosa's private and professional life. She then added that Rosa's letters reveal 'unhappy, intimate and difficult domestic upheavals' and times when her marriage was in danger[4]. Nevertheless, Elsie went on to complete the memoirs using Rosa's unchanged and incomplete autobiography for the first part and her own account for the period from the early 1900s until Rosa's death for the second part. The account was thus part autobiography and part biography.

In 1956, Elsie met Eric Blom for lunch in order to seek his advice about the publication of the memoirs and other unpublished work of Rosa's. Shortly after Janácek's visit to London in 1926, Rosa had made translations of the librettos of *Kát'a Kabanová*, *The Cunning Little Vixen*, and *The Makropoulos Case* in the hope that it would be possible to stage performances of these opera in England. By 1956, none of these had been staged in England and the translated librettos remained unpublished. Eric Blom's initial reaction in his letter of 20 September 1956 was: 'I think the memoirs ought certainly to be published if at all possible: they must be full of period history now just beginning to go far enough back to appeal to older people and to intrigue the younger ones. And I am sure much of it must be extremely amusing.' Elsie duly sent him the memoirs and librettos. Concerning the librettos, his initial response was that he would like to publish *The Makropoulos Case* in *Music and Letters*, a journal of which he was editor. He planned to have it published for the April 1957 issue, but by December 1956 had realised a difficulty that meant he decided against publication. Rosa's translation of the *Makropoulos* libretto was based closely on Čapek's play for which there was already a translation by Paul Selver, and this would undoubtedly mean copyright difficulties.

When Blom was part way through the memoir, his response in a letter dated 15 November 1956 was: 'Most entertaining and interesting. Whether the Memoirs could be published in that form I can't decide as yet; my present impression is that, although they contain much of interest about the early stages of your Mother's career, they stop short just where most people who remember her would want to know what happened – Queen's Hall, and so on.' Then in a final letter in early 1957, he wrote: 'This idea of the memoirs is probably the right one, if you can get somebody to do it. I was rather tempted myself to say I would, if you would let me, but I know in my heart of hearts that I must resist, though it would be the kind of tribute I should love to pay to your mother's memory.' He then went on to explain the large writing commitments he had at that time. He was sixty-eight then, and although he had been a very prolific writer, he was by then slowing down, and he died just over two years later.

After Eric Blom's death, Elsie resorted to Rosa's old publisher, Herbert Jenkins Ltd., writing to the director, Mr Grimsdick, to ask whether they would consider publishing the memoirs. Her letter dated 19 June 1959 began very tentatively: 'Dear Mr Grimsdick, Following your kind suggestion I am sending you the typescript of the Memoirs of Rosa Newmarch. I fear it is a somewhat irregular form of biography and not altogether satisfactory job.' In his reply on 24 July, he damns it with faint praise, saying: 'Her impressions of famous composers and their work, and the important musical events she initiated or participated in are of undeniable value. Nevertheless, we feel that the book suffers a certain shapelessness in an attempt to combine two methods of presentation.' He concluded that it needed to be written in either the first or third person and that it required further editing, but could become a very interesting memoir. Elsie then talked the matter over with her nephew, Michael, who worked for The Associated Press. He expressed interest and concurred with most of Grimsdick's comments, but felt that it would be best done by someone outside the family who could be more easily objective.

Elsie felt that if it were to be rewritten all in the third person, 'it would lose a good deal of the personality which is in her writing.' Nevertheless, she did so and resubmitted it to Herbert Jenkins, but again in a carefully worded letter, dated 1 February 1960, Mr Grimsdick declined to publish it, partly on the grounds that its appeal would not be to a large enough market. Elsie then sought advice from a good friend Lady Jesse Wood, who then wrote to the publishers Victor Gollancz. Gollancz indicated that 'they would very much like to consider the manuscript.' After submitting it, Elsie received a polite but bland reply on 15 July 1960 from one of their directors in which she thanked Elsie for sending the manuscript and said that she enjoyed reading it but declined to publish it on the grounds that they would be unable to find an 'effective market'.

By now Elsie was seventy-two and she must have felt that all her efforts to publish had been to no avail and that further editing on her part would be difficult, time-consuming, and with limited chances of success. Elsie died in 1973 having worked tirelessly to support her mother, especially during the latter part of her life, and to keep her legacy alive. It is pleasing to see that there now seems to be a revival of interest in many aspects of Rosa Newmarch's work.

Notes

1. Reginald Pound, *Sir Henry Wood* (London: Cassell, 1969), p.63.

2. *Horae Amoris: The Collected Poems of Rosa Newmarch* edited with an introductory essay by John Holmes and Natasha Distiller, Rivendale Press, 2010.

3. Zdenka E. Fischmann, *Janáček-Newmarch Correspondence* (Rockville, Maryland: Kabel Publishers, 1986).

4.Philip Ross Bullock, *Rosa Newmarch and Russian Music in Late Nineteenth and Early Twentieth-Century England* (Farnham, Surrey: Ashgate, 2009), p.6.

APPENDIX 1
BIOGRAPHICAL NOTES

Beneš, Eduard (1884-1948) was Czechoslovakian Minister of Foreign Affairs from 1920-1925 and 1929-1935. He went into exile in 1915 in Paris where, from 1916-1918, he was secretary of the Czech National Council in Paris. He was prime minister from September 1921 to October 1922 and became the second president of the Czechoslovak Republic, to Thomas Masaryk following, from 1935 to 1938.

Birkbeck, William John (1859-1916) was a high churchman who devoted his life to increasing his fellow-countrymen's knowledge and understanding of Russia and the Russian Church. Birkbeck was a frequent visitor to Russia, building up a wide range of contacts both at court and among senior figures in ecclesiastical hierarchy. He used his position to campaign for closer relations between the English and Russian churches. His biography, *The Life and Letters of W J Birkbeck* (1922), was written and compiled by his wife, Katherine Rose Gurney Birkbeck.

Chorley, Henry Fothergill (1808-1872) was the author of *Thirty Years of Musical Recollections (1862)*, a lively and often quoted memoir of operatic life in London. In his day Chorley was best known for his weekly columns on musical life in *The Athenæum*. He began working for *The Athenæum* in 1833. Initially he wrote reviews on a variety of literary subjects but within a year he became the journal's authority on all musical matters. By the end of the 1830s, Chorley's reviews earned the journal a reputation as a musical authority that was unusual for a general interest publication. His journalistic peak was in the 1850s when he and Davison were regarded as the arbiters of the London musical scene.

Chudoba, František (1878-1941) was appointed in 1919 as Professor of Czech and Slavonic Languages at the newly formed School of Slavonic Studies. At that time, the school was a department in King's College, London and was expanding its range of Slavonic languages. The newly independent Czechoslovak Government funded the post in the Czech and Slavonic Languages, which Chudoba held until 1923, when he returned to Masaryk University as Professor of English Literature, a post he held until his death.

Colles, Henry Cope (1879-1943) was a musical historian and critic. He studied at the Royal College of Music and Worcester College Oxford and under Walford Davies. He was musical editor of *The Times* from 1911-43. He edited the third and fourth editions of *Groves Dictionary of Music and Musicians* and published a number of other books on music.

Cooper, Anthony Ashley (1801-1885), the Seventh Earl of Shaftesbury and a Member of Parliament campaigned actively for a number of philanthropic causes. These included the improvement in the conditions and hours of work for children, which led to the introduction of the Factories Act and improvement in the treatment of those in lunatic asylums.

Davies, Fanny (1861-1885) was an English pianist who studied under Clara Schumann, making her debut at Crystal Palace in 1885. She performed with Joachim, Piatti, Gervase Elwes, and Casals. Although a classicist, she was the first to play Debussy's Préludes in England and Bax's Piano Quintet with the Czech Quartet. She was popular in Czechoslovakia and promoted the performance of Czech music.

Davison, James (1813-1885) lived most of his life in London. At the age of forty-five he married the twenty-one-year old pianist Arabella Goddard. After the birth of their second son, the couple separated. Many years later, their sons, Henry and Charles, married Rosa's nieces, Laura and Emily Kenney respectively. In his long spell as music critic of *The Times*, Davison wrote anonymously, but according to his biographer, Charles Reid, there is little difficulty in penetrating the anonymity, as for thirty-two years, he was the paper's sole writer on music. The same also applied to his writings in *Musical World*, where his position as editor identified his writings. He also wrote the analytical programmes for the popular concerts at St James' Hall. According to Charles Reid, 'his purpose was to bias two generations against the pre-eminent musical geniuses of his century. Not until well into the present century [20th] was his influence undone.' His critical judgements have been described as both astounding and comical.

Destinn, Emmy, originally Kittlová **(1878-1930)**, was a Czech soprano whose vocal abilities were revealed by her teacher, Marie Loewe-Destinn. She subsequently adopted her surname as a token of appreciation. She specialised in Wagnerian roles and performed the title role in the Berlin and Paris premières of Strauss's *Salome*.

After internment during the war, her powers declined and she retired in 1921.

Dobrovsky, Abbé Josef (1753-1829) was a Bohemian philologist and historian. He was educated for the Roman Catholic priesthood under the Jesuits at Klatovy, but with the dissolution of the Jesuit order in 1773, he devoted himself to scholarship, particularly in Slavonic philology. He travelled widely in Russia and Sweden. He pleaded the case for civil rights for the Czech language within the Austro-Hungarian Empire.

Drtina, Prokop (1900-1980) was a Czech lawyer and politician. He created the Czechoslovak Political Centre Party. He became secretary to President Beneš and was Minister of Justice from 1945-1948.

Gambetta, Léon (1838-1882), was a French Republican statesman, who initially trained as a lawyer. After the Franco-Prussian war precipitated the downfall of the empire (1870), he became prominent in the provisional government. His organisation of a government of national defence to drive out the Germans, his spectacular escape from Paris in a balloon, and his gallant opposition to the Prussian forces won worldwide sympathy. Gambetta bitterly fought French capitulation and briefly retired from politics, but in 1879, he became President of the Chamber of Deputies, and from 1881-2, he was briefly première under President Grévy.

Graham, Stephen (1884-1975) was a freelance author, noted for his travel writing, though he also wrote novels. At the beginning of the First World War, he was in the Altai Mountains, Russia and wrote articles for *The Times* and later two books entitled *Russia and the World* and *Through Russian Central Asia*. Two years after the war, he visited the battlefields and wrote *The Challenge of the Dead*.

Hannikainen, Ilmari (1892-1955) was a Finnish pianist and composer. His teachers were Alexander Siloti in St Petersburg and Alfred Cortot in Paris. He composed a piano concerto, a piano quartet, and many piano pieces. His brothers Tauno and Arvo were also musicians, cellist and violinist respectively.

Hewitt, Sir Frederick (1857-1916) was a distinguished anaesthetist. He was appointed anaesthetist at Charing Cross Hospital in 1884 at a time when anaesthesia was a comparatively crude technique. He was responsible for many improvements in the technique. In 1901, he was appointed anaesthetist to King Edward VII.

Three days before the coronation, he was called upon to anaesthetise the King for surgery on his appendix. He was awarded the K.C.V.O. for services to the King and was the first anaesthetist to be knighted.

Heyner, Herbert (1881 – 1954) was an English baritone, a pupil of Frederick King and Victor Maurel. He sung in English concerts and festivals, including the Promenade Concerts. He sang in a number of performances of *The Dream of Gerontius* and also the part of Amfortas in *Parsifal*. He was a friend of Sir Henry Wood. He lost a leg while serving in the First World War.

Irving, Henry (1838-1905) was one of the most famous actors of the Victorian era; the first actor to be knighted. His original name was John Henry Brodribb. He became a matinée idol. He has been described as handsome, genteel, and gentlemanly, and a perfect specimen of refined English manhood.

Jurgenson, Peter Ivanovich (1840-1903) was born in Reval and was the son of a poor fisherman. He became apprenticed to a master printer in St Petersburg, and was later clerk to the music-publishing house of Stellovsky, before moving to Moscow in 1859 as manager of the firm of Schildbach. Ten years later, he opened a publishing business of his own, with the cooperation and advice of Nicholas Rubinstein. He raised the standard of printing and engraving and published a number of books on music, including works by Tchaikovsky, Arensky, Ippolitov-Ivanov, and others. In order to protect Russian copyrights, he opened a branch in Leipzig, styled Commissioners to the Court Chapel, to the Imperial Russian Musical Society, and the Moscow Conservatoire. After the Revolution in 1917, the firm ceased to exist.

Kocián, Jaroslav (1883-1950) was a Czech violinist who studied at the Prague Conservatory and took composition lessons from Dvořák. He travelled widely as a violinist, but after 1920, confined himself to teaching. He composed a number of violin pieces.

Kolísek, Alois (1868-1931) studied theology in Brno and later in Rome (1892-4). He taught in Moravia and in Bratislava after 1919. He was a friend of Janáček and also of Seton-Watson and he visited London on many occasions. He investigated and lectured on folk music.

Kollar, Jan (1793-1852) was a Slovak poet who played an important part in the national and literary revival of the Slavs in the early nineteenth century.

Laroche, Hermann (1845-1904) was a Russian music critic, born in St Petersburg. He studied with Anton Rubinstein and Zaremba in St Petersburg, and with Tchaikovsky in Moscow. He wrote for numerous musical journals. His most important work was *M.I.Glinka and His Place in Russian Music* (1863) and with Kashkin he wrote *Reminiscences of Tchaikovsky* in 1894.

Lee, Vernon See Violet Paget.

Léon, Mischa (1889-1926) was a Danish tenor whose real name was Harry Haurowitz. His teachers were Jean de Reszke and Sir George Henschel. He made his debut at the Copenhagen Opera House. He toured the US, England and Europe and sung the London première of Janáček's *The Diary of One Who Disappeared*. He was briefly married in 1918 to the opera singer Pauline Donalda.

Mackail, John William (1859-1945) was a Scottish man of letters, socialist, poet, and biographer. He was author of *Russia's Gift to the World* (1915).

Masaryk, Tomáš (1850-1937) was an Austro-Hungarian and Czechoslovak statesman. He was a keen advocate of Czechoslovak independence, and he fled the country to avoid being arrested on a charge of treason. While in exile in London in 1915, he became one of the founding members of the School of Slavonic and East European Studies. He was the first President (1918-1935) and founder of Czechoslovakia.

Miliukov, Pavel Nikolayevich (1859-1943) was the leading organiser and ideologist of Russian liberalism from before the 1905 Revolution until his withdrawal from active politics after the Russian Revolutions of 1917 and the Civil War. He was a founder of the Constitutional Democratic Party (known as Kadets) and represented it in the third and fourth State Dumas. During the Great War, he most boldly asserted the program of the Progressive Bloc within the Duma, particularly in the last months of the old regime. The February Revolution elevated him briefly to the position of Foreign Minister in the provisional government in the spring of 1917. After the October 1917 Soviet Revolution, he was an active participant in the 'white' movement against the Bolsheviks. He was also an eminent Russian historian. After the 1917 Revolution, he immigrated to France where he lived for the rest of his life.

Morfill, William Richard (1834-1909) was appointed reader in the Russian and Slavonic languages at Oxford University in 1889 and then professor in 1900. Possessing an unusually powerful and retentive memory, and being an omnivorous reader, he had a larger acquaintance with literature, both Russian and Polish, than even many educated natives of those countries. He was a fellow of the British Academy. Among his publications was a popular account of the Slavonic literature, written for the Society for Promoting Christian Knowledge in 1883.

Nebdal, Oskar (1874-1930), was a pupil of Dvořák, a Czech conductor, composer, viola player, and member of the Bohemian String Quartet. He was conductor of the Czech Philharmonic Orchestra (1896-1906) and later the Tonkünstler Orchestra in Vienna.

Novikoff, Olga, née Kireff (1848-1925) was a Russian aristocrat both by parentage and marriage. Her brother-in-law was the Russian Ambassador in Vienna. Madame Novikoff was politically active, and as the goddaughter to Tsar Nicholas, was a devoted imperialist. She lived for a time in London, where she established a circle of acquaintances, including politicians. She was an Anglophile who worked to bring about cordial relations between England and Russia, something she lived to see realised in 1914/5. Her most important book was *Russian Memories*, published by Herbert Jenkins in 1917.

Osuský, Štefan (1869-1973) was born in Slovakia and came to the US after completing elementary school. He received a law degree from the University of Chicago. During World War I, he worked for creation of an independent Czechoslovak state. In 1920, Osuský was a co-signatory with Eduard Beneš to the treaty that gave final recognition to the independent Czechoslovak borders, and in 1921, he was appointed Czechoslovak Minister plenipotentiary to France. Later he served in the diplomatic service of Great Britain and Switzerland, and from 1931-1938 was the Czech ambassador to France. After Munich, he joined the Beneš government in London.

Pachmann, Vladimir de (1848-1933) was a Russian pianist, born in Odessa and hailed as the greatest Chopin player in his day. In 1844, he married his former Australian piano student, Maggie Okey (1864-1952), in London. He performed in London both as a soloist and with his wife. He was also noted for his eccentricity, talking to the audience and sometimes having them upon the stage, and after a recital crawling under the piano to look for the wrong notes he had played.

Paget, Lady Muriel Evelyn Vernon (née Finch-Hatton) (1876-1938) was a philanthropist and a humanitarian relief worker, initially in London and later in Eastern and Central Europe, where she organised the Anglo-Russian Hospital, which from 1916-8 cared for enormous numbers of wounded on the eastern front. She was awarded an O.B.E. in 1918 and a C.B.E. in 1938.

Paget, Violet (1865-1935) was a writer using the pen name of Vernon Lee. She was born in France to ex-patriot parents and spent most of her life in Italy, mainly near Florence. She was recognised in her time as one of the most impressive intellectuals of Victorian England, a prolific writer best known for her supernatural fiction and having wide ranging interests in art and music. She was a lesbian and had a close friendship with Mary Robinson.

Palacký, František (1798-1876) was a Czech historian and politician and an authority on Slavonic languages. His magnum opus was *The History of the Czech Nations in Bohemia and Moravia* (5 vols. 1836-1867).

Pares, Bernard (1867-1949) made his first visit Russia in 1898. In 1902, he was appointed as an adult education lecturer at Liverpool University, and in 1907, he founded the first School of Russian Studies in a British university. He was a regular visitor to Russia and met leading figures in the Russian Government. At the outbreak of World War I, he was appointed British Military Observer to the Russian army, but left Russia after the October Revolution. On returning to Britain, he was appointed Professor in Russian History at London University. He wrote several books and founded and edited *The Slavonic Review*.

Riquet, Marie-Clotilde-Elizabeth Louise de (1837-1890) became Comtesse Mercy-Argenteau after her marriage. In her childhood she developed considerable aptitude as a pianist. In 1866, she met Emperor Napoleon III and befriended him and later wrote a book about their four-year relationship, *The Last Love of an Emperor*. In the 1880s, she developed an interest in the music of Russia, translating some vocal music by several Russian composers. By 1885, she was publicising the music by the New Russian School when the individual names were hardly known in their own country.

Robinson, G.T. ((1829-1897) was a gifted architect and a man of many intellectual interests. Many of the buildings he designed are described in Pevsner's *Buildings of England*. He worked in Wolverhampton and Leamington before going to London. Among the Wolverhampton buildings he was responsible for were the Public Baths, St Luke's Church, and the Theatre Royal. The Burslem town hall at Stoke on Trent was also his. One of his daughters, Mary, wrote poems, published as *The Collective Poems, Lyrical and Narrative* (1902) and also a book on Emily Bronte and *Portrait of Pascal* (1927). She first married James Darmesteter, Professor of Oriental Studies at the Collège de France, who translated her poems into French, and subsequently she married M. Duclaux, Director of the Pasteur Institute.

Sand, George (1804-1876) was the most successful female French novelist of her century. Her novels present a large fresco of romantic sentiment and nineteenth century life. Her reputation came into question when she began sporting men's clothing in public. Sand's male dress enabled her to circulate more freely in Paris than most of her female contemporaries could and gave her increased access to venues from which women were often barred. Also scandalous was Sand's smoking tobacco in public; neither peerage nor gentry had yet sanctioned the free indulgence of women in such a habit. These and other behaviours were exceptional for a woman of the early and mid-nineteenth century, when social codes were of the utmost importance.

Svehla, Antonín (1873-1933) was a Czech politician who served as prime minister from October 1922 to March 1926 and from October 1926 to February 1929.

Talich, Václav (1883-1961) was the chief conductor of the Czech Philharmonic Orchestra form 1919-1941 and head of opera at the National Theatre from 1935-44. During his tenure at the Czech Philharmonic, it became a world-class ensemble.

Virchow, Rudolf Ludwig Carl (1821-1902) was a German medical scientist, anthropologist, and politician. He founded the school of 'cellular pathology' and is regarded as the father of modern pathology.

Watson, Sir Thomas (1792-1882) was appointed physician at the Middlesex Hospital in 1827. He rose to become physician extraordinary to Queen Victoria in 1859, and he had been in medical attendance to the Prince Consort at the time of his last illness. He was created a baronet in 1866.

Wilberforce, Albert Basil Orme (1841-1916) was appointed canon residentiary of Westminster in 1894, chaplain of the House of Commons in 1896, and Archdeacon of Westminster in 1900. He published several volumes of sermons. He was a son of Samuel Wilberforce, best remembered for his opposition to Darwin's Theory of Evolution, most notably in the debate in 1860 with Thomas Henry Huxley.

APPENDIX 2
NAMES OF THOSE WHO PRESENTED ROSA NEWMARCH WITH A BLÜTHNER GRAND PIANO.

The names, as given below, are listed in a diary of Rosa's. The presentation was made on 6 June 1929.

Philip Agnew Esq.

Sir Charles Addis

Frederick Austin Esq.

Ernest Auston Esq.

Sir Hugh Allen

Miss Jelly d'Aranyi

Mr & Mrs Wm Bennett

Arnold Bax Esq.

Adrian Boult Esq.

Messrs Baines & Scarbrook

Mrs Charles Bell

Aubrey Brain Esq. (Q.H.O.)

Frank Bridge Esq.

Miss de Bennich

York Bowen Esq.

Eric Blom Esq.

Professor Granville Bantock

Mrs Brodie of Brodie

Mr & Mrs Godfrey Brown

Thorpe Bates Esq.

Allen Blackall Esq

Arthur Bliss Esq..

Mr & Mrs H.C.Colles

The Columbia Gramophone C°

Gerald Cooper Esq.

Dr George Cathcart

W.W. Cobbett Esq

The Misses Colman.

C.A.Crabbe (Q.H.O.)

John Coates Esq.

Miss A. Chitty

Basil Cameron Esq.

Miss Harriet Cohen

Miss J. C. Child

Madame Duclaux

Mrs Frank Dawes

Mrs D'Oyly

Miss Helen Douglas

Miss Fanny Davies

Haydn P. Draper (Q.H.O.)

Baron Frederic d'Erlanger

Mrs Farebrother

Mrs Field

Madame Adila Fachiri

F.L. Gyp (Q.H.O.)

Percy Grainger Esq.

Balfour Gardiner Esq.

Lady Mulleneux Grayson (Miss Louise Dale)

Miss Myra Hess

Copeley Harding Esq.

Mrs Arthur Hinton (Miss K. Goodson)

Walter Hall Esq

Miss A. Hall

Julius Harrison Esq.

Gustav Holst Esq.

Miss Dorothy Haurell

Walter Hansell Esq.

Herbert Heyner Esq.

Messrs Ibbs & Tillett

Miss E. Johnson

Herbert Jenkins Ltd.

Howard Jones Esq.

The Revd Duncan Jones

Harry Kling Esq.

F.B. Kiddle Esq. (Q.H.O.)

Madame Kirkby Lunn

Mrs Cherry Kearton (Miss Ada Forrest)

John Lane Ltd

Lady Lewis

Mr Mewburn Levien Esq.

W. Leveson Esq.

Adolf Lotter (Q.H.O.)

The Excellency The Czecho-Slovak Minister – Dr Jan Masaryk

Messrs MacMillan & Co

Dr & Mrs John McEwen

Mrs Rose Morley

Miss Manuelle

Madame Tatiana Makushina

Robert Mayer Esq.

Robert Murchie (Q.H.O.)

R. Newton (Q.H.O.)

Mrs Robert Newman

Mr & Mrs Norman O'Neill

The Oxford University Press

Miss Mary Paget

J.C. Pantling (Q.H.O.)

Montague Phillips Esq.

Roger Quilter Esq.

Edmund Reeve Esq.

Dr H.W. Richards

Bruce Richmond Esq.

Ernest Read Esq.

Miss Mabel Robinson

J. Roskill Esq.

G.W. Reed Esq. (Æolian Company Ltd)

E.J. Richards Esq.

W.J. Riley Esq.

W.H. Reed Esq.

Mrs Rooth

Maurice Sons Esq. (Q.H.O.)

Edward Speyer Esq.

Miss B. H. Simpson

Mr & Mrs Francis Sanders

Philip Sainton (Q.H.O.)

Miss Johanne Stockmann

Miss Irene Scharrer

G. Stratton (Q.H.O.)

Miss Dorothy Silk

Mrs Saunderson

Dame Ethel Smyth

S. Schwabacher Esq.

Harold Samuel Esq.

Mrs Threlfall

Somerville Tattersall Esq.

Mr & Mrs Lionel Tertis

W.W. Thompson Esq.

Alfred Willink Esq.

Lady Maud Warrender

Dr Vaughan Williams

Miss Florence Whittall

Charles Woodhouse Esq. (Q.H.O.)

William Wallace Esq.

The Misses Willis

Miss Isobel Wartley

Miss Eleanor Webb

Sir Henry & Lady Wood

Miss Tania Wood
Miss Avril Wood
John K. Young Esq.
W.H. Tabb Esq. (Q.H.O.)

In the diary, the initial sentence is in Rosa Newmarch's handwriting, but the subsequent list of names appears to be in another hand.

Q.H.O. = Queen's Hall Orchestra.

In addition, there are signatures on three dates in the diary as follows:-

21 May, Sinigaglia

5 June, Henry Wood

3 October, Frederic Lamond

INDEX